I Took the 3rd Choice

Dennis Jackson

Table of Contents

When, Where, Why, and How 1

Navy Training Center (NTC) - San Diego, California May – July 1975 4

Graduation Day 17

Home on Leave 18

Naval Technical Training Center Corry Station (NTTC) – Pensacola, Florida August 1975 –...... March 1976 20

Dancer 29

NSGA Hanza, Okinawa Japan April 1976 – January 1979 45

Naval Station Treasure Island – San Francisco California January 1979 123

Re-Enlisting in Navy: NTC (Naval Training Center) San Diego, California – December 2, 1981 129

Naval Radio Receiving Facility (NRRF) Imperial Beach, California January 1982 – February..... 1984 134

NSGA Misawa, Japan May 1984 – November 1986 169

NTTC Corry Station, Pensacola Florida December 1986 – March 1987 209

NSGA Homestead December 1987 – January 1989 220

NTTC Good Fellow - San Angelo, Texas March 1990 – June 1990 253

NSGA San Vito, Italy June 1990 – January 1993 265

NSGA Edzell, Scotland (United Kingdom) January 1993 – January 1996 292

NSGA Imperial Beach, California October 1996 - February 1998 315

Retirement Ceremony February 28 1998 350

Acknowledgments 355

When, Where, Why, and How

It was May 5th, 1975, and I was nervous as hell, maybe anxious would be a better way to put it; whatever those feelings were, I had them, and I never felt like this before. Was this going to be a big adventure? Was it going to be fun, or was I going to regret this for the rest of my life? I guessed I would find out and find out fast. Most of the men in my family had done it, and now it was my turn; I had already signed up; no backing out now. My father had told me this would be something I could not change my mind about and say to hell with it; I'm out of here, he said you signed up, and now you are in. WOW! The whole trip, I was thinking, how did I get myself into this.

I had managed to stay away from all the gangs, Crips, Bloods, The Family, and all the rest of them; they were in full swing, gang banging all over Los Angeles, and the police were busy, and I knew that I could go to jail at any time just because I was an eighteen-year-old black male. If the police stopped you and they needed to make an arrest for a crime, you would get punched up pretty good, cuffed, and off to jail even if the person that committed the crime looked nothing like you. If you were taken on a Friday, your ass was not getting out until that Monday if you were lucky. I was an apprentice sewing machine mechanic making pretty good money, one hundred and seventy-five dollars a week after taxes.

I also had a little side hustle selling new clothes which I got from the companies that rented the sewing machines from the company that I worked for, I would work on their machines after hours, and they would either pay me twenty dollars an hour, and I always took at least two or three hours to finish the job, or they would give me ladies clothes which I would sell out of the back of my car at the barbershop or where ever I could find a peaceful crowd of people. I had a new car. It was an orange AMC Javelin with black racing stripes, my own apartment, a gorgeous young lady that I had just proposed to. I had all this going for me at the young age of seventeen, but of all, that got me a lot of unwanted attention by two LAPD officers, and damn, they were all over me.

I needed to get out of the City of Angeles as soon as I could. They had already put a dime bag of some really good Acapulco Gold weed in the glove compartment of my car, and when one of my homeboy's little brother came in the store and told me he saw them doing it, I knew this could be the beginning of the end for me, lots of people were being set up by LAPD all the time, and I did not like the idea of going to prison. I was shopping for some new clothes in one of the clothing stores that lined Vermont Avenue back in those days; I gave the little guy my spare car key and a couple of bucks and told him to take the bag to my best friend's house around the corner which he did. I waited a while before I left the store; I saw the two police officers that had been watching me. They were sitting in their unmarked car parked outside the store in the red zone. I walked to a couple other stores on Vermont between Manchester and eighty-second street just to give the little guy enough time to get to my friend's house.

At that time, all the clothing stores on that part of Vermont Street were owned by Koreans. As soon as I walked to my car, the two officers were all over me. Thank god a lot of people were out on the streets, and they were all watching as the officers slammed me against the car first, then I got the punch in the stomach and a couple of slaps in the face. In the early seventies, the police liked to show off. Then they searched the car and couldn't find their weed boy did they get really pissed off; they couldn't figure out where or how that weed disappeared. (They were probably going to smoke it after their shift was over). They kept asking me where it was, and of course, I played dumber than dumb. After a few minutes, the cuffs were taken off, and I was let go, nose bleeding and the crowd yelling, "leave the young brother alone" some of the people in the crowd were the brothers from the Muslims Temple across the street, and they always made the police real nervous, the cuffs were taken off, and they got into their car and sped off. I got in my car and headed home; they were in front of my apartment in their car, just watching for me; they were really pissed about that weed, guess they wanted me to know that they could have my ass anytime they wanted. And they were at my apartment waiting for me again; there goes my Friday, Saturday, and Sunday. I wouldn't be out until after I saw the judge again, this was my third time seeing him, and he gave me three choices, go to jail, leave the state or join the military.

I had been thinking about those LAPD officers, my family, the girl I thought I was going to marry, and the test I had taken to get into the Navy, which I had to take twice. It was called ASVAB test (**ASVAB** is a multiple-aptitude battery test that measures developed abilities and helps predict future academic and occupational success in the military). Someone thought I had cheated; then, after they figured I did score that high on the test, I was asked what I wanted to do in the Navy, and my answer was I wanted to be a Disc Jockey, and they told me that they had just the place for me and it was in communications that sounded good to me, so I raised my right hand along with all the rest of the guys and repeated the oath of enlistment, I was barely eighteen years old when the enlistment was done.

Navy Training Center (NTC) - San Diego, California May – July 1975

It seemed to be a slow two-and-a-half-hour ride in an old beat-up white navy bus down to "San Diego Navy Recruit Training Center" for boot camp. As soon as the bus stopped and the doors opened, 2 guys dressed in white uniforms came onto the bus; they seemed really cool they told us to grab our bags, exit the bus and stand behind the white line. Once everybody was off the bus and standing behind the line, all hell broke loose; I had never been called so many crazy names so fast; maggot and civilian slime were the two names that really stood out!

It was getting dark, and the temperature had dropped down into the sixties, so to us guys from L.A., it was a little bit chilly; thank god for my bell-bottom jeans and my leather coat. There were twenty-five or thirty of us that got off that bus; they made us walk to a staging area where there seemed to be about 500 guys standing in lines; we were the last bus load to come in that night. We were all told to stand at attention, and then this short little Pilipino guy in a brown uniform came out and stood in front of us. He just screamed some more profanity at us, then told the guys in white uniforms to "get this maggot shit out of my sight."

Everywhere we went, we had to run. The first stop was the barber shop, I was one of the first in there; at the time, I had a fairly decent-sized afro, the barber asked me how I wanted my hair cut. I told him to trim up the edges and knock a little off my sideburns, and he said no problem. The guy took the clippers and went right down the middle of my head and started screaming at me, told me to get the hell out of his chair and get my ass in the back of the line; there were over two hundred guys in line all staring at my head as I walked to the end of the line.

I knew my life and my lifestyle was going to change really fast, and there was nothing I could do about it. We were allowed to make a phone call home, and the only thing we could say was, "I am here, and I am safe," end of phone call. After the phone call, we were taken into the gym and told to remove everything from our pockets. I was so glad I didn't bring any kind of weapon with me. (I left them all in my car). First, we were told to remove everything from our pockets and put all items on the table in front of us, and then we were told to remove all our clothes except our drawers and t-shirts. Lots of knives, a few small revolvers, and some weed were put on the table.

Everything we had on us was placed in plastic bags, and we were told except for the weapons and drugs, we would get our civilian shit back when we graduated boot camp. The guys that had the drugs and pistols, we never saw them again. I was thinking they were going to get some serious jail time; they probably did. Wearing only our underwear, we were taken to the supply center where we were issued three sets of dungarees, one dress blue uniform, which at the time was a regular black suit, a real skinny tie, one dress white uniform, one set of Boon Dockers (ankle-high boots) one pair of dress shoes which we spent most of our spare time trying to keep then shining, some really cheap tennis shoes and five pair of white underwear (t-shirts, skivvies, and socks). In another part of the supply building, we were issued two sheets, one blanket (god, that thing was itchy), one pillow, a pillowcase, our seabag, and a ditty bag with toothpaste, shaving cream, a six-pack of disposable razors and a large netted bag for your dirty clothes. After that, we were divided into groups of seventy and taken to the barracks, where we would live for the next three months and a week.

We were instructed on how to make our racks. It was after 1:00 a.m. before we were able to get into our racks because we made them up a couple of times, and then we had to search each of the metal tubes that made up the post that held the racks together; we were searching for contraband (mainly drugs and weapons), and after discovering a few bags of weed most of which were turned in, there were two guys that were going to try and hide one bag but later changed their minds (gentle persuasion was used and was never again used in boot camp) after that we were allowed to get some sleep.

Week 1 (P-Week)

During the nineteen seventies and probably a lot earlier than that, every day in boot camp was part of a week, we were at day one of week one (Week one was known as P-Week or Processing Week), and we still had twelve weeks, and six days to go, I remember thinking damn this is really going to suck. (The first week was mainly getting all the paperwork, physicals and dental work completed). We were awakened at 0430 by the sounds of trash cans slamming on the deck (floor) and the lids being banged against each other, and it was all done by the two white uniforms who we learned that day were our company commander and the assistant company commander screaming their lungs out. Those that did not get out of their racks were forcibly removed from them, usually tossed out of them by lifting the rack on one side and flipping it over. It took a few seconds for most of us to fully wake up; even though we were standing, I was trying to figure out what was happening.

We were told to shit, shower, and shave the (three - S's) and get in our work uniform. Our company commander was the first second class petty officer to be a company commander in Navy Recruit Training Center San Diego. Usually, company commanders were senior first class petty officers that needed that position so that they could become Chiefs, or they were Chiefs, and for a chief, this was some much needed and not too bad shore duty. I felt sorry for the little Pilipino guys, there were seven of them, and they all spoke broken English; only one or two of them could read and write English, the others understood just enough to get by for now. I know they just didn't have a clue what the hell was going on, but then again, neither did the rest of us.

That morning week one, day one, we learned that we knew absolutely nothing about the navy, and we were going to be retrained on how to dress, walk, talk, run, eat, and especially stand at attention. Whenever we addressed the company commander or anyone other than another recruit, the first word is "Sir," and the last word is "Sir". You always referred to yourself as this recruit "Sir this recruit feels sick Sir", "Sir this recruit needs to use the head Sir".

We were instructed on how to put on our work uniforms; they were dingy blue and made out of some kind of cotton, both pants, and shirt, which we later learned were called trousers and a blouse? Before we left boot camp, the work uniform was changed back to the old bell-bottom jeans and light blue colored short sleeve shirt.

After doing pushups (fifty or so), we were yelled at to get out of the barracks, shown where to stand outside, and then back into the barracks, where we were taught that a bed is called a rack, the cabinet beside the rack was a hanging locker (that's where your dress uniforms were put and it was just wide enough for them and the dress shoes and boots), we were taught the bathroom was called the Head.

Everything was open; no doors on the stalls for showers or toilets, just wide open. WOW, so much for privacy. As we kind of marched to the chow hall, we were called names by the other recruits that had been there longer than us, and Nuggets' was the most common, and we all had totally bald heads hence Nuggets. Before we left the barracks, the company commanders had a few questions for us, like who played football, ran track, and if anybody had been in ROTC?

I was thinking, what the hell is an ROTC? After all the questions were answered, we discovered we did have a few high school stars in our company, mainly track and football. I ran the hundred-yard dash and the one hundred- and ten-foot low hurdles, and let's just say I could move when I wanted to. Our group of people was called a company, and our company number was number (110); we were a real mixed group of screwed-up people from all over the country and seven totally lost people from the island of the Philippines. It seems most of the blacks, and there were about twenty of us, were from Los Angeles, New York, Chicago, Detroit, and one guy was from Indianapolis; most of the whites were mainly from the deep south and the Midwest, We had some serious racial problems the first day or two, but the company commander squashed that shit real quick usually by letting the problem people get all the fight out with push-ups until they couldn't move their arms and then putting the two guys in racks next to each other.

After chow each morning, cattle trucks drove past our barracks on the way to the chow hall; they were full of marines from the Marine Corps boot camp right next door to our camp. Our boot camps were divided by a narrow river which was lined with six-foot chain-linked fences on both sides, topped off with barbwire. The marines were hustled off the trucks with shouts and screaming, then they formed up in ranks and started to march around the parade grounds in double time fashion (like a slow run) while screaming at the top of their lungs, "kill, kill, kill" no cadence songs just "kill, kill, kill". We never had any contact with them other than watching that every morning spectacle; this lasted for about three weeks while their chow hall was being updated. This was the first time I was glad I joined the navy.

The first week was mainly all the medical, physicals, dental checkups (most of the guys had their wisdom teeth removed, mine had not come in yet, so I didn't have to worry about that and after the first night looking at all the blood on the guy from Indianapolis pillow I was real glad they hadn't come in yet. Now you have to remember this was 1975; there were no computers, cell phones, CD/DVD players, and hell, cassettes had just got started. All shots were with the old fashion needles, a lot of shots in both arms, and after the docs finished with us, we all felt like shit (docs were what we called the corpsmen who were trained navy medics), but then it was more push up and a few sit-ups, after that it was time to start filling out paperwork, and it seemed to take up most of the next 4 days, we spent most of the next 4 days with clerks using typewriters and triple-ply paper, and here we were thinking hey if all we had to do is answer questions while someone else did the paperwork this won't be so bad, or so I thought.

The first Saturday, we spent the morning cleaning the barracks from the toilets to the decks. I had never seen a buffer before; they were huge. We got one of the Pilipino guys sit on it to help hold the damn thing down, and it was like trying to hold on to a junkie that needed his heroin. After that, we were led around to different locations of the base that we recruits needed to know about. Then it was off to the parade ground where our lessons in marching, standing at attention, parade rest, and later marching with a rifle would take place until we left boot camp. Learning the basics of basic training, how to make your rack the navy way, and yes, they did check a couple of the racks to make sure a coin would bounce on it. Tying your shoes was no problem for the Americans, but the guys from the Philippines that were in our company, it was an issue as they had only wore flip flops most of their lives along with short pants and a t-shirt in their country; they had it twice as bad as we did, but they did try, and they never quit, and for that I respected them.

Breakfast, lunch, and dinner were a whole new experience for every one of us; you stand in line while waiting to be served, the line was our entire company of seventy guys outside the door with about five more companies of seventy guys waiting to get in. While in the line, other recruits that had been there a couple of weeks before us would make sure we were not talking or fooling around, and they screamed weird things at us like "nuts to butts" they wanted us to get closer in line so we could get other recruits waiting behind us out of the streets, after you were served a good helping of eggs, bacon, and toast along with cereal or cream of wheat you were hurried out so the other companies could get in and eat. While you are eating, other recruits that are now working in the galley screamed, "eat it and beat it." Running was important because if you had to go anywhere by yourself as a recruit, you had to run if you felt sick and had to go see the medics, you had to run if the company commander needed you to deliver a message to another company commander you had to run if you had to go to the toilet you had to run.

Whenever left the company, you had to have a chit (a written note from the company commander giving you permission to be away from the company). We were marched to the parade ground, where we would later learn how to march with riffles and learn cadence songs. We finally got a break; it was lunchtime; we were fed well. Lunch was cheeseburger, fries, and basically the same drinks you could get at any fast food place. While we were eating, other recruits were still running between the tables and still screaming, "eat it and beat it" I was wondering if they had extensive training for that?

After lunch, we all formed up outside the chow hall (galley) and got inspected. I was standing next to the only real fat guy we had in the company; they hadn't sorted us out by height yet, but I was wondering where he would normally be put in our ranks, and I was praying it wouldn't be near me, he had some cake on his face, and it looked like mustard on the side of his mouth. Just as I was wondering what all the bulges in his clothes were, that same little Pilipino guy in the brown uniform came over (he was the battalion commander; I found that out later); we were going to have our first inspection by him, one of many. We were told to stand at attention, so we all stood as straight as we could, and I just knew with this fat kid standing next to me, I was going to be one of the best-looking in the company. I could hear the battalion commander screaming at people, but I just didn't understand any of the things he was saying "straighten out that gig line", "did you shine your shoes with bricks?" and the one I did get was funny to me, but I knew better than to laugh "your daddy should have eaten you when he had the chance." Well, he got to the fat kid before he got to me, and he just started screaming, "what the fuck is this? Did you get all that shit on your face while you were dreaming of your momma's cooking, or did this asshole next to you squirt it on your face after you ate chow" then he got closer to the fat kid if you can imagine that and punched him right in the chest, pieces of cake flew out of the front of his uniform and landed all on the side of my fresh bald head. The fat kid fell to the ground, where he was screamed at by both the company commanders telling him he was not worthy of lying on their deck!

The battalion commander was standing right in my face now, he looked at my name on my shirt, (JACKSON) he asked why I didn't duck when I saw the piece of cake flying at me, I didn't say a word, I knew I didn't know how to address him, and I didn't want to get my chest caved in also. So I stood there with my eyes looking forward (this was a no-win situation, I knew I was screwed); then he asked me if I liked the cake; I told him, "Sir, I didn't eat any of the cake, and therefore this recruit did not know if the cake tasted good or not." Then he smiled and asked me if I didn't trust the cooks that worked in his galley (now you have to remember this guy was maybe five foot four inches, and he had a strong Pilipino accent, and I was trying hard to figure out what the hell he was saying. (You no trust my kooks in da gaaly?) I just knew I was screwed, and then he smiled and called me "Action Jackson", turned, and said something to my company commander. He looked at me for a few seconds and walked to the next guy screaming and cursing, I wanted to let out a sigh of relief, but I knew better.

After the inspection, we were marched back to the barracks, and that's when all the real fun began; we were told to sit on the deck in a circle around the company command and the assistant company commander. After we were all sitting down, we were told how things were going to be, and that we needed some recruits that would be in charge of things in the company, and whoever was chosen would be held responsible for certain things, and if those things weren't completed satisfactorily, there would be hell to pay. That's when volunteers were asked for; nobody raised their hands for anything, so certain people were picked; the one guy we had that was a quarterback on some high school football team was the RCPO (Recruit Chief Petty Officer) he was in charge of us whenever we left the barracks, there was the RLPO (Recruit Leading Petty Officer) the RCPO's assistant, RMAA (Recruit Master At Arms) and the RY (Recruit Yeoman). I got unlucky and was picked for the job as RMAA, I didn't know what it involved, but I was sure I didn't want it. The company commander made it known that when he was not around, the RCPO was in charge and that the RMAA was in charge of the barracks; he stressed that point. After all of that was settled, we went outside to do pushups, sit-ups, and jumping jacks, seemed like we were out there for hours.

The sun had gone down before we were finished, then we were back inside the barracks and had to learn how to tie some knots. That wasn't too hard for me, as my father had taught me how to tie quite a few knots during our many fishing trips. After an hour of learning how to tie knots, we got a fifteen-minute break, and during this break, we were told to shine our shoes and brass belt buckles as we would be inspected the next morning.

Sleep came easy that night; we were all worn out. The inspection was our first of many, and it did not go well for us; we spent the entire day after the inspection marching in ranks, running in ranks, and then exercise until we were all ready to pass out. If one person did not do an exercise correctly, we started that exercise over until we were all counting together.

It was time to learn teamwork, and that didn't come easy for most of us. The first week had come and gone, P-Week was over, now the real training began, and it was not going to be fun. The 3-S's were always the first thing we did in the morning, then form up in ranks and get inspected, and then it was about two hours of push-ups, sit-ups, jumping jacks, and pull-ups. After that, it was time for breakfast, so we marched to the chow hall. The RCPO stood at the head of our formation, and we had a guy called the guide on; he carried our company flag; it was blue with white number 110 on it, RLPO was on the outside in the middle of us. We were four lines across with twenty men in a line, tallest in the front with the shortest in the back. I was in the middle. We also formed up like this for the inspections; there was one Pilipino that was almost my height; he was stood next to me. At the time, I didn't know it, but for a while, he was going to be a problem. Behind me was a real short guy; he was a Mormon; I had never met one before, but after the first day I wanted to kill him, he couldn't march to save his life, and he always kicked the back of my boots when we marched. I only screamed at him once. I got fifty push-ups for that.

The entire second week was spent learning how to do certain steps while marching or standing in formation like "left or right face", "about-face", "left or right quarter-turn", double-time, and half step. It didn't seem that hard to me and most of the other guys, but some of us just had a real hard time trying to march and keep in step. The first step was always with the left foot, and some guys just couldn't get it. I bet they couldn't dance to save their lives. The third week we were issued old M-14 rifles to march with and learned the 16-count manual of arms, where to go from right shoulder arms to left, then to present arms, and finally to parade rest. There was an old M-1 rifle that was filled with cement it was used for punishments; if you dropped your weapon, the whole company would start to march, and you would have hold that M-1 directly over your head for the entire march, most of the punishments were funny as hell as long as it wasn't you getting punished.

One morning one of the recruits forgot to put his dirty underwear in his ditty bag, so they did not get washed (that was a real bad thing). During the morning barracks inspections, his dirty skivvies were found by the company commander in his footlocker. After all the yelling and spitting at the poor guy, we were told maybe we all needed to march for a while; the recruit who had the dirty skivvies was held back inside the barracks. A roll of toilet paper was put on the top of our company flag (none of us knew what that was about). The guy that carried the flag was centered in front of us and was ordered "forward March" then we were given the order "column of two's, right face and forward march" that meant the first two rows of recruits turned right and started marching, after the last two men in those two columns made the right turn and started marching, the next two columns made a right turn and started marching this continued until all the columns were in a straight line two columns wide and forty men per column, then the order was called "company halt" we all stopped. Then the company commander made us split into two separate groups, so the front half of the company started marching, and the second half stayed in place until the first half was at least five hundred yards in front of us, then the rest started marching, that's when the recruit with the dirty skivvies came out, and he had to run around us with his T-shirt on backward over his uniform and his dirty skivvies on his head on top of his cover with the poop stains in the back, he had the old M1 rifle over his head, and he had to scream at the top of his lungs every five steps he took "look at me I'm a shit bird" now most of us wanted to laugh so badly, but we all knew better.

He fell to the ground forty-five minutes into the march and was left there until we came back;

then he was forced upon his feet, and we continued back to the barracks with him screaming again. Nobody ever forgot to put their dirty clothes in the bags after that.

It was now Wednesday morning; we had just left the chow hall, and we were told that we would be going to the firing range; we would be firing M-14 rifles; most of us were grinning (finally, something fun). We were led to some bleachers near the range, where we were instructed on everything about the weapons, from the speed of the bullet and its trajectory till it hit the target, the weight and size of the bullet (round), and the different firing positions. The rifle weighed a little over ten pounds and held a twenty-round magazine, and could fire over seven rounds per minute when set to automatic, the rounds were 7.62mm, and it could hit a target over five hundred yards away, then we were all issued a rifle it would be ours until we graduated from boot camp, I liked mine right away. We were told to name our rifles by the range instructor, so I named mine "Babe", babe and I got along well; cleaning it was a pain in the ass because you had to learn how to take it completely apart, clean each part and quickly put it all back correctly. If for any reason, you ever dropped your M-14, you would sleep with it for a week (I never dropped mine). The first time at the range, we fired one hundred rounds; that would be the last time we got to fire that many rounds, and it was fun. We fired from standing at the shoulder, sitting, squatting, and laying in the prone position at a target that was over two hundred feet away. I will say this much after firing one hundred rounds with Babe; my shoulder was a little stiff; for a guy that only weighed one hundred and fifty pounds, she had a serious kick. We did not go to the range daily. It was only once or twice a week; I wish it was more, but we spent a lot of time with line handling and firefighting training.

At the end of the week, our RCPO got into trouble as we were marching to chow; another recruit from another company just walked through our ranks as we marched, and our RCPO did not chew him out for walking and not running. The RCPO was almost relieved of his position. That morning we had a barracks inspection as usual and had passed it with no problems; when we got back to the barracks, there was another inspection the same as the one we had that morning; we did not pass this inspection, I was told to lay on the deck face down at attention in front of the first rack, and I did, then two other recruits were positioned one in front of me, and one on the other side of the rack, the one behind me was told to push me under the rack, the guy behind the rack was instructed to pull me to the side of the next rack. This continued until I had been pushed and pulled under each of the racks on both sides of the barracks (thirty-five racks on each side). Needless to say, when I was ordered to stand at attention, I had a big dust afro and beard, my clothes were also covered in dust.

The rest of the company was standing at attention during the whole time I was pushed and pulled under each of the racks; the battalion commander was also present (the little Pilipino Chief), our company commander, and the assistant company commander. Everyone there had tears in their eyes. They were trying so hard not to laugh at me. I couldn't stop sneezing for a couple of days. The funny thing is, before we went on that march, we swept, swabbed, and buffed that deck. To this day, I do not know how all that dust got in the barracks.

Then I was ordered outside, where my company commander and several others picked me up and threw me into the dumpster, and I was told to remove everything from the dumpster that was not paper. (Socks, underwear, and food were stuck to me as I tried to stand up; you don't want to know why the socks were in there). We kept the toilet paper roll on our guide-on (the company flag that meant we were shit birds) until the end of the week because we were still having issues; we just could not learn to work together. All of our screw-up and racial issues with each other were about to stop and stop really quick.

We had firefighting training, and it was a real eye-opener; we had to learn how to handle a four-inch hose which seemed like no big deal; however, once water was pumped through it, it became a monster, you could get hurt badly or killed if you didn't know what the hell you were doing with it. If you ever turned on your water hose at home and it was just sitting in the yard, you know how the end of the hose comes to life and goes crazy in your yard? Imagine that your three-quarter inch being two and a half inches in diameter and having a brass end on it that weighs over one pound. Three guys were volunteered to grab the hose after it was turned on with a full water flow; the end of the hose was going crazy; we were all sitting in bleachers watching it, then they tried to grab it, one guy went done after it hit him in the back, the other two were a little more cautious, they watched it and tried to grab it just at the end of the hosed length, that didn't work out well for either of them, both had banged up knuckles, that went on for at least five or six minutes, the company commander and the instructor were crying laughing at them. I had seen the firemen in Los Angeles handle a runaway hose, and I knew how to get to it, but I wasn't going to volunteer that info with anybody at that time.

That Sunday morning, after breakfast, as we marched back to the barracks, a runner gave the company commander a message; he announced, "it was a red flag day" (too hot to exercise or march). It was in the upper 90's. We marched back to the barracks (Scuttlebutt had it that we were just going to clean the barracks and smoke, joke, and drink cokes for the rest of the day like all the other companies would be doing), but we were company 110 the shit birds of the battalion all that was about to stop. We got our normal command in front of our barracks "halt" we stopped and were ordered back inside the barracks and to stand at attention in front of our racks. We stood at attention for about 45 minutes, and it was getting hotter in there. All the windows were closed, only the doors were open, and we were all sweating pretty good. Then the door from the company commander's office opened, and in walked two of the biggest guys any of us had ever seen. They were both Chiefs, but they were not in the khaki uniforms that all the rest of the chiefs wore; they were in the green uniforms like the marines wore back then, and they both looked like mean as hell; we just didn't know how mean yet.

Our company commander and assistant company commander were dismissed, and they left the barracks; then, both of the chiefs turned towards us, and I know I wasn't the only one with the gut feeling that we were not going to be coking and joking the rest of the day like the other companies in the battalion. We were ordered to stand at ease (relax); by now, we had been at attention for over an hour; we were told we had 15 minutes to get a smoke and water break; we all looked at each other and smiled. I was thinking this is not going to be a bad day after all. Damn, I was so wrong. After everybody was done smoking and getting water and feeling kind of relaxed, the shit hit the fan, we were all at attention again, and they told us who they were. I forgot their names, but they were called Salt and Pepper; one was white, and the other was black; they let it be known in no uncertain words how they felt about us again maggots and shit heads were used a lot; they chewed us up and down for about a good 20 minutes, then they closed the doors, screamed at us again for about another ten or fifteen minutes, and that's when the fun began.

We were ordered to put on the work jacket, then the p-coat, then the raincoat, the little black beanie, and then the ball cap. Just putting all that on made most of us sweat like crazy! Then we were ordered to line up next to the racks, one person in front and one at the back, then to lift the rack and start marching in place; we didn't know it, but we were going to march to Georgia and even though we never left the barracks we did not stop marching until our sweat was pouring off the windows and when we thought they were done trying to kill us, we had to do other stuff to help us get in the right frame of mind such as squat thrusts which we did until they got tired of watching us.

Let's just say after a day with those two, most of us got our act together really quick, and the next day our whole company looked like we knew exactly what we were doing, so the toilet paper roll was no longer on our company flag. We were company one-one-zero (110).

We did have a couple of guys that could not make the swim qualifications. No matter how they tried, they just couldn't make it (it was the ten-meter high diving board, and it was over thirty-two feet tall) that got them; it is a long way up there and to jump off into a swimming pool well it sucked and looked scary as hell from way up there a little over thirty-two feet) we had to tread water in the pool for about 10 minutes, take off our trousers in the water and make them into a floatation device by tying the pant legs together and float on our backs for a while also.

They just couldn't get it, so they got a choice of flunking out of boot camp or being set back to a new company and trying again; most took the setback option. We spent the last week of boot camp looking good and feeling good about ourselves. We still did not know what to expect next after boot camp. Some of us were lucky and already had schools lined up; lots of guys were going to be deck apes until they could get a school. (Deck Apes were the nickname for boatswain's mates. These are the people that get to do all the paint scraping, sanding the decks, tying knots, and all the shit nobody else wants to do) Later in my career, I gained a lot of respect for those people.

A couple of days before graduation, I was called into the Company Commanders' office. I was told to bring my pencil that I used to write letters and get my ass in his office ASAP. When I knocked on his door and announced myself "Recruit Master At Arms Jackson reporting as ordered SIR," I was told "ENTER" I did and stood at attention while awaiting orders. I was told to take my pencil and hold it with my two index fingers while my arms were straight out above his head; I was informed of the insane consequences that awaited me if I dropped the pencil on his head while he was reading the new edition of Playboy magazine.

He read a couple of articles for about ten minutes, and I swear my arms felt like I had been holding thirty lb. dumbbells. I was then informed that I could place the pencil in my upper left pocket and then stand at attention. I was given a walking chit and sent to a building I had not been to yet; there was a third-class petty officer that was taking me for another test for my school. I had to learn 5 letters in Morse Code they were T, I, N, R, and A. I was taken to a room and told to sit and put on some earphones (cans); then, a recorded message said this is a test then. I learned the letters, T, I, N, R, and A in Morse code. I had to write the letters each time I heard them, It got me away from marching on the parade ground, and it was nice and cool in this room. I liked it sitting at a typewriter punching the corresponding key as soon as I heard it, and they went faster and faster. I just knew this was going to be fun.

After I returned to the barracks, the recruit LPOs and myself were called into the company commander's office, and immediately I was thinking that we were in some kind of trouble that was not the case. The company commander congratulated all of us and thanked us for helping him with his first company he handed each of us a can of coke, and we all sat down and shot the breeze with him for about 15 minutes, and we learned that he was a pretty cool guy. He told us how we would be the nugs (new guys at our schools and at our first assigned duty stations) and that if we went with the flow, none of us would have any problems and the last thing he told us before we were dismissed how proud of each one of us.

Graduation Day

It was zero dark thirty, and nobody was able to sleep; we were told that after this day, we would probably not see each again for a while. If we ever did again, most of us would get two weeks' vacation time at home then off to our A-Schools; others would get the two weeks off but would report to different ships or shore stations. I was heading to Pensacola, Florida (where ever in the world that was). I had never heard of Pensacola, and all I knew about Florida was that there was good fishing and lots of beaches, just like in California. At 0600, we were up and getting ready for our final march to the parade grounds for graduation, we were all in Dress Whites (white bell-bottom trousers, a white top with the flap in the back, a black neckerchief which took forever to figure out how to fold it and the little white Dixie Cap) and our shoes were shinned so good you could see yourself grinning in them. Around 0900, were could hear the speakers at the parade grounds as we marched to them; we could see all the people that had come to see their sons graduate, lots of ladies UMMMM, it had been over 3 months since I had smelled some perfume other than on a letter, my parents were there along with my two sisters and my babe, it was going to feel real good seeing my family and holding my babe in my arms again.

After we arrived on the parade grounds, we were put in our position. A minute later, we were marching around the parade ground for the last time, and it felt good knowing that as we were given the order "Eyes Right. I looked at the Base Commander and the Battalion Commander. Each of them looked at us like they were proud of their kids graduating from high school; it all felt real good. After the march was over, we heard some speeches and were put at attention then. The order was given to dismiss the battalion; company 110 was dismissed.

After we were dismissed, we were allowed to be with our families for a while. After shaking my father's hand, he just grinned that was all I needed from him. Mom hugged and kissed me and my two sisters also. My babe was kinda shy, but I still kissed her real good and told her I was coming home for a couple of weeks, and we would not leave the room for that time. She didn't say anything. She just looked away. When it was time for the guest to depart, my youngest sister came over and told me that my girl had joined a biker club, my heart sank for a minute, but then I remembered one of the Chiefs saying it the Navy wanted us to have a wife or girlfriend she would have been issued with our sea bags!!!

Home on Leave

My first day home was awesome; my father picked me up at the bus station, and I, along with a couple of others, caught the Greyhound from San Diego to Los Angeles. Most of the guys left the bus terminal and headed for their homes, and we all said our goodbyes promised to keep in touch, but we never did. As my father pulled up in front of the house, it brought back lots of memories, and everybody was there, all the family and lots of my homeboys. Everybody made fun of me not having my afro or mustache anymore, but they all understood. They were all there but not my best friend, the one whose little brother warned me about the police and took the bag of weed back to him, and he only lived halfway down the street.

After everybody left my parents' house I asked my little sister what was going on and she told me my girl, who was my best friend Mark's cousin, had joined a motorcycle club, and she had to sleep her way into the club, I was like damn WOW at least I didn't get a Dear John letter, and we both started laughing my little sister was a little amazed at me for not being mad, and I told her what the Chief had told me "If the Navy wanted me to have a wife it would have issued me one in my seabag," and we both laughed again.

Just as we stopped laughing, my little sister's boyfriend came running into the house; we called him Black A. It seemed as though my new ex-girlfriend and her new biker friend were at Mark's house, and he was telling everybody how he was gonna cut me with his knife. I grabbed a pistol and walked down the street; as soon as they saw me coming, they both jumped on the bike and took off. I didn't see her again for over twenty years. I went back home, jumped into my car and drove to her grandmother's house, parked my car in the flower garden and jumped over the back end of it and used my key, went into the house and got my clothes, left the key and went back home. Sorry about the garden.

The rest of the two weeks were uneventful, just hanging out with the family and having a good time, and eating good food cooked by my mother. One morning I woke up, and to this day, I do not know why, but I had on my white gloves and was running my hand over the fireplace mantle looking for dust and dirt, My sisters and I still laugh about that one. One night my oldest sister came home from a date. It was after two in the morning, and she came in went upstairs and went to bed, a few minutes later there was a knock on the door, it was the guy that she went out with, he wanted to talk to her, he was a little upset about all the money he spent on her, and all he got was a kiss, I asked him how much he spent, and he told me it was over two hundred dollars, I laughed at him and told him he should have taken me out, at least I would have went to a strip bar with him, then I told him to get the hell out, he heard me cock the pistol, and he left. I spent the rest of my leave hanging out with my family and friends, partying and drinking. Most of them were still smoking that good bud. I knew I would probably get the piss test when I got to my A-School, it was killing me not to smoke that good weed, but I didn't touch the stuff, and to make matters worse, I didn't get laid.

It was time to move on. My flight was Friday at one P.M., and I was ready. Before I left, I told my father where the school was, and he looked it up on the map, he was a member of AAA, and when he found it, he laughed his ass off and told me a few things (words of wisdom) first he said: "You're crazy, but you're not stupid if something or somebody pisses you off walk away, keep your eyes open and watch your back, and your buddies backs on base and off base and finally you're gonna be around a lot of red necks, serious red necks and they are different than anyone you have ever had to deal with before with the exception of LAPD so be careful."

Naval Technical Training Center Corry Station (NTTC) – Pensacola, Florida August 1975 – March 1976

My A-School was in Pensacola, Florida. I had never heard of the place, and I did not know what to expect when I got there. I had saved enough cash I hoped to get me through until the next payday, which was the end of the month. WOW! The flight that flew from Los Angeles to Atlanta was on a normal jet. From Atlanta, it was an hour layover, so I went to the USO to hang out and try to find out where the next gate was located. I knew what it said on the ticket, but I just didn't know how to get to the gate, so a very nice lady wrote some instructions for me, and I made my way without any problems to the gate. It was Gate-8. I did not see the normal jets, only little twin-propeller airplanes.

I went up to the counter, gave them my tickets, and was told to have a seat. The plane would be ready in a few minutes, and they would call us when it was time to board the aircraft. Now you have to remember I was only eighteen years old and had travelled on a few jets in my life, but I was not ready for this. It was one of the twin-prop jobs on the runway, and we had to walk down the stairs onto the runway with our luggage. I had my seabag, and it was over my shoulder. There were only five other passengers on the flight, one older couple and a really young couple with a baby.

When we got to our little plane, the co-pilot came over to us and said follow me, we walked to the other side of the plane, and he pushed a button on the wing, and part of the wing opened. That's where we put our luggage WOW (I had never seen anything like that). Then we boarded the plane, I was the last one on, and I sat in the seat right behind the pilot. I put my seat belt on as soon as I sat down, and it stayed on until I got off that plane.

It was a bumpy two-hour flight, and I felt sorry for the baby because it screamed damn near the entire flight. Boy, was I glad to be upfront away from that? The entire flight, I was busy looking out the window at all the scenery. We were not as high up as we were in the jet, and you could see everything. It was awesome. After a while, the pilot announced that we were getting ready to land, and I got confused because I did not see any big airport like in Los Angeles or Atlanta, I saw one little runway and a few buildings, and that was it, a tractor and a few vehicles, I got nervous.

The pilot lined us up for the approach to the runway, and we were down and bounced all the way to the small building, and then a tractor came over with a flatbed trailer attached to it. The co-pilot got out first and put our luggage on the trailer, and the tractor-pulled it to the back door of the building. We got off the plane and walked to the back door, collected our luggage, and we were in Pensacola, Florida. It was hot, not hot like in Los Angeles or San Diego, but this heat was something else, and the dress white uniform we had at that time wasn't making things better. This difference in the heat was going to take some getting used to for me. It was in the upper eighties, and it felt like the nineties.

I didn't know about humidity, but I was learning fast. There was a Navy van at the front of the building, and I was told to get in it. They asked to see my orders, and one of the petty officers called me lucky. We got in and headed for the base. When we got to the base, I couldn't see any ocean anywhere. It was in the woods on the very outskirts of Pensacola. After we turned off the main street, it looked as though the street leading to the base was over a mile long, nothing but trees and bushes all the way. I did notice a little bar before we turned on the "Chiefs Way," which was the name of the street.

Now the bar had beer for five cents, I could not believe that, and I knew the first chance I got, I was going to be a good customer there. The van dropped me off at the quarterdeck, where I handed over my orders and was assigned a room. I was told where the male barracks were located and also what time to report back at the quarter deck the next morning at 0730 for assignments. In other words, I was assigned to a class and then the extra duties such as guard duty.

My room had three other guys in it, and they were all white. I did not notice any other black sailors the entire time I had been on the base. The barracks were all made out of bricks, as a matter of fact, all the buildings were made of bricks, and there were pine trees all over the place. After I got myself settled in and talked to my new roommates for a few minutes, one of them told me I could "find my kind outside the in front where the round circle was" I didn't have a clue what the hell he was talking about my kind, but I decided to go out the rest of the base.

I left out the back door. My room was on the second floor of a three-story barracks near the back door. The first thing I saw when I opened the door was a forest as far as I could see (coming from the city, it really took my breath away). I walked around for a few and found the base gym, bowling alley, club, barbershop, and the package store, a place that sold cigarettes, beer, snack foods, and a few other things. I could see the commissary a little way off, and I decided to head back to the barracks.

When I came back around the front, there were about fourteen brothers all gathered around, most had gotten there a day before I did, and two of the guys were already in class and were giving us the heads up on the place. At that time, I was the only one from Los Angeles, so everybody wanted to know what it was like. We hung out there for hours, then one of the guys said let's go to the galley and get some chow. I was hungry, so I went along, as a matter of fact, all fifteen of us went. I discovered the base also had marines going to school there also, no black marines, though.

The galley was big enough to feed a lot of people, and it was half full by the time we got there. As soon as we walked in the door, it got real quiet. I mean, all the white people were staring at us like we just stole their new Sunday Go to Church Clothes (that's what my new best friend Keith said loud enough for all of them to hear), and we all busted out laughing.

After a few minutes, they all went back to eating, but a couple of the marines kept staring at us. I was too hungry to give a dam, and honestly, I just didn't care. After we ate, we left, and Keith led us to our new spot; it was several picnic tables in between two of the barracks, which was our new hang-out spot. We all got to know each other and where we each came from. Out of the fifteen of us, thirteen were in my class, and we were all that was known as R-branchers. Keith and Dave were both I-branchers who I learned were linguists.

Dave told us all to watch our backs at all times in and out of class because we had some serious racism in our school and everywhere else down here in the Deep South. I had no clue what the hell they were talking about, but I paid real close attention. It was about ten that night, or 2200 hours when we all split up and headed back to our rooms.

I was surprised to find out that none of us blacks shared a room with any other blacks (interesting). There was a lot to learn in Pensacola, Florida, and it was not all about my naval training. I was going to learn a whole lot of new things and fast. I was going to be what was called a CTR (Cryptologic Technician Collections). I didn't have a clue what that meant, but I was cool with it.

There were thirty people in our class, and thirteen were blacks, (you have to understand I did not know too much about racism other than T.V. and the police, in our part of Los Angeles, we were all pretty much the same kinda middle-class blacks and whites and a few Hispanic families). The A-School in Pensacola, Florida, was a top-secret facility, and we were issued badges that were checked each time we went in and out of any gate or major entry point. Our badges had to be on our person at all times while this part of the base was separate from the rest of the base, and it had high chain link fences all around it with barb wire at the top of each fence. I felt like a kid going to junior high school all over again, trying to find out where I needed to be and at what time I needed to be there.

After the first week, we were all settled in, and kind of had a grasp of what was expected of us. Billy (who was one of the coolest people that I ever met) was kind of our unofficial leader who had been in the navy for a while. He just finally got this A-school, he said he was a deck ape for a year, and boy was he glad for this training.

But he had more time in the navy than any of us, and he was a CTRSN (S.N. means Seaman). We were all CTRSA (S.A. means Seaman Apprentices), he was a seaman, and we were seaman apprentices. Most of us would be seaman as soon as we graduated from school. One of our instructors was a marine staff sergeant, he was a fair man and usually pretty cool, and he had been involved in some kind of accident, so he stuttered from time to time. Other than that, he was alright. He earned our respect and trust later on during the six months of class when we had some VIPs visiting the school and one, a Commander in the United States Navy, saw us and wanted to know why we were here and didn't everyone know that our brains could not handle the highly technical stress and training required to make it through this training? Staff Sergeant Truett slowly stood up from his instructor's position and informed the commander that there were only three members in his class that had finished four weeks ahead of the training schedule, and all three were black. I was one of them, and at the time, while the rest of the class was finishing that part of the training, I was instructed to repair manual typewriters, which I was told I could do since I could repair industrial sewing machines this should be a breeze for me so for three weeks I fixed typewriters.

Herald was one of the three, his nickname was Bugeye because when he got drunk, his eyes looked like they were going to pop out of his head, and the other was Billy, Popeye, and Billy both did administrative work while the rest of the class finished that part of the training. The training was learning Morse code, there was an old computerized machine affectionately named Ralph because it sounded like it was throwing up if you missed a character, and when you passed, it made a nice buzzing sound.

We started out with five groups of characters with five characters per group per minute and finished with thirty-two groups of characters per minute, that's what it took to pass that part of the class. There were other things that we had to learn, but due to the nature of the training, I will not go into it except to say it was hard and contained different types of radio theories. Our first day off base on liberty was about the fourth day after we arrived. It was wild, you have to remember this was 1975 in Pensacola, which borders Alabama and Georgia. Do I need to say more? We walked all the way to the end of Chiefs Way street and found the bar that had been for a nickel, went inside there were I think six of us, the bartender quietly and quickly came to us at the door and let us know that our kind was not welcomed and for our own safety we should leave ASAP.

I had never heard anything like that, and I was getting pissed when Billy grabbed my arm and said let's go, we left and caught two cabs, and we went to what I learned was called the blocks (where the blacks lived) we went to a movie and watched the movie "Superfly," I had seen it about three years before at home, it was just coming out in Pensacola. While we were watching the movie, I couldn't help but notice some of the brothers staring at us, and so were some ladies. I kept winking at one of them. She smiled, and I noticed all her gold teeth. I turned around and watched the rest of the movie.

Then Billy said he knew a little bar that was cool and we could all relax, while we were walking to the bar, we saw what I thought was a parade. It was the KKK in full costume. I didn't know what to think.

Billy asked, "Is this the first time you have seen this shit?"

All I could do was nod. He said I was spoiled not to have seen this bull shit up close. I told him we saw it on T.V., but I only thought it was something on T.V. from our country's past, he slapped me on the back, and then he laughed at me, which was starting to piss me off. He could see it in my eyes.

Billy said, "My brother, Let me set you straight on where the fuck you are, there is not much farther south than where we are" I was getting madder and madder, and basically, I was at the point where I didn't care what anybody said it was fighting time and I was going to fuck somebody up!

Billy grabbed me, and he had a good grip on me. I could have gotten out of his grip, but he started telling me to just listen.

Billy said, "Sure, we could fuck these assholes up, but what about the people that live here? After we rip them apart, we could spend the rest of our time on base, but these folks would have to deal with these racist fucks" He practically had tears in his eyes while he was schooling me.

He told me to look at the cars behind the white Cadillac. They were all police cars, and my rage had taken over me hell I was only eighteen years old and had not dealt with racism from this aspect. I had only known the police to be racist. There were poor blacks, whites, and Hispanics, and we sort of lived together. I knew that in Los Angeles, nobody went too far west, like up into West Hollywood where all the stars lived.

I was past screwed up.

Then Billy grabbed me and put his forehead on mine and said, "Relax, this is not anything new, but times are changing!" Then he said, "Let's move on, man, relax and chill."

He nodded at the other brothers that were with us, all of them were from the south. They thought I was really weird not knowing about this shit, shit that they all grew up with. I felt so bad, and I really wanted to hurt one of the guys in robes.

We got a cab and went back to base.

When we got there, Billy said at first, "I thought you were some crazy piece of shit that was put in here with us to spy on us. We are the largest group of blacks that the navy has ever had in the C.T. community." Then he added, "Welcome, my brother."

Then we did the basic dap that was going on at that time.

I sat there with a beer in my hand, thinking of all the things I had just learned about this country. Wow, I guess I was totally spoiled, and I didn't even know those two policemen. I could have shot in the ally and probably got away with it was a whole different story compared to what these people were going through.

I think in just a few minutes, I learned about issues that I could not have even known about.

I asked Billy, "Are all the white people like these assholes."

He shook his head and said, "No."

He said to me, "Today has really fucked you up?"

And before I could answer, all I could do was laugh.

Everybody started laughing as well. I think it was good for all of us as they knew I was for real, just another screwed-up brother from another part of the country that had to deal with racism in a whole new way that he didn't understand. Life sucked!

My brain was trying to deal with the fact that I was just learning what these brothers had been dealing with all their lives.

Then Billy came to me and said, "I need to tell you something that nobody else knows!" he added, "Can I trust you?"

I told him, "Why would you want to trust me? I don't even know what's happening outside the base!"

He said, "You look like you want to cry because of it."

"Cry is not the word," I replied.

He just smiled at me and said, "My wife is white, we have a baby girl, and we are trying to stay separate, so nobody knows what's up."

Before he could say another word, I told him, "I have your back to the end."

He looked me in the eyes and said, "I know, so do the rest of the brothers we have been with all day long."

Then we all laughed and nodded at each other. We all understood each other now, and I was the new guy. I was accepted by them. I didn't even understand that at that time. I just wanted to let Billy know if anything or anybody threatened his woman or his baby, I would be there, without a doubt, and put my life down for them, he looked in my eyes, and he knew it. Now the one thing he forgot to tell me was that he played the bass guitar, and he was damn good at it, his nickname was Bootsy, and that brother could hit the licks on that guitar.

Come to find out, he would play his bass guitar there every now and then, so we were all cool with the owner once Billy introduced us to him. He had a few gold teeth.

Also, I thought, *damn, nobody knows about the toothbrush around here?*

We had a few beers and decided to go back to base that was when Billy told us the real deal out in the town.

He said, "It's hard to find a sister to date out here. Most of them will tell you that you only do two things, one is to get them pregnant, and the second is that you will leave them."

The more I thought about what he said, the more I wanted a southern bell. It had been quite a long time for me, and I needed one.

The next day after class and study period, Billy and I left the base and went to the club that he took us to, and of course, there were three fine-ass babes in there. Billy and I were on them like crazy. The owner of the bar just grinned and laughed, we both tried to lie and say we were not from the base, but short hair and slight mustaches just didn't hide our lies too good. I did manage to get one of them to sit with us. She and I talked, and we even kissed a few times.

Then she dropped the bomb on me and said, "I know you're in the Navy, and you will leave soon, so we could never have relations," before she said that a part of my body was beating up my polyester bell-bottom slacks if you know what I mean.

When she got up to leave, I had to remain seated cause the condition and the thin slacks did not allow me to be a gentleman and escort her to the door, so I sat there looking miserable as hell with Billy and the bar owner laughing their asses off at me. That weekend on Friday, I was one of the "lucky ones" I pulled gate guard duty at the front gate along with Keith, so for thirty minutes, a second class petty officer remained with us, and we got "on the job training" on how to stand and talk to people entering and exiting the base, along with which cars to salute and not to salute. We were also instructed on how to operate the radio in the guard shack and how often we had to report to the main security station on base.

We reported at 1600 hours for duty and did not leave until 0020 hours (12:20). No way to get anywhere that was partying, so we went to the base club to get a few beers. To our surprise, the entire crew was there, the club, which was normally dead, was jumping, and I was starting to feel a lot better. I went to the bar and heard one of the chiefs complaining that all the new students, over 60% were female. The navy was letting large groups of females into the C.T. field, and I can't speak for anybody else, but I was happy as hell. There was going to be a dance contest Saturday night, and the winners would win a bottle of either Jack Daniels or Mad Dog 50/50. I figured I probably would not like the Jack Daniels but that Mad Dog and I could be good friends for a while.

I was sitting with the guys when this awesome redhead came into the club, I know she felt me staring at her, and I was trying not to be too obvious, but I couldn't help it (thank god I had on Levi's that night). She and her friend couldn't find a seat, so they sat at the bar next to the grumpy drunk seaman. He got up, slammed his drink down his throat, and left before he was six steps away. I was in his seat. She had arrived that Wednesday and her name was Sharleen. I wanted her badly, but I had to be cool. When I left the barstool, I told her about the dance contest on Saturday and being bold. I told her that together we would win it. She laughed and looked me right in the eyes and said we would see, then they both got up and left the club. I went back to my seat, and all the guys wanted to know if she had any friends other than the one she came in with. I told them it should be a lot of them on Saturday morning. It was awesome.

There were only two black ladies on the base, and both were married, so I was really looking for Sharleen that morning when I got up and out of the barracks and headed to the chow hall, but I didn't see her at all that morning. Some of the guys and I went to the gym and did a little stretching and lifting for about an hour, then Billy and I went out to town. I needed to get some new slacks for the club tonight, and I wanted a new pair of Levie's. At that time, I had a twenty-eight-inch waist and a thirty-two-inch length, so I brought twenty-eight in the waist and thirty-four in length. That way, I could iron a cuff in the legs with lots of starch. To me, they were awesome.

When we got back to the base, Billy showed me all the spots where everybody hung out in the woods and where we probably shouldn't go (rednecks) just to avoid trouble. His favorite spot was where the dopers hung out. It seemed they didn't give a damn about color, just getting high and having a good night.

He said, "if I am not with the brothers, this is where I will be," and we both started laughing.

It was lunchtime, and everybody was heading toward the chow hall.

That's when I saw her.

Damn!

Did she look good?

That long red hair, those awesome green eyes, and that body, *WOW.*

I winked at her, and she smiled back at me, and I went over to her.

"Don't forget the club tonight," I said.

"I'll be there," she simply replied.

We both smiled, and I went back and sat with the crew, ate lunch, and tried to relax.

Dancer

It was about 2100 hours when we got to the club (9:00 P.M.), and as soon as I walked in, I saw her. It's hard to describe how I felt when I saw her, that long red hair, beautiful green eyes, soft red lips, and a very hot body to go along with everything else. I was glad I was wearing jeans.

Billy said out loud to the guys. "Look at him, he is chomping at the bits looking at her, and everybody started laughing, including me."

She smiled at me, but there were some lame assed rednecks making lewd remarks to the ladies at her table.

I just said to hell with this, she is going to dance with me, and right now, I got up, and Billy told everybody to get ready. I guess he thought I was going to get into it with the rednecks, but honestly, I never paid attention to them.

I just walked up to her, held my hand out to her, and said, "You promised me a dance!"

She never said a word, she just looked me in the eyes, took my hand, and we were on the dance floor. Billy and the guys sat back down then. I didn't pay any attention to the smears and pissed-off looks I was getting from some of the white guys in the club, and I didn't give a damn. I was with this woman, and she was going to be mine. It didn't matter to me that this was a fast record, and I was slow dancing with her. She just kept looking up at me, straight into my eyes. I pulled her tighter onto my body, I wanted to feel her completely, and I did.

I could feel her heart beating, and I'm sure she could feel mine and something else too.

I whispered in her ear, "You are almost mine."

She grinned and held me a little tighter. We slow danced through about four or five songs when I looked up and saw Billy waving at me. He had a beautiful blond sitting next to him, it was his wife, and he had a grin from ear to ear. She had just gotten on base and was in the same class as Sharleen. I stopped dancing and asked Sharleen to grab one of her friends and come join us at our table.

She kind of hesitated for just a brief second, then she said, "OK."

Now back in the mid-1970, we were dancing to Kool and the Gang, Earth Wind and Fire, K.C. and the Sunshine Band, Donna Summers, and the rest of the groups that were popular during that time, so we knew how to party. Billy introduced his wife Janine to Sharleen and me, then he opened a bottle of Champaign, and the whole group put their glasses up.

Billy said, "To, good times and beautiful ladies." We all cheered.

I reminded Sharleen of the dance contest and told her that we were going to do the cha-cha L.A. style, so we got up, and I showed her how it was done. She caught on really quickly, and when it was time for the contest. We won it, hands down. The prize was a bottle of Mad Dog 50/50 and a bottle of Champaign, that's when I got my first nickname in the military, and it was "Dancer."

We partied the rest of the night, and after the club closed around 0400 (4 A.M.), we went to the hang-out spot in the center courtyard. Most of the gang had left, so it was only four couples left. We didn't make much noise if you get my drift.

Around 0530, I walked Sharleen to her barracks, and it was a real warm, muggy summer night, so we sat underneath the back stairwell on a bench and talked until the sun came out. I kissed her as if I would never see her again, and she held me real tightly. When we broke the kiss, she asked if I wanted to see her again.

I said, "Do ships sail on water? Hell yes."

She gave me her room number and the phone number to her barracks. She had already written it down. I told her we would have to hit the club again tonight so we could win the next two bottles of booze, which would be Gin and Vodka.

We both laughed. She asked me if I was always this sure of myself.

I told her, "Not until I met you."

She smiled at me, kissed me again, and went up the stairs.

I watched that hot tight body of hers going up the stairs. When she got to the top of the stairs and opened the door, the air from inside slightly blew her hair, and I almost ran up and grabbed her. I knew the penalty for going into the woman's barracks, as I have always been told, 'you're crazy but not stupid.' I turned and walked back to my room.

When I got back to the barracks, Billy was just saying goodbye to Janine. They had disappeared into the woods. He said they had some business to finish.

"Was it near the druggies?" I asked Billy. We both laughed and grinned.

After waking up, it was too late for breakfast, so we hit the gym. Billy said that he wanted to show me something, so he took me to the head of the gym and said to read the first and second stall walls!

I said, "What??"

That's when I remembered where the hell I was.

"Nigger I'm gonna kill you and your nigger loving white bitch", got my blood boiling.

I didn't care that they threatened me but putting Sharleen in the mix really pissed me off.

He started laughing and said, "What makes you think you're the only one they meant?"

I took a second for it to sink in, but Billy, Benny, and Bugeye had also been with white ladies last night. Then I started laughing but not for long. A chief came in and saw what was written on the stalls.

He said, "Do you think this is funny?"

I replied, "If whoever wrote this tries anything, and I mean anything, trust me! I won't be laughing."

"And you can bet on that, Billy," said Dancer. "Let's get out of here. It must be lunchtime by now."

So we left. I did not know that he had told Janine to meet us there and to bring Sharleen.

They were waiting for us and were already seated.

Billy said, "Please don't mention that shit on the walls in the gym to Janine because she gets really pissed at stuff like that. She is from New York, and she doesn't play that game."

We ate lunch, laughed and talked, having a real good time.

Then someone yelled out, "Didn't you see the walls in the gym!"

Billy and I both stood up, and nobody said a word. Just then, the rest of our group walked in again, nobody said a word. When the guys got to our table, they had Denise and Ann with them. Billy and I didn't say a word about the gym, but they already knew. We all joked in front of the ladies and kept them smiling all through lunch, then the 4 of them left and went to check out the city of Pensacola and its available shopping.

Billy told us to get all the guys together and meet in the courtyard, so that is what we did. All 15 of us were there around 1300 (1 P.M.). He told everybody that we now definitely had to watch each other's backs at all times on and off the base. While we were discussing what could possibly happen and what we would do if anything did happen, the base Master At Arms walked up to us. He was a black Staff Sergeant in the marines. He told us who he was and that he had seen what was written on the stalls in the gym. He said he only had two things to say to us; first, he would not stand for any of this racist bullshit from either side, and second, if he catches anybody writing shit like that on this base. He was going to have their ass, black, white, yellow, or brown.

Then we started to walk away, and he stopped and told us that he had to inform the Commanding Officer. He walked away.

It was the end of September and hotter than when I first arrived last month. This humidity had me sweating like a pig on a regular basis, everybody told me I would get used to it, but I just could not believe I ever would. Billy and Janine had brought an old Volkswagen beetle. Now we had some transportation, it was slow and noisy, but it always got us to where we wanted to go. Sharleen and I had been talking about getting a little place off base to get away from all the racism and nut cases. I guess she had mentioned it to Janine because Billy told me that we were going to find a spot off base on the weekend, and I just smiled. The 4 of us renting a place would be a lot cheaper, plus they already had a car, so it sounded really good to me.

Just the thought of not having to sneak into each other's rooms after all the roommates were gone or not being out in the woods behind the barracks with god knows how many others in the dark with all the bugs and everything else that crawled and crept at night sounded real good to me (making love under the stars is awesome but not all the damn time). I was finding it hard to concentrate in class as I just couldn't wait for Saturday morning to arrive. Friday night, we really partied. Sharleen and I stuck around for the Friday night dance contest at the base club. After we won that, we lit out for our last night in the woods, and it was awesome.

Billy and Janine had a car. It was an old Volkswagen Beetle. They asked me if Sharleen and I wanted to get off base and do something.

"Of course," I said. "Let's get off the base," I called the barracks phone number that Sharleen gave me. She had a good friend that answered the phone. I asked her to get Sharleen for me, and she did.

I told Sharleen what was going on, and she was ready in no time. We decided to go down to the blocks and watch a movie, it was "Super Fly" so we headed there, we were a little bit late getting to the movie theatre, but we had only missed a few minutes of the show. We sat close to the back, where there were more empty seats. I wanted to be with Sharleen, away from all the red necks, and just have her by myself (now remember Pensacola, Florida is in the Deep South). When we walked in, we didn't notice anyone as the lights were already off, the whole theatre was filled with our brothers and sisters, *awesome?*

Near the end of the movie, I kind of noticed that a lot of the ladies in the theatre were staring at us like crazy, and they did not look happy.

Then I heard somebody say, "Who the hell do they think they are bringing those white bitches in here" about that time, Billy handed me the keys to the car and whispered to me that I should bring the car to the front of the building cause we need the get the hell out of here, I agreed wholeheartedly, took the keys, and told Sharleen I would be right back when I got out the front door. I jogged to the car, got in, and drove straight to the front door. I blew the horn twice, and Sharleen, Janine. Billy came out in a hurry, got in the car, and we were off.

Janine and Sharleen were not sure what was happening in there, but I guess the way Billy said we needed to go, made them understand. Billy and I both let out a big sigh of relief as I sped off down the street as fast as that old beetle would go. I told Billy maybe that was not a good idea, and we both started laughing like crazy. We were all hungry and decided to go get something to eat. We went to Mc Donald's and used the drive-thru, headed east on Cervantes Street until we came to Highway 90, and just cruised until we found a nice secluded spot.

It was the first time any of us had seen the Gulf Of Mexico, and the water was awesome. It was a turquoise blue and calm as hell, not like the Pacific Ocean near Los Angeles, which was dark blue and mostly cold, this water had to be in the mid-seventies, and it was November.

We now knew where to go to get away from all the racist B.S. from both blacks and whites. We stayed at the beach until the sunset, and it was beautiful, but we had to get back to base. We all had to be up early the next day for classes.

None of us wanted to go back, but as we all said at the same time, "Duty Calls," we now all knew where to go when we needed to get away, and it was a great spot.

The school was getting more intense, and there were a lot of new things to learn. Staying late in the study hall seemed to be the norm, but on Friday and Saturday nights, we were always at the club having a good time unless we were unlucky and pulled gate guard duty. Christmas in A-School in Pensacola was the first time I was not home for the holidays in my life, Sharleen, Billy, and Janine all went home on leave, and I was still there with a few of the gang that did not go home for one reason or another, I was saving money so I could buy a car and the flight back to Los

Angeles would take all the money I had saved, so I stayed.

I stood a couple of gate guard watches for other people for $20.00 each, that was my Christmas and New Year's Eve party money, and the few of our little group that remained had a decent time. I really missed Sharleen, but I knew she would be back right after New Year's Day, and we would be together again. That Friday morning, we were ready. Billy was behind the wheel with Janine sitting next to him. Sharleen and I were in the back, we wanted to find a place near the base, but that was all we knew. All of the apartments we looked at were too expensive, and renting a house was totally out of the question price-wise, so we started looking at trailers to rent. At the first one we went to, the manager just told us to go away. The second place was something else, it looked like it was behind a junkyard, and none of us even wanted to check the place out.

We went to a really nice looking place that had little fences around each trailer, and each little yard was really clean. It was my turn to go to the manager's office. I knocked on the door of the only house in the place with a big sign that read "Managers Office" no one answered, so I rang the doorbell, this sweet looking little old lady came to the door, she was so innocent looking after.

She asked me if she could help me. I told her that I and some friends were looking for a nice trailer to rent.

She said, "Please wait one minute." I nodded to her, and she came back with a big ass 12-gauge shotgun and started cussing and screaming at me (I couldn't understand anything she was saying, but you crazy Nigga's ain't moving in here). I took off running. I passed Billy in the Volkswagen and had to wait for them on the corner (I guess she didn't like the idea of having blacks renting from her, after that, we let Sharleen and Janine do all the checking, that was one of my scariest times in Pensacola. Janine eventually found us a decent trailer park to live in. Billy and I stayed at the base while the two ladies finished the trailer search.

About three hours later, the BUG pulled up.

Sharleen got out and walked straight over to me and said, "You two, let's go," pointing at Billy and me. Sharleen pulled the seat back, and Billy and I got in the car, and then Jenene drove us to our new trailer. The trailer was double-wide, and it had two bedrooms and two baths with a nice living room, a really nice kitchen, and patio doors leading outside. It didn't take us long to move in as all we had were clothes and a few radios along with our personal items for the bathrooms and another thing, the trailer was located near the rear entrance of the trailer park, which put us within a fifteen-minute walk to the base. That night we had a few friends over for a couple of hours, we had some wine, and somebody brought a little weed, so we had a little party for a little while. I couldn't keep my hands-off Sharleen, so I grabbed her by the arm, and we went to our bedroom,

I was hoping everybody didn't hear the hollering and screaming. Sharleen kept telling me to be quiet! We only left the trailer once that weekend, and that was to go and get groceries, beer, and wine. And yes, there was more hollering and screaming.

I was young!

It seemed as though this was the woman I was supposed to spend the rest of my life with. When I was in class or had duty, I missed her so much. It took all I had to stay where I was supposed to be in class or on duty. I just wanted to be with her and only her. I mean, I had had crushes in high school and just wanted sex, but with Sharleen, I just wanted to be with her. The thought of not seeing or being around her, watching her sleep, bathe, dress, walk, and the way she talked to me like she knew I was hers and she was mine, we both knew that we were made for each other and that we trusted each other with everything from money to each other's bodies. Now the way we felt about each other was not shared by many whites and a few of the blacks on the base, the white guys, I didn't talk to, but the brothers needed to know what was up; first, we were going to be in that school in Pensacola Florida for at least six more months for some of us long for others, and I knew that I needed a woman and I damn sure found her and that's just the way it was.

We ran into most of the racial problems on the base at the club. The rednecks hated us so bad it was eating them alive. Billy told me that was just something that I would have to get used to and not worry about it because those kinds of people are always going to be there, both whites and blacks, mainly the black women and the white men. I never gave it a second thought after that.

We did have one hell of a big fight in the club one night, it was a Friday evening, and I was out of class early, and instead of going home, I had some levy and a shirt in my bag, so I changed in the head at the club with a few of the sailors I knew in another class that had gotten out early when one of the new brothers came in the club with his girl, he and I were the only blacks in the club at that time, and they were dancing and trying to have a good time when one of the marines that were a pure racist and did not care who knew it, threw a big glass ashtray at him, it missed and then shit hit the fan. Three white sailors that were in my class and one marine that was black all stood up. The black marine was named Dereck, and he told me he was waiting to get his hands on the asshole that threw the ashtray for a very long, long time and now seemed as good as ever to give this racist the ass-kicking he needs.

Dereck was six feet six inches tall. Damn, I was glad he was on our side. Now there were five sailors and one marine against twenty-five drunken marines and about six sailors joining their cause.

I just grabbed a Budweiser beer bottle and said, "Let's do this and get it over with,"

Then I saw Harold coming in the door. I shook my head no and mentioned for him to leave. He was back in about two minutes with the rest of the gang, which included about eight more of the brothers and about five white sailors, the odds were just about even now, and it was on. The fight, or brawl, whatever you want to call it, seemed to last forever. It was probably only a few minutes, like maybe five or ten at the most. I got a few good ones in with a Michelob bottle, and I did take a punch to the jaw. I mostly stayed behind Dereck, just where he told me to stay.

Nobody was seriously injured, but there were more of the drunk marines laid out than our guys. A couple of the ones on the ground were the cowards in the navy that decided to get on the marine's side when it looked as though the odds were in their favour. They didn't move or try to get up until the base commander, along with shore patrol, came into the club, whistles blowing and screaming and hollering. Now some of the shore patrol guys really sided with the marines. One tried to get to Dereck from behind. His only problem was that I was there with that damn Michelob bottle, and he pretty much figured out what the outcome would have been, so he backed up with the other shore patrol and stayed behind the C.O. The commander and the Command Master Chief along with the Executive Officer were all there, they were eyeballing all of us and not saying a word when the C.O. did speak it was not what we were expecting.

We were waiting to hear about going to the brig and handcuffs, but nothing like what he was about to say. In a quiet and controlled voice, he told the marines to get out of his club and that he did not want them back in the club for the rest of the month, he already knew the sailors that were with the marines, and none of us could figure that out, and he told them the same goes for you.

Once they were all gone, we started to walk towards the door. He stopped us, told us all to sit down, he pointed to the white sailors and Dereck to sit also, he told the bartenders to bring us all two beers apiece, then he had the X.O. and the Command Master Chief take a seat also, you could tell he had been thinking about this situation for quite a while and what he said was from his heart, and he said, "There are three things I need you, men, to know and understand. First, I will not tolerate racism in this navy, not now, not tomorrow, not ever. Times have changed for the navy and the Marine Corps, and we all have a lot to learn about each other, and those changes are happening as we speak. Third I will not have anyone at this training command or any other command fighting, brawling, or rioting. The next time there will be severe punishments handed out to all! Did I make myself clear?"

We all stood to attention and shouted, "Sir, Yes, Sir."

We all knew that he meant every word that he said.

After that, the X.O. said, "I agree one hundred percent with the C.O. If I see or hear anything else about this or any other racial issues that are insults or threats, I will have that person or persons standing tall before the C.O., and I will not hesitate to be that person white or black! Did I make myself clear?"

We all shouted, "Sir, Yes, Sir."

Then the C.O. looked at the master chief and said, "Master Chief, they are all yours."

The Master Chief replied, "Eye Eye, Sir," then the C.O. and X.O. left the club.

The Master Chief told us all to take a seat, and we did. He said to all of us in a quiet but meaningful way that if the X.O. finds out about any of this unwanted bullshit before I do, it won't be good for anybody involved. Do you understand that? We all agreed, and then he told the bartender to bring us two more drinks and close the club. The Master Chief walked out of the club.

We all sat quietly for a while, then one of the guys said, "I bet the Master Chief is the leader of the KKK." and we all started laughing, a nervous kind of laugh.

Then we all drank up and left the club. Sharleen, Janine, and several other girlfriends were outside the club waiting for us.

We all walked to the woman's barracks and watched the females go upstairs. We went to the male's barracks and watched the guys get inside. We quickly got into the bug and drove to our trailer.

What a night, the sex was hotter than usual too!

The next day at school, it was like nothing ever happened, nobody said a word about the fight, and we all knew all was not well. That next weekend all four of us had no duty, which was beyond unusual, but we didn't complain. We all headed out to the beach. It was still warm, and well, we didn't live on base anymore, but it was a good chance for all of us to get off base. We had new people in a new class, and they had more blacks than we did, so it was good for all of us to get to know each other.

Now Pensacola beach has pink sand. It is something else to see, especially when the sun is setting, but not this night. This night we had other issues, and it started right at sunset. Most of us were drinking wine, beer, or Mad Dog 20/20, which was the drink for us in those days. Cheap in price, but it would make us feel good for a while, then bad for a longer time. We drank it anyway. Our problem was that the sand at a distance seemed to turn black. None of us had ever seen anything like it before, all of us were from the base, and when we looked around, we were the only people on the beach, we didn't think much of it, and I cannot speak for the other people that were there, but I liked not having a crowded beach for a change.

The dark spot on the beach got bigger and bigger and closer to us. I stood up and watched when I stood up, so did Sharleen, I mean it looked like a giant shadow moving toward us, we both walked real fast toward the water, then we ran and jumped into the water as the shadow got closer to us and we could hear a lite crunching sound, the shadow turned out to be sand fleas, millions of them and these were not the ones you catch and use for fishing, these were like the kind that bite your pets but bigger. Not everybody got out of the way in time but when they felt those bites, let's say they moved very fast and into the water with the rest of us, we were shouting at everybody out there. Some listened, and some did not. Those that listened and got into the water were OK. The ones that didn't listen had bites that itched like crazy. I knew that they would listen the next time.

We all stayed in the warm waters of the Gulf Of Mexico for well over an hour, mostly just sitting and talking, waiting for our unwanted guests to leave, and even after they were gone, most of us were having sex in the ocean, and it felt really good, I didn't mind being in the water for so long. Things were going pretty good for us, and none of us expected anything less, but all of us were getting short, meaning our time in school at Pensacola was almost up. Sharleen and Janine only had a couple of months left as they were T-Branchers, whereas Billy and I were R-Branchers we had close to 4 months left.

I didn't want to think about it.

I was sure no one else wanted to think about it either. The thought of being without Sharleen was not something I wanted to think about, especially now that the hardest parts of all the classes we were taking were coming up fast, all the studying and extra studying, and no one wanted to fail. Failure meant that you would be expelled from school and have to wait for an opening and hope to become a radioman instead of a deck ape (boatswain's mate). None of us really knew anything about them but what we were told was that they had the hot, sweaty, manual-related jobs like painting the ships and scrubbing decks, not something any of us wanted.

It was a Friday, and we stopped by the base to check our mail. Sharleen had a letter from her mom. She got more mail than the rest of us put together, her mom really loved and missed her, not to say the rest of our families didn't love and miss us but *WOW*. One day she received a letter, and she wasn't smiling after she read, she looked like she wanted to cry. I walked over to her thinking, hoping I could help with whatever the problem was. I was really wrong on that thought.

Man, was I ever wrong?

Her father wanted to send her brother down to kick my ass and make me stay away from his daughter.

The old man must have put some serious thought into it, like where was the kid going to stay? Just basic things like that, and more importantly, was I just gonna stand there and let someone just beat on me. Yep, I figured lots of thought.

I took a really deep breath and told her that I didn't care what anybody thought about us being together, her parents or mine. I had already told my parents in a letter all my mother said was, "I don't care what your girlfriend or wife looks like, just give me grandchildren."

I reminded her of that, and we both started laughing. I kissed her and held her tight. I noticed there was another page of the letter that she didn't show me. I didn't think anything about it.

The next couple of weeks were busy as hell with school-wise and lots of good sex and beach fun. The partying was cut back for study, but it was still very good with Sharleen, and I was happy. We all had finals on the same day, and it was six hours for Janine and Sharleen, but Billy and I had two four-hour tests back-to-back, only thirty minutes between them for lunch, so the girls stayed on base until we were done. Not one of us was ready for what happened when we got to the trailer. There were police everywhere in our trailer. They forgot to leave someone outside to stop us from coming in. Billy and I walked right in on them and asked what was going on?

Now there were the same police that were in the KKK parade and a couple of Navy chiefs that we had not seen before, so we had to keep our cool. We both turned and walked out. The trailer was trashed, there were red swastikas and KKK signs painted everywhere, our civilian clothes were thrown everywhere, the stereo equipment we all paid for was gone, and there were signs spray-painted on the walls "niggers go home" and "stupid fuckin nigger loving whores".

We were beyond pissed off. None of us could talk. The police officer in charge came over to us and told us that the owners wanted us out of the trailer and off the property before midnight, so we were back in the barracks again and not happy at all. Our time was getting short, Sharleen and Janine were down to three weeks, and Billy and I were under two months. We still didn't have orders yet, but scuttlebutt was all the R-Branchers were going to Okinawa, Japan, and I knew for a fact that Sharleen was heading to Rota, Spain, and my heart was breaking already. I just never wanted to think about it. I just wanted to keep her with me all the time, not to be stationed on the other side of the world where all we could do was write letters to each other and hope the letters got to us.

While we were living in the trailer, a lot of new people came to the base. We now had the air force and army with us, but we were still in separate classes because of the difference in our military branches' missions. It wouldn't make sense for the army to know our mission as they really didn't work in the open ocean, nor did the air force. So, our classes were separated out to marines and navy, then the air force and the army. We, old-timers, were glad we were heading out. The racial problems were probably going to get a lot worse, I just knew the Commanding Officer was thinking the same thing we were, and he was getting short himself. Barracks' life sucked from the beginning, but now it was worse. I didn't have my babe with me. I had three guys in the room, they were OK, but we didn't have anything in common, and I know one of them hated me for being with Sharleen, I just told him to fuck off, and if he had a problem, we should settle it now, he never really said anything else to me after that.

There were a lot more blacks on base now and a few Hispanics, this base prior to us was mainly white, and this explosion of personnel was really going to have one hell of an effect on good ole Pensacola. Now the whole time, Sharleen and I were together. She had a friend that just could not stand her being with me. Now this woman had the orange-red hair and freckles very badly and was kind of straight up and down. I found out that the one roommate I had a problem with which was with her. No wonder he was such an ass. Sharleen and Janene both were down to two weeks left at the school. All four of us were feeling the strain, Janene was able to get her orders changed because she and Billy went to disbursing and showed their marriage license to the clerks, and they were processed as married, and Janene was able to get her orders changed, so the three of us were heading to Okinawa Japan, Sharleen and I talked about getting married, she would stay in the military, I would get out and get my degree, once I had that she would get out and get her degree. It sounded like a plan to me.

I went back to the barracks to get a bottle of wine I had stashed, and on my rack, the second page of the letter that Sharleen's mother had written to her was sitting there for anybody who came into the room to read, I know it was an asshole, and I was going to slap the shit out of him for it, then I screwed up, and I read it, and as I did my heart sank, I couldn't swallow and I was breathing really hard, disbelief and anger made me feel real hot, I just could not believe that someone that did not know me could hate me so much that they would disown their own child, especially a daughter. I was going to kill the asshole when he came back into the room; one of us was really going to be hurt, and I meant to hurt him really bad. I sat in the chair and drank all the wine by myself. I kept reading the letter, and it hurt just as bad, if not more, each time I read it. I couldn't imagine how Sharleen felt.

I knew I had to come to grips with the contents of the worst letter I had ever read; the worst part was it was not meant for me to have read it. I stopped thinking about myself and started thinking about the person that was probably ten times as upset as I was, and that was Sharleen.

How long have they been sending her letters like this?

I wondered how she dealt with this and me and school all at the same time. She was one hell of a good woman. I calmed down after an hour or so. I just knew the asshole wasn't coming back to the room tonight. He knew his ass was going to be mine. Had he only messed with me, I could have cared less, but he messed with the most important person in my life, and there was going to get a serious ass beating. I figured I would wait to get that back on him, but he was going to get knocked out. I meant he was going to go to sleep.

I needed something else to drink. I woke up just in time to get showered and shaved and get my ass in class. I was still buzzing from all the booze I had drank the night before, but I was able to handle it. I had no choice. I needed to talk to Sharleen; I didn't know what to say to her or even how to say what I felt. When I finally got the chance, I turned and walked away from her. I couldn't make myself speak to her, she only had a week left at Corry Station, and I couldn't make myself talk to her. Most of the gang thought I was trying to distance myself from her, and nothing, nothing could have been farther from the truth. I felt like an idiot each time I saw her, and I turned and went in another direction. To this day, I have never felt for or loved anyone as much as I felt for and loved Sharleen.

Sharleen left that Friday; I watched her putting her bags in the navy van that would take her to the airport from behind the admin building. I watched how lovely she was and how everything I loved about her and she was about to leave my life, my brain was telling me to get my ass out there and call a cab, so I could ride to the airport with her, hold her the whole way there and explain why I had been avoiding her, let her know my real feelings that nothing had changed, but I was just scared to come between her and her family, how I could bring myself to hurt her like that and how I could not imagine how anybody could hate someone they way they hated me without even knowing me.

I had a woman that was willing to give up her family just to be with me. I was confused and scared. I would fight anybody and didn't care about the consequences of those actions, but to hurt her by making her lose her family, and trust me, I really wanted to because I didn't think they deserved her. Then I thought about how she smiled when she talked about her family, how she talked about having children, and how happy her mother would be, I couldn't imagine them actually loving a half-black baby, and I knew that would destroy her, I walked away from my hiding spot and went to the side of the gate so I could watch the van drive down Chiefs Way, and I did, I stayed there for an hour after the van passed by and yeah I shed some tears off and on for a couple of days, it probably would have been longer, but I had a lot to do with the last couple of months of class to finish.

After I left the fence, I went to the barracks. The asshole was nowhere to be seen. I was hoping to goad him into swinging at me so I could all but kill him for putting that letter on my rack, but that didn't happen, so I took a shower and headed to the club. The whole gang was there. A guy named Dereck yelled, "Here he comes, and we all better keep an eye on our ladies."

I smiled, and I don't know how I did it.

Billy had just got back from the bus station with Janine, and he didn't look that happy either he looked me straight in the eyes, or we both knew that the best things in either of our lives were gone, mine probably for good and his for the next two months.

God, this was going to suck being without her. There were a bunch of new ladies on base now that the Air Force and Army were now in class on our base. Billy and I just started drinking. All I remember is Billy telling me to stand up so we could get back to the barracks. All of the guys were laughing at me. I didn't know why.

The next morning Billy told me I had just turned down a couple of the finest babes left on the base and that I just kept drinking until I passed out. I guess that's why everybody was laughing at me. I didn't care. I was hungover from hell and starving. We hit the chow hall. I felt better for a while, then I went back to the barracks and hit the rack. I woke up four hours later. I felt much better. I hit the showers and headed to the club, she was still on my mind, but I had to show the fellas and myself I could live without her, no matter how much it hurt. I hooked up with this really good looking sister in the navy, I hadn't seen her before, and she had been in Corry station for three months. I guess I never looked at anybody else when Sharleen was there.

I did cheat on her with other babes, and I didn't care. I was getting short and didn't care. I just wanted to get out of Corry station. I had brought a little sports car a couple of weeks after Sharleen left. I used the money I was saving to get us a hotel room and to rent a car for our last weekend together before she left. I forgot I had it saved, right around four hundred dollars, the car was a gold Fiat, and it was old, but it was easy to fill up with gas, and it worked. Once at the beach, I was so drunk (one of my feeling sorry for myself without Sharleen binges) I swerved it into the sand, four of the guys came over and told me to get out, and then they picked the car up and put it back on the street, I then proceeded to drive home except I swerved off the road again and back into the sand, they picked the car up again, and one of them and we drove all five of us in that car that could only seat two comfortably back to base.

Billy left the next day. Janine was pregnant and having problems, and since he, another brother named David, and myself had already finished all the requirements to graduate, they let him go home on leave early as she was in a hospital in their city somewhere in North Carolina, I saw him again about a month later after I got to Okinawa Japan.

The next week another one of the brothers named Billy Kirk was with me. He also had orders to Okinawa. He was the only person that knew how o felt about Sharleen besides Billy and when I told him I had watery eyes after I let him know about Sharleen and myself, he said that was all he needed to know as he was seeing this gorgeous Mexican babe with huge tits she fit right up there with Sharleen and Janine and he said thanks, then he told me they were going to be married, their class was two months behind mine, I shook his hand and told him I wanted to be the first to congratulate him, he just smiled and told me to thank you as he knew he was gonna face the same problem with her family.

A couple of weeks later, we graduated, and all of us had tickets home for at least two weeks.

Again I found myself at home, and I didn't do much but chill out with my family. My youngest sister was graduating from high school, so that was a big thing. Unfortunately, I would not be home for it, but I let her know how proud I was of her and that I would always try to be there for her. I didn't have to say it. She already knew. My oldest sister was already working and graduated the year after I did, she was going to be a model, and she was awesome. I loved them both to death. I realized what family meant when I came home.

I did party with the gang, and we had fun, made fun of each other, played a little bit of football in the middle of the street, was told who had joined the Crips and or the Bloods, and was surprised it wasn't all of them, but Mikey's mother would have torn him a new ass, Alan's father would have done the same to him, bear and the rest of the group had joined. Those few weeks flew by; I had never heard of Okinawa and didn't know what to expect when I got there. Somehow, I was thinking it would be like what I had seen on T.V. about Hawaii, the hot little babes putting all the flowers around your neck called leis. Well, let me tell you, it was nothing like it.

NSGA Hanza, Okinawa Japan April 1976 – January 1979

Torri Station, Okinawa Japan

We worked inside a building that was surrounded by what was called a Wallen Webber antenna array. We called it the elephant cage. I have to tell you, I thought Pensacola, Florida was hot, when I stepped off the plane in Okinawa, Japan (lovingly called 'OKI' by those of us stationed there in the nineteen seventies, it was something else), it felt as though the heat just burned my eyes and seared my lungs when I stepped off the plane, it felt worse than California's deserted area, and the really bad part was the humidity, it felt twice as bad as Pensacola. My hair was packed perfectly, not a hair out of place, and it was less than a quarter of an inch all over. When I stepped off that plane on the tarmac, my hair stood straight up like it exploded and then went damn near straight, that's when I knew it was going to take a lot to like this place. That's when I started telling myself this must be the place because I am here.

There was the usual old white navy van there; it already had three other sailors in it waiting to go to the base, and I was the last one to arrive for the day, so I was instructed to get in the van and take a seat, the other three sailors were going to the navy base at White Beach, I was going to the Army Base it was officially known as Torri Station, US Army Garrison Okinawa, tenth support group.

That was where the Navy CTs on Okinawa were stationed, the Army Base was where our disbursement office, quarterdeck, and barracks were located. It was a small Army base, but it had a chow hall, a two-lane bowling alley, and its own commissary for grocery shopping. It couldn't have had a garrison of more than 100 soldiers. About 2 miles away and on top of a hill is where we CT's worked. It was a building surrounded by a huge circle of wires. It was named Naval Security Group Activity (NSGA) Hanza Okinawa, Japan. NSGA Hanza was what it was called by all that knew about it. Most of us that worked there were called watchstanders (we stood watches), we worked a schedule back then of two-day watches, two-mid watches, and two-eve watches, and it was called two-two-two and eighty (2-2-2-80).

To explain it better, this is how it worked. We started with two-day shifts that started from six am until two pm. On the second day shift, after you went home and went to sleep as you had to be up and ready for the first of two mid shifts that started at ten pm until six am, and after the second mid-shift, you went straight home to get some sleep before you started you two evening shifts that were from two pm to ten pm, after those six shifts (watches) you were off for eighty hours which came out to be three point three days off, once you got used to it that left a lot of time to party and explore the island before the next shift started.

But I have to tell you. It really takes some time to get used to. I think it took me about two months, half asleep and sometimes just being totally asleep. Now, remember this is Okinawa, Japan back in the mid-nineteen seventies' air conditioning was not a normal thing off base, that included houses, restaurants, strip joints, and the whore houses, but we will get to those areas later. The barracks were similar to what we had in Pensacola, Florida. They had four racks per room with metal lockers to stow all of your clothes from the blouses and trousers that you hung up, Uniforms and Civvies similar to your underwear, socks, and shoes, all personal items including watches and jewelry also were stowed there and locked securely. Then you had a rack with a small nightstand next to it, and that was a normal barracks room.

We all had our clocks and some kind of radio on the nightstand also. Now imagine having four guys in a room, three working shifts, and one off. Someone is always asleep, and one guy is on his break. You couldn't sneak a girlfriend in to have fun with to save your life. Now here is a saying that we had on OKI. "For every one woman, there were around five hundred marines, one hundred and fifty airmen, fifty sailors, and probably fifty soldiers. Good luck finding your own girl".

During my first week, I tried to find out everything that I could about the island. There were quite a few bases on this little island, and Kadena Air Base was the biggest base of all. It was the biggest Air Force base in the Pacific Ocean area, and any of us would almost kill to be stationed there. Torri Station had a club, but it wasn't much, and no one was ever there, at least female wise.

Billy was already on the island and was waiting for Janene to arrive. He already had an apartment not too far from the base. He said he was going to the lemon lot on Kadena to find a car. I decided to go with him as there were busses that ran from base to base, we could have caught a cab, but Billy wanted to save every penny he had. I was cool with that. That was my first time being off the base without being in a military vehicle, all the cars were very small, and most were Toyota's, Datsun's (later to be known as Nissan), Subaru's, and Mazda's, but they all had funny names like the Datsun 260Z was known as a Fairlady Z, and the wildest thing was all the steering wheels were on the wrong side, even though during the time the United States still occupied the island under some treaty or another they still drove on the same side as we do here in the US. I made the mistake of calling one of the Okinawan people on the base a Japanese citizen, that little guy lost his damn mind. He started yelling, "me no Japanese, me no likey," he was killing me, and I was laughing so hard that I had tears in my eyes. He was really pissed off! Billy pulled me to the side and gave me a quick rundown on the people here.

He said that the Okinawans had been getting screwed over by the Japanese when the war started, and we are nowhere screwing them over by taking their land, making our own rules and laws for them to follow. He also told me the fleeing Japanese soldiers told the Okinawans that "the Americans were huge crazy people that would torture and kill the men, rape and kill the women and eat their children," so not knowing what to believe, a lot of the Okinawan families that were on the island during the end of the battle for Okinawa went to the cliffs and jumped into the ocean killing entire families!

I never called an Okinawan Japanese again. When we got to Kadena Air Base, we caught another bus to the base itself, it was a really big base, not as big as the base in San Diego, but it had to be close. I later found out it was one of the biggest American bases outside of the US. We walked for a few minutes, and he said this is it! I was a lot full of junk and some decent cars. Billy walked over to a Toyota that looked like a Celica but was called a ladybug. He grabbed the note that was on the windshield, and we drove to the barracks and the room written on the note. Billy found the guy paid him one hundred and fifty dollars, and Billy had his first car in Okinawa.

We drove to the gas station on base, and he filed up the tank cost him a whole ten dollars, then we drove from one end of the island to the other there were American Military bases or storage facilities all over the island, and we went to white beach in those days you had to be an E-3 to get in the area. It was nice, but it was mainly for camping for the beachgoers.

Then we headed all the way down south and hit Suicide Cliffs, the spot Billy was telling me about. Then we drove back north until we hit Naha, the main city on the island. There were some crazy clubs, then we went back on to Kadena Air Base, and we went to Gate 2 Street. That was a whole different world. We walked around for a few minutes, and then we went back to base. I asked Billy about registering a car and insurance. He just laughed at me and shook his head and asked me what did I see today, and I told him basically the wild, wild west but with smaller people, lots of dirt roads, and things. I never saw before a pit dug in the street where a very dangerous snake called a habu, would fight a mongoose, and all the drunks that walked by would bet on one to win. Strip clubs were everywhere, with guys outside yelling "Cho cho cho" (it was supposed to be shown, show, show), which meant a show with stripers and nude acts of all sorts. You saw all of that during the day; Billy said what do you think happens at night? I told him I didn't know, but I couldn't wait to find out.

Then Billy told me that Janene was pregnant, and he was picking her up tonight at the airport and that I might not see him for a while. You know how it is when you haven't seen your babe, and you need to get to know each other again. Then he smiled and took off. I was walking toward the club, so I could get a pack of smokes out of the machine and have a few beers before I turned in for the night, then I ran into Benny at the bar. He said it looked like not a lot was happening on this base, and I told him everything that I had just done with Billy and not to expect to see him as Janene was pregnant, and Billy was on his way to the airport to pick her up, Benny just grinned.

We had a few drinks and talked about being on this island. I told him that on payday, I would be getting a car from the lemon lot, just a pure beat-up old piece of junk that no one would want to steal, he said cool and that the rest of the gang should be arriving throughout the rest to this week, we both grinned. We were going to party here and have a good time. I asked everybody if they had heard anything from Sharleen, but the answer was always the same NO. After a while, I quit. I quit asking. I did see Janene as soon as she flew in, and she was pregnant and no longer in the Navy.

I never asked why or how she got out of the Navy. It wasn't my business. I was glad everyone was finally getting here, we were finally getting the crew back together. Boy, were we all in for a surprise? We were all called to the quarterdeck, where we were given our watch schedules and supervisor's names. Benny and I were put in section 4. Our supervisor was pretty cool. He gave us his rules, and we followed them,

"Don't bring your ass in here drunk, don't get caught with any drugs, stay out of fights with the damn marines, and don't ever come in late," He said. With the watches we stood, the guy sitting at your position could not leave until you get your butt in that chair to relieve him, "and if you are late, well, payback is a bitch. We all found that out really quickly." Then he added, "I don't give a damn what color you are or who or what God you believe in. Just follow my rules, and you will be fine. If not, I will tear your ass off one piece at a time".

He was a first-class petty officer going for Chief, and I didn't want to get on his bad side, and neither did Benny, so we followed his rules and orders. Now back in those days, the Navy personnel were allowed to have beards. They needed to be well-groomed and neat. I only had a mustache at that time, and I was cool with it at first, and Benny didn't even have a mustache guess he didn't want to deal with keeping it trimmed.

Benny and I were the only two blacks in the section for quite a while, so we became really close. We did get to see and hang out with the rest of the gang but only for a few hours at a time, and that was mainly at the chow hall or occasionally at the club, and that was because of the schedules that we worked. Before I got my car, we had to catch the bus to work and back to the base. If you missed it, your ass was walking or hoping you could catch a ride, and when we first got there, catching a ride didn't often happen, and walking up that hill in the Oki sun or at ten at night sucked ass.

The heat and the mosquitos, along with the other bugs, would make you really mad at yourself for missing that bus! Now our section had some crazy-ass people in it, and it was all guys when we first got there. When the female sailors and marines finally got to Oki, we were the last section to get any, and there was a good reason for that. For the first week or so, we got on the job, training OJT for newbies. We were put in positions that didn't have much going on and sat side-saddle with someone that knew the job inside and out. I got a guy named Dave, he could care less what color you were. He just wanted me to learn and be as good as he was.

I was lucky to have gotten him. He was skinny as hell with a scraggly beard, his work uniform looked like he ironed it with a brick (which was the saying for a wrinkled uniform), and he was from somewhere in the Midwest like Oklahoma or somewhere. Benny got a guy named Craig, and he was just as cool as Dave. I think our supervisor gave us to them for that reason, and his name was Dave. Once we got to know him, it was all good. We had thirteen sailors and four marines. They were pretty cool also. After the second week, we basically fit in. You could tell we were the newbies. Our shoes were shined, and our uniforms were ironed, just like in school and boot camp.

During the first week, our supervisor came over to it was our second mid watch on my second week there. Things were slow, and it looked like everybody was having trouble keeping their eyes open. He came over to me and looked me right in the eyes, and said are you a betting man?

All of a sudden, everybody that wasn't busy stared at me.

I told him, "Hell yeah! I like shooting dice or poker."

He shook his head and said, "No, buddy. I mean real gambling off the hook gambling."

I got a little nervous and said, "Yeah, he is right,"

Then he went to his desk, grabbed a piece of paper., and said, "I bet you five dollars you can't do what I can," he was in his late twenties and kinda chunky. My brain told me anything he could do, I damn sure could do, and probably better, so I said bet, the guys that weren't working were really staring at us now.

Again, he said, "Good," he walked to his desk, grabbed a piece of paper and twisted the paper into a funnel and put the narrow end into the front of his trousers, tilted his head back, and put a quarter on his forehead (I thought what the hell is this all about) then he quickly shot his head forward and the quarter dropped into the cone into his pants.

He looked at me and said, "Bet."

Well, I was still side saddled during OJT, so I took my cans (earphones) off and said I'm ready, he went back to his desk, got another piece of paper and made a cone out of it, and said use your on the coin I don't want you giving my quarter any damn crotch rot, and everybody started laughing, so I put the narrow end of the cone into the front of my trousers, he said you better put in deeper cause if the coin pops out you lose,

I pushed in a little bit farther, reached into my pocket, got a quarter a tilted my head back. He said, "Nope, put your head all the way back like I did mine."

So I tilted my head all the way back and put the quarter on my forehead. He said back farther, so I did; that's when he got me. He poured hot coffee down that cone. I screamed and cussed like hell. My whole section was laughing so hard that some of them fell to the deck crying and coughing. Meanwhile, I was still cussing and yelling.

After I calmed down, I started laughing. Dave came over to me and said you are doing a damn good job. Your OJT is over, and he said welcome to section four, he then told Dave to take me back to base, and I had the rest of the watch off. I didn't know 1 cup of coffee could cover most of my body, my trousers in the front were soaked, my skivvies were totally soaked, I had coffee in by but crack, and my manhood was drenched. I had to walk out of our spaces thru several other spaces where everyone else was crying and laughing at me. The senior officer on watch came over to me. He was beet red, trying not to laugh. The whole thing was caught on the security cameras, so all the people that were in the building got a good laugh that night at my expense.

When we got to Dave's car, he told me to stop, then he opened the door and put two towels on the seat, still laughing, he said, "Welcome, buddy, and enjoy your mid watch off. He laughed all the way down the hill and to the barracks.

When I got out of the car, I was laughing too. They really got me. It never happened again. I thought about what had happened, laughed again, shook my head on a damn Friday night at 2200 hours which was ten o'clock, I ran up the stairs went to my room my roomies were crying and laughing when I came in, I grabbed my ditty bag with my soap and shaving gear, took a hot shower, shaved, went back to my room got dressed and hit the club. Billy and Jennine were there, so I hung out with them for the rest of the night, around 0200 hours, the club closed.

Billy gave me their address since they had moved Off base. I told him I would come over after I got a car, then I stumbled back to the barracks, fell on my rack, and crashed out for the night.

I remember thinking about Sharleen for a second then I passed out. On our last eve watch, Benny's computer made a ringing noise, the supervisor ran to his position, and Craig stepped away from the desk and grabbed the folder that had 'T O P S E C R E T' in red all over it, they gave it to Benny and told him to get each supervisor to sign it and not to open the folder as it was above his security level, and then to get the guard to initial it. We had heard that a lot of the supervisors were in that night for training, so they all had to sign it also, I looked at Dave who I now sat in the position next to his. In case I had any questions, and it looked like he was crying, and he was beet red, I looked around the spaces, and all the rest of the section looked like they were all red in the face. Then it hit me, it was Benny's turn, Benny was gone for nearly thirty minutes before he came back, and he was still nervous as hell. That's when the supervisor opened the folder and told Benny to sign it. It was a form that had ID -10 –T on it, "ID10T." It took a few minutes for it to sink in for Benny. Meanwhile, everyone in the building was laughing at him, including me.

He was gone for thirty minutes, getting the signatures of all the supervisors and a guard. There was a note inside that read, "This is an IDIOT. Please acknowledge and sign and pass it on."

Then Benny started to laugh and pointed at me. Dave and the Senior office both came over and welcomed him to the section. I was wondering which one was the funniest, and I think it was mine. Then Craig was told to take Benny back to base, we were officially part of Section 4 now.

I can't imagine what the other guys had done to them, but we were now part of section four. Benny and I became really close after that, like two brothers that were always trying to outdo each other. If one of us ran two miles, the other would try and run three miles. We were insane, totally insane, and though we were invincible, that kind of insane. Before his future wife got to Oki, we were on break and bored to death. We had heard of a place called white beach where we could rent a boat, so we brought a twelve-pack a piece and decided we would rent a boat.

I have to make this as clear as I can. We did not know a damn thing about a sailboat, every boat either of us had ever been on had a motor and a steering wheel, not a tiller and canvas to catch the wind to make it go and guide it. It would be a new challenge and adventure, so we thought to rent one. We rented the boat for twenty-five dollars, leaving another twenty-five for a deposit in case we wrecked it, and with only our swimming trunks and two cheap foam coolers full of beer and both wearing sunglasses, we pushed the boat out and climbed in it, I got to the tiller first the sail was already up, and there was a good breeze, it took me a few minutes to figure how to make it go straight, but I finally got the hang of it, we popped the beer open, and the cruise was on, we were not going all that fast, but it seemed like we were, then after a couple of beers each Benny wanted to steer. I laughed at him and told him to quit crying and to get me another can of beer, he tried to kick the cooler over to me, but it was stuck between two of the planks on the bottom of the boat, and his foot went right through it, and we both started laughing until he pulled his foot, and the whole side of the cooler broke off, he was really laughing then, I wasn't laughing anymore, that was my beer getting hot, guess I didn't think it was funny, he called me a cheap assed bastard and laughed some more, I let go of the tiller stood up and kicked his cooler same thing happened, and now his cans of beer were rolling around on the bottom mixed up with mine. He didn't think it was so funny anymore, and then I started laughing.

The fight was on! We were both swinging and ducking. We couldn't kick because the boat was so small, then we grabbed each other, both trying to flip the other one over.

It lasted a few minutes, then we stopped, had a couple more beers sat back, and started laughing. That's when I said, "Let's trade places, you can steer,"

He said, "Okay," and we both stood up. I moved to where he was sitting, and he bent down to grab a beer, and that's when I was able to kick him, and I did, square in his ass. It was on again when I tried to stand up. He caught me with a punch to the ribs, and it was a good one. I couldn't breathe for a second, and he knew it, so he was really coming at me, and I ducked. He lost his balance, and when I tried to grab him by the neck, we both went over the side and into the warm water.

Laughing like two crazy fools that we were, we both swam around for a few seconds, then he said you are so lucky none of my beer was lost, or I would have to really kick your ass, I laughed and told him he was on his best day he couldn't dream of how to beat me, and we both laughed again, and when we looked around the boat was moving away from us. I went under and swam as fast as I could to it and just barely was able to grab it. Then Benny pulled up, we were both out of breath, then we both started laughing again.

After our fits of laughter stopped, we both tried to get into the boat at the same time on the same side, but that was not a good idea at all. The damn thing flipped slowly toward us. I told Benny to let go, and he told me to let go, and since neither of us would let go, it flipped all the way over the actual sail was now in the water. I didn't know that canvas, once wet, weighed so much that we both swam to the other side of the boat, and then the sail went under. I tried to grab as many cans of beer as I could, sticking them into my trunks. Benny did the same thing, then we swam nearly a mile back to shore, old papa san, whom we rented to boat from, was screaming and shouting at us and waving his hands in the air, and he was all in Benny's face.

Then Benny screamed back at him to shut the fuck up, "You still have four left, and keep the deposit." That's when we ran to the car and took off. The sail was actually stuck between two boulders on the bottom, and that's why we could get it to flip back over.

On the drive back to base, we were trying to imitate papa san screaming at us, cracking up, laughing, and drinking the last of the beers we managed to save. Needless to say, we never rented another sailboat again. After that, the next month, I did not do much. I was trying to save for a car. I took a cab to Kadena Air Force Base and went straight for the "Lemon Lot" (a place where guys that we were leaving and needed to sell old, beat-up cars).

Now I have to tell you a little something about the cab drivers that drove us around. If you were a black man, they would put James Brown's music or Sam and Dave's "I'm a Soul Man" in the 8-track player. Some of them would even try to sing the songs that came on; I would just smile and shake my head. What really messed the drivers up as if the passengers were mixed, and I mean two or more blacks with two or more white guys, it kind of confused them. Anyway, I found a car immediately. It was a 1967 Toyota Corona. It was a little 4 door model, at one point, it was probably brown, but when I got it, it was rusted completely, the floor on the driver's side had big holes in it, and I had to tie the passenger door shut with a piece of rope, the radio did not work, but all the lights did, it was a stick shift, so I just drove with one foot on the gas pedal the other foot on the clutch and oh yeah, the steering wheel was on the other side. I drove it back to base, and it moved along really well, didn't make much noise when shifting the gears, and hardly any smoke came out of the exhaust pipe.

I had a car, and my thoughts were, 'It's so ugly, no one would want to break into it or steal it now.'

Benny and I had a ride to work and to the different bases. Back then, I could usually just drive it onto most bases without any insurance. I didn't know how much the insurance for it was and did not have any plans to find out. It didn't even have seat belts. I didn't care, and it got us to the site for work and to all the clubs we wanted to go to. It cost me seventy-five dollars and another twenty-five to register for the first year. Out of the three years I was there, I never registered it again.

When I drove it to the barracks, some of the brothers laughed at it. Billy said, "Smart man," they all looked at him like he was crazy. He said, "Who would want to steal it?" We all laughed but not for too long.

After I got to the car, a major cyclone hit the island. Cyclones are just like hurricanes, except they spin in the opposite direction. We were up on the hill working when it hit, we were prepared. We had rations to feed the on shift crews for seven days. It hit hard and fast, most of the major buildings were made of cement on that island after World War II, but a lot of the islanders had houses made of wood, and it ripped a lot of them up badly, so after the all clear was sounded, sailors, airmen, marines. Army guys were volunteered to help with the island clean up, it took about three days to get most of the roads cleared and search through the rubble for any dead bodies, but we never found any.

Then on the fifth day, the cyclone turned around and hit the island again, not as bad as the first time, but it still hit us. Thank god for the monster size generators we had at the site and on the base. Everybody at work was worried about our cars sitting in the parking lot. I just knew mine was totally screwed. When we were allowed outside after the all clear and our reliefs showed up, we went outside and to the parking lot, mine was still there. The passenger seat on the front side had about four inches of water along with the back seats. One of the windows in the back had rolled down. I may have left it down. I don't remember. I never sat in the back. But I opened the driver's side door. The seat was soaking wet, the holes in the floor had let the water drain out of it. I got to input the key in the ignition the car sputtered for a few seconds, and then it fired right up. I was grinning, a lot of the guy's cars would not start, the mind did. I waited for Benny and we drove over to Dave's car. It wouldn't start, so we drove him to his apartment off base, he said he would worry about the car later. He wanted to check on his wife and kids, but they were moved to the base gym where they stayed during the cyclone, so we drove to base, got his family, and dropped them off, he was lucky. He lived in a brick apartment, and it was okay, he even had power.

After we got back to base, there was a little bit of cleaning up to do, and again, we volunteered to help with the base cleanup along with the Army guys, and it was hot and muggy.

The way we were volunteered sucked on of the chiefs on the quarterdeck came to the barracks and just started knocking on all the doors had us form up outside like we did in boot camp, took roll call, and said, "You are the most gracious people, I don't know how to thank you for volunteering on your off time to assist this base and its personnel in cleaning it up," then he shouted, "start picking up all the shit you didn't see on the ground before the cyclone." He called off all the senior petty offices E-5s and E-6s and put them in charge,

I just bet he was going back to his office to eat more doughnuts and drink coffee. There were about thirty of us, and each was handed a canteen full of water and a pair of gloves along with big trash bags. Benny and I were assigned to an E-6. We hadn't seen him before, but he was really cool. He said, "We would get what we could and be careful to keep your eyes open for Mr. habu. Mr. habu is a snake that is gold with black and brown designs on it. If it bit you, you only had a few minutes to get the antidote, or you will die."

I think they grew to around five or six feet and were fast, very fast. Not being a fan of any damn snakes, what he said scared the shit out of me, not to mention those snakes don't make any noise like a rattler. They just struck. I took my time with each leave; I found a small tree branch, and I used it on any leaves, and palm leaves I had to pick up Benny was laughing at me, but when I looked around, a lot of the guys had the same idea.

Benny stopped laughing, grabbed a branch, and did like the rest of us. There was only one Habu found, and it was blown into the bed of one of the army pickup trucks. The Army Security Guards took a car of it with a shotgun, end of Mr. habu. It took about three hours, but the base was cleaned up, and we all went to the chow hall, sweaty and smelling like, well, you get the idea, the chow was good. I had the cheeseburgers and fries, I just couldn't stop thinking about that damn snake, so before I went to the barracks, I went to one of the trash dumpsters and found a big cardboard box, took it back, and cut it so I could cover the exposed floor of my car. Didn't want Mr. habu in there while I was driving.

That night I decided to hit the town. Benny wanted to stay in the barracks I didn't ask twice, got in the car, which I called my "hooptie," drove to Kadena Air Force Base, and went over to Gate two street. They had drinks, three for five dollars in most of the clubs, and I had about twenty-five dollars on me. I wanted to see some nude babes, so I parked the hooptie in one of the alleys and started walking. This Okinawan guy jumped out as soon as he saw me and was yelling, "cho, cho, cho," he meant to show, show, show. That meant there were strippers on stage doing all kinds of wild stuff, and the sign said three for $5. I went in, and the place probably had about ten small tables and a few chairs in there, only half were full. I went to the one closest to the stage, sat my happy ass down, and ordered my three for $5. Just as I did, this little lady, probably in her forties, came over and sat with me. I looked at her, then looked around the rest of the club, and there were lots of empty places for her to park her ass, but she sat next to me.

I wasn't drunk, yet so I asked her, "Why are you here?"

She said, "I think I lub you, you buy me drinky, you feel good with me, I will love you a long time."

I started laughing and asked her to leave, and I said I just wanted to watch the show, she gave me a dirty look and left, then another one came right over. She actually had some tits, but when she smiled, she had some really bad teeth, looks like some were broken, and others just rotted. I downed two of my drinks back to back, then I asked her to leave. She got mad and said something. I didn't understand, and to be honest with you, I just didn't care. I just wanted a good buzz and look at a show.

Then the stage lights came on the stage, and this little tiny lady with no tits but the longest nipples I have ever seen started dancing, she squeezed her nipples and started licking her lips and was trying to shake her ass, but she didn't have one. The music went faster, and she (bless her heart) tried to gyrate her body to it, it just wasn't happening. Then she stopped, laid on the floor, and removed her panties and this thick afro popped out, and it was all I could do not to laugh. I had tears in my eyes trying so hard. I took another shot and downed it. Then I looked back up on the stage. She had the biggest dildo I had ever seen. It was thicker than one of those big gulp cups you get at Seven-Eleven. She licked it for a while, then she spread her legs and pushed it inside her. I picked up one of the shot glasses that still had the whiskey in it just to make sure I hadn't been drugged or something cause there was no way somebody that little could get that in there, but she did it over and over again.

I drank the last shot I had, got up, and walked out of that place. My brain could not conceive how she got it in there. I walked past the next two clubs and walked into the one that looked really packed, got a seat at the bar, and ordered two shots. They actually had a lady that had at least 34c for tits. I was getting excited and ordered a beer. It was a Budweiser. I was kind of happy, and I was sipping it because it cost about four dollars, and I made it last. I looked back at the stage, and the lady was naked, but she had a snake wrapped around her neck. I know I have mentioned I don't like snakes, but what she did with that snake while she was standing on the stage was way too much for me.

I staggered back to the hooptie, got in, and drove the long way back to my base. It was still early, about 11:30 at night, when I got back. I parked the car walked to Benny's room, and banged on his door, he opened it, and I told him everything I had seen. He laughed and called me a liar, then one of his roommates described the club I was in and said, "He had seen the snake show also."

I just barely made it to my room, looked at my rack, walked over to it, and passed out.

I woke up the next morning with the same clothes I had on the night before, including my tennis shoes, and I was hungover from hell. It was almost lunchtime, so I took a long shower, got dressed, and headed for the chow hall. Did I say I was hungover? I really didn't go back to the clubs outside Gate two street anymore unless it was for some special occasion with the guys. The snake around the lady's neck, Mr. habu, I was done with snakes. Just as I was sitting down, Benny came in with a big ass grin, I thought he was going to make fun of my last night's adventure, but he didn't say a word.

After I finished eating, I looked him dead in the eye and said, "What" he just kept smiling, then he finally said, "Debbie will be here next week, and I'm gonna need the hooptie to pick her up."

I looked and him and said, "Sure."

It took me almost two days to recover from that Gate Two adventure. I felt great on the last day of our break, so I found Benny and talked him into going snorkeling behind the base. It wasn't hard. It was something to do to keep his mind off of Marie getting to the island. I went and got the equipment along with two small bags for collecting shells. Benny went and brought two knives, we met at the beach behind the base, and we put on our gear and started snorkeling, the water was nice and warm, we saw quite a few fish, no sharks though, we floated with the tide going out to sea in a southerly direction, but the tide was not that strong, so we went with the flow of the current, we were near a really deep drop off maybe twenty feet or more, so we both took deep breaths and went down as far as we could, there was a lot of cool looking coral, and some really big fish that kind of looked like black grouper. I don't think there were, though, lots of bright colored small fishes and a couple of octopuses. The bottom was filled with red and brown starfish, and when we surfaced, we were both smiling. Then I noticed we were quite a distance from shore, so I started snorkeling back in closer, and Benny was right behind me.

When we got closer to shore, I noticed we were nowhere near the beach where we went in the water. We were on the other side of the base. The current had carried us over there, we didn't even think about it, just kept on snorkeling. We did head back toward the side of the base where we started out but got distracted by the water color being a grayish color instead of the crystal clear blue. We both floated over into it, and that is when I saw a really cool looking brown and blue seahorse, he was about two inches tall and had his tail wrapped about some seaweed. I scooped him into my bag along with the seaweed, he was going to be my new pet in my little ten gallon fish tank in the barracks.

Benny and I stayed in the water for about an hour just having fun and looking at all the different things that were on that rocky area. Then we decided to head back in to get some lunch. The water was warm, and it felt kind of muddy when we got to the beach, and out of the water, we walked back to the back gate of the base, and I told Benny he smelt like shit, and he looked like greyish color, he told me the same thing as we were walking. We saw the reason why we had swum through the base waste overflow area, all garbage and poop went out those pipes, and we just swam through it, and now the sun was baking it on us. I sat down, pulled the fins off, and took off running, Benny was right beside me, and his hair was grey, and man, he smelled real bad, it was terrible, and the worst thing so was I.

When we got to the gate, the guards were holding their noses and laughing at us. Both of them told us to shower and get to medical asap for a few shots, we kept running. I stayed in the shower for almost an hour and used all my shampoo, and that bar of soap was real thin when I finished with it. The worst part was I could not get the smell out of my mind. Before I got into the shower, I put the seahorse in my fish tank along with the piece of seaweed, and he looked happy I had just filled it with saltwater and going to buy a few more saltwater fish since I had the seahorse. He would be my only fish in the tank. Other than the smell still in my mind, I was kind of pleased, and we did learn a very valuable lesson do not go snorkeling any near the base.

After we were all clean and dressed, we did go to medical just to make sure. Both of the doctors were laughing at us for snorkeling back there, then one of them told me about a place off the coast that was really awesome to snorkel. We told him thanks; I was done with snorkeling until he told me that a lot of tourist females usually go there. That piqued my interest, and I told Benny about the place, and we both laughed and left the infirmary and headed to the barracks. We got teased a lot about that little adventure, and our supervisor was the worst.

He said, "Out of the whole damn island, you decided to swim at the back of a military base." He shook his head and walked away, we didn't go there again.

There was a bus trip set up for us to go snorkeling off of a boat by what was known as suicide cliffs at the south end of the island doing WWII. The Japanese propaganda was that the American Marines would kill the men and would do insane things to the women and eat the babies, at least that's what I was told. We were going to snorkel in that area. I didn't like what I saw lots of skeletons of men, women, and children. They were so afraid of the American Marines that they jumped off the cliffs.

The water was warm and crystal clear, and when we swam closer to the cliffs looking down, that's where we saw some skeletons. I didn't go there again. I knew that WWII was insane but seeing this just proved it to me. All those innocent people died for nothing but pure fear.

We were all ready to go back to shore, we would find better places to swim and snorkel, and we did. Debbie finally arrived, and I saw less and less of Benny. I couldn't blame him, Marie was an awesome lady, and she had the nicest body I had seen in a long while, and Benny was always smiling. I was really glad for them, and she was perfect for him.

I really missed Sharleen. Sometimes I would sit on the steps outside the barracks and wonder what if, then I would snap out of my daydream and keep moving on. I volunteered to go out on a short cruise on board the USS Oklahoma City CG-5 when it was first commissioned on February 20th, 1944. It took a little over two years to build it. It was 610'1" long and was 66'4" wide and was supposed to go over 31 knots. It used the old boilers instead of the diesel or jet engines used on today's warships. By the time I was assigned to it, most of the anti-aircraft guns had been removed and replaced by surface to air missiles, but it still had the triple guns on the main deck and the dual guns on the 01 level on the main deck, and I think it had diesel engines installed by the time I was temporally assigned duty (TAD) on board her.

The Oklahoma City was a fleet flagship; in other words, it was the ship the admiral in charge of the Pacific Fleet stayed on and ran the rest of the ships in the fleet from it. The ship itself had a crew of about 900, and the admiral's crew was around 300. I was part of the admiral's staff along with about ten other CT's, which was one officer I had never met, and the rest of us were enlisted. I want to say six of the CT's were stationed in Hawaii that was on board with us, and the rest were our guys from Okinawa. I was a replacement one of our guys had to leave, and I volunteered to take his place, so I arrived two days after the rest.

We flew onboard a couple of days after the ship had left Olongapo, Philippines, and we were not going to hit another port for the thirty-five days I was assigned to her. I thought to myself, that sucks, but at least I was going to be with the other part of the Navy, the seagoing part.

I was taken to the navy base on Okinawa and boarded a helicopter, I had never been on one, so this was something else that was new to me. I didn't mind flying on airplanes, but this was a totally different thing altogether. My seat was a little lowered bench that pulled down from the side, and my feet were on the emergency escape hatch, which was a metal grate with two latches holding it in place, so for the entire flight, a little over an hour. I had to tuck my trouser legs into my socks and sit there with that breeze. We all wore helmets with little microphones in them, I was a little bit nervous about the seat, but I was the lowest ranking person onboard hell, the fleet admiral was on board, and he had two captains and a commander up with him. The closest person near me was the crew chief. I guess he figured I was not a happy camper, so he gave me a playboy magazine to read. Reading a sex magazine was the last thing I wanted, so I lifted my feet and opened it up, laid the book on the escape hatch, and put my feet on it. That was much better.

The crew chief said something in the microphone I couldn't make out, but everybody started laughing, then the admiral came on and said those CT's are some smart people, then I laughed, not because of the book but because I was a little bit scared.

After a while, we could see the Oki boat. It looked like a toy in a bathtub, but once the helicopter started descending, it got bigger and bigger. We landed on the helo pad at the aft end of the ship, and it was a real smooth landing. I was able to breathe again, as I was the last one on, I was also the last one off. Everything was by rank. The crew chief on the way down told me to stay put until he said otherwise. I nodded my head and gave him the thumbs up, the rotors stopped, and the crew chief got out and dropped the ladder, the admiral left first, and in order of rank, everybody else departed, I was last.

The crew chief told me to go to the quarter deck and find out where the rest of my crew were bunked and then go and get some chow.

I asked him, "Where the quarter deck is?"

He smiled and said, "See, where the admiral is now."

I said, "Yes."

He said that is the quarterdeck. Everybody there was in dress white uniforms, and I was in my work uniform. I was told to wait until the admiral left that area and that the crew up there would assist me. When I got to the quarterdeck, I asked a first class petty officer where was the CT's berthed. He said what the hell is a CT, and I told him Communications Teck. He looked at me, kinda surprised, and said wait one sec. He came back a few minutes later and had a seaman with him that escorted me down to our quarters.

Our CT chief was waiting for me. He told me which rack was mine and asked if I had a lock. I took the lockout of my seabag and showed it to him, and he said, "Good man, took me over to my locker." He added then, "Stow your things in here."

He told me he had to get back to our workspace. I asked him where is the chow hall, and he told me, and then he was gone. I put my seabag in the locker and headed off in the direction the chief had told me. When I got to the spot, he told me there were two lines. I got in the line on the right. It was the shortest one. I was starving. I had heard you could always get a hamburger and fries on board the ship at lunchtime, and I was looking forward to it. Also, my stomach was growling like crazy. The line was moving quickly, and I was glad to be in this line. I was really hungry, damn near starvation. I didn't have breakfast and wasn't sure how a helicopter ride and my stomach would get along.

The line I was in was really moving fast, and when we turned the corner, there was a 1st class petty officer standing there with a notebook and a pen, but the other line kept going straight. I started to question myself about being in this line, and I was right to do so.

When I got next to him, he asked for my name and rate, I told him, and he said, "When you get in the office, drop your trousers and skivvies, bend over and put your elbows on the desk, and chin in your hands." I looked at him like he was crazy, this guy was at least six feet six inches tall, and the only fat on him was between his ears.

I said, "What the hell are you talking about? I'm in the chow line."

He looked at me and said, "Son, your ass is in the VD line, and you know it's mandatory to get the shot, so quit your bitchin."

Again I said, "What the hell are you talking about? I just got on board, and I'm part of the admiral's staff."

He looked at me and said, "Am I gonna have trouble with your crazy ass? You know we just left Olongapo."

I then noticed he had on his shore patrol gear, and his hand was on the nightstick. I looked dead in the eyes and said, "Not one bit of trouble, petty officer."

I was trying to figure out a way to get out of this line when I heard "next," and the petty officer looked right at me, so I went into the space, and the doc (a second class petty officer said, "Didn't you get the word – drop your damn trousers and skivvies, put your elbows on the desk and your chin in both your hands" I started to plead my case, but he cut me off and said, "Do I need to get the first class is here to help you?"

I dropped my trousers and skivvies and put my elbows on the desk which had my whole ass totally exposed (I never had a Venereal Disease shot before) and then I put my hands together which really had my ass in the air and that son of a bitch stabbed me, I wanted to scream, but I didn't want to give him the pleasure, he got me about two inches below the belt line and that needle felt like it was as thick as a pencil, of course my cheeks tightened up and he said, "Loosen your cheek muscles."

I said, "Please just get that needle out of my ass," then I got another jab on the left cheek, and it hurt just as bad as the right side. When I stood up to pull up my skivvies and trousers, it felt like I had a golf ball inside the top part of both cheeks. I was so pissed off I forgot about eating. I wanted to hurt somebody, but there was nothing I could do, and when I tightened my belt, that was, let's just say, uncomfortable as hell. I told myself to go and get some air. I was thinking, what the fuck have I gotten myself into? Ridding on a helo with my seat about to escape, hatch, and a double dose of penicillin in my ass in less than three hours? How screwed up is that?

I hobbled up the ladder and found the smoke break area which was not hard to find. You could smell the smoke, so I just followed the smell all the time. I was thinking about my new adventure, a helo ride over the South China sea sitting above the escape hatch legs freezing, then Godzilla making stay in a VD line when all I wanted was something to eat, walking like Red Fox in his TV show Sanford and Son and the pain from the double stab wounds in my ass cheeks what could be worse. My fingers were still trembling as I was trying to light my cigarette when this officer came over to me. He looked at my name on my blouse and said, "Boy! Your ass is mine."

I swallowed real hard, took another hit off the cigarette, and said, "Sir, I think you have made a mistake while clenching my teeth." I just wanted to knock his ass flat out, but I knew what's better than that.

He started reading off the charges, "Missing ships movement, Absent Without Leave on two counts one for not showing up for work detail the day before and today, Missing Muster and Last Night's Watch, the Captain is going to make a real example out of your ass."

I wanted to say the Captain would be the second one today sir, and fuck you, but I knew I had to keep my mouth shut. After he told me to get into dress whites for Captains Mast, I informed him I had no dress uniform and that I was part of the admiral's staff, and I said it loud enough so everybody around me could hear. He looked at me as if I had just lost my mind.

Then he said, "Lying to a commissioned officer will be another charge." I turned and hobbled my ass back down to the berthing area, found a petty officer down there, and explained that I had Captain's Mast but no dress whites to wear. He looked at me like I was crazy, but he could tell I wasn't joking.

Then he said, "Let's see what we can find for you."

I wear a size nine shoe, and you already know I was a thin kid. He found a pair of size eleven shoes, trousers that would have fit the Godzilla guy, and a blouse also, and that's what I had on when I reported to the quarterdeck. My Captain's Mast was going to be put on the 1MC so everybody could find it here. The 1MC was a speaker system that could be heard all over the ship, I have to tell you getting out of my work trousers with these two lumps on my ass was very uncomfortable but I put on the dress whites with no insignia, no rank patch or anything and a little white cap that was also too large for me, hobbled up the ladders out on to the main deck and to the quarter deck, the Captain and the Commander looked at me like I had totally lost my mind, just as the Captain was about to give me the pre Mast ass chewing the admiral walked up, did a double take at me and said son what the hell is going on here, and I told him, "Sir, it all started when I got into the helicopter with you and had to sit over the escape hatch, then the wrong line for chow and ended up getting a shot in each butt cheek, then the commander over there chewing me out for missing ships movements. AWOL and a bunch of other things I have never heard of, not having a dress white uniform and scrounging up this uniform from a petty officer I don't even know who to return it to.

All I wanted after coming on board was some chow and to start working. My day sucks, "Sir, I have enough penicillin in my body to last for fifty years, and I just wanted to have a smoke before I started work." He looked at me again like so many that day, like I was crazy, then he looked at the Captain and said, "This man is part of my staff. He is from Okinawa TAD on this ship" then he turned to me and said seaman Jackson, please go and put your work uniform back on, get some chow and take a couple of hours off, till the swelling subsides, I actually was able to stand tall and salute saying "eye eye sir" then I did an about-face and tried to walk smartly back to the ladder down to the barracks I only made about ten paces before the Red Fox walk returned, I could feel that commander staring at me, and I turned my head and stuck my tongue out at him, started laughing and got my ass out of there.

I could hear the Captain chewing his ass out the whole time. I was hobbling toward the ladder to get down to the berthing spaces so I could get out of this outfit I had on. After I got in the correct line for chow and fed myself, chow was over, so I had to settle for a ham and cheese sandwich, a bag of potato chips, and some strawberry bug juice. I casually hobbled myself to our workspaces. Once I knocked on the door, it had a keypad on it, and I didn't know the combination yet, so I banged on it as hard as a person can on a metal door. There was a sign on the door with the CT emblem on it, a pen and quill, and it read, "In GOD We Trust All Others We Monitor."

The chief that helped me earlier, his bright face red, opened the door and said, "Son, you have had one hell of a day." Then he showed me where my position was. I gingerly sat down, and everybody in the space busted out laughing.

The petty officer sitting next to me said, "The shot should ware off tomorrow but sleep on your side or your stomach." I said. "It would have to be my stomach as I got a shot in each cheek." Then they all busted up laughing again, and even I started laughing.

The rest of the trip was damn near uneventful, most of the crew had no idea what we did on board and didn't ask. They were probably told we had very high-security clearances and not to interfere with us, I did see that ass hole commander a couple of times, and each time he would walk past and not even look my way. I was good with that. For the remaining twenty-nine days, I did my job as best as I could. One of the petty officers whose position was to the left side of mine kind of took me under his wing. We both worked the same schedule, the mid shift, twelve hours on, and twelve hours off every day until I got off. Now two days before I was scheduled to get off the Oki Boat, I was sleeping and had been asleep for a couple of hours, then all hell brook loose in our berthing area. All I remember was my ass hitting the hard deck from the second rack and then seeing one of the brothers charging two white guys and knocking them down.

I was so tired I scooted my ass into the nearest corner, rolled up in the fetal position, and went back to sleep. If you had the mid watch, you were put in what was called "mid sleepers" or something like that. The other people in the spaces were supposed to be quiet, but that never happened, so you just got used to it. On the Oki Boat, I learned to sleep through anything. I didn't know it was more than just those three assholes. It was about forty of the crew, blacks and whites. When the ship's security finally got things under control, they found me lying on the deck sleeping and thought I was hurt. I woke up and told them I was okay, then my chief came over and asked me what had happened. I told him I didn't know and could I please get some sleep.

Later he told me he thought I was somehow involved in the race riot, then he looked at me and shook his head. The Admiral had a staff meeting that day and wanted to know if any of us were involved or in the location it was. There were two white petty officers that worked the same shift and were berthed where part of the fight took place. The three of us raised our hands. Our chief spoke up before any of us could answer and said, "Sir, none of our people were involved, just in the wrong place at the wrong time." the admiral looked at us and asked if we were okay. We all said, "Yes, Sir," then he looked at me and just smiled. I was off the Oki Boat two days later as we headed back to Okinawa on the Admirals Helo. Only four of us were on board, the admiral had his family from San Diego there waiting for him. When we were about halfway to Okinawa he told me that not all my TAD's would be so much fun, and we both laughed. I was just happy to be going back to NSGA Hanza and wanted to find a babe.

Once I reported back to the Quarter Deck on Torri Station, I was told the Captain wanted to see me. I thought to myself, What kind of trouble am I in now? Turns out the chief in charge of the CT's, the Operations Officer, and the Admiral were impressed with my performance. Then I had to tell the Captain about my first four hours on board the Oki Boat. I don't think he heard one word I said about the mission. We both had a good laugh, and before I was dismissed, I told the Captain I wanted to go to Olongapo Philippines to see if the double shots in my butt cheeks worked, he told me I was dismissed, and I could hear him laughing his ass off after I had closed his door. The Oki boat was my first ship, but it definitely was not the last one.

After the Oki Boat trip and back on base, I had three days off. I couldn't find Benny at all, I knew he said Marie would be there, and I knew I would meet her, but there were some more female CT's on base. I didn't care, I wanted to find out about this MAC thing (Military Airlift Command) where I could fly anywhere in the Pacific where there was an official Air Force Base for $10.00 each way, and I wanted to go to the Philippines and to Olongapo City and Subic Bay Navy Base, my next adventure.

Well, it turned out to be true, not just the ordinary scuttlebutt. I could go to Kadena Air Force Base in Okinawa and catch a flight to Clark Air Force Base in the Philippines. From there, I could get a cab or Jeepney for a couple of dollars and go to Angeles City in about 2 minutes or get a cab or bus to Olongapo for about $5.00, and I would be in heaven compared to Okinawa. It was the plan. I had three days off of my normal shift, which I damn near spent two days sleeping and drinking, and yes, my butt cheeks did return to being happy, no needles jabbed into them, just healthy bronze skinny cheeks. I decided I would take three days' vacation time after my next shift, which would give me six days off. I had a whole check that I only spent on a couple of packs of cigarettes, soap, and toothpaste. I had over $200.00 and would be getting paid again this week probably put me at almost $500.00. I had planned on only spending $250.00 for the entire trip, which included meals on base or out in the town, booze, and partying with the Pilipino ladies.

The plan was set, I jumped in my hooptie and cruised around the base looking for someone to hang out with, couldn't find anybody, and then just drove off base. I went over where Dave said he lived, and I'll be damned if they were not all outside sitting and drinking beers. I pulled up, had some beers, and hung out with Dave, his family, and Rodney. I asked if any of them knew about the MAC flights, and they all pointed to Rodney. He had been on two of them. He told me everything I needed to know. I was all set for my trip. He told me about the women there and how to keep my eyes on them and not get robbed. Make sure they're really as drunk as they appear to be and not just faking it. Try and find one that is not working in the clubs, and good luck finding one without any kids. Then we all started laughing.

I asked Dave about living in this apartment. He said they liked it, but he and his wife (she was really cool) were having another kid that would make their second one, and they would be looking for a house next year. I hung out with them for a couple of hours and left, thinking when I got back from the Philippines, I would need to be looking for an apartment. I got back to base and saw this new little blonde lady, I waved at her, and she waved back. I was tired, so I went back to the barracks and crashed.

The day finally came I went to Kadena, signed up for my flight, paid the $10.00, and caught a flight on an Air Force C-130 cargo plane. Other than the crew, there were only three passengers, all enlisted. I was the only sailor; the other two were airmen. This plane was huge, it was normally meant to carry troops and equipment, but it was empty at this time. There was netting stuff everywhere, the crew chief came down and instructed us on emergency escape and floatation devices, handed us a bag of peanuts each, and he sat down, and we were off. Do you know how people say the difference is between night and day? Well, landing in Clark Air Base in the Philippines on Luzon Island compared to Kadena Air Base in Okinawa was like just having the lights turned on in a dark room. The heat and humidity were about the same; the base was a good size airbase, but nothing like Oki. The first thing I did was find the chow hall; the crew chief told me where it was for the enlisted. I got on the correct base bus, and I was there in just a few minutes. I was not sure what kind of food I would have once I left the base, so I decided to get my old standby, a cheeseburger, and fries, along with a strawberry soda.

I had a small suitcase with two pairs of levy's and a couple of short sleeve shirts, and I did bring one pair of dress shoes, my tennis shoes, and some skivvies. I brought a cheap Timex watch before I left Oki. If it got stolen, I wouldn't care. I wanted to get one of those Kodak cameras that developed the picture after you take it, but Rodney had told me to "Try and not look like a tourist." So, I didn't get one. I got on another bus that said, "Main gate," and from there, I hopped in one of the cabs that were parked outside the main gate and I was on my way to Angeles City, and in about five minutes, I was in "Heaven," The people from the Philippines look nothing like the Japanese or Okinawans, the women here were short like them, but that was the only thing, they had noticeable tits and asses, and they smiled a lot.

Now at the time, I was there, the Philippines still had Martial Law, put on by the president at that time, Ferdinand Marcos, which meant there was a curfew and you needed to be off the streets before 23:00 hours or 11:00 PM, if you were stuck in a club then that's where you stayed until 0500 or 5:00 AM, the crew chief told me about the curfew and a decent hotel to stay in, and I went there first it was walking distance to all the clubs, and that was just what I needed.

The lady at the front desk smiled at me and said, "Your first time here."

I said, "Yes."

Then she said, "I will watch out for you, okay!"

I smiled at her and said, "Okay."

The room was $6.00 per night, but I had planned on staying in Angeles City my first night and then again on my last night; that way, I could be one of the first in line to catch a MAC flight back to OKI.

My room was on the second floor, and it was a basic room. It had a nightstand, bed, and sink, but the shower was in the same room, and it just had a curtain around it. I thought to myself, it's better than nothing. Then I put all my cash in my wallet and put it in my front pocket harder for a pickpocket to get to, took the room key, and headed toward what was called Fields Avenue, it was still daylight, and the ladies were already partying, I was so happy, I think I shed a tear or two.

Now the cheapest mode of transportation was the Jeepney or a trike (you have to see them believe they exist). I had never seen anything like those vehicles in my life. The Jeepney was an old jeep re-designed to carry people in it, the back seat was removed, and a bench was put on both the left and right sides, then there was a hard top added to it with pipes to hold it in place, some had a board fixed to both sides and a tube added along the roof on both sides so you could stand on the board and hold on to the roof. I loved it, then there was the trike. It was usually a small dirt bike with a small sidecar added to it, there were cars for taxis, but it was cheaper to just jump on the Jeepney and hold on, give the driver a few pesos, and you were good to go. There were cars and bicycles but mostly the jeepneys and trikes.

Then you had the people pushing carts with food on them, and they usually had a WOK on it with a little gas stove to heat up whatever they were cooking. I really liked the jumbo shrimp. Then there were the folks with the carts for ice cream and fresh drinks, water, and cokes mainly, and there were also stands where you could buy fried and grilled stuff, chicken, fish, and shrimp. I'm not sure what the other stuff was, but it all came on wooden skewers, and rice came with everything.

I cannot forget the kids trying to sell me one cigarette for five cents. Now for the good stuff, not all the ladies on Field street were prostitutes, but there had to be at least twenty to thirty at what was called Girley bars. There were women dancing with bikinis on (did I mention I had a tear or two in my eyes), and most of them looked damn good to me after a year on OKI. I knew I wasn't going to deal with one of them tonight. I had to get up and be on the road to Olongapo first thing in the morning. That was a three and a half hour trip. I didn't want to be hungover, trying to figure out where I was and being by myself. I thought I should be somewhat sober, just in case, I walked into this club that had a real cute little lady with a nice size afro, grabbed her hand, and walked out to the dance floor, and we danced for a couple of songs, I knew from Rodney if I danced with one I would have to buy her a drink, so we got a table, and I ordered two Budweiser's, you could buy Budweiser just about anywhere and that's what we had, her English was pretty good, so we just talked, we danced again, I brought her another beer, and she asked me if I was taking her back to my room, I told her nope, and she got up and walked away.

She was cute but not what I wanted, so I got up, went to the next bar, had another beer, and watched the girls dancing. Then I got myself up, walked down the street back to the hotel, and went up to my room, the same lady was there, and she just stared at me. I smiled and walked up the stairs, it was after 21:00 or 9:00 PM, and I wanted some rest. After I took a quick shower and brushed my teeth still with the towel wrapped around me, there was a knock on the door, I went over and opened it, and there was a really good-looking woman, and she said, do you want me to stay with you tonight I told her to thank you, but not tonight, she huffed and walked off.

About five minutes later, another knock on the door. This time, the lady was really fine, but I told her the same thing. She looked at me like I was crazy and walked away. Just as I was getting into the bed after checking for any kind of bugs, there was another knock on the door, this time, I was a young boy.

I got so mad that I went downstairs and told the lady at the reception desk, "I just want to get some rest. Is that okay?" I went back to my room, double locked the door, put my wallet under my pillow, and lay on the bed waiting for another knock, thinking, *what kind of shit is this? Can't a brother just get some sleep?*

Nobody else knocked on the door. No more interruptions. I went to sleep. I was up around 0700, and it was still hot and muggy. I put all my clothes back in my suitcase and paid for the night, got a cab, and headed to Olongapo. God, I was glad I didn't have a hangover, the roads were terrible, potholes and everything. I had to stop a few times for cows to cross, but everything was all green and jungle like. The three and a half hour ride cost me $10.00 for the cab. I could have caught what was called the rabbit for a lot less, but I just wanted to hurry up and get there. If the ladies looked like what they did in Angeles City or better, I was in a hurry to find one for myself. The cab driver made one stop, and he got out and took a piss on the side of the road, I said if you can't beat them, join then, but I kept an eye on the ground; I didn't want to make anything on the ground that could bite or sting me mad. We did not make any other stops. He dropped me off on

Magsaysay Street, that street was something else, women everywhere. I had another tear, Rodney had told me about a hotel just off Magsaysay street that was fairly reasonable and clean. I walked there, the room was $9.00 per night, and it was clean. I didn't see any roaches. I was happy. I let the lady behind the reception counter know that Rodney from Okinawa said this was a good place. She dropped the price to $8.00 guess she liked Rodney, and not to mention she looked really good. We smiled at each other, I didn't know if she was being nice because it was part of her job, but I thought she wanted to be with me.

She had walked up to the room with me and showed me where the shower was, and it was just like the room I had in Angeles City, damn near identical. I smiled at her again, and she told me her name was Honey, I smiled at her again. Before she left, she told me if there was anything, anything I needed to just let her know. I wanted to ask her if she wanted to take a shower with me, but I didn't. She smiled again at me and left. I unpacked my clothes and did the three S's.

I went back down the stairs, and she was still there, so I asked her where was a good place to go for breakfast even though it was almost lunch. She asked me to wait for a second and then she came back with another lady. They said something in Tagalog (the Pilipino language), and she said follow me, so we walked over to Magsaysay street and went into this restaurant. I told her I would buy her lunch if she wanted, and she smiled and said, "Okay," we talked, and she told me all about Olongapo and what clubs to go into. If I stayed on Magsaysay street, I was cool. That was the only street the blacks and whites both partied on. I think the side of the city for us black was on the east side, she then told me about herself, she wanted to know where I was from so I told her Los Angeles California, her eyes got real big she asked me about Hollywood, and I cracked up laughing, she asked me what was so funny, I told her we called it Holly weird – she didn't get it, and I didn't try to explain.

I asked her what was the best club to go to. She said the third one from this restaurant, that's where she goes, and she would be there tonight around seven. I said, "Okay, I'll be there," she smiled again, and we left. I paid for the lunch. I had what I hoped was a cheeseburger, and so did she. It cost me about five dollars for the both of us, along with a bottle of water, and she had a coke. After I paid, I walked over to the club, and it was kinda like the clubs in Angeles City, just bigger and louder music and a lot more ladies. I knew the fleet would be gone, which meant hardly any sailors or marines would be around, and that meant more fun for me. I was smart like that, I wasn't too smart about that VD line on the OKI boat, but I was over it.

When I walked into the club, I was in heaven, a bar full of women and hardly any guys.

Oh, yea! I was good to go.

There were women on the stage dancing, some sitting together at different tables, laughing and smiling, having fun. I guess they were kind of happy the fleet was out. They were having a break, and when I walked in, one of them came over to me and told me she loved me and she really liked my afro. I smiled and asked her how she could love me. She said she could tell and I almost choked laughing so hard. She kept smiling. I told her to be a good girl and get me a beer, a bud. She said, "Okay, Daddy." I really laughed then.

All the babes that worked in the bar had on the same kind of shirt and black jeans, then there were the dancers, they usually had on daisy duke shorts and a bikini top and had a number somewhere on them, just in case you wanted to make a payment for them to be yours for twenty-four hours, and of course, you had the prostitutes that would come in and try to get an American if I remember exactly. They could only come into the clubs if accompanied by an American, and they would normally be chased out. I sat, had a beer, and wandered off down the street. I stopped at a shop that had some of the best wood carvings I had ever seen. There were elephants, tigers, and all kinds of carvings. I reminded myself to come back before I left to get a chess set I saw carved out of ivory. It was beautiful. I was told it was ivory.

How would I know?

I saw a person I thought was a woman, but she sounded like a guy and had some big ass feet, for a woman, she wanted to know where I was staying so she could come over. I said in a way she/he knew I wasn't playing NO! a couple of the girls in the club chased her/him away, and one girl said, "Ladyboys no good."

After that, I went over to the market and saw all kinds of fresh fruits, fish, shrimp, and meats, and lots of woodcarvings and paintings. I checked that place out for about an hour. I was hot and tired. I walked back to the hotel and took another shower, laid on the bed, and took what I thought would be a little nap. I woke up to all the street sounds from the different clubs the next street over. Jumped out of bed, hit the shower and got dressed, stashed my money behind one of the pictures on the wall in the room, and took fifty dollars with me, I was gonna party my ass off, and I meant business. I got to the club where Honey said she would be, but I had to be cool, so I went to the bar, grabbed a seat and ordered a Budweiser, and proceeded to have a good night, just as the bartender asked me what I wanted, Honey came over and damn near sat in my lap, she was smiling like crazy. I had never noticed that she had a gold tooth before, but instead of having that long black hair, she had a really nice afro, and it looked good on her. I didn't recognize her at first, I ordered her a beer, and she smiled and kissed me on the cheek. She pulled me up and said we had a table waiting. I got up and followed her to the table. All the time she was holding my hand, I was kinda happy. She had on these tight gold bell-bottom pants and almost a see- through black blouse with a gold color bra.

Yeah, I was going to party all night long.

We sat down and finished our beers, and she told me she didn't think I would show up. I just laughed at her and kissed her on her neck, and she smelled really good, like strawberries. I wanted to take her right then and there. We talked for a few minutes then I asked her to dance. They were playing rock music, and I didn't care, so we got up and danced for a long time, then a slow song came, and I pulled her close to me, and I could feel her breast against my chest at first she had her arms around my neck, and all of a sudden she was messing with my afro right on the sides. I told her not to mess up my hair, then she put on hand right on my back, right in the middle where I got the VD shots, and I asked her what the hell is wrong with you, she looked like she was going to cry,

I told her it's okay, just don't be doing that crazy shit, and then she told me that a white man told her that all blacks had horns and a tail at first. I was pissed off, then I took her hand and put it on the front of my pants and said this is the only tail I have. She smiled and squeezed herself closer to me. I had to pull her hand away from my HOOKUP, and then I started grinding on her. Then a fast song came on. I just kept her right where she was.

After a few minutes, I said, "Let's go sit down. I wanted another beer," the waiter came, and I ordered two more buds. We finished them and went back to my room I showed her my horn then, and we stayed there all night and most of the next day. I gave her a few dollars, and she left and came back with breakfast, and we were back in the rack again. I was finally having fun.

She left one more time, and she came back with the clothes that she was going to wear that night we did the same thing partied for a couple of hours then went back to my room, while we were walking back to the hotel, one of the street girls said something in Tagalog to me, I didn't understand what she said, but whatever she said sure made honey mad, and she cursed at her in English, I just smiled and kept walking holding her arm. When we got back to the room, I asked her what that shit outside was about, and she said, "Stupid benny boy said you should be with him and not me." I told her I was not that kind of guy. I like things just the way they are. Before we got to bed, I told her I wanted to go and see more of Olongapo, not just Magsaysay Street and the club. She said, "Okay."

We probably got to sleep about an hour later, I woke up, and she was in my arms just like it was with Sharleen, but not Sharleen, nothing like Sharleen. I rolled over and went back to sleep. We both woke up, got dressed, and went to the restaurant for lunch. I remember having shrimp and rice with fried eggs. It wasn't too bad, and Honey had the same, then we went outside. I wanted to get a cab, and she said, "No, too much money." I told her it was too damn hot and humid to walk. She smiled at me and said, "We'll take the jeepney" I said okay, she talked to the driver, and it was ours for the whole day for $5.00. Back then, you didn't need to convert your money to pesos. I was good with that only problem was no damn air conditioning on a jeepney, but the view sitting in it was awesome.

We stopped at a mama san store and got a foam ice chest and filled it with bottled water and the Pilipino beer called San Miguel, it didn't taste bad, but back then, I was pretty sure there was no way for them to measure the alcohol content in each bottle, sometimes you could drink two of them and be really toasted, and other times you could drink six and not have a start of a buzz, but the price was right twelve bottles cost me $2.30. I was really happy about that. We got back in the jeepney and went to the local beach. It was kind of dirty, but it was still awesome. The water was clear, I had on jeans, or I would have stiped down and gone in for a swim, but not this day. We went back into town to the barrio and hit a couple of the outdoor markets, there was everything from food to wood carvings, and some of the carvings were just awesome. I wanted to remember this place because I would be coming back here again on my next trip.

We went back to our jeepney, had another beer, and went around to a couple of the parks where everybody that wasn't too hung over from the night before was just kind of chilling out. We had a couple more beers. I brought honey an ice cone, and then we walked around a little while longer, got back in the jeepney, and headed back to the hotel. I couldn't wait to get into a cold shower, I asked Honey where she lived, and she told me around the corner of the last part we went to. She said she stayed with her older sister. I said cool and didn't think much else about it.

The next two days were basically the same.

At night, we would go to the clubs on Magsaysay street, have about four or five beers and go back to my hotel room. I hated the idea of going back to Oki, but I had to be at Clark Air Force Base and signed up for any flight that was going back to Oki. I left early, snuck twenty dollars in Honey's purse, kissed her goodbye and got a cab back to Angeles City, and was dropped off at the main gate at Clark Air Base. I caught a base bus to the terminal, signed up, and paid my ten dollars for the return flight, I was told the next flight to Oki would not be until 1400 hours (2:00 PM), so I went to the base club for enlisted personnel, had lunch and a couple of Budweisers. I was sad to be leaving honey, but she gave me a number to call when I came back, and they would get in touch with her for me.

While at the enlisted club, I ate lunch and watched strippers while I ate my double cheeseburger and fries. God, I was gonna miss this country. Back in Oki, I hooked up with Dave and his family at his apartment and proceeded to tell him about the Philippines while we drank a lot of beer, I did tell him about Honey, and he laughed and said she was probably a hooker and we both laughed, I knew she was, but I was cool with it as long as she didn't give me any sexually transmitted problems that required the old needle to ass cheeks I was Okay. Dave told me about a Honda motorcycle. It was a 450cc with some air force guy who was leaving and only wanted two hundred for it. I still had double that amount after my trip, so I told him to take me over there tomorrow to see it, but for now, let's finish drinking. I was really toasted when I left their apartment, and I just cruised back to the base in the hooptie parked in front of the barracks, took my stuff up to my room, and passed out. I'm pretty sure I was thinking of getting back to the PI as soon as I could.

The next morning, Dave showed up in his Honda and said, "Let's go!" he gave me his wife's helmet to wear, and I jumped on the back, and we took off. I thought we were going to Kadena Air Force base instead. We went to a housing area near the base. The guy was really ready to leave. He said his wife and kids had left the day before, and all he needed to do was get rid of the bike and clean the house, so it passed the base inspection for his sign-off, and he was off this rock forever. I walked over to the bike and sat on it. He threw me the keys and said to take for a ride, so Dave and I hit the road. It was fun and easy to ride, not like my cousin's dirt bike in Sacramento that I often drove when we went there to visit. It shifted gears real smoothly, and it handled the curves nicely. I pulled in front of Dave, and we stopped. I asked him why only $200, and he said you heard the man, as soon as he sold it, he's out of here, we headed back to the base housing. I handed over the $200, and he handed me a note of sale and his helmet. I was now the proud owner of a hooptie and a two-year-old Honda 450 with a full tank of gas. Dave and I rode back to his place, had a few beers, and I thanked him for telling me about my new bike, and I left.

I didn't go straight to base, I went to the place Benny and I rented the sailboat. I drove around that area for a while, thinking about how nice it would have been to have Sharleen at the back, speeding along on this new motorcycle. After cruising that road, I made a U-turn and headed back to base. It was damn near lunchtime, and I was starving. I wasn't one for taking guys for a ride on the back of my bike, just didn't like that idea, so if a friend needed a ride, I would just throw him the keys to my hooptie. It was starting to run roughly, probably needed a tune up or something. I told myself we would run it until it died.

There was a guy named Craig who was a part of our watch section, but he was not an R-Brancher. He was a T. He asked me if I could take him to what he called whisper alley and wait about fifteen minutes for him. I said sure, it was still early, about 9:30 PM. I didn't go out until around 10:00 PM, so I got into my new bell bottoms, and a decent short sleeve shirt, put on my platform shoes and went to his room as soon as I knocked on his door, he opened it and said let's go. Craig was really one crazy white dude, I'm not sure, but I really didn't think he cared too much about anything. I did know he had more Playboy magazines than anybody I ever knew.

We went downstairs, got in the hooptie, and I asked, "Where are we heading to?"

He looked at me and said, "Whisper Ally,"

I had never heard of the place, and I said, "Well, let's go."

It was in an area near Naha, some nice looking little houses, Craig told me to pull into the ally, and I did. I noticed some of the houses had red lights on the little patio in the back of the houses, I parked the hooptie under this really big banana tree, and Craig got out and headed towards the back of the houses and knocked on one of the patio doors that had a red light, then the patio door slid open, he unzipped his pants and leaned forward, the curtain was never pulled back, but he had his hookup out, and somebody must have been sucking it for him. I couldn't believe what I was seeing and not seeing. I got out of the car and went closer. Craig told me to wait my turn and get in line behind him, he was standing there getting a blowjob, and he could not see who was doing it. I walked real fast back to the hooptie and got in.

I still could not believe that anybody would let someone get him off without knowing if it was a man or woman. I was trying to wrap my mind around it, and then I just started laughing. I kept telling myself Craig was a real trip. I looked back over at him, and I heard a loud thump on the windshield. I looked up and almost pissed my pants. It was the biggest spider I had ever seen in my life, its body was as big as a baseball, and then those eight legs were pretty long, and it was a brownish color, and to make things worse, it was moving in a circle on the windshield like it was checking me out, I rolled up the window and turned the car on, and when I did that it stopped, I really freaked out, I thought I was gonna shit I was so scared.

I slowly moved my hand to the windshield wiper button and turned it on, I forgot only the blade on the driver's side worked and mister spider was not happy when that wiper blade smacked him on his ass, he jumped and I screamed like an eight year-old-little girl, I never saw a spider that could jump so far, he landed on the hood of the car and it made a thump sound, I quickly got out of the car, tripped over some of the roots of that big ass banana tree and landed ass first on the ground, now I was getting mad, the fear had left and I was pissed, I looked up and Craig was standing there laughing his ass off at me, I told him about the spider and he really started laughing, when I got up I had split my brand new fake Jordash pants from the seam in the middle of the back to right below my zipper in the front, in other words my whole ass was in the wind, I was really pissed and Craig would not stop laughing, meanwhile mister spider had disappeared that didn't make me happy at all because I didn't know where it was. Craig was still laughing. I got up, looked inside the hooptie, and got in. I yelled at him if he wanted a ride back to get his ass in the car. I was mad as hell the whole way back to the base.

I pulled the hooptie into a parking space near the barracks and, with my ass hanging out, went up the stairs to change into a pair of Levi's, sat down for a few minutes to calm down, and then headed for the base club, I really needed a drink. When I got to the club, I parked my motorcycle next to the front door, put my helmet on the gas tank and walked inside and wouldn't you know it, Craig was already there and had told everybody about the banana spider and me, Benny was there with his lady Marie and they were also laughing, I went to the bar and ordered two Budweiser's went and sat with them. Benny asked me what we were doing in that part of Naha, and I told him about whisper ally and Craig getting a blowjob and couldn't see who or what was giving it to him. Benny and Debbie really started laughing, then I told him about my whole ass hanging out, and we all laughed. After the fifth beer, I headed back to the barracks. I parked my motorcycle away from the hooptie, not sure where Mr. spider was, and I was not taking any chances. I stumbled up the stairs, went to my room, and passed out. It was another unwanted eventful day for me.

When I went back to work, everybody knew the whole story about Mr. Spider and me, but Craig had forgotten to mention the reason I met Mr. spider. I wanted to pay back from him, and it took two weeks of careful planning, but I did get even. I had met a couple of the brothers in the Army that I thought were pretty cool, and one of them had what we had in the Navy called collateral duty. He was the base photographer for the guys he worked for in base security. I think his name was Donald, so on that next payday, nobody would give good old Craig a ride down to whisper alley, and he came and asked me, saying no hard feelings. I smiled, and he said, "It's all good. You got me that time."

I told him that I would have my friend Donald with us as he wanted that five dollars or whatever you paid relief. I told him that I had to go to the base PX and get some stuff like soap and shaving cream, but I would be back in time to pick him up. As soon as he walked back to his room, I practically ran down the stairs, got in the hooptie, and found Donald at the bowling alley having a beer, that's where he hung out, and I just knew he would be there. I told him about Craig going to whisper alley and what I wanted to do. He laughed so hard he spits his beer all over the bar and some on me. I didn't care; I just wanted to pay back. I drove him to his barracks, and he got his equipment, put it in the trunk, and we went and picked up Craig.

I introduced them, and we headed to whisper alley and got there just as the sun went down. I pulled into the same alley as that big assed banana tree, but nowhere near it. I guess I didn't want to meet Mr. spider again. Craig got out and walked up to the same patio, and knocked on the glass. Donald got his camera gear out of the trunk and had it set up just as Craig put his money through the curtain. Just the idea of my plan had me trying not to laugh. I looked at Donald, and he gave me the go ahead nod. I walked really fast up to Craig and snatched the curtain aside, and I could hear Donald's high-speed camera just clicking away, taking picture after picture of an at least an eighty-year-old mama san with no teeth giving Craig a blowjob. Donald started screaming, he was laughing so hard. I just dropped to the ground laughing, and Craig turned as red as hell. He was pissed, and old mama san pulled the curtain closed, cursed us out, and screamed you go, you go.

Donald started laughing harder and pointing at Craig now. I will admit I don't have the biggest pecker in the world, but next to that little thing Craig was holding with two fingers, mine would be considered a monster. I looked at him and yelled, "Put that little thing away! It looked like a baby's pinky finger, he got redder and madder," I stood up and said hey pinky you need a ride home he walked to the hooptie and got in, poor Donald was laying in the back seat crying laughing all the way back to base.

When I dropped Craig off at the barracks, he asked me what we were going to do with the pictures, I just smiled, and Donald busted up laughing again, and so did I. Craig walked away shaking his head. He never asked me for a ride again, and I heard he kept going there to whisper ally, guess it was a place he felt comfortable going, and it was the only place he went off base.

Dave had mentioned that his sister-in-law was coming to visit for two weeks. We all wanted to know if she looked as good as Dave's wife. He just smiled when we asked and wouldn't say anything he just kept on smiling. Now Dave's wife was a really nice looking woman, long black hair, her face was very nice and easy on the eyes, she had the body to go with it, plus she was kinda like the big sister to everybody always had good advice for us young'uns as Dave called most of us. I met Dave's best friend. He was more county than Dave, had a scraggly beard, skinny as hell, and looked like his clothes were always falling off of him, but he was cool as hell and twice as crazy.

I got along well with him also, then there was this guy named Ben, I always thought he was a racist but Dave said he just doesn't like most people, Ben didn't say much he was the loner type, and you never knew what he was going to say when he did say something. I think he said crazy shit just to see our reactions, none of them were ever disrespectful to anybody, so this was our biker crew, and we rode all over Oki on the motorcycles, Dave was the only one with the big Honda 750, and at that time it made the rest of our little 450's look like little toys, it was higher, wider and a hell of a lot faster, I knew I was gonna get one before I left Oki. That next break, we had come quick. I hung out with Benny and Marie during the work week when I could.

They were getting really serious about each other, and I was happy for them. They were even talking about having kids. I had to stop myself from thinking about Sharleen while I listened to Marie talk about that subject. We usually hung out for about an hour or two at the club or the chow hall before heading back to the barracks to crash out for the next shift. On the last eve watch, Dave told me not to get drunk and be hung over because we were going to cruise the island the next day and to meet at his house around 10:00. I said, "Cool!" I had a couple of beers in the room. I was just gonna drink them and call it a day, and that's what I did.

I was up in time to get breakfast at the chow hall. I noticed a couple of new females I had not seen before, and I wondered if they were army or navy, one of them was a cute little blonde with really perky boobs; I liked her. The other one looked a little manly. I barely noticed her, the little blonde smiled at me, and I gave her a quick wink, picked up my tray, got in line, and ordered two eggs scrambled with cheese. Some bacon, and two pieces of sausage, when I got out of line to find a spot to sit down when I looked around. The little blondie was gone. I shrugged my shoulders and thought to myself, I will see her again. I ate really fast, took the tray and plate to the drop-off area for trays and utensils, walked back to my bike and fired it up, backed it out of the parking spot, and headed for the front gate, and I was on my way to Dave's place.

I was the last one to arrive, and they were all sitting around or on their bikes. When I pulled up, they all smiled at me, which was really unusual, and that is when Dave's sister-in-law walked out, she had a pretty face like her sister and even the long black hair. The only problem was she was pretty and pretty damn big. She was close to 6' tall and about 195 lbs wearing really tight jeans that looked like they were painted on her, and her boobs I could have used as a scarf, I tried to explain my stomach was hurting and I needed to get back to base and lay down. Her name was Sarah, and she was riding with me today whether I liked it or not, at least that's the look Dave's wife gave me, l looked at his wife and smiled, but on the inside, I was crying like a little girl. Ben started to say something, but the girl he had on the back of his bike elbowed him in the gut, and he only grunted.

Dave handed Sarah one of his spare helmets, and she managed to get in on and walked over to my bike. I put my helmet back on, giving everybody the evil eye, then I felt the back of my bike go down about an inch or two, then these long fingers were on my shoulder. I told her to put her arms around my waist, and Dave and all the rest took off. I put my bike back into first gear and prayed I and the bike would survive. I could feel her boobs pushing me forward. I thought to myself, this is your bike, don't let this big woman push you around on it, so I leaned back into her boobs, and they did feel really soft, I must admit.

We were headed south, that road had lots of curves, and one of them, the second most dangerous one, was in the middle of a tunnel. When I learned she tried to stay straight up, which made me almost have to stop to take the curve completely. After we made it through the tunnel, I pulled over. I was pissed as hell. We almost died when she sat up straight. I was doing about fifty miles an hour, and we came within a few feet of the wall before I was able to break slowly. I had planned to call her all sorts of nasty names after I took my helmet off. If she threw a punch, I was going to throw my helmet at her and run the five miles back to base. I didn't want to be punched by her. I cooled down and thought about it for a second, and I had to let her know how to ride on the back of my bike.

I could feel her heart beating like it was out of control when I did stop, even though those huge boobs when she pulled her helmet off, her face was bright red, and her lips were trembling. I guess she was scared shitless, hell, so was I. I helped her off the bike, and we sat down on one of the curbs. I put my around her and told her, "Look, we're both okay, and I know you are scared, but when we get back on the bike, I want you to sit back a little bit, and then after I get on, lean forward into me and when I lean to the bike you have to lean with me not more or less but just the same as I lean."

She shook her head and said, "okay." She even tried to smile, and then we got back on the bike. She was holding me so tight I thought my kidneys were gonna burst. I had to yell at her to loosen her grip a little, so I could breathe. I thought I heard a nervous little laugh from her. We took off.

We were heading toward suicide cliffs up on in the mountain area. The road had lots of curves, Sarah did as I told her, and we didn't have any more problems. I thought she was turned on after we got to the top of the mountain. Her nipples felt like those deformed oranges that are out of shape where the stem from the tree branch is removed. That portion that stops the orange from being round was just poking me in the back. I have to be honest, and those huge nipples were getting me excited as well.

We caught up with everybody else at the top of the mountain, and Dave signaled a right turn. There was a clearing up there, and it was all dirt, so we all pulled over. He had the big plastic side bags attached to his 750, and they were full of beer and ice. I think he got like two four packs of Budweiser's in there, I needed a drink, and as soon as I stopped the engine and let Sarah get off the bike, she grabbed two beers, brought me one, and said thank you to me. She gave me a big hug and again said thank you. Everybody was looking at me like we had stopped and had sex or something.

I explained what happened, and they all cracked up laughing. Dave then told me that he should have let me know that she had never ridden on a motorcycle before. I gave him a dirty look, and then I started laughing. Sarah was sitting in the dirt, opening her second beer. After drinking our beers, we walked to the edge of the mountain, and you could see the south china sea. We all hung out there for about an hour until all the beer was gone, got back on the bikes, and headed east and down the hill. Sarah was an expert rider now. When I learned she did exactly what I did, no more, no less, and we both were at ease, but those big nipples were still poking me in the back, and every now and then, her hand would slip down and land on my hookup, I could still feel her heart beating. I tried not to think of her hand and where it was as that would not have looked good me trying to get off my bike with my hookup hard as a brick.

We stopped at a little village that had the biggest Koi fish (a kind of huge goldfish) I had ever seen, just swimming around in a pond. Some were orange with gold, orange with black or white, and some were just completely orange. Soon as I saw them, I got hungry. We stopped at the only little restaurant in the village, and everybody ordered Soba noodles, it was noodles with some kind of pork, and this place also gave us boiled rice with it. I gotta tell you, we all sucked with chopsticks, so mama san gave us plastic forks to use as we were spilling rice all over the place. Sarah turned out to be really cool, a really nice lady. She got along well with everybody, and that was awesome.

We all ate and headed back to Dave's house and drank more beer, lots more beer. Don and his ladies left first then the other couple was gone. I was damn near passed out on the couch. Dave and his wife had gone into their room about an hour earlier. I didn't even realize it was just Sarah and me still there. I don't think anything happened. I couldn't remember much after Don left, I know we laughed a lot about our near death experience, and I told her about her nipples poking me in the back. She laughed, pulled up her t-shirt, and showed those huge tits to me. I think that's when I passed out.

It is coming up on the Christmas and New Year holidays in the next couple of months, and I really wanted to celebrate and have some real good fun. I charged $25.00 per watch that I stood for each person, and within three and a half months. I had an extra $200.00. I had planned on going back to the Philippines and partying my ass off.

It just didn't happen that way, and I somehow had volunteered to go out on a thirty-day trip on a fairly new ship called the U.S.S Blueridge LCC-19. It was a command and control ship for the U.S. Seventh Fleet out of Japan. It carried a lot of marines and helicopters. It was also capable of amphibious assaults.

I was again on the navy bus headed down to White Beach, along with several other guys from our command at NSGA Hanza. We met the U.S.S. Blueridge there, saluted the flag and then the officer of the deck and requested permission to come aboard, permission was granted, and there was a yeoman chief that escorted us to our work spaces, this time, I did take my dress uniform and some civilian clothes just in case, I didn't want to try and borrow a uniform again.

The first thing our chief told us was that we would be working 12 on and 12 off, and three of us had the mid watch. It was from 2200 hours to 1000 hours in the morning, and I thought that was gonna suck. He then checked our Identification cards and gave us the combination for the door leading to our workspaces. Then the chief took us below deck to our sleeping quarters. It held thirty-five sailors, the normal layout for enlisted three racks one above the other, a curtain for privacy, a light switch and an air condition vent, and then the locker that we could hang our dress uniforms in and put dress shoes in also I brought my own hangers just in case there were none in the locker, and I was glad I did as my locker did not have one hanger in it.

I lifted the top part of my rack and put my skivvies, socks, and a few books I got from the base library, along with a couple of copies of playboy magazine, my alarm clock, and a spare watch in it, shut it and put my combination lock on it, hung up my uniforms and civilian clothes, two pairs of levy's and a couple of short sleeve shirts along with two pairs of black tennis shoes closed the locker door and put my other lock on it and I was set. To get into the sleeping quarters, you could go through a normal doorway that could be sealed off or a hatch that was a ladder attached to the bulkhead (wall) ten feet straight up to the next level. The spaces had ten showers, sinks, and ten toilets (shitters) at the end of our sleeping area. There were seven of us that would be working the mid watch (night shift) from 2200 hours (10:00 PM) through 1000 hours (10:00 AM). I figured I was only here for thirty days, so it shouldn't be that bad, and after about four or five days, I got used to it.

I had enough work uniforms to last five days, so on Fridays, I would make sure all dirty clothes were in the laundry bag and tied to the back of my rack, the laundry folks would untie the bags, and it went down to be cleaned and was usually back that same day. You had to check to make sure everything came back, and sometimes, things got lost. Your underwear went in a separate bag that was all whites, skivvies, socks, and t-shirts. Your name needed to be stenciled on all items except socks, both bags were also stenciled.

If some part of your uniform came up missing, the best thing to do was head up to the ship's store and purchase whatever was missing. I was lucky on this trip that not one item was lost or stolen. I would go to the gym after my night shift and work out for about thirty minutes to an hour, mostly sit ups, crunches, and some light weights, no more than 150lbs for my arms and 250lbs for my legs, three sets of eight reps, and then after my shower it was usually lunchtime. This ship had really good chow. The only problem was getting there before it was all gone. That took a couple of days to figure out, and I also made sure I was in the correct line for chow.

After chow, I would hit the rack. My alarm was set for 2100 hours (9:00 PM). That was my normal day for thirty days on board the U.S.S. Blue Ridge. During the second week, we had a GQ (general quarters drill). This drill was to practice for combat and or safety conditions, had it been a real combat general quarters, I would have to report to my normal work position and man it until the stand down from general quarters was sounded (the ship had speakers all over the place for all the different announcements but especially for the announcement for GQ. Since I worked the mid shift during all drills, I had what we called sleepers which meant I did not have to do anything for the drills.

During the drills for GQ, all hatches were closed, along with all watertight doors. If you were sleepers, you had to stay where you were if, in your rack, that's where you needed to be. In our berthing area, all the water tight doors were closed, which meant the head was locked to us, but if you are sleeping, what do you care?

During GQ, there is a certain amount of time for all stations to report that they are manned and ready. You could get run over if you went the wrong way during GQ. The port side of the ship goes one way, and the starboard side goes the other way. In other words, everybody is running in the same direction on either side of the ship, if there are nukes on board, it is guarded by marines, and when they come through, they have their side arms (pistols) and shotguns. They only yell once to "make a hole," which means all personnel should be against the bulkhead out of their way. If not, you would be forcibly slammed against it with the butt end of the shotgun, GQ is no joke, and it is taken seriously by the entire crew.

This particular GQ lasted for over four hours; they were normally half of that time. During GQ, chow is served, but it is usually ham and cheese sandwiches with lettuce and tomatoes, a bag of potato chips, and some kind of juice or water. I didn't give a damn about what they ate for dinner that day. I was sleeping, plus I had shit-on-a-shingle for lunch, double helpings since we normally slept during dinner. I had only had that once before, and it was in a boot camp. I remember it cleaning out my system sort of like castor oil did when I was a kid. It was pretty bland tasting (chipped beef in some kind of sauce). I also had a few French fries that were left and coke. The shit-on-a-shingle was covering two pieces of white bread, I was starving, and I ate all of it, finished my coke, and was in my rack twenty minutes before GQ was announced.

Now Hear This, General Quarters, General Quarters, this is a drill.

That's when I passed out exhausted from a twelve-hour shift, a good forty-five-minute workout, and a fat, full belly. About halfway through the GQ drill, I woke up abruptly. My stomach was killing me, and I needed to take a dump.

This was one of those you gotta go now, and I banged my head on the rack above mine when I tried to sit up straight. I knew all the doors and hatches were locked, and there was no were for me to go and relieve myself from the shit-on-a-shingle. About fifteen minutes later, I had sweat dripping down my forehead. I had to go bad. My stomach felt like it was doing flips, I kept telling myself to just squeeze my butt cheeks, and it would be all right, but that didn't help. Now I had the shakes. I was thinking of just taking a dump in my pillow case and throwing it over the side after the drill, but lookouts would spot it, and I would be in a world of trouble. My mind was thinking all kinds of weird stuff like taking a dump on one of the racks on the other side of the berthing area, using their washcloth, and then sneaking back to my rack and getting back to sleep. I couldn't do that. A couple of the guys were still awake. I could hear them talking now. I had been trying to hold it for about forty minutes. My eyes started watering, I was scared to fart, and my guts were just killing me. I looked like I was in a sauna. I tried to lay back down, and that worked for a few minutes, then I started shaking uncontrollably.

I was really screwed up, and I rolled over on my stomach. I thought I was gonna lose it. I started chewing my fingernails, but that didn't help. I grabbed the playboy magazine and tried to read it to help get my mind off of this insanely painful stomach ache and the shakes, but nothing was helping. I tried to say words with Morse code, but that didn't help at all, then my stomach started making those gurgling sounds. I think that's when I started crying, and I lost track of time. I thought I was gonna pass out. It felt like somebody was twisting and turning my intestines. I was sweating, crying, and shaking at the same time. I was thinking about what was gonna happen to my poop chute when I did get to the shitter (toilet). I had brought along an extra roll of toilet paper in case there was none in the stall. For the next thirty minutes, I was crying and sweating, and the shaking was not as bad as it was earlier. I felt like a crackhead, then the announcement to discontinue the drill came "stand down from general quarters."

I slowly moved my legs over the side of my rack and gently lowered myself down. I didn't want anything to stop me from clenching my ass cheeks. I only needed to make it about fifteen feet to the hatch, to the head. When I got there, it was still locked. I almost passed out. Then I heard some noise, one of the sleeper guys got up, grabbed a bucket and his washcloth, and took a dump in the bucket. My teeth were clenched so hard I thought I was going to crack my teeth. When he was done taking a dump, he wiped his ass with his washcloth, threw it in the bucket and slid it back into his rack, and went to sleep. I felt like I needed to give birth or something, and this guy just grabbed a bucket and took a shit in it, I had been trying to hold it for over an hour, almost two hours, and I was still crying.

I was going to try and make it to the bucket, but that's when I heard the hatch lock open, and again I almost pasts out. I made it into the stall, and just as I was squatting, I lost all control of the old sphincter muscle, and I had a blowout. Some guy in the stall next to me said, "Never eat the shit-on-a-shingle. It'll get you every time. I have not eaten any since that incident." I sat on the shitter for so long that my legs went to sleep. I was scared as soon as I got up, I would have to take another dump. After a few minutes, the gurgling stopped, and I was done.

I bet I lost at least ten pounds with sweating and finally taking a dump. I grabbed the door handle in the stall and pulled myself up, my legs were wobbly, but I managed to make it to the shower. They were too old, hand held shower heads. You had to push the button on the side, and the water came out. I didn't have soap or anything. I just took off my skivvies and pushed that button, starting from the top of my head and working my way down. I felt much better, I thought about that experience and started laughing, and I couldn't stop. Again, I never ate shit-on-a-shingle again. I was totally drained, and after I got back into my rack, I slept until my alarm went off.

I never mentioned that incident to anyone after that. When I had to take a dump, I didn't care where I was if I was driving. I would find a gas station, store, or where ever, but I would never hold a poop again. The rest of my time on the Blue Ridge was easy, and I hung out with some of the radiomen and won a little bit of money playing craps. The last week on board was spent in Olongapo, Philippines. I had heard rumors that we might make a port call, but no one I knew had a clue as to where we would be going. We finally were told it would be Subic Bay Navy Base in the PI.

I had duty the first day, and back then, there was no twenty-four-hour liberty for us. When I got off, I went to the hotel where I met Honey, she wasn't there, but her friend said she would have someone to get her. I waited about twenty minutes then this Pilipino guy walked in and asked me to follow him, and I did, he was her brother, we went to Honey's house, it wasn't much more than a one-bedroom with a kitchen, sitting area, and a bathroom, when we got there she looked like she had just got out of the shower which was a nozzle coming out of the wall almost above the toilet, she grinned and said that she was happy to see me.

This didn't feel right, and then I remembered what the crew chief on the Mac Flight had told me she might be your girl while you there with her, but you can bet your ass, as soon as you leave, she will be with someone else that thought stayed in my head, and I couldn't help thinking I got here just as someone else was finishing with her.

We had a good time together while I was there. We hit a couple of clubs in what was called the jungle, that was the side the brothers partied on, the bar I liked, I cannot remember the name of it, but I had alcoves in it, and each one had the name of a major city in the world (that's what we called the good old U.S.A.) they looked sort of like a cave, I liked my cities alcove "Los Angeles" a lot of hot babes were all ways there and all the brothers were dressed to the max. One guy told me about a good tailor that would make me a suit whatever you want. I had a one-piece leisure suit made. It was in one of the playboy magazines in his shop, it was made out of this material that felt like silk, and I had the lapels in gold, and they stitched my nickname on one of the lapels and a bull for my birth month in the black. It had a gold zipper. I had a pair of brown and black platform shoes made to go with it. Everything would be ready for me the next morning.

I went in the next morning after Honey and I left the club, he told me to come back after 6, and I did the suit was ready, and it fits perfectly, the shoes and suit all together cost me $65.00, after I left the tailor shop I went to the barbershop and wasted $5.00. I had them shape my afro and blow it out (they used a hair dryer to make it stand straight) with no curls. While I was sitting in the chair, one of the girls asked if I wanted a blow job for an extra $2.00. I declined, if I was gonna have sex, it would be in bed, not while I was sitting in a barber chair. Then she asked if I wanted to have a manicure. I declined again.

What a place!

After I was done, I walked out the door, and the humidity hit my afro, and it just laid flat for a second and went back to curls. I went back to Honey's house, and we hung out for a while. She wanted to go to the beach, so I gave her brother $5.00, and he went and brought me a pair of swimming trunks, and we went to the beach. It was not clean at all, but it was cooler being next to the ocean. I sat at one of the chairs in front of a bar and ordered a couple of San Miguel beers. Honey and her brother actually went swimming in the water, I had forgotten how the beers tasted, better than the Okinawan beer, but after three of them, I barely had a buzz. I paid $3.00 and got a Budweiser, and then I got a buzz. We stayed there until the sunset. It was an awesome sight, there was an island about a mile away, and when the sun started to set, the sky was blue and orange. It was awesome!

It was time to go back to Honey's house and get ready for my last night, and I had to report back to the ship and stand duty for the last two days. I was cool with that, and I had three days off out of five. Yeah, I was cool with it. After we left the club that night, we stayed in bed until I had to leave. A quick shower, and I was off in a jeepney heading to the base. And I got there, paid the driver a dollar and caught a bus to the ship, faced the flag, and then asked for permission to come aboard from the OOD (Officer of the Deck), went below and stowed my clothes, and put on my work uniform. I had to study for the E4 exam, and this was a good time to do it.

After we departed from Olongapo a couple of days later, two sailors got into a fight about one of the Pilipino ladies, and one guy was stabbed in the hand. One of the brothers in the radio room was talking about it, and he said, "Why would you fight and try to kill someone over a woman that would probably never be yours?" that thought stuck with me.

The ship pulled into White Beach Okinawa a week later, and I was headed back to NSGA Hanza Okinawa. When I got back to base, Billy and Benny asked me all kinds of questions about the PI. I showed them some pictures I had taken with Honey and I, sitting in the club under the Los Angeles alcove, then I pulled out my 1-piece suit, and they were amazing, neither could believe how much I spent to have it tailor-made, especially with all the detail that was put into it. We headed to the bowling alley, and that's when I saw that cute little blonde again, and we smiled at each other. She was hanging out with this really cool brother; his name was Moses, and he always wore those dashikis (African shirts that went down to his knees). Not my style, but he liked it, and that was all that mattered in my mind.

Moses asked me, "Who did I piss off?"

I said, "What do you mean?"

He said, "None of us have been to sea yet, and you have been volunteered twice." Everybody started laughing,

I hadn't really thought of it, and I liked being out to sea. I slept well, for the most part, the food was good, and my job was not bad at all. I was okay with being out to sea, especially when we pulled into a port and I could get laid. I was happy. I had planned on one more trip to the Philippines with Honey, but I got orders to go there for two months just as I got back. I was going to help set up High-Frequency Direction Finding equipment, which I thought was strange since I had not done that part of my job yet. I had been asking about it and what it was, but most answers were very vague, if I got an answer at all.

So, I had to pack my sea bag again and was getting ready to go. I did see that little blonde again. Her name was Kim, and we planned on spending some time together after I got back from the Navy Base in Subic Bay. The day I left, I had time to grab some breakfast on base at Torri Station, and they had Shit-On-A-Shingle. I opted for the bacon and eggs. I just wasn't gonna ever try that shit again. After I ate, I got in the hooptie and drove it to Kadena Air Base. I parked outside as I didn't have insurance on that little piece of junk. I did roll up all the windows and locked the doors. I was wondering if it would still be there when I got back, and I thought, *who cares* laughed and caught the base bus to the MAC terminal.

It was another C-130 cargo plane and hardly anybody on it. It did, however, have a huge turbine engine in it, probably for one of the ships. It took a couple of hours to get there. I read an old playboy magazine it showed Hugh Hefner's new mansion in Hollywood. The pool had a grotto built into it, and it looked awesome. I thought he knew how to live and that had to be the life.

Once we landed, I went to the quarter deck and handed in my orders, and was taken to a secured facility at the end of the base, and there was a small barracks with only about twenty people in it so that's where I stayed the first week, learning about HFDF. After that, I kind of had a clue as to what we were going to be doing, I moved out of the barracks, and off base, I found a one-bedroom little house with a really small kitchen and bathroom that did have a bathtub, and a little living room. It had a small front yard with a garden in the front. The house cost me $150.00 per month, and that included the electricity and water I was happy as hell, I brought a small black, and white T.V from one of the pawn shops on Mag Say Say street, I was gonna give it to Honey when I left, that was my plan.

The place already had a bed, and it was a frame with just a mattress, no box spring, and another mattress underneath the bed. I used it for other purposes. President Marcos was still ruling the PI with an iron grip, and the curfew was still going on, which worked out perfect for me, as soon as the girls from the bar near the house found out I had my own pad, they all loved me and the reason was if they got off work before 10:00 PM they could come over my place and spend the night with me and one or two of my friends instead of having a bunch of drunks all over them at the club until four or five in the morning when the curfew was lifted. They just had to deal with my new buddies and me at my place during the curfew hours.

So every morning before I got ready for work, I had the Iceman come over put a big ass block of ice in the bathtub that I had filled with San Miguel beers that would keep the beers cold well into the late evening (my electricity was cut off as soon as my landlord saw me leave for work), so whatever I had in the refrigerator would be warm as hell when I got home, that's when he would turn the electricity back on. I complained about it, and he said it was his wife doing it. I believed him she was a real bitch, she was also my maid, she and Honey didn't get along at all, they were like two cats fighting all the time. I used to just tell her to get out. I would clean the place myself.

Some nights Honey didn't make it back before the curfew, and I would just have one or two of the other girls. She didn't care, and that's when I knew she had other guys on her plate, I wasn't mad. I understood what it was all about, she had to make a living just like everybody else, I told her as long as I didn't get VD from her, we were cool.

I worked Monday through Friday from 0800 hours to 1600 hours (8:00 AM to 4:00 PM with an hour for lunch. On this base you could have lunch at the chow hall or in one of the enlisted clubs which had girls dancing during the lunch hour also (that was stopped years later because too many wives were complaining about their husbands spending all their money tipping the girls.) Where else could you find this not on any of the bases on Okinawa. This was pure heaven.

My last week was almost up, I put in for an extra three days of leave and it was approved by my command at NSGA Hanza. My time was up with the command at Subic Bay, I really hated leaving, but it was almost time for me to go back to Okinawa. I put all my clothes in my sea bag and grabbed the little tv and walked over to the land lords house, gave him an extra $5.00 cause there was no way I was gonna clean the place, and his wife lost her little mind. I walked over to her, gave her a big hug, and then slapped her on the ass. Her husband and I both broke out laughing, that crazy bitch look and me and smiled. I got out of there and went to the base, locked my bags in the barracks, which was a Quonset hut, and caught the bus to the main gate. I had a little suitcase with two pairs of slacks and two of those leisure shirts that we wore in the nineteen- seventies, one pair of tennis shoes and my brand new black eel skin platform shoes which I wore that day along with a new dark brown leisure suit.

Honey and I were going to meet her family up in the mountains, but I wanted to have a few drinks at one of the bars before we made the trip. We were going to an area called Turlac Turlac, and we needed to hurry. We rented a jeepney for the ride cost me $4.00 for the two-hour drive up there. A regular car would not have made it. After you got off the main road, it was another hour through the jungle, and I was getting nervous as I had no weapons, just a pocket knife. The jeepney driver stopped and said we are here and he smiled at Honey. She paid him, and we got out and started walking. I have to let you know in the jungle, they have a group of little people called Negritos, they used to guard the back side of the base in Subic Bay, and nobody messed with them. They used bows and arrows along with blow darts that had some kind of poison on the tips of the darts.

I really thought this could be a one really bad mistake. In just a few minutes we entered her family's little village it must have had about twenty families living there, most of them had never saw a black man over four feet tall, and here I come, I was sweating like a pig and I wanted a nice cool shower or a bath and a beer, I just didn't understand how poor these villagers were but I was gonna find out and find out really quick.

When we walked into the village, her brother was there to meet us, and he always grinned. Every damn time I saw him, he was grinning, that just bothered the hell out of me, and I wasn't sure why I cared at all about it. I still had the little TV and my little suitcase, but the sweat was pouring off of me I had to be damn near 90 degrees, and it felt like 100% humidity. Most of the houses were built about three feet above the ground on stilts, and we were up in the mountains, so I thought there could not be any floods up here. I asked Honey about it, and she said to keep bad animals out. Of course, I had to ask what bad animals were, and she said, "Snakes, big mean pigs, spiders, and other things." I thought she should have told me this before I came all the way up here.

The main street, if you could call it, a street had the only shower and the toilet, and it was public for all to use it was in a small building about the size of our guard shacks at the main gates at most military bases. The shower was on one side, separated by a bamboo wall, and the toilet was on the other side of the little building. To make the shower work you pulled on a string and water would drop out of the showerhead at the top of the little building it was kinda like being in a light rain, in other words, there was no real fast water pressure, the shower head came out of a pipe in the center of that little room. There were no locks on the little bamboo doors, just a lever you pull up to open, and then you pull down once inside to keep it closed.

After she showed me that, I knew this was gonna be a long-ass three days. We walked to her family's house, and I met her mother, father, two sisters, and that grinning brother of hers. I also met her eight-year-old daughter, who she never mentioned. I was good with everything and I gave her father the little TV. Her whole family was happy as hell when I did that, my mind kept thinking, "Really."

The houses were simple, all made out of bamboo, the walls were about six or seven feet high, and there were no windows, just another section of what I thought was the rest of the wall that was connected, so when they pulled on a rope the whole side would open, it was pretty awesome honestly when it rained, they would partially open it so it was at an angle and the water would run off into their gardens which were all over the place, the walls were the same on all four sides.

When I gave her father the TV, it made him the second most important person in the village. The most important guy had a generator that had extension cords running to most of the houses, just enough for a few lights in each house, most of the houses had butane cookers for the stoves, and there were no refrigerators. They used chipped ice like I did in my bathtub at the house I rented, and they only got ice once a week. Honey told me most of them use the river that ran through the back of the village for bathing and fishing water to drink. My Los Angeles mind was trying to comprehend how in the 1970s people were still living like this.

Most of the younger women ages fifteen to thirty would leave and go down to Olongapo or somewhere in Subic City to work as prostitutes, so the ones that were here were babies and over forty, I had just turned twenty, and this was working my brain. After I gave her father the TV, they ran an extension cord to it and, with the rabbit ear antenna, were able to get two channels, they only used the TV twice a day, and when he did use it, everyone would gather in their house or lean against the wall to watch either the news or I love Lucy in their Tagalog language.

After she put my clothes in her father's house, her brother gave me a pair of short pants to wear, but I told Honey I needed a shower, so she took me to the little building and I took off my clothes, handed them over the little wall and she handed me this blue bar that was used as soap, the wrapper on it said 'AJAX', they used it to wash clothes and their bodies.

Everyone watched me taking a shower. The walls on two sides were only like four feet high, so I waved to the little ones, and the others watched for a while, then went on their way. After my shower, I was given a towel and a pair of shorts to wear along with what we call shower shoes. They were way too small, but wearing my tennis shoes or platforms just wouldn't work.

Honey rubbed some concoction on me that kept the mosquitoes away and it really worked, kind of smelled like fresh oranges. I did not ask what it was. That night we had some kind of fish and rice for dinner, the fish still had the head on it with the eyes and everything. Again, my mind said this is different. I was waiting for a fork or spoon to use, then I noticed everybody using their fingers, so I dug in. She had given her brother money to buy us some beer and bottled water, so we had twenty-four bottles of San Miguel beer and lots of bottled water which were tied together at the neck of each bottle with this very thin twine and then tied to a rock to keep them cool in the river, guess where I hung out?

It was Honey with her father and brother at the river, having a beer or two before the sunset, and we needed to be back in the village before it got dark. Martial law was for the entire country, and you could be arrested or shot if you were out after 10:00 PM. I stood by the wall in the back of the house to have a cigarette and there was her mother smoking a Pilipino cigarette. She put the lit end of the cigarette in her mouth and smoked it like that. I asked Honey what the hell that was about, and she told me during the war, if the Japanese soldiers saw the embers from a cigarette, they would fire two times at the ember, and you would be dead. Her mother and father were in their early 60's, so there were there for that part of the war, hiding from the Japanese if her mother was caught, she would become used for sex, and her father would have been used for had to slave labor or just killed.

I had whole new respect for these folks living up here on top of a mountain with a river running through the village. We all talked most of the night, they wanted to know about Los Angeles, California, USA, and I told them about Hollywood with the walk of fame, American football, baseball, and all that stuff. I was making myself homesick. They wanted to know what my family looked like, what kind of car I have – everything and really wanted to know about the food I liked to eat. I said hamburgers with cheese and French fries, they all laughed, and then it was bedtime.

There were no beds. Everybody slept on the floor on these thin little mattresses, but I got used to it real fast. Without any lights at night, walking around the house was kind of dangerous. I accidentally stepped on someone's hand the first night, trying to get to the back part of the house so I could relieve myself of the beer I had drunk that day.

Honey and I slept in this area that was curtained off with dark mosquito netting, nobody could see anything anyway, and her daughter wanted to sleep in the same area as her mother and I. She was a cute, smart little girl. Her name was Maria. It was different having Honey laying next to me and not having sex. Instead, I had a baby girl there holding my hand while I slept. I woke up to all kinds of jungle sounds, mainly birds and the sounds of the little children playing outside, and it was peaceful. I noticed I was the only one in the place and the clothes I wore. Yesterday's were washed, cleaned, and folded. I quickly searched for my wallet and passport. They were under the mat where I left them.

When I looked at my watch, it was 9:00 AM. I had a pair of short pants on and wanted a shower and to brush my teeth. I called for Honey, and she came immediately, grabbed my hand and took me outside to the location of the shower. They had a big tin bucket filled with water and she told me to get in. Once in it, she told me to take off my shorts. I did as instructed and then was given the second best bath I could remember ever having. Her older sister washed my hair, and Honey took care of the rest of me.

Honey's daughter watched me the whole time I was there. She was either holding my hand or trying to sit on my lap. I think she thought I was going to be her new father, but that was not going to happen. She was a great kid, just not mine. There was going to be a big party tonight, so after my bath and a breakfast of fruit and some kind of bread, I went off with Honey's father and brother to do some fishing, now they were talking in my language.

I thought I would get a stick with some kind of line on it. Her father unrolled a net that was made out of some kind of twine, and I was given an end to it, her brother at another end, and the father was in the middle. We walked into the cold river at a bend in it and slowly walked back to the shore, holding the net under the water. We only caught about ten little fish, so we changed locations. I wasn't sure about being too far away from the village, but you had to do what was needed to get food. We must have walked down trails that followed the river for about an hour, and then her father said this is far enough in Tagalog, their language, and her brother told me we were getting close to the Negrito's area and you didn't want to be there without and invitation, it could be really bad.

I nodded my head that I understood. We made our way out into the river and again slowly walked in toward the shoreline. I could tell we had some bigger fish this time and we did, they all went into the bucket, and her father told me it was enough, and we needed to save some for the next time. I thought there would not be next time for me. This was enough, the heat and humidity made it hard to breathe, we were probably one and a half miles from the village, and walking felt like we had run ten miles, and as hard as it was to breathe, I still wanted to smoke a cigarette.

Once we got back, there were three other groups of men that had gone out fishing, so there was lots of fish for tonight. I asked her brother what other meats we were going to eat? He said we will go to Negrito village and trade chickens for a small pig. I was thinking I'm taking my pocket knife just in case one of those little fellas gets out of control.

After we gave the fish to Honey's Mother and Sister, Honey gave the three of us bottles of water to drink. We were saving the last case of beer for tonight as I was planning on leaving the next morning. For the rest of the day, we sat in the house and chilled out until 3:00 PM, that's when everybody in the village gathered around the house. Honey's father unplugged the string of lights from the generator and plugged in the TV. Honestly, I didn't think they would get any reception for a TV channel up here, but he was able to pull in the two different ones. I kept moving the antenna on the TV until it was a pretty clear picture, and it was 'The I Love Lucy Show' in Tagalog. I was amazed.

After the show was over, the TV was unplugged, and the lights plugged back in. They would turn it back on after 6:00 PM to watch the news and again, the whole village gathered around the house to peek in at that little TV. They were all hoping to hear that their president would be killed or run out of the country, that didn't happen until the mid-1980's when president Ronald Reagan told President Marcos he needed to leave. After the news about ten of the villagers, including Honey's father, brother, and myself, went to the Negreto village. They were all carrying a chicken each. I wasn't carrying a squawking, screaming chicken anywhere. I had my pocket knife in my front pocket and a bottle of water. I did pick up a fallen branch and used it as a walking stick. It was gonna be my bat if I had to use it against something or someone.

We got to the village after about an hour trek on a much better path than what we used to follow the river. It only took us about forty-five minutes to get there. Once we made it to the center of the little village, I freaked out. They were cooking what looked like a small baby with long arms, it had a stick stuck up the butt, and there was no head. My brain went straight into fighting mode, I put my hands in my pocket for my knife, but Honey's brother grabbed me and said, "No, is a monkey, not baby." I was so pissed off it took a few minutes for me to calm down a little.

When I turned around, we were surrounded by all these little black people with afros. I smiled at them, they were not these savage little monsters I had heard about, but they were little people. Honey's father held up his chicken and started speaking in another version of Tagalog I had not heard him use before. Her brother told me he was letting us know we needed a pig and had ten chickens to trade for one. All the Negrito's were looking at me like I was deformed or something.

At five feet nine inches, I towered over the Philippi 'no's' so I guess I looked like a giant version of a Negrito with short pants and a t-shirt to them. I smiled at them, and it was all good after that. I dropped the stick and took my hands out of my pocket. We stayed for a few minutes, they traded the chickens for a ten-pound pig. Honey's father carried it all the way home and that damn thing made more noise than the ten chickens all by itself. I was from Los Angeles, California, and had never thought about how we got ham and bacon. I found out that night after we got back. It was right around 8:00 PM and there was already a hole dug in the ground with rocks and sticks on top of the rocks.

I went into the house with Honey while they gutted the pig and cut it up everything, but the bones were eaten that night. Honey's mother put the fat from the pig in a pot with a little bit of water that was going to be eaten later as a treat, sort of like pork rinds. I have to say I was starving and Mr. Pig hit the spot for me. I was just hoping I would not have the same reaction like I did with shit-on-a-shingle, but once Honey handed me a beer, I forgot all about that experience.

That night Honey grabbed my hand and we walked into the jungle. She took off her clothes, and well, it was on. I was making my own jungle noises. That next morning, we were up early. It was time to leave, so I had to say goodbye to everyone Honey's daughter was the last one I said goodbye to. I kissed her on her cheek, she hugged me and ran off to Honey crying, then Honey kissed her and told her to be a good girl and mind her grandmother.

Honey's brother, Honey, and I each had a bottle of water and my little suitcase. We walked down the trail to the road where the Jeepney was waiting for us. We quickly got in and headed back to Olongapo. The driver had cold beers in an ice chest waiting for us. I knew this was the end of Honey and my relationship, don't get me wrong, it was fun, the sex was good, going out to the village in the jungle to see how she was raised and hanging out with the villagers was cool and the clubbing in Olongapo was great.

It was just not with Sharleen. I knew I had to find Sharleen or somebody exactly like her, that was a tall order to fill for any woman in my eyes, but she was who I wanted to be with. When we got back to Olongapo, I kissed her goodbye and went back to the base, grabbed the rest of my stuff, and headed back to Clark Air Base so I could make my way back to Okinawa. I was already thinking of my next trip and I was thinking about going to Singapore, Hong Kong, or Mainland Japan. I would just wait and see how things turned out for me.

When I finally got to Clark Airbase, I went straight to the MAC area to see what time the next flight to Okinawa would take off. I would not be for three more hours, I left and went to the base club and had an early dinner double cheeseburger, fries, and a Coke. It was better than McDonalds. I was thinking of all the different places I could go to eat in Los Angeles, but none had this scenery, bombers, jets, and I don't know how many US Military people and some in uniform from other countries. I did see a few British Airmen.

The heat and humidity were the only downfalls and I got over that really quickly. As I headed back to the MAC terminal, the thought of other countries to visit was still on my mind. I usually thought of other places to visit when I was starting to get homesick, and I knew catching a MAC flight back to the states could and probably would take weeks each way. These quick flights from islands and countries over here in the pacific were damn near all pretty quick and easy with the exception of Hawaii, and everybody wanted to go there, mainly officers that could afford it. I knew I couldn't, so I never bothered to try.

The plane took off on time, another C-130 cargo plane, and again only a few of us were on board, the crew chief said these flights were mainly to keep the pilots up to date on their required flight hours for training, he told me they also have to do what's called take off and landings, another requirement for them, not just the pilots but the entire flight crew each person had a job to do on the plane during these exercises.

When the crew chief asked me what I did in the Navy, I told him I was a CT. He didn't ask me anymore questions and basically avoided me the rest of the flight, giving me time to catch up on my sleep in the long-netted seats. I woke up as we landed at Kadena Air Base. I called the quarterdeck at Torri Station and they sent a van to pick me up and bring me back. My division chief was there waiting for me, I had never really met him personally, but he was awesome when I did get the chance to speak with him. I liked him right away. He was an R-Brancher like me, only he was a Senior Chief (E-8). I was just getting ready to test for 3rd Class Petty Officer (E-4) and if I passed the test and all other requirements (physical training – so many pullups and pushups and the mile and a half in a certain amount of time). He told me I received straight 4.0's from all the TAD (temporary assigned duty) trips that I had been on and did not have any problems with the physical fitness portion of the test. The only thing I needed was to study all of the test info and I did.

I was still low enough in rank that I never knew why I was doing the things that I did, that was the information I would not be privy to until I made second Class Petty Officer. I just wanted to make third Class Petty Officer, with more benefits, and the pay was a lot better. I thanked the chief, and he said, "Son, you have your shit together. Now stop the unauthorized MAC flights, or I am going to have to stop you!" I almost passed out. I didn't know I needed the authorization to catch a MAC flight.

He then said, "Don't worry, you're not the only one that didn't know you needed to get permission and it does take weeks or months to come down the chain of command, we need to know where you are twenty-four hours a day seven days a week," then he looked at me and smiled and said "I know you understand what I am saying." I said, "Yes, Senior Chief, understood." You never said sir to any enlisted person, especially a chief. If you were not in trouble, you could be after doing that.

I went straight to the bowling alley, saw some of the gang there, and got a lot of questions about what was happening in the PI. I told them what I could about the job I was doing, the babes in Olongapo and about going up into the mountains in the Tarlac region and the Negritos cooking a monkey. Everybody laughed when I said I kept my hand on my knife.

Three days after I got back, my section went on break, I got up and went for my daily morning piss, and I thought I was gonna scream. It felt like razor blades were shooting out of my hookup. It did make my eyes water a little. I took a quick shower and shaved, dressed, and went straight to medical, and there I was told I had VD. I was pissed!

'The doc', that's what we called our guys that were more like a doctor than most real doctors, they did everything from ex-rays to giving meds, most didn't do operations, anyhow doc asked me where I was the last time I had sex, and I told him the PI, he didn't ever take a culture, then he told me to milk my penis and that he would have to stick this long assed thing that looked like a one foot cue tip swab inside my penis, but he said he knew the strain I had. So here I go again, bent over a table with my trousers and drawers down around my ankles, my elbows on the table and my chin resting in both hands, and then I again got the double shot, one in each cheek. I was thinking to myself just before I screamed when the first needle blasted into my upper ass cheek on the left side, "Honey is not my Honey anymore." I knew what she was when I first started dating her. I had no plans on marrying her and taking her and her little one back to the states. This just made it easier for me.

Then after the doc was done destroying my butt cheeks, he said that someone had mentioned that a couple of us had been there, and he would like it if there was no record of this in our records.

Then the doc said it would all be gone in a week or so and not to have sex during that time. Sex was the last thing on my mind after getting those two shots in the ass, that would be the last time I was going to visit Honey, maybe some other babe but not her. We were done.

The next two months I spent working and studying for the E-4 test. All the material was classified, so I could not bring any out of the site to study, so I would go in three or four hours early on my evening and mid watches just to study and then work my eight-hour shifts. After almost three years, I was now a new third-class petty officer, and a lot of things changed in my life. My pay was better, I could buy a better hooptie and get it insured along with my motorcycle, I had a little more responsibility in the section at work. I was now one of the guys training new folks coming into the section and I was able to put in a request to move off base.

All of the gang that arrived in Okinawa when I did that were able to test made E-4 and it was great, we had to get our new rate badges which had a feather and a quill with a chevron underneath, this designated that we were CT third class petty officers. There was a ceremony where the commanding officer presented you the document stating you had been awarded this new rank and then after the ceremony your rating badge or stripe was pinned on your left shoulder.

At our command there were a lot of petty officers and everyone that was already an E-4 or above got to pin it on you, it was a tradition of the navy, each senior petty officer got to punch you on your left shoulder to make sure the rating badge would not come off, for us CT's our insignia on our rate badges was a quill with a lightning bolt with one chevron underneath it, and by other ratings we were called CT1 for a 1st class petty officer, CT2 for a second class petty officer or in my case it was CT3. So now most of the gang I had come to Okinawa with were third class petty officers, we hit the base club hard that night.

I had a mid-watch so I was able to sleep off most of the alcohol that I drank the night of the celebrations, some folks did not have that luxury and even though they new they had to work the next morning they still got totally lit at the club. We were the ones some of the guys the new guys came to with their questions about work, pay and just about anything they could think of, if we didn't know the answers, we would find out for them.

Dave and his wife had found a really cool place to hang out at off base, it was like a watering hole, a little lake with huge rocks surrounding it and about fifteen feet deep in the middle, it had a rope tied to a huge tree and you could swing right into the middle of it and let go of the rope and drop into the cold water.

It was very secluded, I asked Dave how he found it and he said he and his wife were just following some off-road trails one day on his Honda 750 and the last trail they tried lead to this spot. Dave said not many people knew about it and they were trying to keep it a secret, I was good with that.

Two days after I got back from the PI one of the army guys from our base was found dead behind the back of the base, he had been bitten by a sea snake. The sea snakes in the China sea are very poisonous and if you do not get the antidote quickly the poison from its bite will cause death.

No one was sure how he got bitten as the snake's mouth is small and its fangs are back in its mouth not like most snakes. It could bite your ear or between your fingers and the soldier was bitten between his fingers.

We all thought he must have been messing with it because whenever we saw sea snakes, they usually tried to get away from us as quick as they could, I usually went in the other direction whenever I saw one of them. I'm not big on snakes, you could say I would hurt myself trying to get away from them.

After that none of us CT's were allowed to go snorkeling or scuba diving alone, it needed to be at least two personnel at all times. I really felt sorry for him and his family back in the states, but as I was going to learn people could and did get killed in the military and there was no war or policing action, just the fact that our military people could die or be seriously injured in a foreign country far away from home for really crazy reasons like this one or accidents on the job while conducting training, car accidents and even being hit by cars.

I finally met Kate. She was very pretty and fun, had nice perky boobies and a little round ass. We were a couple in no time, she liked riding on the back of my Honda and shortly after I made third class, I went looking for my own apartment or house. There was no discrimination in Okinawa, as long as you had money, you were good to go to them. The Okinawans were all Gijin's (Gi-Jing) or outside people.

At first, I rented an apartment where Dave and Andy had recently moved with their families. We were all on the second floor of a three-story complex. It was really different. The electrical cords were the same and a few items I had, like my stereo, and a black and white TV, worked just fine. TV off base was the same as on base, we only had three or four channels, and one was the military's channel showing news and new military equipment, no regular TV shows. The other channels were in Japanese and they did have "I love Lucy" in Japanese.

The apartment I rented was a one-bedroom, living room, kitchen, and a bathroom. It cost a little over $300.00 a month, but the military paid for that amount and a little bit more to help with food called COMRATS (commuted rations) pay. If I remember correctly, once I moved off base, my check increased by almost $500.00 a month. It was always a party in that complex. Drinking and hanging out after work was what we did, and a lot of motorcycle riding all over that island.

I had my own place and I was glad to get out of the barracks. Having roommates was not big on my list and as far as I was concerned, it really sucked and usually didn't work out well for me. Billy and Janine were in the same apartment complex, only on the other side of it facing the road, our side faced the south china sea, and it was awesome to wake up and see that from the front windows of the apartment. I hardly ever saw them as Billy was on a shift that worked opposite mine, but we made time whenever we could to hang out.

There was a trash dumpster that was located beneath a garbage chute on each floor, to empty your trash, you just carry the trash bag to the end of the hallway, open this heavy metal door that had a latch on it, and it also had a spring attached to it so the door would slam shut if you let go of the handle and a latch to hold the door open while you threw the bags in it. The door was waist high and damn near four feet diagonally so you could get big boxes in it, I thought it was a great idea, but the roaches would be all over the place as soon as you open the door, so once you drop the trash bag into the chute, you had to unlatch the door and let it go asap.

Dave's wife always complained about the roaches and one day, we were all hanging out on the walkway when Dave decided to take care of the roaches once and for all. He had a five gallon gas can filled with gas, and he said he was gonna cook some roaches. We all laughed at him, and he asked us to come on and check them out. We all grabbed our chairs and sat about six or seven feet away from Dave and of course, we brought the beer with us, and we sat down. Once Dave was sure we were all there and seated, he turned around and poured the entire five gallons into the chute and bent over to see if he could see the gas sitting on the trash bags, which back then were just the paper bags that came with our groceries, none of us thought about the fact that there was no opening at the top of the chute and that turned out to be a big problem for Dave cause he threw a lit match into the chute, quickly unlatched it and closed the door, nothing happened, he opened the door, put the latch on and looked inside the chute, nothing happened no flame, nothing.

He threw a second match and for just a few seconds, nothing happened and that's when we all discovered what a backflash was, the latch was still on, holding the door open, and crazy assed Dave was bent over looking inside the chute when the backflash happened, he screamed, and we all screamed, the flame shot straight up the chute but some came out charging right at Dave, he screamed again, we screamed again. Billy spit beer all over Dave's wife when he screamed.

Dave turned around toward us. His beard, eyebrows, and eyelashes were singed off his face and some of his hair was on the top. If his head was still smoking, he had the craziest look on his face, and then he smiled at us. It took a second and then we all lost it, tears in our eyes we were cracking up laughing at him, his t-shirt was just smoke black, he said I think I just pissed myself, that was it for me I fell out of my chair onto the floor laughing so hard. Kim fell on top of me and Billy got out of his chair, checked on Dave then sat on the floor. He was laughing so hard he looked like he was crying. After about an hour, we all stopped laughing, and it was because we kept seeing it in our minds and had to start laughing again. Janine was the first one to do it and it kept going from there. Yep it took an hour for us to stop laughing at him, then the joke started, but not until his wife checked on him one more time. She punched him in the chest and started cussing him out, calling him an idiot, then she laughed, and we all started laughing again. He was teased about it for quite a while.

We had an inspection coming up and our chief told Dave not to participate due to him not having eyebrows or eyelashes. It was hot as hell out there that my white dress uniform was sticking to my body because I was sweating so bad. I was lucky there was always someone that was overweight standing in front of me within arm's reach. Once they locked their knees trying to stand straight, it wasn't long before they would start to pass out. I, along with several others, would assist them over to the base ambulance that was always ready (standing by in case someone passed out from the heat). The guy standing next to me grabbed his right arm and I grabbed his left arm. We escorted him to the ambulance. He was put on a stretcher and went into the back of the ambulance where the air conditioner was working full blast. I tried to get in with him for the ride to medical. One of the army med techs told me, "Nice try, Son, get out." So, we stood in the shade during the rest of the inspection, to assist the guy that was gonna faint. We both got an outstanding on the inspection and we were never inspected.

Kate had some family emergency, so she left the next morning and got a MAC flight back to the states and to Tampa. She would be gone for three weeks. It was my section last eve-watch and then it was three days off for us, and we had a new guy, Kris, who moved into the apartment complex. He was in the navy as well. He was a radioman, not a CT like the rest of us. Kris was known for having some good weed, came to find out, he was getting it from one of us CT's whose grandmother was sending it in thru the mail in care packages stashed inside the thirty-five mm film canisters, and she would send twenty of the little canisters at a time. Will was the dealer's name and he sold that stuff to the army guys on the base. He never tried to sell it to us. He knew better, he would not have gotten busted if he had just stayed with the Army guys, but he started selling to the Air Force folks, and that was the end of his Navy career and selling weed. He got a dishonorable discharge and ten years at Ft. Leavenworth, which was a seriously hard core prison.

Kris wanted me to take him to Naha Airport to pick up his girlfriend who was coming to visit him from the Philippines and boy was he excited. When I asked him where he met her, he said he was in Olongapo, and she was down from Manila visiting her family. I said cool, we got in the car drove to the airport, and went inside as it was too damn hot to be outside.

We only had a few minutes to wait and then it landed, we all walked to the door leading outside to the tarmac. Once the truck with the ladder pulled up and the door opened, all the passengers came out and walked toward the door we were standing at, that's when he saw her and Kris started yelling like crazy, he was so happy. I couldn't tell him that every time I went to the club outside the gate in Subic Bay, I saw it here and there. I would let someone else do it, he was just so damn happy.

Once we got back to the apartment complex, he took her up to his apartment and almost forgot to grab her bags. I had to shout at him to come down and get her bags. He had a look on his face like *you didn't bring them up?* I smiled at him and headed to base. I needed to let everybody know that she was here and not the virgin that he thought she was. All the neighbors came out to meet her, she looked like she was gonna faint when she saw three of the other neighbors that I didn't know, but the three of them looked like they did recognize each other. I just smiled. He paid over $900.00 just to get her papers passed thru in the Philippines and then another $300 just for her plane ticket. I guess he didn't know that she was a hooker or if he did, he was probably hoping none of us knew her.

After she had been there for a couple of weeks, Kris was late for work, and his supervisor came over to pick him up. She let his supervisor in the house and that was when Kris got busted. He had a couple of weed plants on the counter. Because it was just a couple of plants and he was a radioman, he only lost one stripe and got thirty days restricted to the base with no pay for the thirty days. They gave his Honey a free MAC flight Back to Clark Air Base in Angeles City. The only problem was she left her cat at Kris's old apartment. Dave's wife went over and fed it and cleaned the litter box.

When Kris got off of restriction, he screwed up even worse. He grabbed the cat he had brought for his girlfriend, who was gone, by the neck and tried to throw it off the second floor. He ended up with over twenty stitches in his arm. I guess the cat decided it couldn't fly, and it dug its claws into his arm. The more he shook it, the more it dug its claws in his arm, he was screaming, and the cat was screaming too. It took Dave's wife to get the cat off of his arm.

The commanding officer heard about the incident, and Kris lost his privilege to live off base, I guess the CO was a cat person. Kate was still on emergency leave, after she left most of the guys. I hung out with in my section who were transferred or either got out of the navy. I moved out of the apartment complex and got a house about two-thirds of a mile from the base. It had two bedrooms, a kitchen, one bathroom, and a little living room with a sliding patio door. It didn't have much of a patio, just about a four-foot by six-foot slab of cement. I had brought a futon couch and chair. It was burgundy and black vinyl (everybody called it pleather for fake leather). I didn't care, I loved it. I could sleep in the couch and it was more comfortable than the cheap ass bed I had brought, but the good thing was the roof was flat and it had a stairway leading up to it from the outside of the house. I had two beach chairs up there and I ran wires for two of my speakers up there so I could listen to my tunes while sitting up there. I also had a fan and umbrella. Life was good then. I met this Army babe named Karen. Her boobs were damn near as big as Mari's. I don't even remember her face, just the hooters, and she loved having good sex, especially on the roof.

She and I lasted about a week. It was almost time for Kate to come back and we were both getting tired of each other. She liked country music, which I couldn't stand it at that time, and she wanted more than I was willing to give. It was over. About a week later, I got a letter from my oldest sister, and I was shocked, my mother and she wanted to meet me in Manila, Philippines.

I was so happy, I put in my leave request immediately for two weeks of vacation time for two weeks in April, the day before my birthday, I had not used any for quite a while and I was told by the clerk that it would take a couple of days for the Captain to approve it. I was at work when the request chit was handed to me and it was approved. It was signed by the Commanding Officer, the division officer, the division chief, and my supervisor. Let's just say I was happy as hell!

I could have cared less about the Philippines, I was just glad to be seeing my mother and sister after work. I called them home and let them know I would be able to go. They would arrive the day before I got there, the day before my twenty-first birthday. I hadn't realized it was that close to my birthday.

I got a roommate just for the time I would be gone, that way he would share the rent. He was a really cool brother. I think he was from Atlanta, Georgia, and he hardly spoke, but I had a suspicion that he was a pothead. I didn't really care. He was leaving a month after I came back from the Philippines. I would get the hotel room as I would be there a day before Mom and Sis. I just knew it would be fun, both of them liked to laugh a lot, and I knew my sister would get me up to date on what was happening in the hood. When the day came to start my vacation, I caught MAC flight, $10.00 both ways which was just awesome. Kim and I had just broken up the day before I left. I think she had a thing for Moses, that's right, Moses. I kissed her and told her I wished her the best.

The next day I went to Kaden Air Base on my new Honda 750 and parked it on base at the terminal. The crew chief had told me to park it in the hanger where the C-130's were parked and I did. Got on the plane and was at Clark Air Base outside of Angeles City, I caught a cab to Manilla for $15.00, and the cab driver was pretty cool, he had his hair done in a Isrow (Israeli afro) big curls shaped like an afro. He played the old Temptations, James Brown, and Kool and the Gang all the way there. We stopped a couple of times for piss breaks and some lunch which I sprang for $5.00 for both of us to have shrimp fried rice, and I had a couple of San Miguel Beers, and he wanted Coca Cola. When we got to Manila three hours later, it was around 6:00 PM. The driver dropped me off at the Manila Hilton. I had to use my passport to check-in and when they saw my last name and I had a small afro I had been keeping packed for about 2 months, they thought I was some part of the Jackson 5. I got the room next to the presidential sweet on the sixteenth floor and only paid $16.00 a night. It had two bedrooms and a nice little living room with big patio doors that opened up to the swimming pool area. The hotel had one hell of a good club and a large conference room, restaurant, and clothing store. It was all there.

My mother and sister were also on the sixteenth floor in a room down the hall from mine. After I checked in, I went to see my mom and sister. They were dead beat from a thirteen-hour flight. We all hugged and talked for a few minutes then I let them get some rest. I left them and went down to the club in the hotel, it was closed, but the bar portion was open. Lots of Japanese, Australian and American business people were in there. I strutted in with my new tailor made burgundy and black three-piece suit with burgundy and black eel-skinned shoes. I just knew I was the bomb!

I had a few Budweiser beers which were ice cold and tasted so damn good. Just as I was finishing the second beer, this dance troop came in with the traditional Philippine dresses and some long assed bamboo sticks about three inches thick and about six feet long. I was thinking, *what the hell are they gonna do with the bamboo poles*. I had been to this part of the world and seen some strange floor shows in the strip clubs. I got another beer and followed them into the center of the club. A couple of the other guys at the bar were right behind me. I wanted to see what kind of freak show this was gonna be. I was always interested in seeing what other cultures do and they had some nice looking little ladies there. We all walked over to the area that was set up near the stage where all the band equipment was, then one of the ladies turned on a record with I guess it was some traditional music for them, and it was on what they did was amazing, and it is called 'Tinikling' or the 'Bamboo Dance'.

Two guys put these two by four pieces of cardboard about three feet long in front of them on the floor as they knelt down, they both held each end of two bamboo poles. Stevie Wonders's song 'Higher Ground', started, and then the show was on. The two guys smacked the bamboo poles on the ground then made the poles touch each other, and the ladies put their feet in between the poles without getting their ankles smashed. It looked like the little girls jumping rope in the hood. Only they used the bamboo poles as the rope. I asked one of the ladies that was in her costume what is this called, and that's when I learned of 'Tinikling' the guys would make the poles clap together fast and slow and the ladies were put their feet between the poles without being hit, the whole group was good. The lady I was talking to told me when the show really opens, they would only use traditional music, not Stevie Wonder, she was really good looking and while she explained the dancing she was just smiling at me like crazy, I had to smile back, and she had all white teeth no gold or silver like the girls at the clubs in Angeles City or Olongapo, she was different, educated and classy.

I watched them for a little while, then I went back upstairs, put on my swimming trunks and went out to the pool, put my towel on a chaise lounge, and slowly walked into the water. It was a pretty good-sized pool up there on the, and it was on the sixteenth floor. The sun was going down and I wanted another beer, magically a waiter came over to me and handed me a Budweiser. I was amazed, and I remember thinking, *this is the best service I've ever had.* I later found out he was the brother of the sexy little lady I was just talking with that did the bamboo dance. She called him and said if you see a black American, please make sure he has a Budweiser beer to drink. The whole area on that floor had a wrought iron fence about four feet tall surrounding it. It was pretty cool to sit in the pool and see the city of Manila. It was more than that. It was awesome.

This Australian couple came out to the pool. They told me this was their first time in the Philippines and asked me how long I had been in the hotel. I told them I had just arrived earlier today, and they told me it was their honeymoon. I congratulated them, finished my beer, and left. I figured they wanted some alone time in the pool, and I was the only other person up there, so I left, went to my room, and took a nap. I woke up about an hour later, put on my new one piece elephant eared black silk with gold lapels tailor made suit, it zipped up in the front with a hidden zipper that went down to my crotch (I didn't want to drink too much beer with it on, had to unzip the whole thing just to take a piss) and my new black and brown platform shoes, fluffed out the afro and I was ready to go, just had to put my wallet in my front pocket as there were no back pockets. I didn't want to wake my mother and sister. I knew they needed sleep, I knew just how they felt after a 13-hour trip, when I made the trip to Oki I think I slept about three or four hours on the plane, "Me just no likey flying." I was never a big fan of flying and to this day, I still dislike turbulence. That bumpy feeling is not high on my happy list.

I went to the bar, ordered a Budweiser, and found a seat near the dance floor just in case my sister wanted to get down and boogie, and I knew she would, there was a Pilipino band there. I can't remember their name, but I swear the lead singer sounded just like Stevie Wonder when he was singing some of Stevie's songs.

I didn't have long to wait for my sister. She came over to the table I was sitting at and said, "You are probably wondering how I found you,"

I said, "Yeah," and she was informed where I was by one of the receptionists, she said they all giggled when I asked if they knew where you were, I just hunched my shoulders, and we both laughed. She and her mom were in the restaurant and were ready to eat.

I asked my sister, "If Mom had ordered yet."

She said, "No". I was very relieved. I quickly got up and walked as fast as I could to the restaurant, where she was sitting with that long beautiful silver grey hair. I smiled at her when she saw me. I hugged Mom and then pulled out my sister's chair for her and then I sat down. I tried to explain to my mother that the food here is not like what you get when you order in a restaurant back home, she looked at me like I was crazy, and she let me know that she had plenty of friends that were Philippinos back home in Los Angeles that worked with her and they told her what to order.

I was freaking out, thinking they had told her to order ballute, which is an egg that is fertilized for months underground and still in the shell and boiled. The smell alone is something most Americans have never experienced. She said she ordered jumbo shrimp, rice, and a salad. I just shook my head and tried not to laugh. She smirked at me. I just shook my head, my sister caught on really quick to damn near everything and she ordered exactly what I did, a well done cheeseburger with French fries and a Budweiser beer, that's when my mother told us we needed to experience the culture of the country that we are visiting. I just smiled at her. Now in Manila, when we were there, the country, as I mentioned earlier, had President Marcos as their leader, and that man was no joke, lots of Philippinos were called in for questioning and never returned, and their families never heard from them again, and at this time he was up for reelection. Let's just put it this way he had been president ever since the end of World War II and was not going to lose an election.

Most people liked breathing air and so he really had no one to run against. But during the period we were waiting for our food to arrive we lost power in the hotel, it was only off for a few minutes but when the power came back on, the air conditioner, fans and lights came back on, and my mother, sister and I along with other Americans were the only ones sitting upright in our chairs. Everybody else had ducked under the tables and were getting up, both my mother and sister stared straight at me like I knew what the hell was going on and all I could do was shrug my shoulders and smile at them.

When the waiter came with our plates, Mom asked him, "What in the world makes everybody get under the tables?"

The waiter replied, "Marcos is running for President, and he has some opposition party members having dinner here. Most people thought the Army would come in and shoot him," then the waiter put our plates and drinks on the table my mother was still staring at him, but sis was staring at the jumbo shrimp. They still had the heads on them and the whiskers or antennae were moving due to the fan blowing down on us. After Mom finished talking to the waiter, she looked at both my sister and I, and we were both staring at her plate. It was killing me not to bust out laughing cause I knew what was gonna happen as soon as Mom saw the shrimp's whiskers moving, and boy she was loud when she screamed and then she yelled, "Hell no!" she jumped up out of her seat and had backed up against the wall, both my sister and myself busted up laughing I had to hold my sides and tears we coming out of my sister's eyes.

Mom moved her chair back when she screamed and it all happened so fast then the tears started pouring out of my eyes, we were the only black people in there, and most of the Philippinos thought we were somehow related to the Jackson Five, so you can imagine how concerned the staff there was, the manager of the hotel came running over to our table, and even the cook came to our table to see what was wrong. I wanted to explain to them that we are not used to seeing shrimps with the head on, but I couldn't stop laughing, so my sister had to try and explain in between her bust of laughter every time she looked at Mom. Once we all settled down and assured the manager and the cook it was alright, Mom ordered the cheeseburger and fries. They had to remove her plate from the table before she would sit back down. I don't think we went more than two minutes at that meal without one of us busting up laughing along with some of the other people that were there eating their dinners.

That was the first for Mom, but deep down, I knew it wouldn't be the last thing that would freak her out while we were on vacation in the good ole Philippines. Mom ate her cheeseburger real fast and said she needed to go lay down. I got up and pulled her chair out for her. She got up and gave both of us a kiss on the cheek and walked straight to the elevator. That was the last I saw of her that night. After Sis and I finished our beers, I got up, grabbed her hand, and said, "We gotta hit the club. They have a really good band and they be jamming."

She said, "Okay," and we got up and went to the club, and the seat I was sitting at was still empty. We sat down and I ordered us both another drink, we sat there for a couple of songs laughing at Mom's reaction at dinner, then she said, "The lead singer sounds just like Stevie Wonder."

I said, "That's what I thought." she got up, grabbed my hand, and said, "We gotta dance,"

I said, "Sure," and the funny thing we did was 'whatever moves we did on the dance floor', the Philippinos would imitate us, so we did the 'cha-cha LA style' and it took them a while to get those moves down, but a lot of them did. We had a great time the lead singer came over and asked me if he could dance with my sister.I told him he would have to ask her and she did dance with him, just as I was heading back to our table.

The little cutie that was doing the bamboo dance grabbed my hand and said, "Lets dance," she and a couple of her friends joined me and Sis at our table, her name she told me was Marie, and she said not Maria but Marie. I told her that was my mothers middle name and she smiled like you wouldn't believe like I had just asked her to marry me, that shit made me nervous for a few minutes, but with another beer and some more dancing I forgot all about the nervous issue I had, Marie and her friends asked my sister about the United States and Los Angeles and they kept telling Sis how beautiful she was. Then I told them all to dance, by now we had a couple of guys from the band had joined us and of course the lead singer. I didn't have the heart to tell him he probably didn't stand a chance of getting lucky with my sister. I knew she never dated guys that were shorter than her and she was only five feet two inches, but he kept trying and I finally said lets all dance and they did 'whatever we did for dance moves'. We had to teach them the 'cha-cha' the way we did in Los Angeles back then and it was awesome.

Sis had a great time, then Sis said she was tired and went back to her room with Mom. Marie stayed with me for that night. I had asked her about her boyfriend and she said she had an Australian boyfriend that was in his late sixties, and he only gave her oral sex. I almost spit my beer on her trying not to laugh. She said no kidding, only him giving her oral sex, and they had been together for two years. I asked her if she would be in trouble if she spent the night with me and she said he gets drunk and falls asleep around nine PM. I said okay and then I took her back to my room. There was no time for oral sex, she wanted the hookup, and I let her have it, and we were both happy. She fell asleep in my arms, and I – Well, I was happy.

Then next morning, she got up and I ordered room service. I asked for American bacon and scrambled eggs and two glasses of orange juice. The way she was acting you would have thought we were on our honeymoon or something. She wanted to take the three of us on a tour of Manila.

I said, "I would check with my mom and see what she wanted to do. I had never been in Manila, and it sounds good to me."

Marie said, "Just tell them about pickpockets and people trying to steal." I told her not to worry about that.

I called Mom's room and asked if they had eaten and to see if they wanted to check out Manila, and Mom said, "Oh yes, that sounds good."

And she was happy that we had a guide, so about ten AM we were in a cab checking out

Manila, we went to the big outdoor markets, the first thing Mom saw what she and the jumbo shrimp started laughing then Sis. I saw what she was looking at and we started laughing. I had to explain to Marie what had happened at dinner last night, and then she laughed.

The outdoor markets where the locals shopped and they usually shopped daily not like we did once a week. Most did not have refrigerators and if they did, there were problems with the electrical grid staying on twenty-four-seven, so no one wanted their food to spoil. It was best to get fresh fruits and veggies daily. At the end of the markets were the clothing areas, mostly t-shirts with all kinds of designs on them and shorts, tennis shoes, and dresses. After the clothing stores were the wood carving and they were awesome. I brought a Philippino beer keg made of wood with all kinds of intricate carvings of a typical Philippino village with mountains in the background. Mom and Sis both brought wooden jewelry and a couple of dresses. We pitched in and brought Marie a dress. She was so happy, she kissed Sis and Mom on their cheeks.

We walked around two different outdoor markets. At the last one, I noticed this guy staring at Mom's purse. He looked away when he saw me watching him, he walked away, and I later saw him talking with another guy. I was hoping I would not have to give them a beat down as we were leaving and heading back to the cab, the guy he was talking to walked right up to my mother, and he had a box cutter in his hand. I knocked the box cutter out of his hand and pushed him away.He didn't get a chance to get the blade thru her bag before I had him. Neither Mom or Sis saw anything. Most people just kept walking past us, Marie said something to him, and he looked like he was going to pissed on himself. Marie grabbed Mom's arm and we got into the cab. I asked Marie what she said to him before he took off running, and she said, "You fucked with the wrong people. He is from US Military."

She smiled at me.

I asked her, "If she would have any problems if she went back,"

She said, "Hell no, they will probably run if they see me thinking you will come for them."

I smiled and told her, "I would"

She said, "I know."

Marie asked my sister, "What happened?"

Sis just looked at me and said, "How did you know?"

I told her, "I saw another guy staring at us, but when he saw me, he walked away, so I figured he had some friends and went to one of them. What they would do is cut the bottom of your purse or bag, and when everything falls out, they all start grabbing your stuff and run off with it," and I told her, "It wasn't going to happen to them."

She smiled.

I gave the cab driver an extra $2.00 to step on it back to the hotel and he did. We took the back streets and got to the hotel in no time, he probably knew what happened. I didn't bother to ask him, it was over, and everybody was okay, except for the guy I helped go to sleep. After I pushed him away, I hit him in his jaw, my crew and I later called that the punch from Cuba cause that wasn't the last time I would do it, and they also learned it.

Once we were back in the hotel, we went to our rooms and agreed to meet for dinner at six PM. Mom was still shaking up and didn't understand how I could get so violent so fast and knew what I was doing, my sister later told me, and I replied to my sister, "You know where I learned it from in South Central Los Angeles."

She smiled and said, "She didn't want to tell Mom," (my sister once watched something similar, but not with a pickpocket but with some serious rednecks that decided to drive to our high school and beat up the blacks catching the buses home). It didn't work out too well for them. They had enough folks, just not as violent as we were, that was how I had to grow up, and its still with me today. I think I'm not sure if I were to swing at somebody now that my arm wouldn't fall off. I got old and I am now writing this story. Once we got all stuff we had brought put away, we went out to the swimming pool. It was nice Mom, Sis, Marie, and I were just chilling out and enjoying the view of the city of Manila with the mountains and jungle in the distance.

We had a few drinks and played in the pool until around six PM, then we all left, showered up, and went down to the restaurant for dinner. We were all wearing jeans. I laughed, Sis told me if we needed to get under a table, nobody wanted to be in dress clothes, and I just laughed again. Mom smiled at me, and Marie laughed. We all ate, and had a few more drinks except for Mom. She hardly drank any alcohol. She did like lemonade, we had all had steaks for dinner this time, and it was pretty good. Marie wanted to get back to the room, and to bed, since she would not see me for a couple of days. I agreed she said she would be waiting for us to return the next evening. I smiled at her and she asked me if I didn't believe her, and that's when I reminded her of her boyfriend. She looked me right in the eyes and she said, "I will be here."

I kissed her and said, "Okay," then we got busy, and I mean really busy. I guess after that adrenalin rush for the both of us, we needed to work it off, and we did. I remember screaming her name and my name. Boy, that was a good sex session!

After we finished, I had Marie call the front desk and leave a wake-up call for us at eight AM so we could get an early start to the bus station to catch that rabbit bus down to Olongapo, then a quick cab ride to the Subic Bay Naval Base. We said our goodbyes to Marie the next morning and caught a cab to the bus station in Manila heading to Olongapo and it was a Ribbit bus. I had been on one of these buses with Honey and I didn't like it one bit. The driver we had, I would not have gotten in a jeepney with him let alone a bus. I was hoping this one would be better, we boarded the bus, and it was a little more than half packed. Mom got a seat near the middle of the bus and she didn't get the window seat. I went to the back where they had stacked big bags of rice and my sister sat next to me. I told her to keep an eye on Mom, it's going to get funny, and she looked at me like I was crazy.

The bus was only half full when we departed Manila, but on the first stop we made. There were only four or five people that got on and a few chickens, and I was surprised they were in cages. After they loaded, we went about forty-five minutes before we made our next stop. There was a rest area there, so I got off to use the restroom. When I got to Mom's seat, I asked her if she needed to use the rest room cause I didn't know when the next stop would be our if she would want to stop at the next one, she got up and went to the ladies' area, and I went to the one designated for men. Then I went and grabbed a few beers for Sis and I and the Philippino version of seven-up for Mom got back on the bus, and we were off again. The bus started to head up a mountain and the driver never slowed down.

The road was winding, and it was a cliff on the passenger side. I was so glad Mom was paying more attention to the people on the bus than looking out the windows. She used to freak out really bad when my father would take us up to Santa's Village, which was near Lake Arrowhead in Southern California up in the mountains. She would sit in the back seat with her eyes closed. I bet that was why she was looking at the people and chickens on the bus, but I knew she hadn't seen anything like what was yet to come.

There was another stop at the top of the mountain road we were on and the road split between the mountain, so most of the Philippino women got out of the bus and went to the side of the bus that had bushes and did her business there and the men went on the other side of the bus. This was normal for them. Mom's eyes were big as those old silver dollars. I was trying not to laugh, then the lady with the baby sitting next to Mom pulled out her tit and started to breastfeed her baby. Now Mom was looking for another seat. I barely giggled then.

After everyone was back on the bus, maybe twenty minutes later, there was another stop, just on the side of the road, and we hadn't started going back down the mountain yet. We pulled over and there were about four more people and four piglets, and a heck of a monster sized hog. They just put the piglets on the bus and they started running around under the seats and making all kinds of noise. Again, Mom's eyes told the whole story about how she felt, breastfeeding, chickens, and now baby pigs. They tried for about fifteen minutes to get the hog inside the bus, it didn't work. I was just barely past giggling when my sister started cracking up laughing. I remember trying not to look at Mom but it was killing me. I wanted to laugh so badly, but I felt so sorry for Mom.

No air conditioning, baby pigs running under the seats, and now the chickens started cackling, then one of the guys outside trying to push the hog inside pointed an overhang, and the driver pulled the bus under it. One guy had a rope, I thought they were going to kill the hog and tie it to the top of the bus, but no, they tied the damn thing on top of the bus, and it was screaming. I couldn't hold back my laughter and Mom looked like she was going to pass out. My sister had tears in her eyes from laughing so hard. It was about an hour's drive to the next stop and I was wondering how they were going to get the hog off the roof.

I was sure it was going to the slaughterhouse, but I just couldn't figure out how they were going to get it down. We found out at the next stop. Once at the next stop, people came running to both sides of the bus trying to sell things to the passengers, that's when my mother and sister got their first smell of ballute. There are some foods that smell really bad, like chitterlings and kimchi (a Korean delicacy). They both smell like a-port-a-potty that hasn't been cleaned in a week, but ballute, when the top of the egg shell is knocked off the aroma if you are not used to it. It will make you want to gag, and the lady with the breastfeeding baby, put some pesos out the window and got one. I told my sister to put her hand over her nose cause in a few seconds, this whole bus with all the other smells was going to get fifty times worse and man, did smell like the outhouse from hell.

Sis and I were not laughing anymore. It was getting hard to breath and even though I wanted to laugh, I didn't want the smell of ballute getting in my mouth. Mom got up and signaled for me to come over to her and I did, and we, along with my sister, walked out of the bus and got as far away as we could to catch our breath. I think my sister was about to puke and we got off that bus just in time. Then I saw how they were going to get the hog off the bus. They had a bulldozer and the bucket was raised. They pulled the still screaming hog into the bucket and it had to have been five of those guys, but they got it into the bucket. The bulldozer backed away from the bus and lowered it to the ground, I thought they were gonna take the little pigs off as well, but they stayed on the bus, a truck came over, and the hog was loaded into the back of it, probably on its way to the slaughterhouse.

There were no cabs to get us to Olongapo at this stop, so we had to get back on the bus with all the windows down. The smell of ballute was just about gone, but it was still in our minds, and it stayed in my mind until we got to the base, and I took a shower. After about an hour, we pulled into the bus station at Olongapo Mom used her hand and signaled me to come to her when we were getting off and she looked like she was going to cry. I kind of pushed people out of my way so I could get to her and see what was wrong, she said "you need to stand in front of me" and I asked why and she said "I have peed on myself" I got right in front of her and we walked step by step until we got off the bus I was so mad at myself for laughing at her, when we stepped down off of the bus she pushed me away and said "gotcha" I looked at her and she had not pissed on herself and she and Sis were laughing at me, then I started laughing.

We got a cab to Subic Bay Naval Base and I had already called and reserved to rooms for us to stay in, sort of like a very nice hotel room. We would be there for two days. Once we were all checked in we all wanted a shower asap. I knew my poor Mom was in panic mode alpha once we stopped at the second bust stop. She never again wanted to see how her Pilipino friends back in Los Angeles grew up in their little villages in the Philippines.

Marie was there waiting for me at the front lobby when we finally got back to Manila. She ran up and kissed me and hugged Mom and Sis, then Mom's adventure on the Rabbit bus began. We all laughed so hard just thinking about her on that bus with the piglets, breastfeeding, the hog, and people pissing on the side of the road, but the best was the look on her face when she got the first sniff of ballute. We had dinner at the hotel and Mom and sis went to their room to get some sleep. Sis and I partied most of the nights that we had left of our two-week vacation. Mom sat by the pool most days and read her books, and relaxed. The day before they were to depart, they slept most of that day as they had a long plane ride back to Los Angeles the next morning.

Marie and I went to the bar, had a few drinks, and went back to my room. I knew this would be the last time I would see her also, so we both made the best of the time we had together. The next morning, we were up and dressed early. I went to Mom's and Sis's room just in time to see their bags being loaded onto the cart. Mom had tears in her eyes as we walked to the elevator and headed for the main lobby. Their cab was waiting to take them to the airport, so we hugged each other, and they were off. I kissed Marie and got into one of the waiting cabs and headed off to Angeles City to catch a MAC flight back to Okinawa. I didn't have to wait long, probably about twenty minutes, and I was on another C-130. After the plane landed at Kadena Air Base,I felt exhausted and I was ready to get to my place and crash out, that's just what I did, and I still had two days off from work. I just planned on relaxing. I was a short timer on Okinawa and in the navy as my enlistment would be up in a couple of months. Lots of my friends were leaving. Benny and Marie had already left for their next duty station, Billy was gone, all my good friends in my section were gone, and there were a lot of new folks to replace them all, but I was a short timer and really didn't want to really get close to anyone else, just wanted to do the rest of my time and say Adios.

I still had a couple of friends that I hung out with, and they were the same as me short timers, but all in different sections. I had hooked up with this new seaman apprentice and she was hot. I thought when she wasn't with me, she was with someone else, and I didn't care. I never even bothered to ask her, the sex was good, and she can cook, thats all I needed for the rest of my time in Oki. I didn't bother selling my hooptie. I just left a note on it at the barracks that whoever wanted it could have it. And since I was an E-4, I was able to have my furniture and motorcycle shipped home by the military for free. It was all shipped to the Long Beach Naval station. I shipped everything a month and a half before I was scheduled to leave Oki for the out-processing center at Treasure Island in San Francisco, California, and that process would take almost three weeks.

All I had left in the house I rented was my bed and a couple of those plastic chairs, and of course, my bathroom items, along with a little radio that was also my alarm clock. The babe I had was pissed off because I had all the rest of the furniture along with the stereo shipped out. I told her to kiss my ass if she didn't like it. Hell, she didn't help with anything. All she had to do was cook every so often and clean up after herself, so she packed the few things she had there and left. I wasn't even mad, but I forgot to get the house keys and didn't even think of it until later.

That evening I got a cab to take me outside Kadena Air Base and hit a couple of clubs on Gate-2 Street. I was home right as it started to get dark, the cab driver was playing country and western music and I asked him to please change it or just turn it off, nothing but sad songs, and it was depressing. He called me a baka gi ging. I said, "*okay.*" I told him to stop two streets from my house. I got out of the car and ran, didn't pay him anything.

I went into my house and I could see him driving around trying to find me, but I was already home, sitting on the roof in one of the two plastic beach chairs. I had whiskey, listening to the little radio playing Japanese music. Once he left, I put the base radio station on and was jamming by myself. I was drinking the last of the Saki I still had and was pretty buzzed when all of a sudden I noticed I had company on the roof with me. He came right up the stairs. It was a big ass stray dog, a bull mastiff, he was that dark brown and kind of dirty. He walked right up to me and rested his head on my leg. I had never seen this dog before and panic mode alpha hit me. I could feel my heart beating fast. I was thinking if this thing bit me, he could get a big chunk of my leg before I could scream. I almost passed out.

I shook my head several times with my eyes closed, but when I opened them, he was still there staring at me. I finally took a deep breath and slowly, very slowly moved my hand toward his head. He didn't move or growl at me and I softly patted his head, and he looked up at me, then he sniffed my cup with the Saki in it. I asked him if he was thirsty and hungry he just looked at me with those big eyes. I gently moved to get up, and he moved backward and sat down. I went downstairs and got a bowl of water and I had some baloney in the little refrigerator and I took it all back up to the roof. I put it down near me, and he slowly came over and started eating the baloney. I thought it was bad. I had it before I left for the Philippines and never bothered to toss it out. He ate it and then drank the whole bowl of water and then put his head back on my leg. I had his slobber all over my leg, but I knew I had just made a good friend.

I had to go back down and get a couple of beers. I didn't know if he would drink it or not, so I took the bowl that had the water in it down to fill it up for him. When I got back, I put the water down, sat my butt down, and started drinking one of the beers. I usually drank them fast, so they didn't get too hot. The dog stared right at me and licked his lips. I didn't have any more food to give him, just my cereal that I ate before work and some ramen noodles, but he wasn't getting any of that. It was all mine. I sat my beer down to turn the radio up and the damn dog knocked the can over and started lapping up my beer. I didn't get mad I just watched him as I had never seen a dog drink beer before. I remember thinking to myself, this dog is cool as hell, and drinks beer. What a new friend I have!

I had my first day shift in the morning and I knew it was a little after ten PM. I needed sleep, so I picked up all the stuff, left the chair, and whistled for the dog to follow, and he did. I took him in the house and locked the doors. I figured I'd put up a note at work to see if anybody lost a dog. I passed out.

When I woke up, the dog was sleeping at the foot of my bed. I let him out of the back door before I went to take a shower and left the back door partially open as there were no real thieves in the area, and I expected him to go home.

When I got out of the shower, the dog was laying on the floor by the front door. I got dressed and went to work. When I got back home from work my ex-girlfriend was sitting on the floor and the dog was sitting in front of her. He would not let her leave and she was crying like crazy. I was already aggravated as hell because my relief didn't show up in time for me to catch a ride down the hill, so my tired, hot ass had to walk home, and this is what I came home to.

She said she had left some clothes and wanted to take them back with her, but what she had in her sea bag was most of the food I brought to last me until I moved back into the barracks. I knew then and there I had a new best friend. I emptied the sea bag put all the stuff away, walked into the bedroom, and checked to make sure she didn't try to steal anything else. When I walked back into the kitchen, she started yelling and screaming about how I was holding her against her will and was going to rape her. I smiled at her and asked her if she wanted me to go and get the police or the master at arms to see what they would think of the situation. Then I asked her how she got here from the base and she told me she had walked. I knew that was bullshit as she wouldn't walk anywhere.

I later found out her new boyfriend brought her to my place to get food for their apartment. Yep, I loved my new best friend, I called him to me, and he stood up and walked over to where I was standing. I told her to get up and get her ass out of my house, and that I never wanted to see her again. She asked if I was going to give her a ride back to base and I looked at her like she was crazy. The reason she really left was I had no vehicle to take her places. She walked back to base. The nearest phone booth was right outside the main gate. She was trying to walk out the door and I told her to leave the keys to the front and back doors. She threw them on the floor and I walked her to the front door. I never saw her again and I didn't care.

After I slammed the door shut behind her, I opened two cans of beef stew and poured them both in a bowl and fed it to my new best friend. I put mine in the oven and opened up two cans of beer, took two more plastic bowels and poured water in one and beer in the other. I sat on the plastic chair and drank the other beer and just stared at the dog as I ate my dinner. I was wondering who he belonged to and why he wasn't with them, then the idea hit me, someone left and was probably sent to another duty station and couldn't take their pet with them, I felt sad for him and them.

After he ate and drank both the water and the beer, I grabbed two more beers and the plastic chair and headed outside to go up on the roof. He was right behind me. I forgot to get his bowel, so I had to go back downstairs, he sat by my chair until I came back, and I poured his beer into the bowel and sat down and drank mine. He laid down right beside me, and farted once, which I thought was going to kill me with the smell. Then I laughed at him and you know what, he looked like he was smiling back at me.

I wasn't even mad at my ex. I had to remember to ask how much it would be to take him back to California with me the next morning at work. Again I got up to let him out the back door and I went, did the three S's shit, shower, and shaved. When I got out, he was laying on the kitchen floor waiting for me, I had cereal, and he had another can of beef stew. I was kinda glad I was leaving to go to work because I knew I didn't want to be around when he farted again. That last one almost made me cry.

I had told a coworker about the dog and he seemed to be interested in taking him if I couldn't afford the plane fare to get him home with me. I didn't know where or how I was going to keep him, I knew I could stay at my mom's house, but she already had a couple of dogs, and I wasn't sure she would let me keep this monster there. She probably would because she loved dogs and he didn't pee or poop in the house, so I was hoping she would help me out with him until I found my own place when I got back before I joined the navy. The company I worked for said there would be no problem getting my old job back.

One of the guys in my section let me borrow his car while he was out to sea for two weeks. He was leaving in two hours for a white beach to board an old destroyer. I now had transportation to get to work and to the base. I had to promise I wouldn't take it to any of the strip joints out in town and I would leave it on the base with the keys at the Quarter Deck before I left, and I made that promise to him. He knew I was a man of my work and he handed me the keys. So that last eve-watch, I had transportation. I stopped on base, went to the little px and grabbed two six-packs of Budweiser four cans of dog food, and headed home to my best buddy. When I got there, he was laying on the front porch. I forgot to turn on the fan in the living room, where he usually stayed while I was gone. I liked having him around I didn't have to lock any of the doors. He scared the hell out of the Okinawans and he would snarl and bark at them, not Americans, just the Okinawans. I named him racist.

That night we ate and drank a few beers. I would talk to him and it looked like he understood what I was saying, probably just me being drunk that night. The next morning, I took Racist to the base, but they didn't have any dog collars big enough to go around his neck, so I went to the base auto shop and found a piece of chain, one of the guys the worked in there couldn't believe how big Racist was, he really helped me out, he had a long piece of chain that they used on the gates around the base, and he cut it and made a collar and leash for me, I gave him $5.00 for it and we put the chain around Racist's neck, and it was perfect. Now, I weighed about one hundred and sixty pounds back then, and I was pretty sure Racist weighed just as much, if not more. I took him to the Navy barracks and everybody wanted to pat him, he loved that. We spent about an hour there drinking beer and hanging out with everybody there. None of them could believe how big he was. We had one Japanese American that was also a CT and Racist just didn't like him either, as soon as the guy got close to Racist the hairs on his back stood straight up, and he started snarling.

To this day I still don't know why he didn't like the Okinawans. He must have been mistreated by them, I never knew why. We left the base and headed to my buddy, Franks's house. There was no place to park near the front of his house so I had to park down the street. I put the chain around Racist neck and we walked towards the house. There were a lot of dogs on this street, most were in houses and as soon as they saw Racist, they all started barking like crazy. Racist didn't blink an eye he walked right by my side and payed no attention to them at all.

Just as we got to Frank's front yard, a dog, I later frond out was an Australian Collie, ran up on Racist, it looked like the dog on TV named Lassie only bigger. I was getting nervous because I didn't know what the hell Racist was going to do, I tried to walk faster but Racist just kept his normal slow pace, I didn't want to piss him off by pulling too hard of the chain because it would choke him, I yelled at the Collie to get out of here, and that's when Racist turned toward the Collie, I let go of the chain, and Racist was on the Collie, and with one paw he slammed the Collie to the ground, then he turned and walked back to me and sat down. It looked like he just slammed a rag doll to the ground, all the neighbors there watched the whole thing and it happened right in Frank's front yard. I was hoping this would not make his family dislike Racist.

Before I could knock on the door, Frank opened it and said, "Dude, that dog is fucking awesome. I love this dog." Then he said come on in and we got to meet his family, his wife, older son, and a ten-month-old little baby girl. We sat at the kitchen table and I told Racist to lay down, he walked by the front door and laid down. Frank grabbed some beers and we started talking, they asked me all kinds of questions about Racist, and I just told them the truth. I didn't know anything except he has been staying with me for almost a week, and I told them about my ex-girlfriend that was trying to steal food and how Racist kept her in the kitchen sitting on the floor until I got home also that he didn't like Okinawans or Japanese people.

We all laughed, then his wife made a real small gasping sound, the little girl had crawled over to Racist and she was making those baby sounds and laughing she grabbed his nose, his ears, and that went on for a good five minutes then Racist licked her arm, and with his head, he nudged her near his belly. She grabbed his skin and laid her head against his belly and went to sleep. We were all holding our breaths and once the baby was asleep Racist laid out flat like he was protecting her, and we all started to breathe again.

Franks's wife had tears in her eyes, I thought she was mad, because none of us actually didn't know what the dog would do, then she said, "Look, the baby is smiling in her sleep, and how beautiful is that?" I thought, *Racist had licked her to see how good she was going to taste.* That's when somebody banged on Franks's front door. Racist gently nudged the baby over and stood straight up staring at the door, Frank walked over, and I called Racist to me and told him to sit. It was the owner of the Collie dog, and he was pissed.

The first thing he said is, "Whose dog is this?"

I said, "Mine, why?" with an attitude.

He told me, "I was on the report that he would see to it that Racist would be put to sleep." I looked right in his eyes and told him that ain't going to happen.

He asked me if I knew who he was and the first thing out of my mouth was, "I don't give a damn who you are." He was screaming and yelling. Half the people on the street were outside Frank's house, I told him I had my dog on a chain, and we were in Frank's yard, so again how did my dog attack his.

At the time I didn't know it but this guy was an Air Force senior officer. Then Frank started telling the officer, that his dog had been a problem since he moved into the base housing, it attacks all the neighbor's dogs and his runs around like it owns the area, then I said not anymore and we all started laughing. two minutes later Shore patrol and Air Force security showed up, Racist was still sitting near the chair I was sitting in. Frank and I followed the Air Force officer out to their cars, they told the officer that witnesses said his dog attacked Racist in Franks yard and I had a leash on Racist.

The officer asked me my name and I told him my name, rank and who my commanding officer was. The officer looked me right in my eyes and said that my dog was going to be put to sleep. I told him if anything happened to my dog, he would have a permanent size 9 footprint on his ass. He stormed off, the Air Force Security guys asked me to take Racist out of the housing area and I said we were just leaving. They all had big grins on their faces, I heard them talking and one of them said, "It's about time some dog kicked that collie's ass." I started laughing. I got Racist in the back of the car and drove off. When we got home, we went up on the roof and had a few beers, it helped to calm me down.

The next morning, the Command Master Chief came over and asked me what happened, he said the Air Force officer had filed charges against me and Racist. I looked at the Command Master Chief and said, "Really!"

He smiled and told me not to worry about it, just don't take the dog to that base housing again. I asked if Frank was in any trouble, and he said, "Hell no!" and told me how Frank wanted Racist, but Racist was not allowed in the base housing. I told him I would just have to take Racist back with me to the world. He grinned and said, "He is a good dog. You have a good day and left."

I didn't take Racist anywhere but to the barracks after that. The day before, I was getting ready to leave for the states and out of processing I couldn't find Racist. I went to the base to return the car I had borrowed and asked if anybody had seen him, and no one did. I caught a cab back to the house and that's when I found him he was in the back dead, someone had poisoned him. I was pissed. It was a good thing I didn't have a car at that time is all I will say about how I felt.

The next day I walked to base after giving the keys back to my landlord and went to the barracks. My flight back to the states was in three hours, so I went to the chow hall, had lunch, and then hung out at the barracks. Everybody was sorry to hear about Racist and wanted to know what caused it. I told them he looked like he was poisoned and I wasn't sure who would have done it, but they all knew about the Air Force Officer that complained about Racist. I just don't think that guy had the balls to do anything.

I never knew who did it and that is probably best. I shook hands with the guys and hugged the babes. There was one there that had gotten out of the navy but stayed in the area. We were friends and she came on base to wish me well. She had gotten a job off base in one of the really posh clubs that the Japanese went to when they came to Okinawa and her tips in a couple of months were more than her yearly Navy pay. I hugged her and that was it, back in a navy van headed for Naha International Airport to catch a flight back to the world.

Naval Station Treasure Island – San Francisco California January 1979

It was February 3rd, 1979, the weather was nice and cool, not like Okinawa or the Philippines. I was standing at the quarterdeck at Naval Station Treasure Island in San Francisco, California. I had the biggest smile. I was getting out processed with an honorable discharge from the United States Navy, and I was feeling very good. I was told by one of the clerks that out-processing would take two to three weeks. I just didn't care. I was ready to become a civilian again, I knew the first thing I would do when I got out would be to go back to the sewing machine company. I used to work for and get my old job back, then find an apartment somewhere back in Los Angeles and that would be that.

After I handed my orders shown on a map where the barracks and everything on the base was located, I left the quarter deck. I was in my dress whites and ready to get out of them, so I went to the barracks and checked in. This was similar to boot camp, open bay barracks. There were thirty or more racks in one room. There was a stand-up locker to hang our uniforms and a foot locker next to the rack for underwear and stuff. I took everything out of my sea bag and put everything where they were supposed to go, my civilian clothes I hung up in the locker with my dress uniforms. I took my medals and put them on the top shelf of the locker, and then reported back to the 1st class petty officer in charge of this area.

He told me that since I was a third-class petty officer and getting out honorably I had no curfew for liberty, which meant I could stay out all night if I wanted to. I just needed to be here at 0800 hours each morning for work details. I looked at him like he was crazy. "Work details?" He said, "Don't worry, you're a petty officer. You'll probably be in charge of people picking up litter or something, and it's usually only half a day. You will be assigned a date for a physical and stuff like that" He said, "You won't be working every day and weekends are yours."

I said, "Cool!"

Then he asked me if I was sure I wanted out, and I said, "Hell yeah!"

He laughed and said, "I see on your sleeve, you are one of the communications guys.

I said, "Yep!" Then he started telling me about how things were here in the real world, people losing jobs because of businesses closing, gas shortages and only being able to get gas on certain days depending on the last number on your license plates. I just couldn't believe him, then he said being stuck on Oki, your probably haven't heard of any of this and I told him all we got was Japanese stuff on TV except for the military stuff on the radio and some of the new songs, that was all I knew, he just laughed. I was thinking to myself this brother is nuts.

Then he told me that everybody processes out here from the pacific, honorable and dishonorable, stay away from the ones that got dishonorable, they are trouble and that most of them had done serious brig time and were getting kicked out and most of them are pissed off at the navy. I told him I would keep that in mind.

He said, "Cool, good luck and stay out of trouble."

I went outside to the phone booth and called Mom to let her know I was back in California up in the San Francisco area. I could hear her telling everybody in the house that I was back in the states and up in San Francisco. She told me to call my aunt because she should still be here in San Francisco, a part called Daily City. She gave me the number and then tried to tell me about the family, but I was running low on change and I wanted to call my aunt to see if I could kick it with her and her husband who I really got along with very well. We hung up the phones and I called my aunt. She said she knew exactly where I was and would come over tomorrow around 12 PM to get me, and I said, "Cool!" I don't know which of us was the most excited, then I told her I had just talked to Mom, so I was out of change and needed to hang up.

She said, "See you tomorrow at 12 PM."

I said, "Later to her."

I left and found the chow hall, had a real cheeseburger and fries with a 7-up and chocolate cake and I was damn near done for the day. I found the base club and had a few beers then headed back to the barracks to change and then watch some TV.

I never realized how much I missed things that were normal to a lot of Americans, like having TV shows in English. I went to the beer machine in the back of the lounge area and brought one more beer, that's when I met Ron, another brother getting out with an honorable discharge when I asked him we both laughed and he said, "Yeah, honorable," he went to the beer machine and grabbed a bud also and sat down. I asked where he was stationed and he said on a ship out of Hawaii. I told him that had to be cool, he smiled and asked where I came from and I told him, he looked at me and said I wouldn't wish that on anybody I said your right there that's why I'm here and we both laughed, he had spent some time in the PI when his ship pulled into Subic Bay

Olongapo, and after hearing that we talked for a while he had just gotten here and put his stuff in the lockers and was just as tired as I was. I told him about my aunt picking me up tomorrow and I said I would ask if he could tag along, and he said, "Cool."

All his family was in Los Angeles County in Norwalk. I couldn't believe it. I told him I was from South Central. We were best buds after that. That night was something else for me. I was not used to that many people coming in at all times of the night, all were getting processed out, at around 0200 in the morning, there was some shouting and cussing going on, Ron and I both screamed as loud as we could and to them to shut the fuck up at the same time, there was no more noise after that, I never knew who it was, but at 0600 we were all awakened by the first class petty office that was at the front desk. He went to all the guys that were getting out honorably first and told us to get dressed in work uniforms and wait outside, none of us knew what the hell was going on, one of the two guys that were arguing earlier was caught trying to leave the base without his id and he had blood on his clothes, once they checked us all they found the guy he had stabbed, dead in the same room as us, most of us slept right thru the whole thing, that was the last night Ron and I slept there we stayed at my Aunts house after she came and picked us up that after noon, her and her husband were leaving that night for a business meeting he had in Texas, he worked for the Shell Oil company and would be gone for almost two weeks, they let me borrow their car which was beyond cool, it was a Fiat convertible sports car with a stick shift, Ron and I were set we never spent another night at the base, they had a very nice house in Daily City about thirty-five or forty minutes from the base across the Golden Gate Bridge. Every weekday morning, we would be on base at 07:45 and would be on work parties. I never saw the guy that did the stabbing, the guy he stabbed died that night. There was no way in hell either of us was going to stay there at night.

We went to some of the clubs in San Francisco the first weekend we were there, we just didn't know where to go, most of the ones we went to on the first night out were full of guys and that was not either of our thing so we caught up on things we really missed like going to Taco Bell and other fast food places, checking out movies that we never heard of, one of my aunts friends showed up and when she found out we were staying there and as she said were both straight, which neither Ron or myself understood what the hell she was talking about we asked her for the address of some good clubs that had ladies in them and she told us, when we got there most of the ladies were just a little too much for us, the one came over to me and asked what I would do for her and after I told her what I had to say, Ron and I were asked to leave the club, if I wasn't drunk I probably would not have said what I did, but after I said it me and Ron busted up laughing and he kept pointing at her, all I said was I would be nice to her and I wouldn't call animal control, she looked like one of the monkeys that I saw in the Philippines and I just couldn't stop laughing, the bouncers were cool and one of them couldn't stop laughing, Ron and I called it a night and went to my aunts house, we laughed all the way there. I didn't see my aunt's friend for the rest of the time we were there. Our last work detail was watching guys with sticks that had a nail attached to it picking up cigarette butts and then I had my physical that lasted about an hour, then I went back to the work party and told Ron it was his turn. He came back and was mad at me. He yelled, "Why didn't you tell me they were going to do the finger in the butt thing?"

I laughed and said, "I figured then did it when I came in the navy, and they are going to do it when I got out," we both laughed.

The next day we were on a bus to downtown Los Angeles. We both had on tailor made suits from overseas, mine was a one-piece black silk with the elephant ear bellbottoms it had big gold lapels that were made out of some gold material, and it had my nickname on the left lapel in black silk and a black bull with Taurus under the bull on the other lapel. I had black and brown platform shoes and my afro was way out there. Ron's mother was waiting for him and she rushed him out the door and into her car. We barely had time to exchange phone numbers. We were going to hook up tonight and party real hard.

A few seconds later I thought I heard my sister's voice, but I couldn't see her, then I heard the voice again, she told me to look around and asked if anybody was dressed like me, then I looked no one was wearing bell bottoms or platform shoes no big afros when Ron and I went out in town in San Francisco we just wore our dress uniforms and had our hair packed we never noticed how everybody was dressed. I felt so stupid, I walked as fast as I could on those platforms to the men's room and changed into jeans and tennis shoes, ran to the door and my sister had the door open, and we took off.

After that I looked at everybody and everything. I was thinking how everything could change so fast. That first night Ron called, he was going to stay home with his mother for the first night. I said, "Cool," my brain was still reeling from all the changes at home. I had a little nephew and he was named after me. My father now smoked a pipe. Damn nearly all my friends were there, and Mom had so much food on the table I couldn't leave if I wanted to.

This is the only part of my two year civilian life that I will tell you, the second night we were home, Ron and I decided to get as much weed as $20.00 would buy and I had an old Cheech and Chong album and it still had that giant rolling paper in it. I had asked my sister if she would take us to the Vermont Drive-in and she said, "Okay." Ron and I were already drunk as two skunks by the time we left Mom's house to go to the drive-in. Once there, I unfolded the giant rolling paper, we carefully put the weed in it. It was the same size as an album cover. Ron and my sister were in the two front seats, and I was in the middle of the back seat. Once I had rolled it all, I looked at Ron and said, "Light My Fire," he lit his cigarette lighter and lit mine. I was leaning back and puffing away. The next thing I saw was the paper was on fire, a little flame at first, so I puffed harder, it flamed on. I was still puffing when it caught my mustache and beard on fire. My sister picked up my jacket and put the fire out. Ron was spitting beer all over me, laughing, and I was still puffing. All the weed had fallen on my lap and on the floor of the car. Then I heard my sister laughing. She said, "You guys are crazy as hell."

Ron said, "My beard was still smoking when he handed me a beer." About twenty minutes into the movie, I had to take a piss. The only problem was I couldn't walk. Ron had some rolling papers and we must have smoked at least three points apiece, now not smoking week for those four years in the navy and then coming home and drinking all that beer and smoking. I was ripped, Ron was just as bad. My poor sister had to get us both to the men's room. She had to help each of us out of the car, she got Ron out first, and he leaned him against the hood of the car backward. I knew if he felt like I did, the whole world was spinning like crazy.

After she got him out she had to try and get me out, I fell out of the car, and she had to help me up. Ron tried to help her, and we both fell again. Once she got us both up, all the cars around us were blowing their horns a laughing at us, weed smoke was still pouring out of the car by the time she left with Ron to take him to the men's room. I was trying not to fall again while I was leaning on the car and people were still blowing their horns at me, they got back just in time because I couldn't hold the pee back much longer and it was really hard staying on my feet.

I was thinking about crawling but they showed up just in time, my sister got Ron in the back seat and I put my arm around her and somehow, she got me to the door of the men's room. I put my hand on the wall and made it to the first urinal, but now I had a problem with the buttons on my jeans. I was just about ready to piss on myself when I jerked the top part of my pants and the buttons opened. I finally got my hookup out but then I had problems standing, I put a hand on each wall then I remember feeling pretty good about being able to stand, then I pissed all over the place. I was too scared to let go of the walls because I knew I would fall down, and I was swaying, so that piss was going everywhere. I started laughing and with my hookup still out made my way to the door, when I got there I remembered to put it back in my pants I didn’t bother with the buttons, I opened the door, put my arm around my sister's shoulder and somehow she got me back in the car. Ron was in the back seat laid out, I passed out as soon as I sat down. From this day, I do not remember getting home.

Re-Enlisting in Navy: NTC (Naval Training Center) San Diego, California – December 2, 1981

I was a civilian for roughly two years and a little over two months. During that time, I had six jobs, and all of the companies I was working for shut down or sent their production work overseas. I still had my Honda motorcycle that I brought home from Okinawa, Japan. The king, and queen futon couch set, and most of my stereo equipment. I had to sell the rest. I guess the first-class petty officer in Treasure Island was not lying. I found it hard to make ends meet in Los Angeles, so I reenlisted in the Navy.

I was able to keep the same rank I had before I left, but I would be considered a new 3rd class petty officer when I re-enlisted. I had lost my seniority. On December 2nd, 1981, I went back to the recruiting center in downtown Los Angeles and then rode on probably the same raggedy white navy bus that I was in for the ride to boot camp heading back down to San Diego, but this time it was not for boot camp, but indoctrination, this part of the base was called NTC or Naval Training Center.

This is where all of us that were coming back in the Navy on the Pacific side of the country went. We pulled in and were taken to the uniform distribution building to get new uniforms and bedding for our racks. Most of the guys were like me, only out for a couple of years and couldn't keep a regular job to save our lives. Some of them had been told just like I was that our old job would be there waiting for us when we got back home, the one I had no longer existed. The company had gone out of business. We all made jokes about not being made for the civilian world. I felt as though that one joke was really a fact.

None of that mattered now, and we were all back in the Navy. There was one chief that came back in. He said he was tired of waiting for the U.S. Postal Service to call him back and he needed to feed his family. After we were all situated, it was time for physicals again and the good old piss test to see how many of us were going to be able to stay in the Navy. All of us were E-4 or above in rank, so we didn't have a curfew for liberty. Only four out of forty-five people failed the first drug test and we never saw or heard from those guys again.

The barracks were open bay and were terrible, some of the windows were missing and the decks were scarred up really bad. We were going to be here for the rest of December and some of January, the two coldest months in California. It took damn near a week before we were able to get plastic to cover the windows and by then, most of us had caught a cold, so in between going and getting paperwork done. We were also at medical and they gave us medicine that had Codeine in it, which would show up on the drug test as positive, but when twenty-two of us all had the same thing someone figured out it was the cold medicine that the docs had given us at medical, that had most of us worried for a few days. After the 3rd week in indoctrination, the chief I mentioned earlier had gotten a letter from his wife telling him the U.S. Postal Service had offered him a job, and he went temporally insane, that's what we called it, because as soon as he read the letter. He went straight to the assistant to the commander that was in charge of indoctrination and said he needed to get out and be a civilian again.

The assistant to the commander was a lieutenant and you could tell by the way he talked he didn't want to be here, like it was beneath him to be doing a babysitting job of enlisted men returning to active duty, so when the chief went to his office and told him that he needed out. The lieutenant basically to him to get out of his office, the chief went next door to the commander, didn't knock or anything, just walked into the commander's office, grabbed the trash can, put it in the chair in front of the commander's desk and pulled out his pecker and pissed into the bucket, he then put the bucket on the commander's desk took a step back, put his hookup back in his pants and said, "I'm done." He was out of the Navy in forty-five minutes and on his way to his new job with the U.S. Post Office.

The last week there we received our orders. They gave us what was called a dream sheet to fill out for the commands that we wanted to go to. I was hoping I would get overseas but not in the pacific. I wanted to go to Europe, either Italy, Spain or England. Greece would have been great, but I didn't think we had a base there. At the time, most CT's were stationed at shore bases, not on ships. We would not be given our orders until after Monday, and this was a Friday and we had just been handed our paychecks.

I had met this really cool white friend named Chris, and we pretty much hung out together. Hell, we spent our last few dollars at the base club buying each other beers. We walked to the disbursing office to cash our checks. It was more than I remembered it being, and I was a little bit happy about that. After we got our cash, we headed to the base bowling alley, bowled a few games, and had some beers, then headed to the chow hall for dinner. I wanted to get a good buzz going on and after dinner, we caught a cab to the Gas Lamp District, which at that time had some really good strip clubs. We pulled up to one and went in. It was only around nine PM, and the place was jamming.

The dancers were doing their thing and Chris and I had the biggest smiles. When we were in disbursing, we both asked for lots of one-dollar bills that were for the strippers, and we had to pace ourselves as we planned to be there all night. We were drinking Budweiser's back to back and watching the ladies, the shows were nothing like the Philippines as far as how wild the ladies were, here in the states, you couldn't touch the dancers in the PI. You could have sex on the stage if you wanted, I never did, but you could if you were drunk enough.

After a couple of hours, I was really buzzing. Then all shit hit the fan. All I remember was Chris pushing me out the door and toward a cab, and we went straight to base. I did remember seeing a guy that was flat out on the floor when Chris told me lets go, and I must have blacked out because I didn't remember walking into the barracks. The next morning, Chris told me the guy laying on the floor was put there by him. The guy was talking shit about niggers in the bar and had asked Chris how he could stand to be sitting next to a nigger watching white women dance nude. I asked Chris if he had punched him, he said, "Hell no." I used the Budweiser bottle.

Then he laughed and said, "Dude, how long were you out of the navy?"

I said, "A couple of years."

He said, "In the mornings when we muster did you notice how they have us hold our hands out?"

I said, "Yeah," and he told me that was to see who had busted knuckles, and they knew you were in a fight. I just nodded my head and said, "Wow."

We didn't go off base to any clubs after that, plus we would be given our orders and neither of us wanted any more problems. I liked being a petty officer, and so did Chris. Going to a new command as a seaman was not a good thing. You would usually be involved with some kind of work party or galley duty (working in the ship or base kitchen) until you were put in a watch section. We just stayed on base and usually at the bowling alley and bowled a few games, had beers and then went back to the barracks.

Chris and about a third of the guys in the barracks got their orders that Monday morning. Chris got a destroyer stationed in Yokosuka Japan, and he left that day. We went to the bowling alley. First had a few beers. I shook his hand and that was the last time I ever saw him, he was a good friend. I stayed at the bowling alley, had a few more beers went back to the barracks and relaxed in the TV room. I wasn't the only one. Almost all of the rest of the guys that didn't have orders were there doing the same thing.

That next morning, I got my orders, and I had mixed emotions. I was to report to NRRF Imperial Beach, California. I had never heard of Imperial Beach, let alone NRRF. I didn't even know what the letters stood for, I read the orders again, and it was right there in big, bold letters 'Naval Radio Receiving Facility'. I had three days to report to the base.

I put all my clothes and stuff in my sea bag and caught a cab to the bus station. An hour later, I was on a gray hound bus headed back to Los Angeles it took a little over two hours due to all the stops the bus made. I hadn't called my family to let them know I had got my new orders I figured I would surprise them. I knew Mom was going to be very pleased I was only going to be an hour and a half from her and not on the other side of the world.

I caught a cab from the bus station and it was during rush hour, it took forever to get to Mom's and Pops' house, and when I got there, my little sister opened the door and looked at me like what the hell are you doing here for a few seconds then she jumped into my arms, my little nephew was in his crib, and my mom's dog was barking at me like crazy, that dog and I never really got along, it was one of those toy poodles, but I did respect her because one day my nephew had crawled to the back door and it was open, the dog had grabbed his diaper and was stopping him from falling down the stairs. I was home for that, but she still barked at me whenever I came in the house or left. I don't think she was glad to see me but glad I was leaving. I told my sister I was going to be stationed in San Diego and only an hour and a half from home, she had the biggest smile, my nephew's dad was there, he had joined a gang called the Crips. I guessed he didn't have much choice since he had family in the gang, and if you weren't with them, you would have problems.

I slapped him five and grabbed a beer and sat down, they had a lot of questions about Imperial Beach, and I couldn't answer any of them. I finally asked my sister if my Honda was still in the garage and she said Pops wouldn't let anybody near it. I said, "Cool." It was sitting next to his pride and joy, a twenty-two-foot boat he used for fishing with his buddies.

I got up and turned off the alarm for the garage and opened the door, put the battery charger on my Honda's Battery and walked back inside the house. My mother showed up a few minutes later and I opened the door just as she was going to put her key in to unlock It, she looked and me and gave me the biggest smile, dropped her purse and hugged me. It felt so good when she hugged me, I smiled. Then Pops and my other sister came home. We were all together again and it felt good. I didn't do much while I was home except work on my Honda. It didn't look like it did when I brought it home from Okinawa. I had a custom paint job on it. It was dark blue with a desert scene that had three topless women on the tank all of them raising their arms toward a dark starry night. Each of them and the scene were on both of my side covers and one on the back fender.

I checked the oil, gas and chain, I had a Harley ducktail on it and a fat rear wheel tire, and the exhaust pipes were a single exhaust four-into-one and it sounded really nice with a deep kind of growling sound. I had a lot of engine work done to it and the damn thing would get up on the rear wheel real quick for a Honda 750. I had the short T-bar handlebars, so I didn't have to lean forward, just sit back and relax. I also had most of the engine parts chromed that I could afford, the seat was dark blue leather with a diamond design on it and the part that I sat on was 3 inches lower than the passenger part.

It was fast and beautiful. I never gave my bike a name, just never thought about it. I stayed home that night and the next morning. I waited for them all to go to work, and kissed my little sister and nephew goodbye. I pulled my bike out of the garage, tied my sea bag to the bar on the back of my seat with Bungie cords and headed for the 5 freeway south to Imperial Beach.

Naval Radio Receiving Facility (NRRF) Imperial Beach, California January 1982 – February 1984

The weather was a little bit cooler than I liked, so I put on my leather riding jacket, boots, and Levi's. My helmet had the same design as my gas tank, and by the time I got out of Los Angeles county. I ended up behind a biker club. They were just cruising about fifty-five miles per hour, I still had my base sticker on the front fender from Okinawa, and when the last bike saw me, he slowed down and got behind me. I guess when he saw I was in the Navy, he shot past me and rode to the front bike, then they all moved over and gave me the left lane. I checked to see if I could see any highway patrol cruisers, and I couldn't see any. I sped up, and when I got near the middle of their pack. I hit the throttle and passed the rest of the pack on one wheel. I was probably doing about ninety miles per hour. They all flashed their light and gave me the thumbs up. I dropped the front wheel back down and hauled ass.

I slowed down to about seventy until I got close to San Diego County. I stayed on the U.S. 5-freeway heading toward the U.S. Mexico border, I did make one stop at a McDonalds for lunch and a quick bathroom break, and I was in Imperial Beach. I just couldn't find the base. I saw a navy sticker on the back of a truck, and I followed it, the truck stopped at an apartment complex and when the driver got out, I asked him how to get to NRRF. He smiled at me and asked if I was one of the new guys. I said that would be me.

The way he explained the directions made me feel stupid, the base was right on the beach, and he told me to make a left at the corner and I would see it. I made the left at the corner and drove straight and there was the big antenna array. I followed the road along the beach and had to make another turn because that road stopped and then went right to the base. When I got there, I noticed there was only the actual station, no barracks, and nothing else, so I parked my bike, and walked into the array, as soon as I got to the door and pressed the button. The OOD came out and met me, he said that he was sorry that no one told us, new guys, to report to the base at Coronado, which I had passed about thirty minutes ago, and he told me to follow him to the base, and I did.

I walked up to the quarter-deck, and handed my orders to one of the clerks who was a CTA 1st class petty officer, he asked if I knew how to get to the site, and I said that's where I started. He laughed, not at me but the fact that unless you actually lived in Imperial Beach, you would not know to go to the Coronado base first to report in.

Once all the paperwork was done, he handed me a map that showed where the barracks were, the chow hall, barber shop, and right now, the most important part of the base, which at the time for me was the base club. I needed a beer, i was told to report in dress blues to the sight on Monday morning at 0800, i said, "Cool," and headed straight for the enlisted club. After a couple of beers, I went to the barracks. A second-class petty officer said he was wondering if I would go to the sight first and I told him I did, and we both laughed. He asked if that was my bike and I said it was. He then told me I might want to look for an apartment in IB (imperial beach) because when it rained here, the strand usually floods two to six inches, which meant I would be driving with the Pacific Ocean on one side and one of the waterways on the other side of the street. I smiled and asked how long that would take to get approved. He usually said a month, and I smiled. He told me I would have two roommates. One was a seaman apprentice and the other a seaman, so be nice to them. I outranked both of them. I had no intentions of staying in the barracks. I wanted my own place.

A lot of people noticed my bike, mainly because of the design it had, and I got a lot of nice comments like I wish I had any of those babes you got on your tank. I usually replied so do I and would laugh with them. I stayed on base until Monday morning when I headed out to the strand. I had my dress blue uniform in a leather backpack, i didn't want it to get messed up, when I was allowed entry into the sight. I headed straight for the head and changed into my dress blues. Handed my orders and identification card to the Officer of the Deck and waited for him to come back. He then led me to the sight commander's office, where I knocked hard on the door and stated my rank and name. Then I asked for permission to enter, and permission was granted. I entered and handed the CO of my orders, then I stepped back two steps and stood at attention.

Our commanding officer was a was a full Commander and after a few seconds, the CO stood up, checked my uniform out and my hair cut, (I had the high and tight cut going, no more afro for me), he smiled and welcomed me to the command, he saw in my orders that I had helped with some work on an HFDF (High Frequency Direction Finding) system in the Philippines and he asked me how that went, I told him, "It was great because I learned something new and it got me out of Okinawa."

He smiled and shook my hand and called in the chief of the command, who led me out of the CO's office and took me on a tour of the rest of the sight. He told me I would be assigned to section two and would be standing the 2-2-2-80 watches, then he asked me if I wanted to move off base.

I replied that I did, and he said good man, he took me to another room and I had my picture taken and was given a lanyard with my ID card attached to it. I was allowed in most spaces in this command, I guess my clearance had been raised to a higher level then what I had in Okinawa.

Then I was taken to the area where I would be working and met another CTA petty officer who helped me fill out the request chit to move off base. I stayed on base the first couple of months even though my request to move off base was approved. I needed to learn my new job, and the weather was pretty bad. I saw what they meant about the strand flooding, riding the bus from Coronado base to our base in Imperial Beach while the strand was flooded was bad enough. I really didn't want make that ride on my motorcycle. Plus, I needed to learn my way around the San Diego area, I don't remember going there as a kid with my parents at all, and it was something else back then. After boot camp, I caught the straight bus home to Los Angeles and never had the chance to check San Diego out at all, so that is what I did, and I tried to drive home at least once a month to see my family and friends. After the second month, I moved off base into an apartment in Imperial Beach. It was a nice little two-bedroom place, the complex was mainly filled with sailors that also worked on the base, and it was only a five-minute ride to work. My father and little sister helped me move my stereo and my mama san and papa san chairs. I had saved up enough to get a color TV and some cooking devices and plates, Mom gave me my old blanket and sheets but I had brought a queen-size bed, so the sheets and blanket she gave me were of no use, so I had Pops to take them back, this was my second bachelor pad in the United States, and I was happy with it. There was covered parking so my bike wasn't too exposed to the elements. I kept the Honda clean as hell. I liked the compliments it got.

Once I moved off base, the Navy also provided me with extra monies for rent and food. It was called 'Subsistence Allowance'. It wasn't much, but I was able to get what I needed. I no longer ate the beef stew out of the can, it brought back memories of Racist, and I really missed him. But I did buy a lot of canned meats like chilly, and there was this one can of meat, you just heated it in a pot on the stove, pour it over two pieces of bread, heat up some mac and cheese and It was all set. I also liked the total dinners that you put in the oven for like 45 minutes, and that was basically what I ate as a single sailor. I decided to get a roommate to help with the bills, but that didn't work out too well for me, my roommate's name was Barry. We got along fine at work when I saw him, I thought he was pretty cool. He had a little Toyota and it fit him. Barry was probably only five foot six inches tall, real light skinned and had really thick curly black hair. He could have passed for a Porto Rican.

Barry would tell a lie in a minute if he thought he could get away with it and he told one that would burn him really badly in the end with me. We didn't party at the same places as he worked straight day watches and I was on the 2-2-2-80 schedule. The day he moved in, all I had in his room was a mattress and that was for friends that needed a place to crash out when they were too drunk to drive or if they had found a friend and needed a place to take her for the night, so the next day he went out and brought his self a brand-new bedroom set with the twin night stands and a queen size bed with a headboard.

My bed was a queen size, but I didn't have a headboard. I did have the twin nightstands I had found at goodwill, and they were both real wood. His bedroom looked really good once he got it all set up. The rest of the stuff in the apartment was all mine, from the stereo to the $29.99 bar-b-que grill outside the front door. He had a girlfriend about the same height as he was and she was very pretty, but she had a mouth on her, and she really was demanding. She wanted Barry to leave the navy and get a normal job. He only had a couple of months left to serve in the navy, so that was his plan to get out of the navy and marry her. Like I said, she was a bossy little cutie and a nurse at that time, I guess he thought he had the best he was going to get.

I had a nice friend that was a tall babe about two inches taller than me from south America. I think she was from Brazil, she had a body that was awesome, that long shiny, thick black hair down to her butt and a smile that drove me crazy, the only thing wrong with her was she had bad acne scars on her face from when she was a child. She and I were mainly booty calls for each other and we were both happy with that arrangement. She was an artist, she welded stuff into these weird figures and people brought them from her.

I always thought they looked like some sort of cool looking junk, but she made a decent living selling them, so who was I to complain. She had come over several times to visit me and a couple of times, she was there before I got home, only a few minutes before me, and each time Barry had tried to hit on her, she always told me each time, and I just laughed it off. She said he is such a cute little guy and I told her when he first moved in, he liked to walk around the apartment naked, and I had to check him on that because I didn't walk around naked neither was he. He asked me what the problem was and I told him a naked roommates wasn't going to happen and if he didn't like it, he could move out and he laughed and said it's all good, and he started wearing shorts like I did.

I told my girl about him and she laughed and asked whether his penis was so big that he thought he was impressing you or something walking around with a roommate naked. I had to tell her the truth, it looked like my little nephew's pecker, and my nephew was only about four years old and we both started laughing. Each time I told her that when she saw him, she would look at me and hold up her pinky finger, and we would both would laugh. He never understood what we were laughing about. My girl came over one night while Barry and his lady were there. When I got home, my girl was sitting on the couch and she was fuming.

I asked her what was wrong, she grabbed my hand and we walked into my bedroom she shut the door and said that woman is a bitch and she thinks she is better than me. I told her she probably thinks she is better than everybody, especially Barry. She looked at me for a second and then we both started laughing. She had brought her backpack full of clothes because she was going to spend the next two days with me after that she was going back to her country and she wasn't sure if she was coming back to San Diego, she had a job offer in New York that she couldn't pass up.

I told her to stay in my room. I had put some jazz on the stereo and Barry's girl came out and said, "Hi, we were listening to their music."

I looked her right in the eyes and said, "Not anymore, you're not," she huffed and went back into the room with Barry, and they started arguing. I laughed and went back to my girl and told her to relax. I needed a shower and we would be going to the club at the 32nd Street navy base. She smiled and said, "Cool." (32nd street navy base was the main navy station in San Diego. It had all the different clubs, stores, and ships back then).

I got in the shower and cleaned up, put on my jeans and my jump boots and a nice shirt polo shirt. She had changed out of her shorts and put on jeans also. I told her we would take my motorcycle, she loved riding on the back of it, and I liked having her there. Those long legs squeezed me real nice and she always held on tight. As we were walking out the door of my room, we could hear Barry and his girl still arguing. I knocked on his door and told him we were leaving and not to wait up for me, and don't touch my rib eye steaks either. Then they really started yelling at each other. We left, got on my bike, and made the thirty-minute ride to the base.

After I checked my girlfriend in at the quarter deck, we headed to the Acey-Deucy club, it was for E-6's and E-5's only, and it was always a good time in there, very few fights, and the food was good. We partied until after one AM, and it was fun. I knew a few of the guys there that were bikers also and we all had hung out a couple of times. When it was time to leave and we were getting on the bike, one of the guys told me not to let this one go, my girl smiled at me and held on to me tighter than normal. We had quite a few drinks after we had our dinner which was steak sandwiches with fries.

The entire night with her was perfect. When we got back to the apartment, Barry's girl was gone, and he was sitting on the couch listening to jazz looking sad as hell. He apologized for the arguing and then he asked me what he should do. I looked at him and said, "Do you really, really want my opinion?" My girl laughed and I walked with her to my room, we didn't go to sleep for a long time and we had fun together. My girl stayed with me for the next two days and Barry went over to his girl's Mother's house where he had to sleep on the couch. I didn't see Barry's fiancé for a couple of weeks, and when I did see her, she would just go into Barry's room. I was good with that, if they were listening to music when I came home. I would turn off my stereo and put the TV on, that would start another argument between them. I loved it.

Now here is the crazy thing, Barry had told her everything in the apartment was his, he stayed with me for one week after he got out of the navy and he was nervous as hell the whole time, and every time I asked about his new place, he would change the subject. He kept asking me if I was still on the same schedule, and I told him nothing had changed because he left the navy and I did remind him his part of the rent was due. He had planned to move out at the end of the month so he wouldn't have to pay for any days he was not in the apartment and I understood that.

On the day he was moving out he did his normal thing and put the rent money on the little kitchen table in an envelope and I put it in my pocket on my way to work. I didn't tell him, but I took most of that day off. I had asked my Chief if I could because I didn't trust Barry and the chief smiled at me and said, "That is the smartest thing you could do, so just show up for muster and then leave, that is just what I did and muster lasted all of twenty minutes." I figured he would have gotten his stuff and would have left by then, but when I got back to the apartment there was a medium-sized U-Haul parked in front of our apartment, right in my parking space. I parked my bike in front of it, Barry had the stereo blasting so loud that he didn't hear me come inside.

I looked around and his girlfriend was in the kitchen wrapping my plates in the newspaper. I looked at her and told her to just stop what you're doing right now. She got mad and told me that I wasn't keeping anything that belonged to her man. Again, I told her to stop. Then I found Barry he was packing the two speakers I had in my bedroom. I went back into the front room and turned off the stereo and when he looked up my face was right next to his. I guess he thought I was going to knock the shit out of him and I probably should have, but I didn't, I just told him to tell her the truth.

He started sweating. I grabbed his arm and drug his ass into the kitchen, where she was still wrapping my plates up, getting them ready for the box she had on the sink. I still had Barry by the arm when we walked into the kitchen, I told him to tell her now or we were going to have a very serious problem, the kind of problem that he couldn't win. He made a gulping sound and told her to unpack all the stuff she just spent the last twenty minutes wrapping in the newspaper because the only thing that was his in the apartment was the bedroom furniture. She told him to quit playing around because she just got their new apartment in Mission Valley with two bedrooms and they needed all of his stuff that she was packing up now.

She told him she felt sorry for me because Barry and I were friends, and all I had was that old ass bed, but all of this stuff was going with them. He looked me in the eyes and cleared his throat and told her that the only thing in here that was his was in his bedroom and that he just forgot to tell her everything else was mine. Had he been cool about it, I would have given him some of the plates and utensils to help them get started, but Barry was going to take all of my furniture and everything if I would have still been at work. What an Alfa Hotel (Ass Hole). She looked at me and said she was going to call the police. I told her to go ahead, then they could both spend the weekend in jail for attempted theft since this was Friday, and the judge would not see them until Monday morning.

It took her a few minutes for her to comprehend what was going on, Barry had planned to steal my stuff and she was helping him! She got in her car crying and took off. Barry looked at me and smiled. I put my hand out and told him to give me the key to the apartment, then I helped him put the two mattresses in the U-Haul. He had to carry the two nightstands by himself, and they were full of his clothes and stuff. After he put the last of his clothes in the U-Haul. I slammed the door shut and locked it, turned my stereo back on and closed the curtains. That was the last I ever saw of him. Somebody later told me he was a bank teller at one of the local banks. I just laughed.

Imperial Beach was where I met one of the coolest chiefs that I had ever known. He had the big belly that chiefs still had in the early nineteen-eighties, he would tell jokes that were actually funny and he had seen the world. He knew all about the Philippines, Oki, Singapore and Japan. Some days I would stick around after work and listen to him, he would tell me about Japan and its people. He said that the Japanese were short little people, very proud, and still loved their emperor.

One day I got into work early and he told me to make coffee. I told him I didn't drink that stuff and I didn't know how to make it. He got up, grabbed my arm, and took me to the little office that had the coffee pot and showed me how to make coffee and because he had to show me how to make coffee I had to drive to the donut shop and get him two glazed donuts. I put my hand out for some money and he turned his back on me and walked back to his office. I heard him yelling at me that I better not late for my watch.

I hauled ass on my bike to the little bakery and got him the two glazed donuts, I had to have them on a napkin so he could put them on his fat belly while he was sitting down. He got all the new guys with the donut thing. One weekend a few of us went to Tijuana, just checking out the streetwalkers and getting drunk in some of the clubs. On the way back, we passed this guy that had all kinds of clay stuff and I saw a fake turd. It looked very, very, very real. I had to sniff it just to make sure it was clay. We waited before we used it, the chief had two different sections that he worked with, so we all wanted to be in on this. The day came, I got in early and put coffee in his cup. I had the fake turd wrapped in a napkin inside a little paper bag like the chief explained he wanted if he was a little bit late coming in to work.

We had a brand-new Seaman, and he was to wait for the chief in the parking lot and ask the chief all kinds of questions to hold him up outside while we got everything ready. When the chief walked into his office, we all ran and stood outside his office door. We wanted to hear him scream and probably throw the fake turd on the floor. We waited a good five minutes while he took off his jacket and sat down. You could hear the chair complaining. It always creaked and moaned when he sat down.

We could hear him rolling it toward the desk in the back of his office where the coffee and the fake poop were waiting for him. I guess it took a couple of minutes for it to register exactly what he was looking at. Instead of two glazed donuts he had a big brown turd on his napkin, his coffee was there, but not the donuts, he screamed, then he started cursing then he screamed two names and mine was first and a guy named Jeff. We were the ones that normally pulled the pranks on people. We were just trying to get even for all the pranks we had to endure.

The chief's face was red as hell when we walked into the room. Jeff had the two real glazed donuts in a bag in his hand. If the chief was really pissed, we were just going tell him he got the wrong little bag. He was laughing so hard when we walked into his office, he was trying to act like he was pissed, but he couldn't keep a straight face. The chief told us to walk over to the wall that had a calendar on it, he told Jeff and I, each to grab a marker. I thought I was going to have to do some old school writing that I would not put a fake turd on the division chief's desk, nope that is not what happened, he asked what were our days off and to put X's on each day that we had off for the month. He then told us that for the days with X's there better be two extra donuts on his desk, then he asked who's idea was this. I stepped forward and told him it was mine and that we got the offensive turd in Tijuana last week, but it took time to set everything up. The chief had stopped laughing a few minutes earlier after he had us put the X's on the calendar, he then proceeded to chew us out, telling me that I was trying to undermine his authority, and Jeff was trying to incite mutiny (which was a very serious offense, people used to get hung for it). He told Jeff to leave and close the door behind him, I swallowed hard, I just knew my ass was in some serious trouble. He asked me what he should do with me, I tried to answer, but he shushed me, then he asked how I would like to get those very large X's off the calendar for Jeff and myself. I was wondering what he had planned for me.

He told me to sit down and I sat down. He told me that there was another person that should get the fake turd treatment. I was hoping it was not the Commanding Officer of the Division Officer, but he said nope none of them. I want you to get the new female officer that is in charge of the CT Administration. I couldn't believe he said that. She was pregnant and looked like she was ready to deliver any day. I reminded the chief of that fact, and he told me the X's looked very good to him, all those tasty donuts just waiting for him. I asked how long did I have to pull the stunt off and he said two days and only two days. I said to roger that chief, it will be done.

Then I left and went straight to Jeff to let him know what we had to do and when. We both went outside and busted up laughing. Seretly, I was hoping that this gag would not mess with her pregnancy, she was new here and always kept to herself, so I didn't know how something like this would affect her.

On the second day, just as the chief had ordered, Jeff came in with a paper plate and poured a little bit of coffee on it, just enough to stain it. We knew she had just walked into her office, so we had a few minutes to set everything up, he quietly put the paper plate on the deck right in front of her door, and I put the fake poop on the plate, stood up and banged on her door three times, then I took off running as fast as one could on the slippery deck, made it to the corner and turned just in time, she called out to enter two or three times before she opened the door, then she looked down and saw the poop on the deck. She yelled for the chief to come to her office ASAP, we were all trying not to make too much noise laughing.

Our chief should have been an actor. He walked right up to her and asked how he could be of assistance. She could only point to the deck where the poop was. The chief told her someone was totally inconsiderate and he would have to look into it. He picked up the fake poop in his hand and we could all see him right outside her door. He looked as serious as hell, he proceeded to then he licked it, the sound she made had us all thinking she passed out or something, she had backed into her desk, she shouted at us then we couldn't hold back the laughter any longer, then the chief informed her it was fake. None of us got into any trouble for that one. I think the chief smoothed things out with her by giving her one of his donuts. Then she busted out laughing. She had tears in her eyes like the rest of us. The chief made it back to his office before he started laughing. We were all glad she had a great sense of humor, I got along well with her after that.

I had met quite a few ladies at the work site and to be honest, I could have been interested in most of them, but I was home and stationed in a small beach town on the west coast of the United States and I was going find my new version of a civilian Sharleen. I was picky when it came to the ladies. She had to look very nice in and out of clothes and not be too much of a bitch. I went to the beach a lot, checking all the young ladies that went there. Most of them were military brats (people whose families were in the military and they had been to different stations all over the world), so that was out, then I thought of going to San Diego, and I did.

I met a really nice civilian beauty and I wanted to make it work, but she worked for Continental Airlines as a flight attendant and so her never being around didn't work out too well for us. Then I met a woman that had just moved to Imperial Beach at one of the biker bars, it was called ye old plank. I had gone there with a couple of guys from the base that had really old Harley Davidson motorcycles, so I was good there for a while, this place was a dive from hell and it is said to be the most southerly bar on the west coast of the United States. Imperial beach is only one town away from the border with Tijuana, Mexico that city is called San Ysidro.

I did a cruise down to the border with some of the guys and we parked our motorcycles on the American side and walked across the border to party in Tijuana, but I didn't like paying for sex at least not with money, dinner maybe, but not with cash. I had a few one night stands, mostly with older ladies that I would meet in San Diego, and that was working just fine for me until I found out the last one. I dated was married to a marine corps officer. I damn sure didn't want any problems, so I stopped dating the cougars I met in San Diego, just stopped going out there to party.

Right after my first year being stationed at IB (Imperial Beach), I decided to go up to San Francisco with a few of my old buddies in Los Angeles that still had motorcycles. I just knew it would be fun, so when one of the guys named Red called me and asked if I wanted to cruise up there, I said, "Hell yeah!" I had been going back to Los Angeles every other month to see my family and friends, but the gangs were getting worse, and so were the drugs and I didn't want to get caught up in any of that shit, not at all. I took off the last three watches and had six days off.

I rode to Los Angeles and hooked up with the guys. We waited until after the six PM rush hour, and then we got on the US 5-freeway headed north. It rained the whole way from LA to San Francisco damn near seven hours. I was wearing my leather riding gear with my riding boots, neck warmer, helmet and gloves. I also had one of those long crazy straws which went under my neck warmer from a flask with whiskey right to my mouth. All I had to do was drink. Once we got there, we headed for one of the biker clubs and everyone needed something strong to drink. Keith had made the trip with us, all together, it was about twenty-five of us on Honda motorcycles, and most of the guys had hotel rooms. Keith and I went to my aunt's house and crashed out there. I didn't like parking my motorcycle in San Francisco, to many hills, and all it would take was someone to come by and barely touch your bike and it would be laying on its side.

The next morning Keith and I went to McDonalds had some breakfast, and headed back to the same club we were at last night, we got there and the party was already started. We didn't have any patches on our jackets as we were not in any club, but there were enough of us in numbers for safety and there were more of us than the club had members. Beer was only fifty cents, and we were happy, one of the barmaids called her friends and the party got better. I could smell the weed, so I stayed near the door. I could not have drugs in my system or I could be busted if they gave me a piss test when I got back to IB. We partied all day and most of the night, a couple of the ladies decided they needed a ride to their apartment. Keith and I were glad to give them a ride, we stayed at their apartment that night and most of the next day.

Sunday morning, we all met at the club, said our goodbyes to the members and headed back to Los Angeles. It rained the whole way back seven hours and I was feeling a little sluggish. Everybody pulled off the freeway at the off ramps closest to their homes, not me. I stayed on the freeway until I reached imperial beach another two hours. When I got home, i could hardly breathe, i figured I was coming down with a cold. I went to the Coronado base to have a beer at the bowling alley. I don't remember anything else because when I woke up, amd I was in the Naval Medical Center San Diego. I was in the contagious disease ward for spinal meningitis, I was totally lost. I had been there for over twenty-five hours.

When I woke up, these two lieutenants came into the room and started looking at my fingernails, something about the lunula and how in blacks, it is not as prevalent as it is in white people. Just as they were showing each other my fingers, another doctor came in and had me roll over onto my side. He told me not to move and that this was going to sting a little, it felt like a little pinch in the middle of my back. I didn't know it, but I just had a spinal tap done. About an hour later, my command chief came into the room. He took one look and me and told them all that I had the flu. He was furious. First of all they had me in an open bay room. I had a very high security clearance and should have been in my own room. What if I started to talk about work related information boy I never saw him so mad, he looked down at me and said, "You're going to be just fine son. I'm going to have another doctor come in and check you out, and move you out of this area into your own room."

I was really happy about that, I just wish he would have come in before I had the spinal tap done because they told me I had to stay laying on my side for the next 8 hours or I could have back problems. I didn't want to ask them what kind of problems. I just said, "Okay," and I passed out again. When I woke up, I was in a room by myself and one of the ladies from work was sitting in the chair next to my bed. Her name was Carrie. She was a 3rd class petty officer I had met a little after I arrived at IB, she was a good-looking woman and she was easy to talk to. I asked her how long I was sleeping and she said a couple of days.

I needed to pee so badly and my mouth was as dry as the California desert. I was groggy as hell and I slowly sat up looking for the head, then I put my legs over the side of the rack and slowly eased myself out of bed and started to walk to the bathroom. Carrie told me to slow down, I still had the drips in my arm and whatever it's called with the bags attached to it.

I didn't realize the only thing I was wearing was one of those white gowns that your whole ass sticks out of, I slowly walked to the head, and Carrie was moving the cart with the drip bags on it with me. It took me a minute to figure out that I needed to pull the gown up so I could piss, I think she saw my hookup, and I just didn't care, it felt like I pissed for five minutes and I was thinking to myself is it ever going stop. I was getting nervous, that's when I realized I had company in the room with me and I was showing all my goodies, i just didn't care, after I finished I went back to the bed, and there was Carrie's cousin sitting in the room and I have to tell you she was absolutely gorgeous. I laid back down and passed out again.

Whatever was in that drip bag was working very well, I slept like a baby for days. I was in that hospital for about three weeks and I really needed a shave and a good haircut. I again had an afro and a scraggly full beard. Carrie was there the day I was released and fit for duty. She drove me back to the Coronado base so I could get my motorcycle and go home. I asked her if I had done or said anything stupid while I was in the hospital, and she told me not to worry. I asked her if I was seeing things or was there another beautiful woman in my room. She smiled at me and told me it was her younger cousin that was down visiting her. I asked if her cousin was married, and she laughed and told me her cousin had asked the same about me. I felt so much better.

After I parked my motorcycle in my parking spot at the apartment, I slowly walked into the apartment, took off my boots and helmet and laid on the papa san foo ton couch, turned on the TV and went to sleep again. The next day I felt great. I didn't trust my digestive system with any alcohol, didn't want that kind of mess while driving my Honda around. I stopped and got six roses for Carrie and a thank you card. She took good care of me and didn't laugh when my whole ass was out in her face at the hospital. When the door opened, that's when I saw her cousin again. *Damn, she was fine as hell, a perfect thirty-six, twenty-six.* I was happy in more ways than one, if you know what I mean.

Carrie told me to sit down and asked if there was anything I wanted to drink. I stuck with water, nothing else. I said hello to her cousin and asked her name and she said Bella. I nodded and told her my name, then without thinking, I just blurted out damn, you are fine she smiled and said thank you. Carrie came back into the living room and had a glass of water for both Bella and I. Then she filled me in on all the happenings at work that I missed out on, who left, who got busted for smoking dope and those kinds of things that were no mission related to the job. She told me I was still in section two and she had been assigned to my section, so we would be seeing a lot of each other.

I was thinking I wanted to see a lot of Bella, they were both from the Midwest, in a city I had never heard of and wouldn't care to visit after Bella told me how cold it gets, me no likey cold weather, not one bit. I kept staring at Bella, and then I asked her if she wanted to go for a ride on my motorcycle and she had the biggest smile when she said yes. We got up and told Carrie I would bring her back. I just didn't tell her when.

We went straight to my apartment, so I could give her my spare helmet to wear. In California the law then was if you're on a moving motorcycle, you had to have a helmet and I didn't want any trouble with the Imperial Beach Police, word was they weren't happy with the navy folks and would provoke you if they thought they could get away with it, we were told to obey their orders and stay away from them if we could.

After I put the spare helmet on her, we headed out of IB for Interstate five and once on it, I told her to hold on real tight. I should have done that earlier, I could feel her breast against my back and I really liked that. I got the speed up to about eighty-five miles per hour and I could feel her holding tighter. She was awesome on the back of my Honda. This was going to be good, really good I just knew it.

I slowed down, and we got off the interstate, turned around and got right back on it until we got back to the IB off ramp. We stopped at the McDonalds and I brought a couple of cokes for us. We sat inside and talked. We talked for a few hours and I told her I needed to get her back to Carries house before I got in trouble. She smiled at me and told me, it would be no problem. I took her back anyway, Carrie's husband was an Air Force office and I didn't want any trouble with him. I had not met the man yet, but Officer was all I needed to know. I probably wouldn't like him anyway.

I still had one more day before I had to start my shifts again, so I went to the phone booth and called Carrie's house, her husband answered and I said hello I would like to speak to Bella if she is available. He didn't say anything, two seconds later Bella was on the phone, I asked her if she wanted to go for a ride to the mountains and she said, "Yes." I was at their place in less than five minutes, and I brought the spare helmet. I had put my saddle bags on the bike, an old sheet, a couple of bottles of water and some chocolate chip cookies. When I got to Carrie's house Bella came out the door, I didn't even have to knock, she hopped on the back and we were off, did I mention that the back part of my seat was elevated about four inches higher than where I sat, her boobs were right at the top of my back and again they felt good being there.

Bella leaned forward and held on tight, I didn't speed in IB, but at this moment, I wanted Pop a wheelie and haul ass, but I didn't. God, this woman was pretty close to Sharleen in my mind right now and I was going to find out as soon as I possibly could. She was only eighteen, not old enough to take into the civilian clubs off base, so I pulled on the base at Coronado and we stopped at the bowling alley. I had a beer and brought her a coke. I asked her If she wanted to bowel a game and she said no.

She wanted to ride on the back of my bike up in the mountains. Guess what we did, we rode up and into the mountains, it wasn't really like the ones off of Los Angeles. We were in the San Ysidro Mountains. I didn't go real fast, but fast enough for her to enjoy the different views, we pulled over after about thirty minutes, and I grabbed the saddle bags and we walked around, found a kind of flat spot, and I put the sheet down, with the food. Bella had on some really tight jeans and I liked that. She didn't mind showing her cleavage either. I asked her how she liked being in California and she said it was nice and she wouldn't mind living down here. I didn't catch that clue until a couple of weeks later.

She asked how I like the Navy. I told her I liked it so much I came back in after being out for a couple of years. She looked at me with this surprised look on her face. Carrie had told her that as far as she knew, I had been in all the time, I told her about Okinawa and she said I see why you got out, we both laughed. I leaned over and kissed her, she kissed me back, yep she was really close to Sharleen, real close. She was really cool, not demanding or anything and that was a good thing for me as I only had the stuff in my apartment and my Honda and a couple of hundred dollars in the bank, which if I had not gone to the hospital for so long, I would have spent it on something.

We hung out there in the mountains until it started to get dark, I just lost track of time talking to her. I packed everything in the saddle bags, even the trash (my father taught me to leave nature the way I found it when I was a kid, and I still do that today). We got back on the bike and went back to Carrie's house. I wanted to ask her to stay the night with me, she probably would have, but I had a couple of things I needed to get done. I had already gotten rid of the afro and beard, I just kept a goatee. She said she liked it, so I kept it neat and clean. I also had to iron my work uniform and shine my boots. If I had her in the apartment, I would not have done any of that and I knew it.

She got off and kissed me goodbye. She tried to walk away, but I grabbed her arm and got another goodbye kiss, fired up the bike and went home. I kept thinking about how she could be so much like Sharleen, but then I remembered that Sharleen was the same age as Bella when I first met her. Bella had told me she felt safe when she was with me and I liked that, I didn't try to force myself on her (I wanted to, but that just was not my style) and never was. I finished the last thing I had to do, which shone those boots, you could see your reflection in them, and I kept them like that, it was my thing. I always wanted my clothes to look good, especially my uniforms, it was almost time for me to test for second class petty officer and I wanted it bad, especially the pay increase. I would need that to have Bella live with me, she had hinted she wanted to stay here in California, and each time she said it, she looked me right in the eyes and smiled. Now I was never a rocket scientist, but I can take a hint.

Bella was supposed to leave the next month and I would have taken the test and found out the results before then. I wouldn't be paid then. It takes three months after you get the results back from the test before you would get paid. (that's to make sure they didn't make any mistakes and to see if you can handle the advancement in rank. I didn't get to see much of Bella during the days I had to work; I was hoping that his Air Force brother-in-law of hers hadn't brought any of his Zoomie (that's what we called those guys) friends over to meet her.

I don't think I would have handled that too well back in those days. I was still quick tempered and could and would have gotten into a fight over a woman that I thought was all mine, even though I wasn't totally sure she was all mine. But she was going to be! I stayed after work each day studying for the exam, I didn't have any problems with the mile and a half run, sit ups, pull ups and push-ups that were also part of the test, I always during those days. I always did more than what was required, it felt good except for the running part.

On the last watch, which was an ever watch, I called Bella from the base and asked her if she wanted to go to the base at Coronado and go to the bowling alley. She said, "Yes," I had just taken the test and felt really good about my scores. I just knew I passed it and would soon be a second class petty officer, one of the best ranks in the enlisted ranks for people that are fairly new. You have just enough rank to have respect from damn near half of the command and not enough for the headaches of being in charge.So I took her on base to celebrate. She had on a jacket and those tight jeans with another blouse that showed off her beautiful twins perfectly. Again as soon as I pulled up, she came out of the door, I handed her the extra helmet and we were on our way to the base. She didn't know she was going to meet some of my friends from work. Most of them couldn't believe that she was only eighteen years old. I ordered two beers for us and Bella smiled at me. She was just happy to be out of her cousin's house. We stayed out until after midnight. Most of my friends had already left, usually, after the final watch, we would just go home and crash out hard from working six times in five days, but I had told them I was bringing my new lady on base to meet them. They later told me I was a lucky man, I knew I was.

I knew I wouldn't find Sharleen. I thought to myself that Bella is my Sharleen now, and that was it, I told her she was staying with me tonight, so I had her go to the phone booth in the bowling alley and call Carrie to let her know she was staying with me tonight. I really liked Carrie, not so much her husband, he was just different from the black men that I knew and I knew a lot. I never met anyone like him. It was the way he acted, the things he said and how he said them. I didn't dislike him. We just were on two different pages and I will leave it that.

After Bella made the call, we had one more beer each and got on the Honda. It was a very nice night and you could see what looked like thousands of stars up in the sky. We took our time crossing the strand, pulled into Imperial Beach and went straight to my apartment. I think as soon as I closed the front door, we started kissing, and in no time, we were in bed making love and we both needed that release.

We fell asleep as soon as we were done. I didn't know about her at the time, but in my mind, she was going to be my wife. I had told her about how our duty station rotation worked, it was two overseas and one stateside. I told her how most military wives hung out together on base most of the time while the husbands were working or out to sea. She said she could do that and we both smiled at each other. After that night, she only went back to her cousin's house when I had the mid watches (10:00 PM to 6:00 AM). I didn't have a phone yet and I didn't want her unable to get help if something went wrong.

I got a phone my next payday. I drove her to the park outside the Naval Hospital in San Diego. I told Bella we were going to have a picnic at the park near the Naval hospital and she was excited to go. We packed up a few sandwiches, I had a couple of beers in the saddle bag for each of us, we stopped at Mickey D's (McDonalds) and got burgers and fries. Back then, I could drink beer with my food.

It was a good drive up to San Diego, not too warm. Once we got to the park. I pulled up on the curb and drove the bike to the spot we wanted, stopped, and Bella got off first. I put the double stands down for the bike. It was on a flat spot, so I didn't have to worry about it falling over or anything in the grass. Every time I looked at her, I wanted her more than I did the day before, she never really wore much makeup, just lipstick and that was it. Yep, I was a lucky man. Bella put the sheet down a little bit away from the bike, like I had shown her before (we didn't want the bike to fall on us). I pulled out the beers and we took our time drinking them. I was telling her about being in Okinawa and some of the crazy things we did like my mother and sister visiting me in the Philippines. She was laughing her ass off. All of a sudden, we heard these two very famine guys walking toward where we were chilling out on the sheet. The closer they got to us, the louder they got and they were arguing about something. Bella and I both sat up to watch them.

One was crying, they both had on these Daisy Duke short pants, and had their shirts unbuttoned, but the bottom part of the shirts was tied up over their stomachs. The one that was crying was about five feet six inches tall, white with short curly blonde hair. He was just crying and walking as fast as he could to get away from the other one, that was about five feet ten inches tall and was skinny as hell, I was trying not to laugh at them, but I couldn't help it.

Bella's eyes were shut and I told her to open them and look, as soon as she did as I asked she started laughing so hard that she started to cough. I pat her on the back while I was laughing. When the two guys got about six feet from us, the guy that was crying slapped the shit out of the one that was cursing him out, that was it for me. I couldn't take any more. I tried to close my eyes so I didn't have to see them, but Bella elbowed me and said look. The one that slapped his friend and actually climbed on his back and was slapping him/her on top of her head.

The one that was getting slapped just kept putting his hands up and wiping his nose. It was too much. I got up, helped Bella up and we packed our stuff. I grabbed the empty cans and trash and put them in the trash can. Bella had the sheet folded and was hunched over the bike, laughing, I had tears in my eyes when I got on the bike and then Bella got on. I started the bike and we slowly drove off the grass to the street. The two guys were still cursing each other out and we kept laughing.

We went back to my apartment and had another beer each, then I told her I wanted to take her to Los Angeles to meet my family. She asked me when and I told her next month after I get paid, as there were things we needed in the apartment like, more pots and pans, sheets, a color TV and other stuff. Bella smiled at me and said, "Cool."

She didn't know that my sister and a friend of her's were on their way to our apartment right now. Sis's friend had a Honda 750 also. This was going to be fun. We were going for a good little ride. I was looking out the window when my sister and her friend showed up on his Honda. I ran out the door and gave her a big hug. I guess I should have told Bella. She had a look of being piss and sorrowful, I hugged my sister again, grabbed her hand and we walked to the apartment.

Bella was standing in the doorway. I looked and her and said say hello to my oldest sister. I could tell she was pissed before I told her who Sis was. Both of my sisters were and still are absolutely gorgeous. It took Bella a second to say hello. When her brain figured out that this was my sister, she broke out in the biggest smile and then they hugged. My sister's friend was pretty cool. I liked him. I never saw him after our ride that day, guess she dumped him, I never asked.

I told them to come in and rest for a few minutes, they did, and I made sure everybody used the toilet before we left. We left Imperial beach and got on interstate five for a few minutes and then headed west to I think it was the Otay Mesa Mountain Range and crossed the border into Mexico. We then headed east toward Tijuana, Mexico. In some places, the road wasn't paved. It was just packed dirt and there were places that smelt like pure poop. We drove thru a few little towns where most of the guys were carrying weapons. I'm pretty sure my sister and her friend were both packing pistols, I had a Smith and Wesson nine-millimeter and an extra loaded magazine for it stashed in my oversized oil cover on my Honda, it was easy to get to, and I could grab it while driving. We were not too worried about the guys with weapons.

We did stop at a little shop in the second town we passed thru and by then, everybody needed to go to the men's and ladies' rooms. I wanted to tell them it would probably be better to pull off the road somewhere away from the little towns and go there, but both my sister and Bella were not having that. My sister's friend and I both said, "Okay," at the same time. We pulled over to a public restroom if you could call it that and they both hopped off the bikes and went inside. They both came out with a look like they wished they would have done what I was thinking.

We stopped in Tijuana at the McDonalds near the border on Revolution Boulevard, had a quick meal and crossed the border back into San Ysidro, San Diego and headed back on Interstate 5 back to Imperial Beach, that was about a four hour drive and the sun was starting to go down. Sis's friend pulled up alongside us and pointed north. They were going straight back to Los Angeles, I nodded and we both did the two fingers on the right hand down. When I got off the off-ramp, he put on his emergency lights for a few seconds to say goodbye, I waived and they were gone.

When we got back to the apartment Bella and I were both tired as hell. I think it was the bouncing around on the dirt roads and all the dust. Thank god we both had on full face helmets. Once we got off the bike, we both looked at each other and laughed. We were covered in dust, my Honda was totally filthy, that would be taken care of the next morning and Bella was going to learn how to clean a motorcycle.

At one point, I had asked her if she wanted me to teach her how to drive the Honda. She said, "Hell no, it's too damn big," I laughed when she said it, but she was right. A Honda 750 was not a bike for beginners to learn how to drive. A Honda 350 would have been the one for her to learn on. I was never big on spooning in the bed bet with Sharleen and Bella, it just seemed so natural and it felt good. After her first delivery was done, I decided to make a quick run up in the hills. Just as we got to our little picnic spot, it started raining and of course, driving on the dirt roads, we and the bike were covered in mud again.

The next morning, we went and cleaned the bike at the Coronado Base near the car repair shop. After that, I filled up the gas tank, and we headed back to Imperial Beach. We went to the pier and walked around the beach area, they were having a sand castle building competition, and it was really cool to see all the different sand sculptures. I liked the mermaid with the big tits. Bella just shook her head and said that figures.

We had a good day until we got home. Her mom and family were worried about her and wanted to know when she was going back home. I told her she should go and let them know that she was coming back to California to stay here with me in Imperial Beach. Carrie left the next week and was gone for about a month. I couldn't wait for her to get back here to me. Carrie kept me up to date on her and plus, Bella called her once every two weeks. Long-distance calls were expensive back then, and we both knew we couldn't talk every day like we wanted to.

While Bella was gone, moms and pops came down to visit me along with my little sister and my little nephew. Pops brought the old family tent since he had just brought a new motor home and didn't need the tent anymore. I said, "Thanks for the tent," and asked when he got the motor home. He said he started looking for one after I got back in the navy. Since I didn't eat at his house anymore. He could afford it, and we all laughed. I told him I was thinking about asking Bella to marry me, and he smiled and said that's probably a good idea. I said, "Yes, I am going to ask her as soon as she gets back." I parked my Honda in one of the guest parking spots and he put the motor home in my spot. I only had a one-bedroom apartment, so he and Mom slept in the motor home, and my sis and her baby boy slept in my room. I slept on the futon couch. That little kid was so cool. I was hoping Bella would one day give me a son.

We all talked that night about the old neighborhood back in Los Angeles. Pops said it is almost completely Hispanics from all over central and South America. There were no more white neighbors and the few blacks that still remained owned their homes and were at that time not moving. I told him, "Times are a-changing." They all left the next morning and headed for a campsite somewhere in northern San Diego County, pops shook my hand and then told me how proud he was of me, that shocked me, then Mom hugged me and kissed my cheek, then she bit it and told me that was for when I left for Okinawa when she saw she was going to start crying I gently bit her cheek. Guess she got even, we both laughed my little sister hugged me, and I told her little man to be good, and I gave him a piece of candy, he liked me.

I had a few friends that rode bikes on base and they showed up later that day. It was four of us all on Honda 750s cruising to one of the biker clubs in one of the poorer parts of San Diego. We got inside and had a good time.

Members of the club only paid a quarter for a beer, since we were not members and did not want to, we paid fifty cents for each beer. I was cool with that, and they were all ex-military, so they understood why we didn't want to join any club. We could not spend the time that was needed to join a club. We were having our last beer when this biker babe came in waving an old ass pistol looking for her boyfriend, one of the members tried to tell her he wasn't her, and she shot off a round into the ceiling. We all scrambled behind tables and couches, looking for a place to hide from this crazy bitch.

She fired off a couple more rounds into the ceiling and left cursing her man and everybody in the club. After she left, one of the members went into one of the back rooms where her boyfriend and another crazy looking biker babe was hiding. I never went back to any biker clubs after that. I did go to a couple of bars where they hung out, but not a club. We left and went back to IB, the other three went to one of their apartments to keep drinking. I told them I had had enough, and I went to the beach, which was about a five-minute walk from my apartment, and just sat on my bike watching the ocean. I had a good buzz going when this hooker came up to me and asked if I wanted to party. I politely told her my lady would not like that, she smiled and asked me if I wanted some weed. I was getting pissed off, I had already told her no, and I said it nicely, again, I said no thanks.

She had the nerve to get mad and stomp off. She came back in two minutes with, I guess, her pimp or dealer. I got off my bike and pulled open the oil fill cover off my bike and stood there. They both turned and walked away. I never saw her again. I still had a month before Bella would be back. I had to figure out what to do in my off time to stay out of trouble.

The work string went by slowly, but like all watches, we all put out 100%. My supervisor came over to me at the end of my second day watch and told me I was going to the next inspection. I was pissed. I just stood one with our section. Why did I have to go to this one which was for the other two sections that were not at our inspection? He told me to chill and just go with it. He asked if my Dress Whites were ready. I told him I had just got them out of the cleaners, and he said good, your will not report for the mid watch tonight. I said roger that, and then my relief came in. I explained what was going on, walked over to my supervisor, and said thanks. He just smiled at me.

He then told me we were going to have some company starting with our next string of watches. I asked if I could ask who, and he told me, we were going to have a couple of guys from the Canadian Self Defense Forces working with our section. They just increased their numbers down here in IB, and we will have three of them. I said, "Cool," then he told me I was going to be having one of them sit with me side saddle until he gets the hang of how we do our thing. I said, "Cool." The next morning, I stood tall during the inspection along with my supervisor.

I thought that this is strange he and I both here. At the end of each inspection, there would be an awards ceremony if there were any for the CO to hand out, my supervisor and myself were two of five to receive awards, I got my first good conduct medal and a command letter for best improvement, my supervisor got his second good conduct medal.

After the ceremony my supervisor walked up to me and told me congrats and always try to go with the flow, I shook his hand and he told me I had to nights mid watch off also, I was more excited about not working tonight than I was for the medal. I went to the gym and changed into civvies got on my bike and headed off base. On my way home I passed a place that Hapkido training, I thought what the hell is Hapkido, so I stopped went in, this hot little Korean lady in very nice outfit told me it was Korean Self Defense, I asked how much it was and how often would I be training? She told me it would be $30.00 a month and I would have one of the best Hapkido instructors in the world teaching me, I smiled at her and told her to sign me up, at sign in the cost was $45.00 that included my new Dobok (uniform) I said cool, she smiled and I paid the money, on my way home I was thinking this would be a good way to stay out of trouble and learn more than what my father and uncles had taught me about street fighting.

I would start on my first day off at the 6; 00 PM class, there were two things that stood out in the class besides me paying $30.00 a month for the master to literally kick my ass anytime he wanted, however he wanted and to me he liked doing that to class, we learned quickly or he would stomp you, this guy had to be in his late sixties or early seventies, to look at him you would think if a breeze blew on him it would kill him.

He didn't just kick my ass it was every one of his students male or female. One of the Canadians from base joined the week after I did, he had the same name as one of his countries Presidents and he got picked on a lot about that, but he deserved it he was a cocky assed person. We had to stand in front of the class and show how well we learned the different techniques the instructor had taught us, if you screwed the technique up once, he would come out and show it to you again, if you screwed up a second time that's when the ass kicking would come in, he would use the technique against you, and sometimes if you did everything correctly he would still kick your ass.

Sometimes, I would go home with a bloody nose or a puffy eye, or the worse was when he did one of the pressure techniques. That shit would hurt for days. One day the Canadian guy was in front of us, showing us one of the techniques the master had just shown us. This guy had the flu or something, and his technique was all screwed up. The master made him do it three times.

Earlier, the master had told him that he looked sick and to go home. The Canadian said he was okay and that he was staying. The master just smiled at him. I knew that when he smiled at you, that was not a good thing, I knew from experience, and for me, it was usually a bloody nose. The Canadian had to do a flying side kick from a standing position. In other words, he had to jump forward and twist his body as he jumped in a forward motion so he would go forward and up off of both feet and then his left leg would swing around with the heel part of his foot, making the strike. We usually had to stand in a circle around whoever was showing the technique. This time, the master made us sit in a circle but not as close as we usually stood.

The first and second time he jumped forward and twisted his body, he farted, we all knew the penalty for laughing at someone during this part of training and it was seventy-five pushups and sit-ups for each time you laughed. I had tears in my eyes and so did the rest of the class, each time he farted, he was told by the master to start over, I think the master was trying not to cry laughing also, but you couldn't tell by his little old dude eyes.

I was sitting next to this older blonde woman that had just gotten divorced, and she wanted to know how to protect herself. She was as white as white printer paper, but after his second fart, she leaned into me and had her hand over her mouth, trying not to laugh. I was already having my own problems trying not to laugh, but when she put her head on my shoulder, and I could hear her groaning trying not to laugh, I almost lost it.

The third time the Canadian guy got almost to the end of the technique and when he landed, he shit on himself. He had a total blowout. It looked like a fire hose was spraying the wall behind him. It was that watery shit like after a two day hangover. The blonde next to me had her head on my shoulder until the blowout happened. She sat straight up and then fell flat on her back, laughing. If this wasn't so funny, I would have been staring at her tits, but I couldn't. I totally lost it, fell on my back and laughed like crazy.

While I was laughing and the blonde next to me was laughing, I looked around for the master. He was sitting by the door with his back to the class laughing his ass off too. The Canadian looked at all of us and said, "What's wrong with you people? I didn't feel well." The blond, the rest of the class and myself were screaming with our laughter, I looked for the master, but he was nowhere that I could see him. About two minutes later, the master's assistant came in and told us that class was over for the night. The Canadian had run off to the men's room. We were still laughing ten minutes later, and just when you thought you could stop laughing, somebody else would laugh and you started the laughing fit again. It took about twenty minutes before we could all stop and get up to leave.

The blonde was holding on to me so tight with her hand. I could feel each time she was starting to laugh. Like I said, after about twenty minutes we were able to get up and head for the changing rooms. None of the guys stayed in our room longer than it took to get our civvies and get the hell out of that room. I held my breath. I met the blonde again as I was walking towards the exit door. She was still crying and told me her name was Stacy and that she owned one of the tropical pet stores in the area. I told her my name and that I was in the navy, and just as I looked away from her boobs and looked into her eyes, we both busted up laughing again. I made it to my bike, fired it up, put on my helmet and drove home in my dobok (uniform), still laughing all the way to home.

When I made it to my apartment, I undressed and got in the shower. I almost fell down thinking about that crazy assed Canadian and his blowout.

I tried to think of anything else that happened during the training, the blonde's boobs, Bella's boobs, anything, but nothing helped me. I was in the shower cracking up for another ten minutes before I could turn the water off and head to the kitchen. Damn Canadians. After that, I called him BRAVO OSCAR (phonetics for BO for Blowout.) he didn't speak to me much after that, and I just didn't care. He didn't come back to class after that either. Bella came back to me just in time because I was going to have to find a sexy female partner if it would have taken her another day to tell me she was on her way. I did have those needs that had to be satisfied all the time if you know what I mean.

Bella came back and I asked her to marry me. I just had enough to buy a little gold band, and she was happy as hell with just that. She knew how little we got paid and what my monthly expenses were because I let her handle the payments that needed to be paid, and I kept the rest in the Navy Federal Credit Union. I did also get back into the U.S. savings bonds for twenty-five dollars per month. After that, we had enough to go out and have fun. We never got the chance to go to Disney Land in California, she would have loved that, but the gangs were out there killing each other also. That was not a trip to take at that time. When Bella got back, we didn't leave the apartment for 3 days. She screamed the first night in bed, and I screamed the last two nights. I felt sorry for our neighbors, I didn't have the best bed and it was making just as much noise as we were.

After I went back to work, I had the Canadian guy that I was going to teach how to do the job we did. He was an awesome guy, nothing like the BO guy in Hapkido class (which I quit going to after I got my blue belt). I couldn't stand to pay to get my ass kicked anymore. The second month after Bella got back, I took her to the same place in the mountains that we went to on our first ride on the bike and asked her to marry me. I wasn't on my knee, we were laying on the sheet that we always used, and I was flat on my back, and she had her head on my chest.

Bella sat up and looked me in the eyes and asked if I was for real. I told her I was, I told her that I wanted her to be the mother of my kids and to be the woman that had my back twenty-four seven like she knew I had hers. She said, "Yes," I smiled at her and then, just because I couldn't help it, I grabbed one of her boobs and squeezed it and got up and grabbed her. We kissed for a while, I drank a couple of beers and she didn't want any, so I gave her the bottle of water. I asked her about her family back where she was from. She said they were expecting a call for her to tell them that I had asked her to marry me, so she knew what she was going to do as soon as we got home.

I smiled as she called our little apartment home. I smiled longer. The first day I got back to work, I talked to my supervisor and told him I had asked Bella to marry me. He congratulated me and had the biggest smile. He had bet his wife that I would ask Bella within the first week after she got back, his wife said it would take me longer. We both smiled. On the next break, Bella and I were married. I told her I would make up the honeymoon as soon as I could, she said, "We will spend three days after our marriage in Imperial beach, and we will rent a hotel near the Hotel Coronado, and we will spend two days hanging out at the beach there that was good enough for me."

God, I loved this woman. After we were married and came back to the apartment, most of the folks in my watch section wanted us to come to the club on the Coronado Base, and we did. Bella met everybody I worked with, from the watch officer to the new Canadian that I was teaching, most of the guys that were married brought their wives along and Bella finally had some female friends in Imperial Beach. They hung out sometimes when they could while the children were in school. Bella was very happy, and I felt so good about her and how she blended it so easily.

After going back to work, the Canadian guy kept asking me about my bike, I thought he was going to ask to ride it and that answer would have been a big "Hell No," it turned out to be that he had just brought an older Honda 450, but he really didn't know how to drive it, I told him I would help him out. I learned how to ride a motorcycle when I was twelve years old, my cousins in Sacramento, California had them, and whenever we visited them, we usually stayed at least three or four days, and that's all we did as kids were ride the dirt bikes in the hills there. Now my Canadian friend was a brave little guy, and he really wanted to learn how to drive his new bike. We started at parking lots after six pm after the rush hour and he learned how to shift the gears, how to use the breaks without killing himself, how to handle the back tire spinning by holding the front brake and putting power to the throttle so he could do a burnout, I wanted to teach him how to lean into turns, so we went up to the mountains, probably about thirty-five minutes from IB, he looked nervous.

I told him to relax and take turns slow and that I would be in front of him. I wanted him to see how I leaned the bike to either the right or left, depending on which way I was turning. As long as we were doing thirty miles per hour or less, he did great, but my bike didn't like going slow like that for turns. It was hard to stop from falling, so I sped up some to about forty-five miles per hour, we were on a road that was one lane each way, and with a cliff on the side we were driving up, I had to speed up just to keep my bike from falling over when we got to a curve in the road, I looked back, and he was right behind me, then we got to a curve that did a double twist after I got through it looked back, he was nowhere to be found, I thought he just slowed down like he had been doing all day. I went to the top of the hill and stopped, put my bike in neutral and pulled out a beer from the right saddle bag, popped the top, and took a long swig of a can.

I looked back down the hill and didn't see my Canadian. I kept looking for about another two minutes, then I thought if something had happened to him, what kind of paperwork would I have to do and what kind of trouble would I be in because I brought him up here and he lost control and went over the cliff.

I took one more drink of beer, poured the rest out and put the empty can back into the saddle bag and slowly drove back down. I didn't see anything. When I got to the last turn I had seen him at, I turned around and as slowly as I could I drove back up, I noticed that the barb wire fence was missing in one spot so I pulled over and that's when I found my him. He was tangled up by his arms and part of his back and I know this seems to mean, but thank God. Otherwise, his ass would have gone down the hill, which at that point was damn near straight down with ledges sticking out.

I'm not sure how he did it, but his bike was about 8 feet away from the fence. My guess was that once he hit the dirt, his bike went down, throwing him off, and he rolled into the barbed wire and knocked down the poles that just barely held the wire in place. I was standing with one leg on solid ground and the other part on the fence. I bent down and slowly grabbed his jeans and slowly pulled him toward me, when I got my hand on his belt, I put my other foot back on solid ground and pulled him back up and over, then I had to untangle him from the barbed wire. I did stop for a second and pulled another beer out of the saddle bags on my bike and sat down for a few swigs. He weighed more than I did and was about four or five inches shorter than me, so this wasn't easy for me and he was unconscious. When I grabbed my beer, I also grabbed the old sheet and a bottle of water. Once I had untangled him from the wire enough so that I could get his whole body back on solid ground, I removed his helmet and then I opened the bottle of water and poured it over his head.

Trying to untangle a person that is wrapped pretty good in barbed wire is hard as hell if they can't help you. After a few seconds, he opened his eyes and the look of fear was still in them. I told him, "You're alright, just don't move, okay? Don't panic and move," he shook his head and that's when I found out what happened to him. He panicked when he had to lean his bike into the turn, lost control, and the bike went down and that was all he remembered. All of a sudden, he started feeling the pain from the wires cutting into his back and his lower arm, where his leather jacket was ripped. I told him not to panic because if he did, the wire was going to cut deeper into his arm. I needed his help to get the wire off his arm. I already had his legs clear.

The wire that had his arm was also digging into his side and back. Basically, after I got his legs and his head clear, all he would have to do was slowly lift his body while I held the one wire that was digging into his back, and I could pull it under him and he would be out. Once he was out, he told me once he saw the mountain, he started to panic like he had never done before and about how scared he was during the whole time until he passed out.

Then he asked me not to let anyone know about this incident and for the first time, I kept my word about something that was this serious and funny at the same time. I never told anyone. He stood up. I offered him the last beer, he was bleeding but not bad at all. He declined the beer but did drink the last bottle of water. I picked his bike up and checked it out, I asked him if he could ride it back down and he shook his head yes. I pulled his bike forward to put it on the double stands and started it. The bike fired right up as if nothing had happened, but the gear shift was bent and would only go up as high as third gear. This bike had five gears. Needless to say, on the interstate, we were only going about fifty miles per hour, but coming back down the hill, we were on the side closer to the mountain instead of the cliff, so we took it real slow and got back to IB and my apartment, I told Bella what happened.

She had him take off his jacket and shirt. All of the bleeding had stopped, but she still put rubbing alcohol on him. He screamed, and I looked into his eyes and I screamed. Bella thought I was crazy. I was, I couldn't understand what would make a person try to do something that was beyond their abilities, especially having a fear of heights like he had. Later I found out that he was attached to their Air Force division of the Canadian Self Defense Forces.

Until now, I never mentioned this to anyone. Bella had put six band-aids and one small six-by-six-inch gauze on him and had taped that onto his arm. This Canadian had a lot of guts and I admired him for that as it must have taken as he had to try and ride up that mountain. I offered him the foo ton couch to sleep on that night, but he wanted to get back to his apartment near the Coronado base. Bella gave him a couple of aspirin which he quickly swallowed down, drank a glass of water, and got on his bike and headed home. I knew he would be alright.

That night Bella told me I had some crazy assed friends, and we both laughed. I asked her if she was hungry, and she said, "Yes," and we got on the bike and went to the McDonalds. From the day she came back to me, I knew she was mine; I didn't know if when she went back home to tell someone, it was over or what. I didn't bother to ask and I didn't care. When she stepped off that plane at the San Diego airport, she was mine. Carrie picked her up from the airport because I had to work. It was my last ever watch than three days off. After the incident with the Canadian, we just chilled out a lot, every now and then, we would go to the base and hang out, but mostly on my days off, we just rode somewhere on the bike for a little picnic or stayed at home.

The next day one of our neighbors in the apartment asked Bella if she wanted to come to an Avon party, so I had to clean the bike by myself. That was cool with me as she would get to meet the neighbors and have a few friends. When she came home, she was excited as hell and told me she wanted to sell that product, it sounded sort of like a pyramid scheme to me, but if that was what she wanted to do, I was fine with it.

She only worked with it for a couple of months as we had no car at the time and had to deliver the Avon stuff on the Honda. I know we looked funny with two big trash bags full of the products tied together, one hanging off each side of the bike and they were between the two of us hauling ass on I-5. One day I remembered the tent my father had given me, it was for that time very high quality, it slept six people with room to spare, it had three screened windows with zip-up covers for each one, it also had a huge door with both the screen and the material that the rest of the tent was made of and it zipped open or closed and lastly when the material part of the tent was unzipped all the way, you could put two poles there to hold it up and get shade outside of the tent. At the back of our base was a nice beach. No one was allowed on it unless you were one of us CT's and you requested permission to go on the beach. We all knew the guards because we also pulled the duty to guard the beach, so everybody was cool with me and some friends from the base going out there and spending the night.

It was better than trying to drive home drunk, and our people were having problems with the Imperial Beach Police. The first time we went to the beach, I had to invite a friend of mine because there was no way I could get Bella and all the tent parts on my bike. He was another new black

CT that was cool as hell. He had spent some time in the Philippines and married this really nice little lady from there and he was in my section. I had wanted Bella to meet them. They had one little boy and a very pretty little girl who had just started walking, and his son was around five or six years old. My friend had the nickname of COKE, one of the popular sodas at that time due to the fact when he first got in the navy, he was totally buffed and looked like an upside-down Coke bottle, but he had been in for about five years and only worked out when he had to (he got chunky), he smoked those fat assed cigars we called stogies, and when he laughed you could hear it a mile away, they were good people.

One day we were all at the beach, Coke and I were playing catch with a football in the water with his son, both Bella and Coke's wife were getting everything ready to put on the portable bar-b-que grill we brought and the little girl was sitting next to them, Bella went to Coke's car to get the hot dog buns while Coke's wife walked out to the water. We heard this loud scream, the little girl had grabbed one of the hot coals off the grill, Coke got to her first, then he and his wife rushed the baby to the hospital in Imperial Beach, I kept his son with us and we stayed at the beach with the tent and stuff. They returned in about forty-five minutes. The little one had only burned a little part of her thumb and index finger, but her whole little hand was wrapped in a bandage.

Coke was okay, but his wife was still mad at the baby girl. I personally was thinking, why didn't she bring the baby to the water with her? But the kid was fine and back to playing in the sand. Two weeks later, they had to go into child protective services on and off base because of that incident. We partied out there all night, grilling burgers and hot dogs, a few more of our section workers showed up and we spent the whole night there. Thank God! we were able to walk to the bathroom outside the building and it also had an old shower, so we were fine until the next morning. Everybody had serious hangovers except for the kids.

Cleaning up the mess we made and packing everything into Coke's car was rough for me. Bella was laughing at how slow I was moving and I drove my bike back to the apartment just as slow. Coke helped me put the tent away in our apartment, then he and his family went home. I was amazed I didn't have a headache. I just felt like the world was still spinning. Bella made us breakfast. After that, we both took a shower and went to bed. We slept half the day away, but I felt better when I woke up. We went to Taco Bell for dinner and then back to the apartment.

The next day I pulled out the old fishing equipment that pops had given me, I just needed to spray a little WD-40 on the reels and then they worked just fine. We walked to the pier in IB and did a little bit of fishing. We had some old frozen shrimp that we used for bait; we caught a few croakers. They were called that because when you pulled them out of the water, they made a croaking sound. We didn't keep any of the fish we caught that day, but it was fun just to be fishing again. I felt relaxing to me, plus I had a beautiful young woman standing next to me that was mine, all mine and I was hers.

I was starting to get short here in Imperial Beach. It was amazing how fast time went by while I was stationed there. We camped on the beach, rode the bike all through the mountains and hung out with some pretty cool people. We tried skinny dipping at the beach one night, but the Pacific Ocean late in the year was just too cold to really stay in the water for long. There were about eight or nine of us, but nobody wanted to stay in the water, we had a campfire going to cook hot dogs and lots of beer and sodas we had it made. I brought an old station wagon that someone at Bella's church was selling. I think it was a Dodge and it was green with fake pieces of wood on each side. it was a real piece of junk, but I knew if anybody hit her, she would be alright in it. It was a monster. One morning Coke and I decided to go fishing, so he brought his family over to our place. We left them there, headed straight for the bait shop, got about four dozen shrimp and went to the pier. There was this little Pilipino lady named Sandy. She was always fishing there, but today she was in my spot and she had at least four rods and reels. She was taking up all those spaces.

The pier was getting crowded and this old guy came up with his gear. He looked at Sandy, shook his head and said watch this. I can get her to move. He put his gear down, pulled up his left pants leg and pulled off his false leg, I had seen him out here many times and never knew he had a false leg, Coke and I were just staring at him, and he smiled at us and winked his eye. He hopped the few feet right next to Sandy and put his fake leg and foot on the ground next to her. She started yelling at him in Tagalog and reeled in all her lines, put all her gear in the grocery cart she took from one of the local supermarkets and quickly left.

Coke and I were laughing so hard that we had tears in our eyes. We hurried up and took those spots. Sandy was hogging and got ready to fish. The old guy said he lost his leg in Viet Nam. He was a regular on the pier and told me Sandy would do things like that, hogging the spaces and also, she would not throw the small fish back. Whatever she caught, she kept. We all started laughing again. He said, "It's bad luck to the Filipinos to be near any kind of body prosthetics." I was thinking it's good luck for us. We were catching a lot of croakers, then all of a sudden nothing. The old guy said this could only mean one thing and we both looked at him, wondering what the hell he was talking about. He grabbed his deep-sea rod and reel, put one of the croakers he had just caught on a big hook and slung it over the side. In just a few minutes, his rod bent almost in half, and everybody near him started reeling their lines, so Coke and I did likewise.

He yelled over to me to grab the gaff. I was thinking, why would he need a gaff here? Then we all saw what it was. At least a six-foot thresher shark and this shark was putting up a real fight for its life. I was hoping it didn't go under the pier because the line could get cut by the barnacles on the post that hold the pier up. The old guy started walking down the pier back toward the beach, Coke and I followed him and the pier there was very long. It felt like he was fighting that thing for over an hour, probably about fifteen minutes.

He was yelling at the folks in his way, telling them to reel in as he had a shark on the line and they all did, once we were off the pier and on the beach, he kept walking backward, dragging the shark up on the beach, that's when it hit me about the gaff. I was thinking this is a shark a thrasher shark and it has a long tail that could knock the hell out of a person in a boat and it could probably do the same thing on land. I stood about two feet in front of the head of the shark and gaffed it in the gills, and Coke grabbed the gaff with me and we both pulled it the rest of the way out of the water.

Just as the old guy laid his rod and reel down, this guy from one of the restaurants ran over to him and paid the old guy fifty dollars for the shark. The old guy gave Coke and ten dollars apiece because we helped him land the shark. By now, everybody on the beach had come over to see the shark. I grabbed Coke and said let's get back to our spot, we didn't have the gear to catch a shark, but it would be nice to try. We did catch a couple of halibut and four really nice sea bass, which we kept and put on the grill when we got home. We had gone to the pier in the station wagon, so when we got back to the apartment, Coke was putting his gear into his car. I ran into the house to tell the girls about the old guy catching a shark and getting paid for it.

Bella looked at me like I was crazy, the Coke repeated the same thing when he came in the house a few minutes later as he had been outside smoking one of his cigars. Bella and Sally couldn't believe the fish we caught and I cleaned them for dinner. We had rice, halibut and sea bass for dinner. It was good. After that, every chance I got, I was fishing. When Bella was at church with her cousin and her cousin's husband, I was on the pier fishing, don't get me wrong, I do believe in God, just in my own way.

I was usually fishing for sea bass or halibut, but when the fish stopped biting, I would through one of the smaller sea basses on the line and try for the thrasher shark, I could always use the money the restaurants along the pier would pay for one of these sharks, the rest of the time I was in IB I only caught two of them, and one was too small I had to throw it back, the second was perfect and I got sixty-five dollars for it.

The last time Coke and I went fishing on the IB pier, we had about three dozen live shrimp in a bucket in the back of the old station wagon, we got to the pier and there was hardly anyone there. We couldn't believe our luck. We fished for about two hours and didn't catch any sharks but halibut and sea bass again and we had almost a full case of beer on ice in the ice chest. When we were done, fishing Coke had to drive us home. The beer, sun and all that fishing got to me. I was totally drunk and having a great time.

Coke told me if we didn't leave now, we would have to walk home. I said, "Let's go," we packed up the old station wagon. There were only a few pieces of bait left, so we gave them to the folks that were still there when we left. I don't know how Coke did it, but we made it home. I passed out first. Bella just shook her head and laughed at Coke and I, and he must have passed out right after I did. About two hours later, we woke up to the smell of fried fish and tater tots. I was starving and so was Coke. My time in IB was almost over and I had filled out my dream sheet. I wanted somewhere in Europe, no more Pacific Ocean locations for me. I was told I would be getting more training back then. Your second school was called C-School and it would last nearly six months in San Angelo, Texas, to learn how to be an analyst for my particular field.

About three days later, I went out to the car and was going to take it to work instead of my Honda. It was going to be one of those normal hot San Diego days, according to the news reports I watched on tv as I was getting dressed for work. Once I opened the car door, an awful smell came out of the hot car. I quickly closed the door and got on my Honda and rode it to work. I thought something had crawled into the car and died. I would check the car when I got home.

I got off work right at 4:00 PM and headed home. Once I walked through the door, Bella told me about the smell in the car. I changed into my civvies and went out to try and find out what it was. I couldn't find anything, and the entire inside of the car had that smell. Then I thought to myself, we hadn't used the car since Coke, and I went fishing, so what could make it smell so bad. I couldn't see anything and as it was an old station wagon, you could see under all the seats in the front and back rows. I went back inside the house and grabbed a flashlight. I had left all four doors opened so it would air out a little. When I turned on the flashlight, I found a small shrimp wedged between the brace that held the back seat in place and the carpet, it had turned brown and since the carpet was brown, it had to find it.

I went inside and let Bella know what the smell was and I showed her the little shrimp. It was less than an inch long and instead of it being almost clear. it had turned brown. I put it in the garbage disposal and ran cold water in the disposal and I let the disposal do its job, Bella grabbed Lysol and a bucket of warm water and we both cleaned the seats and the carpet with sponges. After that, we used a room deodorizer to help get rid of the smell. We sold the car back to her church a couple of weeks after that.

After we both calmed down, I called Mom and gave her the good news, Mom had always told me she wanted grandchildren, but she wasn't going to take care of them, watch them for a while maybe but not full time. She was happy when I told her about me getting married and the baby on the way after I hung up the phone with her. Bella called her mom and told her that I had just asked her to marry me and she let me know that we were going to have a baby. They stayed on the phone for quite a while. I told my friends at work about the marriage and the baby, and they were mostly happy for us. A couple of guys made normal jokes about how she was going to change on me and I wouldn't be happy. I gave them the evil eye. I didn't hear any more of those jokes again.

The British and the Argentinians went to war over the Falkland Islands and I got extended at NRRF imperial Beach. I wasn't upset about it. Six more months, I could do that standing on my head. We got orders for NSGA Misawa Japan. I had been to Okinawa and really didn't like it there. I thought Japan would probably be a much better place.

We got married a couple of weeks later. Bella was now close to nine months pregnant when we were ready to leave Imperial Beach and head for Japan. We had two weeks' leave, so we spent the first week with her family. I got to meet her family and got along well with most of them. She had a stepfather that let me know what would happen if I ever mistreated her, I looked at him like he was crazy and just walked away from him, plus he showed me the pistol he had in his pocket.

I was thinking by the time he got the pistol out. I could probably beat him with it. Bella was proud of me just walking away, plus I had a baby on the way and didn't want any family problems. I had to wear my dress uniform for that flight. I had on my dress blues (the bell bottom trousers with thirteen buttons and the loose shirt with the black neckerchief with the little white cap. I really liked that uniform. I thought it looked good on us sailors that were in good shape. My new mother-in-law had some of her neighbors over when we got to her house. I came in with a bottle of wine and some really good whiskey.

Bella was passed out. She didn't drink any of the booze, but her mother's friends did. They wanted to see how the buttons on my blue dress trousers. There are thirteen buttons that hold the flap in place, with an extra button on the back of the flap. I knew they were checking me out and Bella said that they were earlier. I tried to take Bella's nephew fishing, but the weather was cold as hell and part of the lake was frozen. We went back to the house and warmed up and played games for a while. We stayed with her mother for about five days and then flew back to Los Angeles, California and stayed in pop's motor home. Bella liked that we had our own little spot. After we left Los Angeles, we caught a flight out of Los Angeles International Airport to Narita International Airport in Japan.

NSGA Misawa, Japan May 1984 – November 1986

Once we reached Narita International Airport, we walked to the USO and I showed them my orders. They told me where to go to catch a mac flight that would have us landing in Misawa Air Base in a couple of hours. I went out there expecting to see the ass that was sitting with us on the flight in, but he wasn't there, we got to the area for the flight, and I was surprised to see how many military people were there all trying to get to Misawa Air Base, we got our bags and boarded the plane that was going to Misawa Japan.

Once we landed in Misawa at the Air Force Base, there was the normal navy white van waiting for the navy personnel. Bella was the only spouse. Once we got to the quarter deck, I was handed a voucher and given two days to get settled in at a hotel until our on base quarters were ready for us to move into. We were told it was never more than a two week wait. Once we got to the hotel, it was temporary housing on base, kind of like a hotel with a little kitchen.

We had about three thousand dollars on us that Bella had saved as I asked her to. We brought a two-year-old Toyota station wagon. It was grey, I thought it was awesome and plus, it had plenty of space for all the baby stuff. We got our own base house which was a two-bed room, one bath with a shower and bathtub. It was on the second floor. I had an assigned parking space which was cool as hell, there were spaces for guests, but each unit had its own parking space. The only problem I had was the couple below me, the husband was air force and he sucked.

He or his wife didn't speak to anyone and I think they thought they were better than the rest of us because he was an Air Force E-6 like a staff sergeant. He was an Alpha Hotel (Ass Hole) to most of us, he would call and report about every little thing. If someone parked in his spot instead of telling them that was an assigned spot, he would call and report the car and the person to the base security. If you didn't shovel the snow in the area assigned to your unit, he would report that also, if your pet pooped in his portion of the back yard, he would call, music too loud after 22:00 hours I just couldn't stand him, but we all had to get along.

In northern Japan, it really snowed a lot in the winter and could get very damn cold (me no likey). We were issued parkas, long johns and extra thick socks. Most of the winter days, I wore most of those items along with my work uniform. Once we got settled into our apartment, Bella was now going on her 10th month being pregnant and her new doctor was worried about her taking so long to deliver the baby. I took Bella off base and we found a place to have a picnic and try our luck at fishing I will never forget. I handed Bella her rod and reel. I had it all set up. The only thing I needed to do for her was to put the hook on the line, I told Bella not to move while I was tying the hook to the line and she smiled at me just when I thought I was finished with tying the hook on, the baby kicked Bella really hard and she jumped pulling the rod and reel upwards which in turn ran the hook right through my right index finger, I couldn't get the hook out by myself and my finger was bleeding just enough that I needed to cover it, I cut the line, looked at Bella and her eyes looked like they were going to pop out of her head, she was scared of the hook that went into the left side of my finger and was sticking out of the right side, of course, the blood didn't help much. After I cut the line, pulled out one of my brand new fishing rags and wrapped it around my finger as best as I could, I actually had to remove the rod and reel from Bella's hands. I helped her up, and got her into the passenger seat of the car, grabbed all the equipment and put it in the back of the car, climbed into the driver seat and drove the forty-five minutes back to the base hospital and then home, the hook only hurt when it went through my finger, while I was driving back to base to the hospital my finger was throbbing the whole way.

Once we were back on base, I dropped Bella off at our place and watched to make sure she was okay going up the steps and made it into the front door. After that, I hauled ass down to the hospital. The doctor I had was pretty cool. He gave me a shot in my finger and almost immediately, my finger grew too damn near twice the thickness as it normally was. Then he cut the barbed part of the hook and then he pulled the hook back through my finger. I did feel the hook being pulled out of my finger and it was not a nice feeling.

After the hook was out, I got another shot in the same finger to stop any infections. I couldn't feel the second shot and my finger stopped throbbing. It was just numb. I was put on light duty for three days. By the time I got back home, Bella was crying like crazy and trying to apologize. I had to calm her down and let her know that I was okay, my finger was bandaged up really good and they gave me extra dressings for it. Once I got her calmed down, we got her out of all the clothes and got her in bed. She went straight to sleep. On the tenth day of the tenth month, my baby girl was born, I thought I was going to be in the delivery room, but Bella would not dilate enough, so they did a caesarian section. I had to leave the room and wait in the waiting room, I was pacing back and forth like crazy, hoping they would both be okay.

There was another couple there with a one or two-year-old and the mother looked almost as ready to deliver as Bella did. I guess she was going in after Bella was done. The guy asked me if this was my first baby and I said, “Yes,” he smiled and said, “This is one of the best hospitals in the world for delivering babies.” I smiled at him and said thanks. I sat my butt down and waited. About forty-five minutes later, a nurse came out to me with my beautiful daughter. She had my eyes and a perfect little body with a head full of thick curly black hair.

The nurse handed my daughter to me and my heart felt like it would explode when I looked at her in my arms. I asked the nurse how Bella was doing and she asked me to follow her to Bella’s room. The nurse told me that Bella and my lovely daughter would have to stay in the hospital for at least four days. I think my face dropped. I was getting ready to complain when half of the folks that worked with me showed up at Bella’s door. My daughter didn’t know how many new aunts and uncles she had. The folks in my work section were close, I mean really close and that’s the way our supervisor wanted it. He arranged with another section supervisor to have at least four extra folks to come in when my baby was born, so a third of my section would be there with me when the baby was born.

I didn’t know anything about it, that made me even happier, all of the ladies that showed up wanted to hold the baby but the nurse took her out of my arms and gave her back to Bella for a few seconds. Everybody stopped talking and just looked at Bella and my daughter, two of the girls cried. I was about to also when one of the guys I had gotten close to named Freddy gave out cigars and then they all patted me on the back and started talking and laughing, calling me pops. Bella just smiled at us, the baby went to sleep and the nurse kicked them all out of the room. She let me stay for a few more minutes and then I had to leave. I did watch them take a blood sample from my baby, and that was the first time she cried, and it was only for a few seconds and then she went back to sleep. I did shed a few tears then.

Both Bella and the baby were asleep. The nurse told me to come back tomorrow and that I might want to get myself some rest also. My supervisor was also there, they were all waiting for me in the waiting room, he told me I had ten days of leave I could take since she had a C-section and if I wanted more to let him know, I looked him in the eyes and said thank you, then I thanked them all for being here, I got big hugs from the ladies the guys all shook my hand and we all walked outside and smoked the cigars.

They all followed me home and had all kinds of gifts for my daughter, Bella and I didn’t want to know what the baby’s gender would be. We brought neutral baby clothes for her, that changed quickly. Once we all got to my house, I couldn’t believe all the presents they had for my daughter.

I was overwhelmed by these people, they were my family here in Misawa, Japan and it was like that until I left.

No one stayed long. They all had to get back to work so the folks that went in for them could go back home. There was even a present from our commanding officer and his family. I didn't open anything I just tried to put things in the baby's room neatly so Bella and I could get to her little crib. My daughter weighed a little over seven pounds and was the normal length for her weight, but that little head full of hair was something else. She had lots of big black thick curls.

Each of the four days I was at home, someone from the section would come over and hang out with me, just to keep me company. I went to the hospital each day and stayed as long as I could with Bella and my new little me, she had my forehead and eyes, and she had Bella's nose and lips. I just knew she was going to be a heartbreaker when she grew up. That first night I went and brought myself a bottle of Chivas Regal whiskey. I had a couple of shots each night before I went to sleep until they came home. We named my daughter Dena the second day after she was born. I was going crazy thinking about all the things I wanted to do for and with them when they got home. I chewed all my fingernails off. I brought myself tv dinners for the days they were in the hospital. It was food and I needed to eat.

Dena had a little rocking horse and lots of stuffed animals to play with when she was able to play with things. We got all kinds of diapers, some of the cotton cloth ones but lots of the disposable ones that were the newest thing in baby diapers. I was glad for them. I went to work on the third day just to tell everyone to thank you and let them know about both Bella and Dena's condition. The baby was doing fine with eating and gaining her weight like she was supposed to. Bella was doing great also, just had to take it easy for a couple of weeks with the stitches.

I actually stayed home for fourteen days due to the fact Bella couldn't do much for that time. I cooked and learned how to mix the baby formula so that we had enough baby food for the kid to eat for two years. I practiced mixing the formula while they were in the hospital. The cotton diapers were beyond my understanding. Bella had to show me how to do that when they came home.

I kept myself busy until they got home and I have to tell you this, the day I brought them home, it was cold as hell and the snow had frozen. It was slippery as hell everywhere. I had to be careful driving due to the black ice on the base roads. The morning I went to pick my family up, I had on jeans, an undershirt, sweatshirt, long johns and those thick socks along with my jump boots and the parka. It only took a few minutes to get to the base hospital. Bella was wheeled out to the car in a wheelchair. I had the baby in a little pink and red baby carrier which I put in the middle of the back seat so I could see Dena through the rearview mirror while driving. It took a minute for Bella to get in the car. I held her by one arm as she slowly put one leg in at a time and then lowered herself gently into the passenger seat.

We were home in just a few minutes and that was when Bella and I had our workouts. I carried Dena up the slippery stairs holding on to the little baby carrier that was given to us at the hospital. I had already brought one just for my baby girl, so now she would have one that stayed in the car. I held the stair rail with one hand and the carrier with the other and I had on my hand warmers and the thick gloves that matched the parka. Once I parked the car, I left it running with the heater on and got out by myself and went up the stairs to unlock the door. I left it slightly cracked so I could hurry and get my little one in fast. I went back down the stairs and slipped just a little. I didn't want to bust my ass on those stairs.

I slowed down and held on to the handrail the rest of the way down. Once I was back downstairs, I opened the back door, grabbed the carrier with Dena in it and slowly went back up the stairs, I pushed the door open and walked over by the heater and put the carrier with Dena in it on the floor near the heater but not too close to it. I took some of the little blankets off of her so she could move her arms and legs, then I went down the stairs for Bella. She was able to walk to the bottom of the stairs but getting up the stairs was not going to happen. I carried her up to our front door, praying to God the whole way that I didn't slip or drop her. It wasn't that she was heavy, but it was just everything was so damn slippery I had to take my gloves off to be able to grab her, and my fingers felt like ice cubes and I wasn't sure I was still holding her by the time we made it to the second floor. I gently bent down so Bella could let her legs down and still holding her with one arm, I opened the door. We both let out a sigh of relief when she stood by herself.

Bella slowly walked to the couch and began taking off her hat, scarf and coat. She looked over at our daughter and just smiled. I will never forget the look on her face. She said we made one beautiful baby. I choked and smiled at her. I was teary eyed and just nodded my head. In base housing back then, we were not allowed to paint the walls any color other than what they were when we moved in a dull white, so I couldn't paint Dena's room any baby colors, but once I called home and let my family and Bella's family know there was a new baby girl in the family more stuff came in the mail. Dena had all kinds of stuff hanging off the walls and tacked to the walls. She had a little wooden crib with little ponies carved into the wood. It was cool as hell. For the first two weeks, it was put in Bella and my room, but after that, Dena was on her own at night and she slept a lot and was growing fast like babies do. Those first two weeks, I did all the cooking, cleaning and everything else. I don't think Dena cried one time during the night. Thank God! She was such a good baby.

Bella did all the diaper changes for the first couple of months with those cotton diapers. After that, I would change here if I was home when she needed to be changed. One night after Dena was about two months old, I took her out of the front door and held her so she could see the stars. I told her that her family could see those stars from their homes far, far away and that one day she would meet most of them on both sides of her family.

I don't think she cared too much because she stared at the sky for a minute, yawned and then looked up at me and smiled, closed he eyes and went back to sleep. I quickly got her back inside and closed the door. I went back to work and everybody asked about the baby and for me to bring in pictures of her. The commander called me into his office. He wanted to know how Bella and Dena were doing, and I told him just fine. He smiled and congratulated me, then told me to get back to work.

It was getting close for the E-6 exams in a couple of months and I needed to study, that meant I would go into work for at least three hours early for study time and then work the 2-2-2 and eighty like in Imperial Beach, then I would come home and help Bella out by taking care of Dena so she could get some rest and a much-needed break. I was off base one day and saw a beautiful little Fairlady-Z by Datsun (what we called a 280-Z back in the world). It was a 1978-year model with everything you could get on a car back then, I had to have it and for the price, I just knew I had to get it two thousand dollars with only a couple of thousand miles on it. That way, I could drive it to work and leave the station wagon for Bella and Dana to use when they wanted. It was my favorite color, burgundy with black trim. I brought it, and Bella was really happy, she would have her own car now. We took pictures by the temple in Hachinohe. It was beautiful with lots of trees and places to sit and just made you feel relaxed. Bella would take the baby here sometimes while I was at work, she was happy she had the Toyota to drive now and it made since with a baby.

I took the exam in early October 1983 and felt really good about my scores. I had done all the required physical testing with no problem, even the run, which was done in the gym, I forgot how many laps it was around the gym, but it was a lot. The actual written test lasted four hours, I used all four of those hours checking and double checking my answers and like I said, I felt good about it, now that the test was over, I didn't have to do the extra study time and I was able to spend more time with Dena and Bella, one day I took them to this little town north of the base. It was known for having the largest Koi fish in the region, so we went and had a good time and Dena just looked at everything. Her little eyes took in everything.

After Dena turned four or five months old, I would take her to the barracks, where all the ladies would take her from me. Dena never cried. She liked all the attention, these trips would last two or three hours on my days off to give Bella her own time and I think she enjoyed it.

On September first, nineteen-eighty-three, a South Korean passenger jet KAL-007 was shot down over international waters when it strayed into Soviet waters. It was shot down by a Soviet fighter jet, and all passengers perished, it caused a lot of tensions with all the countries in the area and we did not report on it until after the Japanese did.

By this time, we had a new commanding officer, he was a Captain trying to make Admiral and he was pushing all of us so he could make it, pushing us hard and after this incident, he really made life hard for us, instead of doing a 2-2-2-80 hour work schedules changed to 1-1-1-32. one day watch then eight hours after the day watch we had a mid-watch and eight hours after the mid-watch we had and eve-watch then we got 32 hours off, that lasted I think 2 or 3 months, it caused all kinds of problems for everybody except the senior officers that were in charge of everything and the folks working straight day watches.

The junior officers and us enlisted were burnt out after the third week, families were pissed and it was just too much for a lot of families, 2-2-2-80 was hard enough to get used to, but this new schedule sucked ass. Bella and Dena hardly saw me and on the 32 hours off. I slept most of that time and then started the schedule all over again. Bella had recovered from giving birth, but we had plans that had to be put on hold, like going back to the world to introduce Dena to our families. I couldn't let her know how long it would be before we could take our vacation and she was pissed. I had never seen her like that before. I was too tired most of the time to even try to calm her down. All I could do was eat and sleep, then go off to work again. Bella was always at home with the baby, so on my one day off, I would take the baby to the barracks for a couple of hours and she would disappear as usual with all the girls in the barracks. They would take her to all their rooms to show her off. My baby girl had so many aunts and uncles in the barracks that it was crazy. When I was ready to leave, I had to go and find her. And she just loved all the attention and the toys, which were usually stuffed animals. I'm pretty sure she got lots of candy also.

Dana was one happy little baby. She didn't cry much and always had a look in her eyes that she wanted to do something. On my day off, after I took her to the barracks and returned home, i would put music on and grab her little hands and we would dance. I would bend down and put her feet on mine. She would just giggle and laugh. It usually only took a few minutes after that and she was asleep. Bella had a chance to get some rest on those days that I took Dena to the base and stayed up and played with her.

When Bella was around 8 months old, I got a call from my mother back in Los Angeles and she really gave me some serious news. I had another child, another daughter that was just a little over two years old. Mom told me the baby was mine and looked just like me. What could I say? I had to tell Bella I just didn't want her to go totally crazy dealing with all the stress she was already under. I guess I had enough time away from my family that I didn't think about how it must have affected other people. Bella needed to be home just long enough to see her family and friends and to show them Dana. I didn't realize that, and I didn't know that a total blowout was about to happen.

After I got home from an eve watch one evening and as normal, I walked in the front door of our apartment and little Dana woke up immediately. It was kind of weird how she would do that, wake up just as I walked in the door and put her arms out for me to pick her up and play with her. I used to put all the pillows from the couch on the floor right next to the couch so we could both fall off the couch onto the pillows and Dana loved that she would just laugh and giggle then I would put her on the couch and tickle her until she had tears in her eyes, then I would take a lollypop and unwrap it and put it on the edge of the coffee table.

Usually, Dana would crawl to the table and grab the table leg to pull herself up just enough to grab the candy, this one night, I did the normal, except I held both of her little hands so she could stand up. My little Dana walked about eight or nine steps to the table and grabbed the candy and put it in her mouth. I was so happy my baby girl had taken her first steps, she was around nine months and usually crawled everywhere, but she just slowly walked to the candy. Bella and I both held our breaths and just watched her.

Dana had the candy in her mouth as she was looking at me. Then she realized that she was standing and fell down flat on her little butt, never taking her hands off the candy. Bella grabbed her and started kissing her, telling Dana that she had walked, then I grabbed Dana and just kissed her little cheeks, she smiled, and me, and then all shit hit the fan, at first Bella started crying. I thought it was because Dana had finally taken her first steps by herself, but that was not the case. Bella was pissed off at me and started screaming and shouting. Both Dana and I looked at her like she had just lost her damn mind. Before I could say anything, she left and went into the bedroom. I sat down on the couch with Dana. Bella was screaming at me, and at that time, I didn't know why. The next-door neighbor called to base police.

Bella was still screaming when I opened the door, and the police immediately rushed me out of the front door. The security officers checked both of us for bruises. None of them asked us both if we wanted to press charges against each other, and we both said no.

I told them she was under a lot of stress and really wanted to go back stateside. I was told to move into the barracks by my division chief, who arrived a few seconds after the security police did. I told him I wanted to leave the car with her and asked him for a ride to the barracks. I packed my work uniform and left with the chief for the barracks.

The next morning after I woke up, I had been assigned temporary duty on a ship leaving out of Yokosuka down near Tokyo. I was allowed to go back to our house and get more uniforms and say goodbye to Bella and Dana. I caught a MAC flight to an air base in southern Japan, and from there, a Navy van took me to the ship that was waiting for several other CTs and me. I was on that ship for forty-five days, mainly in the Sea of Okhotsk, which at the time, the then Soviet Union declared the majority of the Sea of Okhotsk as theirs. They sent ships and bomber aircraft to scare us out of there, but the commanding officer of the ship I was on had nerves of steel. We cruised thru that area as he owned it.

We pulled back into Yokosuka on the forty-fifth day, and I was on the next available MAC flight back to Misawa, which was not until the next day, when I got off the ship I got a room on base and put my civvies on, caught a cab off base went to the first little bar I could find. I had the cab stop at the first bar outside the gate. I just wanted to get slightly tipsy and go back to base. It didn't happen that way. When I got inside the bar, there was country and western music playing, and I really didn't care at that time what was playing on the jukebox.

I had ordered a Sapporo beer as they had run out of Budweiser. After the third beer and all the country and western music, I was thinking about Bella and Dana, but the music was all about how some guy's woman had left him and did him wrong. I couldn't take the music anymore, so I went to the jukebox, put in a couple of quarters and pushed the buttons for Michael Jackson's Pretty Young Thing and Billie Jean. I waited for another thirty minutes before the two songs I wanted to come on. When I first walked into the little bar, there were only six people in there, including the bar tender, but I was the only black person. Once Michael's songs came on, I felt better and just when I was getting in the groove, one of the white sailors started cussing and having a fit, his friends were trying to hold him back. I just looked over at him for a second and looked back at my beer which was almost empty, and when I got up to get another one, one of the white sailors said this nigger must be crazy. I turned around and yelled, whoever said it to stand up and be a man!

They all stood up and came at me. I walked as fast as I could to the biggest one of them and gave him an upper cut, then I pulled him down on top of me. He was so drunk he just fell right down on top of me and damn near covered me completely. His friends were kicking and punching him, they were all really drunk. I heard the bar tender screaming into the phone and that's when I made my move. I crawled out from under him and went under a table we had fallen onto. They were still kicking his ass as I crawled away and made it to the front door. I walked out the door and was halfway down the street when two shore patrol jeeps pulled up. I ducked into another bar, had a few more beers and caught a cab back to the base.

I went to the chow hall and had dinner, then back to my room and passed out. The next morning, I woke up kind of hung over, got showered and shaved, put on my uniform and went to the chow hall, had some breakfast, and then went to the quarter deck and waited for the van going back to the MAC terminal in Yokota Air Base. While I was at the MAC Terminal, I brought a little teddy bear for Dana I knew she would love it. When I got back to the Kadena Air Base terminal, I brought a dozen red roses for Bella. I hoped whatever made her lose her mind on me was over with, and everything would be okay.

I caught the base bus from the Terminal to the street our apartment was on and grabbed my stuff, and was let out on our corner. I walked up to our door and opened it. I immediately put my sea bag over my face so Dana would not know who I was looking up at me from her playpen. When I got inside, I threw my sea bag on the floor and said boo. I couldn't breathe for a few seconds. Everything in the front room was gone. There was nothing, no couch, no 60-gallon fish tank I brought a couple of months before I left for the trip, no coffee table or end tables with lamps on them, nothing and all the kitchen stuff was also gone. I quickly checked the rest of the apartment. The only thing left was two of my four speakers, the stereo and my clothes.

I walked back into the front room and put the teddy bear on top of my sea bag. I dropped the roses and just sat down on the floor. My mind was trying to process what in the hell was going on.

I sat on the floor for about an hour. All I could think of was where was Bella and Dana. I found a note on the counter in the kitchen that Bella had written. It said she was sorry, but she needed to go back home, her and Dana were just fine and that she left my stereo and some of the cooking utensils and also left me two hundred dollars in the bank, we had close to four thousand dollars, it also said when I get out of the navy I could come and visit Dana. I was pissed and not your normal pissed. I was mad at her and the whole world. *How could she take Dana from me?* With a whole two hundred dollars, I couldn't get a flight out of Japan to Hawaii, let alone ack to the USA. I was numb, and my brain had just frozen until someone knocked on the door and it was still wide open.

I was with one of my co-workers, his name was Randy. He explained that after the argument and because the base security police came, it was reported to some spousal abuse people on the air force side who contacted Bella and the rest is history. I was even more pissed after hearing that. I thought if I hadn't gone out to sea on that last trip, maybe I could have straightened things out, but deep in my heart. I knew she still would have left. She was just as stubborn as I was.

My main problem was not seeing my little Dana grow up because I knew how bad the job situation in the states was, and I wasn't going thru that again, losing a job a couple of months after I started it. Randy also told me that I needed to report to disbursing the first thing the next morning to set up stuff and also. I had two weeks to clean up the apartment and move back into the barracks, but that thought had not crossed my mind.

The realization that they were gone was finally sinking in, my brain was slowly thinking of the things that I needed to do, and getting a drink was the first thing I thought of. I told Randy I was going to the base club to get a drink and he went with me. I only had two beers and then I went to the barracks to check in and get a room since I had no bed to sleep on. Then I drove back to the apartment and put my stereo and speakers in the back of my Fair Lady-Z along with my clothes. I left the station wagon in the parking spot. I would figure out what to do with it later.

The next day I had to go to the disbursing office to see how much money would be coming out of my check each month. Dena was my daughter and I was going to make sure I took care of her. I was told to make a payment to Bella for three hundred each month. I was still an E-5 (second-class petty officer) and now living in the barracks, I had my own room, but I would lose the money for having my family with me and it was close to half of my monthly salary. That sucked badly!

I was a new (frocked E-6) which meant I wouldn't be getting paid for my new rank for another three months. Rap music was just getting to us in japan by the new younger sailors. Some of it was okay, but some of it I just didn't understand, a lot of hatred for the police and white people. I just didn't understand it, and one new black sailor had his hair cut with letters in it, that really screwed up some of the senior personnel. I was called in twice to see if I knew what was going on with that sailor. I had to be honest and tell them that I didn't have a clue about what was going on back in the world and about hairstyles. I had been gone too long. This was about the time young black males started wearing their trousers down low and could hardly walk. I didn't know anything about all of that. I was starting to feel old and I was only in my mid-twenties. I started hanging out with my crew, and it was fun, but I was back to drinking a lot and I mean a lot. We were finally off of the 1-1-32 schedule, so we had our eighty hours off, and it was something else in Japan.

A McDonald's opened up in Tokyo and I was one of the few people that had been to Tokyo, so Randy and I decided we would catch the Bullet train down to Tokyo from Misawa and find the McDonalds and get food for our crew. I told them it was about a four and a half hour ride of around three hundred and sixty-six miles each way, so we were going to get a hotel room for one night and bring the food back the next day.

When we got ready to go, three other guys decided to tag along with us. I guess they were all tired of the Misawa and Hachinohe area and wanted to see Tokyo. I still had the station wagon (I just couldn't sell it, yet every time I got in it, it reminded me of Bella and Dena). We all piled in it, and I drove to the train station in Hachinohe, we all got our tickets to Tokyo and we were off.

Not long after we boarded the train, I met this really pretty young Japanese woman she was dressed in business casual clothes, she asked if we could speak English as she needed the practice, and she paid for most of our beers on the way down, and she was nice, but no boobies, which to me was a total turn off. Randy was six foot three inches tall, and he was the tallest of all of us, and she asked a lot of questions about his height, then she wanted to know where each of us were from back in the United States. I don't know how much we helped her out, but she really smiled at me when we got off the train in Tokyo, and she kept staring at me like she was waiting for me to say something to her. I smiled at her and we both bowed our heads. Then I turned and we all walked toward the train exit.

I wanted to find the McDonalds before we got our hotel rooms, and the lady we talked with on the train told us to go to the Ginza district, and it would be in the large shopping center, she was absolutely correct. I should have kissed her, but holding a woman who had boobies that didn't show through her blouse freaked me out after leaving Okinawa. Now picture these five Americans, all over five feet nine inches tall, walking down the streets of this upscale district of Tokyo, Japan, in the early nineteen eighties. We all felt like giants compared to the Japanese people walking on the same streets as us, we got plenty of dirty looks from the guys, but lots of the ladies were checking us out.

We were all excited to be down there. The lady on the train explained that Tokyo was considered the northernmost part of Japan as the emperor had to be in the highest part of Japan, it just didn't make much sense to most of us, but then again, none of us had ever had an emperor either and we just didn't care. We walked past a car dealership and this guy came running out and trying to speak to us, but none of us spoke Japanese good enough to understand. My whole knowledge of the language was to ask for beer, some Japanese food and tak san push- push, which meant sex to the ladies that hung out with us military guys.

After a few minutes, this one Japanese guy walked by and explained that the man in front of the car dealership wanted to take pictures of us standing near his cars, we took about two or three pictures standing near three of his cars and that was it. He gave us the equivalent of about twenty dollars each in yen (the Japanese currency), which was like two hundred and twenty yen per dollar and it was close to four thousand two hundred yen each. It was enough to get about four or five beers each, so we were all happy to make money. After that, we found the McDonalds at the location the lady on the train gave us. It was weird trying to read signs as they were all in Japanese or Nihongo, which looks crazy to Americans like English must look crazy to the rest of the world.

We found the shopping center that had the McDonalds in it and then we walked around the area. I was looking for a hotel for us to stay in, we found a hotel not too far from the McDonalds that we could afford, and then we found a bar and that is where we stayed for a little while. I wanted to get some rest and chill before we hit the clubs, I think each of us had a little over two hundred dollars each in our pockets and partying was the first reason for being here. The burgers and fries were secondary.

We hit the little bar, had some drinks and tried to flirt with some of the ladies there but no luck for any of us. I guess they weren't interested in gigging (Gi-Gings). The next morning, we were all up early. We ate breakfast in the hotel and walked to the McDonalds. We brought over twenty cheeseburgers and just as many little boxes of fries, caught a cab to the train station and headed back to Misawa.

The train was probably half full when we got on it, so there was plenty of seats available. We all sat in two rows facing each other. We were having a good time on the ride back smoking and joking. We were about thirty minutes away from Misawa when this really small Japanese guy came over to us waving a little Japanese flag and he started shouting at us. None of us understood what the hell he was saying and he kept on for a few minutes until one of the conductors came over and got him away from us, when he turned around we all noticed that his face and neck on one side was badly burned and he had a hand where his elbow should have been, we couldn't stop staring at him. The conductor came back and bowed to us and in his broken English, explained the guy was a Hiroshima survivor.

None of us cared that it was a war that the Japanese had started, not us. I thought he was lucky to be alive. When we got off the train, he was sitting by the exit door and I don't know how but we all said Hiroshima and Nagasaki. We each whispered it in his good ear on our way out, he was pissed and we all laughed and exited the train. That was all we talked about in the cab on the way to the base. Now, remember we were on the train for over four hours and then a fifteen-minute cab ride back to base? Those burgers were cold as hell, and so were the fries. No one cared until we ate the burgers. Damn, nearly all of us spit the burgers out into the napkins we had.

The only thing real was the fries. The burgers were made of soybeans and it was disgusting as hell. When somebody realized it was soybean instead of beef, we all started laughing, I never went back to McDonalds in Tokyo again and I don't think anybody else did either. I still had a couple of days to have the apartment cleaned, and most of the racism, at least on the outside, was gone. We worked hard and partied just as hard as black and white. The day came when I finally officially moved out of the apartment. Even though I had been living in the barracks, I still had to go thru the checking out procedures, and after that was done. I moved the station wagon and parked it in the barracks parking lot. A couple of the family guys asked me about selling it. I just couldn't at that time. I still thought about Bella and Dena most of the time when I wasn't getting drunk and partying. Everything I mailed to Bella or sent to Dena, Bella would send to my mom's house. After a few months, I quit trying to write, but I still sent things to Dena, which were also sent to mom's house. Moms kept it all wrapped up and in the garage.

The partying for us could have been anywhere or anytime in the barracks, especially if it was snowing. Somebody would just go into a friend's room, crank up their music and it was on. Since I was one of the senior personnel living in the barracks, I was put in charge of it. My job was not to let the parties get too out of control and to make sure if someone had a watch near a party, the noise was kept to an acceptable level. All I can say is I did my best. At this time, we had lots of female sailors in the barracks. I had my own room, most E-5's and E-6's had their own rooms and it was wild. That is where most of the parties took place. It was too expensive to live off base unless you lived with a Japanese girlfriend and a lot of the senior 4-6's did that, they just requested to move off base and it was usually granted.

I am sure I mentioned that we partied and now I will tell you just how much. We partied in the barracks, base club, off base in the towns surrounding the base and also at Lake Tawada, which was a lake in the middle of a volcano and speaking of volcano's when I was in Japan. You could count on small tremors from earthquakes at least once a month, sometimes more than that.

But back to the partying, Lake Tawada was the favorite spot if the weather was good enough to drive up there to the lake. During the times that we partied at the lake, we had at least six of the Datsun Fairlady-Z's and about four or five of the little Mazda sports cars and we would usually race up the mountain to the lake if we saw the Japanese police we would slow down if we were on our way up the mountain, down the mountain it was a different story, at that time the police drove these little two-cylinder cars about the size of an old Volkswagen beetle and even going down a mountain they never stood a chance of catching us, plus going down the hill usually meant we were done partying and were usually pretty drunk. Not long after Bella and Dana left, a lot of the guys in my section at work decided we would have a bar-b-que at the lake. That was the last time I drove my Toyota station wagon, and it was packed with an old bar-b-que grill, most of the cases of beer and lots of food.

I had a lady in my Toyota that would soon become Randy's wife with me on the way up the mountain, she was new to our command, and I was explaining how everything worked and she kept asking questions about some of the guys. I was way too old for her. I think she was probably eighteen or nineteen, but she had a cute face and a pair of boobies on her that kept me looking at them. It was really awesome when we hit a bump on the road to watch those lovely twins move around in her blouse. God, I missed Bella.

This was one of those days that we actually had sunshine and heat outside, most of us were in jeans and t-shirts, but you can believe we all had some kind of cold weather gear in our cars. Most of the Fairlady-Z's were 2 seaters, and the Mazda's were also. Once we got to the lake, it was time to unload the cars. Some of us had brought steaks to grill, and most of the guys were happy with hamburgers and hot dogs. The park at the lake was set up with the same kind of picnic tables that we have here in the United States, so we had plenty of seating. Randy had just brought his Fairlady-Z. He had left before most of us to secure a spot for us. When I got there, his car was blocking two of the benches and he was sitting on a third one.

We had plenty of space, I pulled up and Randy moved his car. I parked where he had parked long enough for everybody to unload the stuff out of the back and then I parked very close to the benches, opened the back of the station wagon and turned on the music. The station wagon had six speakers in it and a cassette player. I left the key inside and everybody took turns playing their tapes. We arrived around nine that morning and planned to stay until it got too cold or whenever the booze ran out.

Everybody but me parked in the designated parking spots that were near the lake. I mean just feet away from the water and it was awesome to see all those sports cars parked there like that. We all took pictures of them with the water in the background. It was awesome. We partied our asses off. Some of our group were still drunk from the night before, so after about an hour, they were just as drunk, if not more, than the night before and it was all good, no fights or arguments, just good fun. About two hours into the picnic, one of the guys got into one of the Fairlady-z's and just took off. We all thought it was the guy that owned the car as he was really spinning the back tires, then the car took off and that's when we noticed it wasn't the owner of the car, it was Bugeye, we all stood and watched, we all knew that Bugeye didn't know how to drive.

We called him Bugeye because when he got excited, it looked as though his eyes were going to pop out of his head and that was the way he was looking now. Once he had taken off, he looked as scared as one of those animals being chased by a lion. He was in one of the Fairlady-z's that had an automatic transmission, so he didn't have to shift gears just put it in drive and that's just what he did. The cars were parked about ten or so feet away from the tables that we were all sitting at. I had my fold up chair and when Bugeye passed me the first time, I could swear he was saying help me. That's when I spat beer all over the new girl that was sitting next to Randy and both were facing me. Randy stood up and saw what was happening and he screamed for everybody to get out of Bugeye's way.

On the other side of where the cars were parked was a small little mound of sand probably about three feet high and on Bugeye's third pass around us, he hit the mound and went airborne. I'm not sure who screamed first. I know we were all screaming and hollering at Bugeye and each other, then we all took off running to get away from the car. Bugeye hit the mound at probably forty miles per hour and the car flew for a good five or ten feet. When it hit the ground, Bugeye lost control completely and T-boned one of the other Fairlady-Z's that was parked there that's when things got real interesting. Bugeye had passed out during his short flight, we managed to get him out of the car and we carried him to one of the tables and laid him on it.

The brother that owned the car Bugeye took for a joyride was pissed, but he held it together and said he had insurance, but the owner of the car that Bugeye hit wasn't so cool, we had to hold him back for about thirty minutes before he calmed down. Bugeye was so drunk he didn't have a scratch on him and he said he just passed out when he hit the mound, probably from fear and being so drunk. The guy that owned the car that was hit was pissed, it was his first car and it was an older Fairlady but in really good condition until this happened. This brother was probably eighteen or nineteen and he was known to be a hot head, now Bugeye was about five feet five inches and probably weighed one hundred and thirty pounds soaking wet with bricks in his pockets. This young guy was about my height and weight about five feet nine and one hundred and sixty pounds. I promised him that Bugeye would get him a newer Fairlady-Z and everything would be okay. I just needed him to chill and relax.

Needless to say, that was the end of the picnic for us that day. The new babe rode home with Randy. Both of the wrecked cars started and were able to get back down the mountain and to a repair shop which was not too far from the base, I had Bugeye in the station wagon with me on the way down the mountain and he slept until I woke him up at the barracks. Like I said, we partied a lot.

That night most of us were at the bowling alley partying, and every time somebody mentioned the lake, we all busted up laughing, even the guy that owned the car Bugeye took. We all had tears in our eyes from laughing. Imagine a bunch of drunks chasing a drunk in a car, then running from the same car. I knew we had to keep an eye on Bugeye. He didn't have the little man syndrome. He was just crazy as hell, but one of the best people I knew at his job and he had a really slick-looking little mustache, but again when he was drinking, and was insane or just in the wrong place at the wrong time. There was another new black female at the command. I think she was one of the administrative CTA's and she had just made E-4. We were all in somebody's room. I can't remember who's the room it was, but we were partying like usual. It was mainly just the guys. I think Randy and his girl were there. The new girl came into the room. I'm pretty sure she was good and drunk because she didn't say hello or anything. She just looked at all the guys and said somebody is going back to my room right now because she hadn't had a man in two months and somebody was going to give it to her really good.

Now, this new girl was probably six feet tall and when I looked at her like the rest of the guys, I looked down and her feet were twice the size of mine. I quietly grabbed my beer and a few more out of the refrigerator and made my way past her and out the door. Randy and his girl were already outside, then the rest of the guys charged the door trying to get out all at once and they all made it except poor little Bugeye. We all stood down the hallway a bit just to see what was happening, then Randy and I crept up to the door and looked inside. She was still standing there and Bugeye didn't even know she was there. He had his back to her and was pouring himself some more Suntory Whiskey. The girl was skinny as hell. She just looked at Bugeye and said you'll do, she grabbed him by the back of his shirt and turned toward the door. I ran for my life.

The next morning, we didn't see Bugeye at Breakfast and we started asking around if anyone had seen him and no one had. At lunchtime, he showed up in the chow hall. He looked like he had been run over by a train. Randy, his girlfriend, and I were sitting at a table when we saw him slowly walk to the chow line. He got a sandwich and some fries and sat down next to us. We all put our heads down. I could hear Randy trying not to laugh, I had tears in my eyes and Randy's girl got up, saying she had to use the head.

I looked at Bugeye. He didn't have any marks on his face, but being as dark skinned as he was, you could really see his arms were bruised. I started to say something, but Bugeye cut me off and just said one thing. He asked why did we let her do that to him? Randy busted up laughing and I almost choked on my cheeseburger. Bugeye looked like he had tears in his eyes. I had to leave the table and go outside. Randy and his girl were not too far behind me.

Randy said he told Bugeye to meet us at the bowling alley once he got his self-straightened out. We all busted up laughing, then Randy's girl said poor little Bugeye and we busted up again. Bugeye and showed up at the bowling alley later that night. He looked scared and timid, we tried not to laugh, and he screamed, "It's not funny," then he busted up laughing, but it was a nervous laugh. I was volunteered by the gang to talk to her. I explained she had actually had sex with someone that didn't want to have sex with her and that she had forced herself on him, it took a second, but she finally got it. She explained that when she gets drunk, she wants sex. I told her that if she just chilled out, she could have sex here in this part of Japan and if she couldn't find a sailor that there are plenty of lonely air force guys, she smiled and said thanks. I let Bugeye know he was in the clear. He couldn't thank me enough. A couple more months went by and I still had no reply from Bella. I had written her a lot of letters trying to get her back, but most were sent to the return address and I always put my mom's address on every letter I sent. The realization that she wasn't coming back finally set in. I sat in my room one night and just got wasted. I stayed locked up in there the whole day. The next morning I went to chow and Randy said we needed to talk. I knew what it was about and I let him know that I knew I had to get over it. He just put his hand on my shoulder and said he knew it was a hard thing to do, then I tried to smile.

I asked if his girl still wanted to buy the Toyota and he said she was just waiting for me to let her know when I wanted to sell it. I took all of Dana's baby stuff out of the Toyota and gave it to one of the guys whose wife had just had a baby girl. He thanked me and smiled. I sold the Toyota to Randy's girl for fifteen hundred dollars and I put in for a couple of weeks off and requested to take a MAC Flight to South Korea at Osan Air Force Base and just hang out. I wanted to get some new clothes tailor made and I had heard that was the best place to get it done. I had been saving my GQ and Playboy magazines, that's where you could find the latest styles back in the world and I planned on being totally in style when I got back. I was close to one year left in Japan and was getting ready to be the new First-Class Petty Officer (E-6) and the first out of our gang. I had been there before in Osan but strictly for work purposes and had hung out in one of the bars and met some pretty cool people that were South Koreans. One was mama san, she owned the hotel I stayed at. She was something else. She owned a hotel, changed money with a better rate than the banks, knew the clubs to go to and I'm pretty sure she was a madam.

While I was waiting to take my leave days, I got hooked on the little gas engine remote control cars, thanks to Randy, that took my mind off of Bella and Dana. I brought one for less than one hundred dollars with remote and everything. Those little cars would do almost if not forty miles per hour and got to speed real fast, Randy and I would drive to the port in Hachinohe, which was mainly for fishing boats and vessels of that size. The port had a stretch of flat cement that was about a quarter of a mile and that's where we went running and race the cars, my car was made for sand and rocky roads, but Randy's was a flat out street racer. We had fun with them and let other guys know about the cars and Hachinohe the last day before I was to catch the MAC flight to Osan. There must have been about ten of us with the remote control cars heading up to Hachinohe, but we all forgot the most important thing, the frequencies the remotes used, mine and about six others, could not be changed. Once we got there, everybody test started their cars by just getting the engine to start when you wanted to shut it off until you were ready to race.

We were probably about three hundred feet from the end of the pier and away from the boats. Once we all had our cars out and were ready, Randy had the first race with a guy who had the exact same car as I had, mine was blue, and he was red. Randy's car beat that red car with no problem. I wanted to tell him that his car had no chance, but the guy had a big mouth and liked to brag a lot, so I let him lose twenty dollars on his bet. Then it was my turn with another car like mine. It was yellow with cool black stripes.

I set my car down and turned to get my remote, the other guy started his car, and my car took off doing forty miles per hour straight off the pier, it was nothing I could do. The other guy turned off his remote, but it wasn't his remote. It was the guy that Randy had just beaten. He had left his remote on and put it in his trunk. Something in his trunk pushed the lever forward when he threw it in the trunk, so my car being on the same frequency, just said goodbye to me. I stood there with my mouth wide open watching one hundred dollars doing forty miles per hour until it hit the end of the pier and disappeared into the ocean. I grabbed a beer and started drinking. Everybody else was trying not to laugh, then I busted up laughing and they all also did. We later found the remote in the guy's trunk jammed in a way that made my car just haul ass. He apologized and gave me the money for my car. I think he was afraid I was going to kill him. I just kept laughing. I needed to get out of Japan for a while, at least this part of Japan.

That night I packed for my trip to Osan, South Korea, which was the next morning, and all I packed for one week was two pairs of Levi's, a couple of Polo shirts and some underwear and my old tennis shoes, a tooth brush, and deodorant. All I had to do the next morning was get my butt to the MAC terminal on the base and get out of Japan. I had come to realize that Bella and I were finished. It was a hard thing to get over losing my wife and my baby girl, but there was nothing I could do about it, so I decided to just let it go and get on with my life. The day Bella and Dana left was the day that child support was put through via our disbursing office. The amount was considered for an E-5, but I didn't want my daughter to want anything. I didn't even know the money was coming out of my paycheck until I got paid and it was painful.

That next morning I was up, showered, shaved and dressed, ready for my getaway. I called the quarterdeck to check out on leave, got into my Z and drove it to the MAC terminal. I waited for a little over an hour, and then the flight was there and I was off. I had a suitcase and not my sea bag as usual when I got on the plane, it had one giant engine inside it, and it was completely strapped down. I sat as far away from it as I could, put my suitcase next to me and tried to relax for the flight.

About two hours later, we landed at Osan Air Force Base. Once I got off the plane, I caught the base bus to the front gate and from there, I caught a taxi to Mama San's hotel, it took about ten minutes, and when I walked into the little lobby, Mana San came from behind the counter and gave me a big hug. She remembered me from the late nineteen seventies. I hugged her back and then she gave me the room I had the last time I was there, in the corner near the back of the hotel right next to the stairwell on the second floor. I could see from the hotel room window two different streets and the partying on each and quick emergency access in case I needed to get out fast.

After I unpacked my clothes, I went back downstairs and asked Mama San where and who were the best and most affordable tailors I needed new clothes. She looked me up and down and said your right, she wrote something down on a piece of paper in Korean and told me to hand it to the cab driver outside (her nephew), and he would get me to the right places, unlike the Philippines most of the South Korean tailors were really good and used the material you requested back then, no cheap thread that would fall apart after the first or second time at the cleaners.

So I got into the cab and we went about five blocks. I handed the driver enough Won (North Korean currency) and told him to keep the change. I went into the little shop armed with my newest and most current edition of men's magazines from the west coast of the world. I had bent the pages of the suits and the TUX that I wanted to be made, I showed them to the owner and in really good English, he asked me what color and how much time did he have to get everything done. Each of the suits were different in design, and I let him know other than the tuxedo, I wanted all the trousers to have a one-inch cuff, the colors for the double breasted suit with the long coat were to be black, and the normal suit was grey and the last suit that was double breasted and burgundy.

I asked how much and he said three hundred and eighty dollars for everything. I told him that was too much. He said I would have a vest for all suits, suspenders, and waist band for the tuxedo. I told him I would pay four hundred dollars for all of that plus a full length burgundy leather coat that would unzip a little more than halfway to shorten it to a leather dinner jacket. He thought about it and said, "Okay," then he showed me the different material that was available. He had wool, cotton, leather, and all kinds. I went with what was in the magazine. I liked the wool for both the tuxedo and the black double breasted suit. My burgundy suit was made of light silk. The other two suits were cotton for the hotter weather places I wanted to go to.

All the suits had the tailor's label inside along with my name right above the left inside pocket, and the same for all the vests. I gave the tailor fifty dollars to start. He took my measurements, wrote everything down in Korean on a sales slip, handed it to me and said four days. As I was walking out the door, the tailor told me to stay on this side of the street and go five shops down and just look in the window. I nodded and walked out and went where the tailor told me to go. It was a shop that made shoes. I had a pair made for each of my suits as close to the same color as I could. I would find some shiny dress shoes in the catalogs from the world for the tuxedo. I did not want leather or gator on my shoes, the shop owner showed me eel skin and that's why I went with, a burgundy, black and grey the burgundy and grey shoes had the front part of the shoe that covers your toes colored black, the rest of the shoe was the two colors that I wanted, I paid I think equivalent of twenty dollars per pair of shoes.

The tailor knew that when I wore the shoes, they would be with either a suit or the trousers, so he suggested socks the same color, two pairs for each set of shoes, one pair real thick and the other pair of socks really thin. I got those for free because I ordered three pairs of shoes. They would also be done in four days. He measured my feet in three different places, from the back of my heel to the tip of my big toe, across the ball of the foot and around the ankle. I had never had a pair of shoes made, then he had me put each foot on a piece of cardboard and he used a marker to trace my foot on the cardboard. I would pay him after we made sure the shoes actually fit and I was happy with that.

After I was done ordering new clothes. I went to one of the local bars and had a couple of beers, left and went back to my hotel room. I had a bottle of Jack Daniels in my luggage, and I planned on drinking it while I took a really long bath and that is just what I did. After I was done with the bath, I decided to have a little more of the whiskey and chill out in the room.

I was in no rush to go out that night. If I did go out at all. I must have passed out because around eleven PM, I was awakened by a slight knock on the door. I got up, put a towel around me and answered the door. It was a pretty little Korean lady and she wanted to know if I needed company for the night. I smiled at her and told her I thought she was beautiful, she smiled and then I told her not tonight. She looked at me smiling and left. I laid back down and just when I was starting to get back to sleep, there was another knock on the door again. I got up and put the towel around me and answered the door, this time there was a gorgeous looking lady with one hell of a body she only had a full length coat on and she smiled at me and opened her coat, she had nothing on under it. She said that a girl had come to my room, but she knew that I needed a real woman. I smiled at her and thanked her but declined to have company tonight.

She smiled back, kissed me on my cheek and then left. I was hoping I could finally get some sleep as I turned and was almost in bed again, but there was another knock on the door. I was getting pissed and when I opened the door, it was a young teenage boy. I slammed the door shut, got dressed and went downstairs to find Mama San. She was not there, but I talked to the lady behind the counter and she said Mama San told them to take good care of me. I calmed down and I told the lady I just wanted to sleep tonight. She said she didn't think I would have any trouble finding a woman. I bent over the counter and kissed her on her cheek and said, "Thank you." I just wanted to get some rest, then I went back upstairs and got back into bed and passed out.

There were no more knocks on the door. I remember thinking about what a country was before I fell back to sleep. I woke up late, around ten AM or so, and I was starving. I did the three S's and got dressed and went downstairs to ask where was a good place to get something to eat. As in the Philippines, back in those days, you needed to keep your money with you and stay as alert as you could at all times. That was normal for me coming from Los Angeles. I had gotten used to noticing everything in my surroundings and everything looked the same as it was the day before, except that really good-looking lady that knocked on my door the second time was sitting next to Mama San. I smiled at her, and Mama San said, "You don't like ladies and you don't like boys? What do you like?" I told her, "I loved the ladies and if I wasn't so tired last night, I would have had both of the ladies but not the boy," she smiled and said something in Korean to the lady sitting next to her. She smiled at me and said if I was older, she would do me. We all laughed. Then I asked her where could I go to get something to eat and she told me to get in the cab outside. I did and she came out and said something in Korean to the driver he nodded at her and we were off, we stopped at a little restaurant, I paid the cab driver. I could have easily walked to the place it was only two blocks away. I paid the cab driver and went in. There was an older couple sitting under the fan and two really fine ladies behind the counter. I was the only customer there. At first, I thought the place was closed, then the old couple got up and went into the kitchen and one of the ladies came from behind the counter and asked me to follow her to my table, I did.

She was very nice looking, with just the right amount of lipstick and really nice tits on her. From behind, she wasn't bad looking either, with long straight black hair and a very nice little round ass. Just as I sat down, my stomach started talking to me with loud gurgling sounds, the lady smiled at me, and I smiled back. She handed me a menu that was in Korean. I smiled at her and said, "I don't speak or read Korean," she put her hand over her mouth and said, "Sorry," then she read some of the menus to me. I stopped her and asked for a hamburger, no dog meat and shrimp with rice. She looked at me and said no dog, only beef. I smiled at her again, hoping I would be eating beef.

The burger was good and so was the rice and shrimp. I told myself I would be eating here again. After I finished eating, I walked to the counter to pay for my meal and I also asked what clubs did she go to. She smiled and gave me the name of a club, I asked her to write it down for me and she did in Korean. I thanked her and told her to let the chef know the food was excellent and walked out. The cab was still there waiting for me.

I got in and told him to take me to the outdoor market. We were there in five minutes. I got out and paid the driver and walked into the market. There was everything from food to wooden furniture. I was in there for hours just looking, I saw two things that I would buy the day before I would have to leave and they were small grandfather clocks about three feet tall they looked just like the five and six foot ones, and the price was less than one hundred dollars for both. They had some really cool sweat suits, I also saw what was the latest things back in the states the Cabbage Patch Dolls, they were five dollars each. I brought four of them and they had the sneakers that people were paying over fifty dollars for back in the world for five dollars. I would get myself some of those also. I thought even if I partied my ass off, I would still have a good amount of money left for the second part of this trip. I think I was in the outdoor market for a good three or four hours. There was so much stuff to see and look at, I had to stay away from one corner and that was because they were cooking kimchi and it was a warm day with no breezes. The smell was something I would never forget, just as bad if not worse than chitlins.

When I walked out, I saw the same cab driver I had since I checked into the hotel and walked over to his cab and got in. I went back to the hotel with the small stuff I had brought. I needed to change some dollars for the South Korean currency which was called Won, I gave Mama San one hundred dollars to exchange for the Won. The amount of money she handed me after the exchange made me feel like I had a lot more than what I should have had, but it was a good exchange. I paid her for a couple of Budweiser's and went up to my room. I watched a couple of old American movies that were in Korean for a while and then took a good long nap. I wanted to be ready to party that night. After I woke up, it was shower time and fed the belly time. After that, I hit one of the clubs and it was jamming. I somehow hooked up with this one lady with long black hair and a nice little body.

We danced for quite a while, after the dance she started with the buy me a drink thing and I did. I brought her a couple of drinks. But I didn't really care too much for her and got up and danced with another lady who I stuck with for the rest of the night. I took the second lady back to my hotel and just as we were about to go up the stairs, the first girl I danced with came into the lobby and started pulling the other one's hair and screaming at her. I didn't touch either of them and I didn't have to because Mama San came into the lobby and said something to both of them. The second lady stayed with me the other one started crying and trying to speak with Mama San, but she was ignored.

Mama San pointed to the door and the first girl left in a hurry. Mama San told me not to worry she won't be back. I smiled at Mama San and went up to my room with the second girl. The one I had in my room was my age, mid-twenties, very nice and easy to get along with. I shut the door and we just talked for hours. She had a daughter and had her own place not far from the hotel and asked if I wanted I could stay there for the rest of my stay in South Korea. When we woke up the next morning and got dressed, I decided to move my stuff into her place and we had a good time. We went to a few clubs and hung out.

On the day my suits were done, I went back to the tailor shop and tried them all on. They all fit perfectly. Along with the suits I got three suite bags. One was just for the tuxedo and the other three suits went into the remaining two bags after I paid for them. I went to the place where my shoes were made and they were awesome, the burgundy shoes were the same color as the suit and the grey ones the color was so close to the suit. I was pleased with all the clothes after I paid for everything, I took them all to my girl's house, then she and I went to the outdoor market and I brought three of the small grandfather clocks and the cabbage patch dolls for my little Dana, I even brought my new girlfriend's daughter a doll, once I had everything I wanted in one place I got it all together and my girl and I left for the post office on the base. Once we were on the base, I took the clocks and toys to the post office and mailed them to my mother's house back in the world. I kept my suits and shoes with me.

I took my girl to lunch on base and we talked for a while, then we got back into the cab and headed for the MAC terminal. We kissed again and I lugged all my clothes inside and headed back to Misawa, Japan. The flight back to Misawa Air Base was less than two hours and non-eventful, there were only four of us on the flight, but the c-130 had another giant engine in it. I kept my eyes on it the whole way back to the base. I kept thinking if this thing were to shift or break the cables holding it and it came my way, there was nothing I could do to stop it. My only chance would be to try and get out of its way.

I had to think of something else, so of course, I was thinking of Bella and Dana. I was thinking about this trip and how it was supposed to be with them in Osan, Korea. I was thinking of all the things they would have seen and done, the clothes we could have gotten for them. Once back at Misawa, I put everything in the back of my Z and drove back to the barracks. Walking up the stairs to the second floor of the barracks seemed kind of strange. It was quiet in the barracks, scary quiet.

There was no music playing. No doors opened with people having fun. It was like no one was around. I walked into my room and hung up my suits, grabbed all the dirty clothes and headed downstairs to the laundry room. I wanted to get the washing out of the way. I still did not see anyone and I had to walk thru the lounge. It was like a ghost town in the barracks. It just didn't feel right nothing did. I thought it was just me, then I ran into Sarah.

I was still a frocked E-6 which meant I had all the responsibilities of an E-6, just not the pay or the actual rank yet. I still had around a month left before I was officially an E-6. Randy came over to see if I needed any help and as soon as he saw the apartment, he said, "Oh, I see you're done." I told him I needed to clean the carpets, and he said, "No, you don't." Then he suggested we go off base and tie one on, to help me get over the fact that my family was gone and I said, "Let's go." It must have been after ten PM when we got to the first little bar, not many people in there so we ordered the local Japanese beer Sapporo one each, now Randy was still a basketball player and really didn't drink much, so after the fourth beer, he was toasted, but he kept drinking alongside me, and I was getting really hammered, about that time about eight Japanese Self Defense Forces guys walked in. Randy and I paid no attention to them at all, I figured we would order another beer and head back to the base.

The new guys in the bar were already drunk and getting rowdier by the minute, then I heard one of them yelling at Randy and me. I glanced over at them and then turned back to the bar. Randy had quit talking about an hour ago, he was just trying to stay conscious and he looked funny as hell, swaying on the bar stool. I kept waiting for him to fall so I could grab him and get to the car. We had taken my Z that night and it was parked about a half of a block away.

Three of the Japanese guys started pointing at us, I looked over at them and they were making gestures like they wanted to arm wrestle with us. I shook my head no and started to laugh, then one of them started screaming at us, again I just glanced at them. I finished my beer and got Randy to his feet and was heading towards the door, which I could tell was the only way out. I was trying to hold a guy that was over six feet tall and open the door. Just as I got him out of the door, I handed him my keys and told him to go and get my car, that's when one of the Japanese guys kicked me right above my ankle. It hurt like hell. I pushed Randy out the door and another Japanese got in front of the door like he was going after Randy. I quickly pushed Randy through the door and screamed at him to go and get my Z, he stumbled out and then one of the Japanese guys pushed the door closed and kicked me in the leg.

The other two got side by side, Randy was out the door, I was hoping he was getting my car and driving it to the front door, then one of the guys put his head down and started swinging his arms in a down and up kind of motion. I didn't know what he was trying to do, but I was glad he was doing it. I grabbed his head and introduced his face to my knee and I jammed my knee into his nose. The other two started doing some kind of Bruce Lee karate stances. I backed up a little and swung at one of the other two and actually hit him in the jaw.

I ran right up to the third guy and grabbed him by the nape of his neck and his belt loop on his jeans from behind. There was a thick rug over what I thought was a window. I didn't figure out that there was no window until the third time I tried to toss his ass through it. I remember thinking I must be losing it, or this is one thick piece of glass. Neither of the first two guys got up again and the third one just lay there moaning and bleeding. I went to the window and pulled the curtain back and it was a solid brick wall. I was now tired as hell and I hoped the other part of their group didn't want to have any issues with me. I stumbled out of the door and went looking for my car, I couldn't find it.

Randy had driven his drunk ass back to base. I sat down, thinking I would just need a few minutes rest and then I would walk or catch a taxi back to base. That was when the police showed up. I stood up and put my hands out, waiting for them to put on the handcuffs. They just ran inside past me. One of the Japanese policemen came over to me and in broken English, he asked me what happened. I tried to explain the guys wanted to arm wrestle and fight. He laughed and said well, they did not win either. He asked me to get into his car and told me that I would be taken to the Misawa City Police Station, where they would call the base and have someone come and get me. I said, "Thanks." Once we arrived at the station, my adrenalin rush was gone. I was tired and totally drunk. All I wanted was to get back to my room in the barracks.

The command master chief showed up about twenty minutes later, and just before he showed up, I had refused to sign any documents that the Japanese police tried to get me to sign (since most of us in the military cannot read or write in the Japanese language you just don't want to sign any documents that you cannot understand) just as the master chief finished signing whatever documents he needed to get me out of there. I asked him if I was in any trouble as all I did was try to defend myself, he looked at me seriously and said, "I don't know. We have a new commanding officer and he is trying to prove something," I think I started crying thinking about Dana and Bella. I finally let it all out. I remember asking the master chief. It was a big trouble and he said I doubt it. The police are not charging you with any crime, I said cool, I was given a breath test for alcohol and I was way over the limit.

Two weeks later, I had my captains mast (instead of getting a court martial and possibly kicked out of the navy. I opted for captain's mast where just the captain passed sentence on me. The military back during the days I was in, you were guilty usually until proven innocent. I was charged with drunk and disorderly, public brawling, and damage to private property (I was charged with breaking a window – there was no window, just a curtain.) There were three other people going to captain's mast before I had my turn.

I was the only black sailor having mast that day. The guy had drunk and disorderly charges and resisting arrest. He was let go with a stern warning from the captain. The next two guys were drunk and disorderly in the break room and broke windows with the pool balls from the pool table, trying to fight other sailors in the break room, they also got a stern warning and that was all. All three of them were dismissed and let go. I, on the other hand, was not going to be so lucky.

When my turn came, I marched in front of the captain, who was standing behind a podium with the command emblem on it and he read all the charges. I was not allowed to speak until he asked me what I had to say about the charges. Now there was no mention of my getting my shipmate out of the club, no mention of the Japanese soldiers being drunk and starting the fight and the fact that there were no windows in the bar, and that the Japanese police did not press any charges against me. When he asked if I was guilty I said, "Yes sir, I was drunk, I did end up fighting the soldiers by myself, but there were no windows in the bar," he looked at me for a minute and then said "I will not tolerate my people being drunk and disorderly in public and destroying private property, you are the dinosaurs and will not continue to behave in that manner."

Then the master chief looked at me and nodded, that was my que to ask the captain to please be lenient with me and I did. He looked at me again and pronounced my sentence. I would be reduced in rank to E-4, sixty days restriction to the barracks (I still had to go to work, but my off time was spent in a room for people on restriction). I would, after that, be sent to alcohol rehab near Tokyo for forty-five days. I would pay for the damages to the bar and any medical for the three Japanese soldiers. You could hear everybody gasping in the background. I heard someone quietly say this is bullshit. I know the captain heard it also, then he told me I was dismissed with sentencing to start immediately. I saluted, did an about face and headed for the barracks.

As I was walking out of the admin office, the senior marine corps officer told me he would have made me a gunnery Sargent (E-7) instead of a frock (E-6), I tried to smile, but I was mad as hell. I kept thinking I should have taken the court martial. By the time I got back to the barracks, everyone already knew the outcome of my captains mast, and all of the black sailors were beyond pissed off I mean very mad, a couple later wrote the main judge advocate general's office citing racism, our captain did the same thing to other black sailors during the next five months.

I did my forty-five days in the restricted barracks, I was allowed to go to work and the chow hall. Those were the only two places that I could go unless I got sick or injured, then I was allowed to go to sickbay. During those days, I met this beautiful little English lady, nicknamed Gabby. She would sneak into the barracks and be with me. She was in the middle of a divorce from some air force guy and living with friends until the divorce was finalized, then she was going back home to England. Needless to say, her and I hit it off perfectly. The first twenty days I was in the restricted barracks, there was no one there to sign in and or out during my restriction. There was a log book that I had to sign in and out of. Since I was the person that was responsible for the log book and in charge of the barracks (I guess no one thought about that), I just signed myself in and out.

I would call Gabby as I was getting out of the showers, which was at the end of the hallway on the third floor and the phone was right next to the door. I would tell her to come over and she would. I would sneak her into my room, and we would have fun for a couple of hours, and then I would sneak her out of the barracks. If anyone ever saw us, they never reported it. That went on until I had to leave the last few days of January nineteen to eighty-six, I had been released from restriction for two days and headed for the Alcohol and Drug Abuse Center (Naval Hospital) in Yokosuka, Japan, for forty-five days of treatment. Those two days I was off I spent in my room in the barracks with Gabby, she worked in the officer's galley as a chef, and they loved her cooking, but her divorce was final and she was headed back to England to stay with her mother for a while until she found a job and got her own place. We both promised each other that we would stay in touch.

I packed my sea bag with what I was instructed on one dress blue uniform, which I had to get back from the base cleaners as I had to have my E-6 rank patches removed from all my uniforms and replaced with E-4 patches. I took three work uniforms. I also had my burgundy suit, with my shoes that matched the suit, along with my full-length leather coat. Japan in the winter is cold and I planned on being warm while I was there. I checked out of the barracks with orders to US Naval Hospital Yokosuka, Japan and drove my Z to the MAC terminal where I had a ticket for a flight to Yokosuka. The flight was around two hours on a medical aircraft, nothing like the C-130's I was used to getting on at MAC terminals. There were only three of us as passengers, a lady going to the same part of the hospital as I was, but she was a dependent and another dependent that was laying on a stretcher that was attached to the wall inside the plane. There would have been room for ten of us, but with the stretcher pulled down from the bulkhead of the plane, that took up four seats.

There was also a nurse there for the lady in the stretcher. The poor woman had stomach problems and I had to feel sorry for her, she hadn't used the toilet in quite a few days as we all found out during the hour and a half flight. She had gas problems really bad, and again I felt sorry for her. She kept apologizing to the rest of us and to the nurse also. I had a cheap Walkman cassette player and I put the earphones on and tried not to think about her, which was hard as hell to do because she was moaning and crying the whole trip down to Yokosuka.

Once we reached the Yokosuka Navy Base, an ambulance took the lady with the stomach problems to the main part of the hospital. The other lady and I went to an entirely different part of the hospital. It was somewhere near the back of the hospital and was its own separate entity. We checked in and were taken to the barracks, one side of which was for the females and the other for males. This place dealt with all forms of addiction, drugs, food and alcohol. The lady that was on the plane ride down with me became a friend of mine while we were at the facility.

Once we were both checked in, we had the little plastic wristbands put on us that said navy hospital. We were taken to another part of the facility where navy corpsmen went through our bags to make sure we had no drugs or alcohol, then we were taken to our barracks. I was told where my rack was along with my locker, which was just tall enough to put my suit in. I had to unzip my leather coat and I rolled up the bottom half of it so it fits in the bottom with my shoes. Then, I hung up my dress blues.

After that, I was told where to go for chow and showed around the part of the facility that we were allowed in. I was told I would be given this pill every morning called Antabuse, which would cause me to puke my guts out if I had a sip of alcohol. I had made my division chief a promise that as long as I was in Japan, I would not drink alcohol again unless I was leaving. I was given two or three folders with information about alcoholism and the steps. It was just like what you see on tv about people going to rehab centers. We were placed on the honor system for everything. We were told we were restricted to base for the first two weeks until we were evaluated (yeah, right). The weather was a little warmer than in Misawa. During the daytime, you could probably get away with wearing a light jacket if you were going to be outside for a little while. There were clubs and places to eat everywhere I noticed on the drive from the base to the hospital. I was going to make the best of my time here.

On the first day we met the two guys that were in charge of us, one of them had just made E-4, the other was an E-6 and he was leaving soon, and an E-4 was basically in charge of us. We had a guest come in and share their stories about being a recovering drunk. Some were really sad, one day, a retired black navy chief was a guest speaker. He had made chief two times before he retired and married his Japanese wife. He had been in the navy for twenty years before he retired. His story was very colorful and full of the drunk stories most of us shared.

I was talking to one of the guys in the group before ours in the barracks and he told me to try and be as sincere as possible and you will get out of here. There were no second chances. If you failed the courses, you could be kicked out of the navy. I got real sincere, especially when I had to give my final story and write a list of all the people that I needed to apologize to for my behavior as an alcoholic. My list must have been three pages long (most of the names and places I made up hell all my friends drank just as much as I did if not more.) the guy in charge once told me that either I was the most sincere person he had ever met or that I should have been an actor instead of a sailor.

After my third day there, the same guy that told me how to get through the courses asked me what I was doing that evening. I told him I was just going to chill in the barracks. He shook his head and said that I would probably be the only one in the barracks until after midnight. I looked at him like he was crazy, then he explained about the honor system and that everybody left after the instructors did. I was amazed. He said come on, I'll show you around, and I put on a pair of jeans, tennis shoes, and my leather jacket and was ready, then he pointed to my wristband. I said, "What," he came over and used a pair of tiny plyers he had on his Swiss pocket knife and just barely clipped the little button on the top of the clip that held the wristband on. Then he explained that all I needed was a little piece of gum in the morning to put it back on and it would hold. I was amazed.

We left the base, both showing our ID cards and we were in Yokosuka. He said he never swallowed the Antabuse pills but hid them under his tongue. Then he would spit it out in the trash can next to the door of the barracks. I asked him if he still drank, and he said just enough to get by. I told him I was done drinking until I got out of Japan, and he laughed and roger that. We went to a place out in town and got burgers and fries. Then he left to hit his favorite bar. I just walked around for about an hour, then I saw a club with rabbit ears on it. I thought it was the Playboy Club, but it wasn't after that I caught a cab back to base. I wanted to remember where that club was as I planned on going there as soon as I got paid until it got too late. Then I caught a cab back to base and went back to the base and just chilled the rest of the evening. That's when the lady that was on the plane with me came into the lounge area and we started talking. Her husband made her come to the facility, or he would have divorced her, I told her my story and we both shook our heads and then laughed. She hung out with me just talking until around eleven PM, and she went back to her barracks and I went and hit the rack.

I'll say her name was Sharon, the lady that flew down here from Misawa with me. She was about five feet two inches tall and had a decent body. She was in her early thirties and nice to talk to. We hung out when we could. I never told her about getting off base. I didn't want her to start drinking again. She had said she wanted to stop to keep her marriage and I understood. Every day was the same, getting up doing the three S's, taking the Antabuse pill, going to the classes, then sharing new parts of our life story. I was getting scared I would run out of things to say. One day I went over my trauma about my dog dying after the police ran over her with his motorcycle and he only stopped for a second and then took off. Things like that kept me going through the course.

Two weeks later, I got paid, it wasn't much as I was paying over three hundred and fifty dollars for Dena and I had to pay a hundred dollars a month until I had paid off the Japanese soldier's medical bill. I probably had close to two hundred dollars in my pocket for the next two weeks. Good thing was that I quit drinking. That night I put on my three-piece suit and my burgundy leather overcoat and headed out. I had a small afro, not my usual high and tight military cut and I hit that bunny club. I got there around nine o'clock and was ready to party. I walked up to the bar and ordered a rum and coke. I canceled that real quick and ordered sparkling water and just sat back at the bar and checked out everything.

It was full of mostly older Japanese guys. The ladies were dressed just like the Playboy bunny girls with the little outfits on and bunny ear headgear. One really stood out. I think it was her long hair that kept me checking her out, along with the fact that she actually filled out the top part of her outfit, which wasn't saying too much as she was like the rest of the ladies, just a little more in her chest area than the rest.

During this time, I had read an article in one of the magazines in the lounge area about how much the Japanese ladies spent on makeup and I couldn't believe it was over two hundred dollars a month. The girl I was checking out was named Kimiko. She and I were going to be good friends. I could tell by the way she was smiling at me.

I sat at one of the tables, which meant I would have to pay for my drink and the girl that sat at my table with a drink. I pointed at her and gestured for her to come over. She smiled and came right over. I ordered myself another glass of Perrier water which was over three dollars a glass back then. She ordered a rum and coke, which was right at ten dollars in yet. I winced a little at a price, but I figured she would be worth it. She sipped her drink slowly as we talked. I had planned on buying her two drinks and then heading back to base and letting my mind absorb how much I had spent on her. While we were talking, she asked me where I was from and when I said Los Angeles, she really smiled. I found out her father was a businessman and she was going to their version of a collage. She also had her own apartment in Yokohama, which was a little over a thirty-minute drive from this club.

Her father lived in Tokyo and he didn't know she worked at the club. She had her own car and everything. After we talked for a couple of hours and she finished her second drink I got up to leave, she gave me her phone number and I promised I would see her at the club again on that upcoming Friday. Her English was really good and it told her that she smiled at me and had a perfect smile.

I got up and left, but before I did, I kissed her on her cheek, the navy still allowed us to have full beards back then, and I just had the mustache and goatee, and I guess my goatee tickled her, and she giggled and smiled at me, then I got up to leave she walked me to the door. I caught a cab outside and headed back to the base. The cab was close to three dollars and I had to keep a close eye on my cash. I figured I had enough to meet her back here on Friday and have a few drinks and that would be it for what I could spend until the next payday.

The week was full of classes and of course, our typical AA meetings and I remember the main instructor telling me again. "I think you're a great actor, or you just don't belong in here." I knew I had to complete this class, or I could have possibly been kicked out of the navy and I damn sure didn't want that. So, I kept acting. I didn't go off base during the weekdays, but during the weekend I was out there with Kimiko. When we were not at the club, we were at her place having fun, I let her listen to my music and she said she loved it. When we went out to eat, she paid for our meals and she was cool with it.

One weekend I brought her breakfast stuff from the base, bacon, extra-large eggs, sausage and wheat bread. I had enough to last us for two of our weekends together and she loved it. I would say we were great together for the time being. Then I saw a picture of her with her father at the beach when she was a little girl. Her father's entire back and both arms were covered with tattoos, the kind only certain elements of a Japanese gang had.

The day she told me that she wanted me to meet her father was next to the last time I saw her. It was close to graduation time from the facility, it was going to be on a Monday morning and I would be leaving the next day. I spent Saturday and Sunday with her and I kept trying to figure out how to tell her I was leaving for good. She knew something was wrong with me and kept asking me what was wrong. On Sunday morning, I told her I would be leaving the next day, and I didn't want to tell her earlier and screw up our last day together. She smiled and kissed me. She said she knew this day was coming, but she didn't want to think about it.

It was near the middle of March 1986 and I was headed back to Misawa. I wasn't looking forward to going back before I left. I asked if I had requested to stay in Yokosuka and assist with the AA classes, and my request was turned down. Once the MAC flight landed in Misawa, I grabbed my bags and went out of the MAC terminal and caught one of the base buses back to the navy barracks. I had just over one year left here and boy, was I counting the days. I went back to the barracks and I was surprised I still had my own room. I guess someone overlooked the fact that I was now an E-4 and no longer an E-6.

Who was I to complain?

I checked back in at the quarterdeck and was informed that I would be placed in a different section and the section I was in was on their second day of the eighty hours off. I was okay with that. I went to my room, unpacked my stuff, and headed to the chow hall. I saw a few of the gang sitting in there, so I got some chow and sat with them. They all asked about being at the alcohol anonymous facility. I told them everything, being on the honor system and hanging out in Yokosuka and Tokyo, and they all looked at me like I was crazy.

I stayed off of the commanding officers radar and I was glad I was still on the two-two-two-eighty watch schedule. I only had to see the commanding officer on the day watch and only for about one hour while we had to give the morning brief. The section I was in had a lot of new folks, so I was still in the position I had before I was reduced in rank, I was just not in charge of anything and I was good with that. I didn't want anyone's eyes on me.

I saw the base JAG officer once and she told me she wished she had known I was the petty officer that was up on those charges and then she put her head down and walked away. I was the only black petty officer on the base with my last name. She knew that I knew about her off-duty activities, which would have probably gotten her in trouble. I didn't say a word about her or who she dated in her off time. It wasn't my business and I really didn't care that she only dated her same-sex, I just didn't care one bit.

I ran into Randy and all he could do was apologize. I told him he had nothing to apologize for and he said if I had not gotten him out of there, both of us would have lost our stripes and been E-4s. I kind of laughed and said, "I know."

There was a new black female and she was a new E-6. I asked her how she was doing and she just gave me a big hug and said welcome back. She started asking questions about the rehab facility, saying it sounded like a better place than Misawa. Her name was Janet. We got along well. I told her the worst thing you could probably do to a drunk is to send him there (Tokyo area) and not really have any security to watch over him or her. She just smiled at me, gave me another big hug and then she gave me the rundown on what had happened during my forty-five-day absence.

I was shocked at the things she was telling me. The young guy I had mentioned earlier that had the hair cut with his initials on it was in the brig for rape which I could not believe because his girlfriend could have been a model and the woman that accused him was caught in the bathroom having sex with him, she was not very attractive, but she did have big breast. I had told him quite a few times to always lock the bathroom door when he was in there. Now he was up on rape charges, and we all knew that was a lie, that woman had been around with all the younger guys, black and white. He was royally screwed, especially with the commanding officer that we had.

A lot of the crew tried to file reports about the commanding officer being a racist, I don't know how far those reports went and I really don't think anybody above us cared. There was also a policy being enforced about the noise in the barracks (which meant that the twenty-four-hour parties were stopped, along with hanging out in the hallways if your roommate was trying to sleep.) The barracks were not the same like I came back to a brand-new place or one of our training facilities.

I was put in a different section when I went back to work, it had about six marines in it, and the supervisor was a marine, he was cool as hell. He said me, "If I had not gotten busted, I would have been his supervisor," we both smiled at each other and he said, "Welcome to the section." two of the marines in the section loved to prank each other, especially on the mid watches. I remember one of them lost his cover (his cap) and he couldn't find the entire eight hour watch, and nobody else had a spare that he could use. He didn't care about it during the watch, but to leave the workspaces and have to walk out to the parking lot without it was driving him crazy.

Near the end of the watch, somebody found his cover. It was in the freezer part of the refrigerator. It was upside down, filled with ice and a big asset turd in it also. The sailor that found it couldn't stop laughing, and he took it to the section officer, who tried his best to act pissed off about it when he had the section supervisor report to him to find out who had taken a serious dump in the missing cover.

He then handed our supervisor the cover with the frozen turd in it. None of us could stop laughing and the culprit was never discovered, but we all knew who had done it. The guy that owned the cover took it to the head, got the frozen ice filled turd out of it and cleaned it. We were all crying and laughing when he walked back into the spaces with it in his hand. He put it under his desk so no one could get to it. Both of those marines were crazy and I liked them for it. Our supervisor had just gotten divorced and was having a little bit of a hard time with it. He and I talked a lot about it.

They didn't have any children, but they were high school sweethearts that had gotten married and he thought she was happy. She had cheated on him with some air force guy. I just reminded him of my situation, losing my stripes for fighting and that usually calmed him down. He said he is damn sure he didn't want to go through what I did. I really didn't think his commanding officer would have cared as long as he would have taken it off base.

A lot of us were getting short at Misawa. Almost time to leave and we had to fill out our dream sheets (stations we wanted to be stationed at) again. I put in for Europe, Spain, England and Italy. I would have to wait until I was ready to leave Japan before I found out where I was going next. I had just taken the E-5 test again and would not get the results until I was at my next duty station. Sarah and I became good friends with benefits (just booty call friends). Gabby's husband was getting out of the Air Force and she had to leave the base also. We still had a couple of months together. We kept our affair quiet and went to Love Motels. Our favorite one was shaped like a small old English castle. It had about 20 different styled rooms. They were not exactly cheap but just expensive enough that not a lot of people from the base had ever gone to them.

The room Gabby and I liked was really cool. You had to walk up a flight of stairs to enter it and once inside, you could either walk back down to the main level, or you could strip butt naked and go down a warm water slide that ended up in a hot tub. I learned my lesson the first time we got there, Gabby and I both stripped off our clothes and dropped them down the stairs, and I went first down the slide balls and first into the hot tub. I laid on my back on the way down, and it only took a few seconds to get down into the hot tub.

But before I go any further in, I want to explain something, hot tubs usually are set for the temperature to be between ninety-five to one hundred degrees. Now it was cold as hell outside and Gabby and I were both wearing parkas and cold weather clothes. Once we took all that off and I went down the slide on my back holding my legs, so I was nuts and butt first. The minute my testicles hit that one hundred and five degree water, I couldn't scream. Gabby was crying and laughing at me. She said my eyes looked like they were going to pop out of my head.

Now, remember I didn't drink anymore. I will tell you this, once I hit that hot ass water, I'm pretty sure I got out of the tub faster than I went in it. My legs and butt were ok, but my testicles were a different story. Imagine being so cold that part of your body just felt as if it shrunk and all of a sudden it was too damn hot. After a few minutes, I could scream, I looked at the temperature gauge for the tub and it read forty-one centigrade that, is a little over one hundred and five degrees Fahrenheit. I thought they were partially boiled. Gabby was still laughing twenty minutes later. I just laid in the bed with an ice filled towel wrapped around my nuts, we only had two hours for the room and I wasn't horny anymore. After Gabby was able to talk to me without laughing, she came over to me and gently pulled the towel away from my family jewels. I didn't want to look at them in case they fell off or ran away from me. She looked at them over and said, "They don't look like you have anything wrong with them," I asked if I still had skin left and she started laughing again. She walked over to the little refrigerator and grabbed a little bottle of Suntory Whiskey and handed it to me. I told her, "I couldn't think of a better reason," the bottle was the size of the ones they give you on airplanes. I gave it back to Gabby we still didn't have sex. I guess my hookup was pissed at me, but it was going to happen, so we just laid in bed and chilled for the rest of our time in the room.

When I stood up, I was kind of worried about putting my underwear on, but my nuts were ok. I smiled at Gabby, who watched me the whole time I got dressed. Once I had my parka on, she couldn't hold her laughter any longer. She laughed the whole thirty-minute drive back to the base. Once I pulled up next to her car at the officer's club, she got out and kissed me. We promised to try again next week, just in a different room. She was still laughing when she got into her car. Then I started laughing and I kept on laughing until I pulled into the parking lot of the barracks.

I went up to my room and crashed out. When I got back to work, we had a temporary section officer, our lieutenant junior grade went home on leave for a week, so we ended up with one of our newest officers to join the command. She was a lieutenant and very nice looking. She would be a section officer for section three after our (JG) junior grade came back. She smiled a lot and not just at me. She was just a good officer to work for, not as stuffy as most of the junior officers. She understood if we trusted her and did our jobs well, it would only help her look good. She was one of the few back then to understand that, I later found out she had family in the military and that was where she learned how to be a good officer.

Gabby's husband had gotten out of the Air Force and she had to leave the base also, she went back to England and promised to write to me so we could keep in touch. I believed her when she left, Sarah was still around for booty calls so I promised to write Gabby back and we did. After about three weeks, I ran into the new lieutenant at the air force enlisted club sitting at the bar. I walked over to her to let her know this was the enlisted man's club. She smiled at me and said me, "Let's go." I knew it was against the rules, but I went outside with her. Once we got outside, I told her about our Commanding Officer and how he is a stickler for the rules. She looked at me and smiled, then she told me a lot of things that were going on that none of us enlisted should know.

One thing was that our JAG officer was a lesbian. I told her we all knew that and she only slept with an air force officer wife's. She smiled and said the CO would be leaving soon for a better command. I didn't know that, then she shivered it was cold outside. I said, "Let's go to my car," as she had walked to the club, we got in my Z, and I started the engine and turned the heater on. Before I could say anything, she leaned over and kissed me, two minutes later, we were out of the front gate headed for the love motel.

The motel was, to my surprise, packed, there was only one room left, so I paid for the two hours and we took the last room. It was weird. It looked like a dungeon and it had a basket above the bed, she and I both stood staring at the room. I said this is really kinky and we both laughed. Now she was almost as tall as me, with nice large breasts and a big ass with a little waist, she probably weighed about 145 pounds, she opened the little refrigerator and gave me a bottle of water and she took two of the Suntory whiskey bottles, downed one and put the other in a glass with a couple of ice cubes, we got busy. We took a break and we both looked at the basket. It had a place for her to sit in and it unscrewed down this pole onto the bed. She looked at me and said, We just have to try this." I took another drink of water and said, "Let's do it."

I helped her climb into the basket. There was an opening in the bottom of the basket so my hookup would go right into where it was supposed to. We were both laughing and giggling, she let go of the pole and held her legs straight out and she spun right down on top of me, but the damn basket kept going down. I couldn't breathe. I was trying to tell her to get up and she was enjoying the feeling. To me, it felt, my the skin on my stomach was going to be ripped off if it twisted once more, then it stopped. We figured out if she stood on the bed, the basket would automatically go up and when she sat back in it, it would go down. We did have fun, we were almost done showering when the time-out buzzer rang, we hurried and got dressed and both at the same time said we just had to try again in another room.

We did visit the castle shaped love motel a couple more times. Then she was switched to another section which worked totally opposite my schedule. She got the worst section and was asked to straighten it up. Neither of us was happy about it, but we both knew it was for the best thing for us. We managed to get together two more times for trips to the love motel before I transferred out of Misawa. We had the King's Room and the last room was just a normal room. We enjoyed being in the love motel. It was fun and exciting. I spent my last two nights with Sarah before I left. Most of the guys I hung out with when Bela and Dana were here were already gone. They only had two-year tours as they were not married. Just before I got my orders, I was informed I had Made an E-5 again, but I would not be put on the rank until I got to my new duty station.

I took my Fairlady-Z to the shipping area. I was hoping it would be ready for me to pick it up by the time I got to my new duty station. Making E-5 again made me happy, but I knew it would have a long wait to get my E-6 back. I had orders to NSGA Homestead Florida after another C-school to become a senior analyst (I had been doing Senior Analyst work for the last two years at Misawa minus the AA time in Yokosuka). The school was back at NTTC Corry Station in Pensacola, Florida. I was good with that. I would be there for three or four months and the school was not too hard for me. A lot of the gang from Misawa had ordered there also.

NTTC Corry Station, Pensacola Florida December 1986 – March 1987

I stayed at my parent's house for a little over a week and then I was driven to Los Angeles International Airport by my father. He was amazed that I was going to school for something that I had been doing for years. I explained that times and things change, and he just shook his head and smiled. While I was at his house, I learned a lot of my childhood friends were either dead or in prison. I was glad I left for the navy. I had a layover in Atlanta for an hour, then a small jet to Pensacola, not the little twin engine I was on back in the seventies. I guess a lot of things had changed. When we landed, it was colder in that part of Florida than it was in Los Angeles. It was in the upper forties, but the smell of trees and the ocean was awesome compared to the smell of smog in Los Angeles. We still had to depart the plane via a ladder and walk down the tarmac to get inside the airport. It only took a few minutes to get my bags. After that, I went outside for a smoke and saw the white navy van. I walked over to it to see if I could get a ride to Corry Station. The driver said, "Sure, no problem." He said he had been there for over thirty minutes and I was the first sailor he had seen. He dropped me off at the NTTC Corry Station quarterdeck, where I handed in my orders and was told what barracks I would be in and where to go for morning muster.

The last time I was here, there was no morning muster. I found out that was just for folks waiting for their classes to start up. I was in the same barracks as my first time at the base. I was on the first floor with all the other petty officers. I went to the bowling alley, and there I found Bugeye, Randy, and his new wife. I have to say I was happy to see them, we all hung out there for most of the day, Randy and his wife had already gotten a place off base and headed home, Bugeye and I went to the chow hall for dinner and then back to the barracks. There was a note on my room door. I was to be in dress whites the next morning and report to the commanding officer's office at zero-eight-thirty. I was wondering what I had done now. I didn't have a drink other than the one in Misawa after we found out the captain was leaving and I only had one.

I guess I would find out the next morning. The next morning, I got up, did my threes, put on my dress blues and went to the administration building and reported to the commanding officer. I knocked hard on his door three times, I heard him say enter. I did and stood at attention and said the normal, petty officer Jackson reporting as ordered, sir. He had my records on his desk. He stood and said welcome to NTTC Corry Station. I said thank you, sir. He was straight to the point.

He wanted to know about my incident with the Japanese self-defense personnel, I told him exactly what happened, and I tried to make it as quick and concise as I could. After I finished, he looked at me and shook his head, then he told me there was nothing he could do about my punishment, but he did notice that I was out of uniform. I said, “Sir, I do not understand. Isn’t the dress uniform supposed to be dress blues?” and he said, “It is,” and I said, “Then, sir, I don’t understand. The captain told me I was wearing the wrong rank, and he handed me my second time around E-5 advancement paperwork.” I smiled, he shook my hand and said, “Congratulations,” I smiled, he said, “That will be all,” as I did my about face to leave his office, he said, “Do not lose it again.” I said, “Yes, sir,” and exited his office. I was smiling all the way to the uniform shop. I had to get all new rank patches, one for my dress blues and five for all of my white uniforms, along with the one for my dungarees. I went back to the barracks after that and grabbed all of my white working uniform shirts, took off my dress blues and put folded the shirt, hung up the trousers and headed to the base cleaners where they would sew the new rank patches on my uniforms.

Since I was at the captain’s office, I was allowed to miss morning muster and was back in civvies heading to the cleaners. I saw Bugeye and he told me he had gotten almost ten thousand dollars to re-enlist and was going to buy a car. He said he got his driver's license back home before he came to Pensacola. I told him good luck and got a nice car. He ended up buying one of the new Toyota. Once I got back to the barracks, I had another note on my door. I was from the shipping department. My Z will be in New Orleans the next Friday. I was so glad I had stayed at home with my parents and didn’t go out partying as I saved most of the money I had when I got to Los Angeles. I had over three hundred dollars in my wallet after I brought all the new patches for my uniforms, and payday was the same day as my Z’s arrival. I was really happy.

Classed started that Monday and our classes were eight hours long from Monday through Friday, so we had the weekends off. I was glad to hear that there were close to twenty of us in the class, most of the guys and ladies in the class were awesome and a few of us had already been in the senior analyst positions at previous duty stations. None of the classes were easy for me even though I had done the job before. All of us spent extra time studying in the area where the classes were held, and you couldn’t take any of the classified material out of those areas.

After Bugeye brought his new Toyota, we decided to go to one of the new clubs that had opened in Pensacola, it was awesome, and I learned that times had really changed. You saw blacks and whites partying together and mixed raced couples having a good time off the base. I was amazed. I will never forget they were playing a song by New Shooz, 'I can't wait', the song I played when I drove my Z off the base in Misawa for the last time. I saw this gorgeous looking lady that had a body that had me staring at her. Her body was what I had been thinking of a lot, just like the lady I had when I was first stationed in Pensacola. The only difference was she was a black woman.

She smiled at me when she noticed I was practically drooling at her. I walked over and asked her to dance. She said, "Sure," and I was with her for the rest of that night. She had a friend with her that was not too bad looking and Bugeye was with her spending part of that re-enlistment money. He brought most of the rounds. I had to make him let me pay for a couple of the rounds, the ladies were happy and so were we. I got the lady's phone number I was with. Her name was Glenda, and I planned on seeing her again depending on how much it cost me to go and get my car and the insurance for it. Glenda gave me her phone number and address. I wasn't expecting to get the address too, but I smiled at her and told her she would be seeing more of me. She smiled, Bugeye and I had to leave. It was almost midnight and we had classed the next morning. I called her the next day after class was over from the phone in the barracks. I let her know I might be over to see her on Saturday after I picked up my car from New Orleans. Every Friday, we had a test, and you needed to have gotten at least eighty percent correct on each test, if you didn't, and you failed two tests, you were kicked out of the class and sent to your duty station. I only had one test that is in the eighty percent range the rest were well in the ninety percent range. After the test, the class was dismissed and you had the rest of that day and the weekend off.

I left for New Orleans right after Bugeye finished his test, he drove me to the airport and I caught a flight to New Orleans. It was a one-way flight and a little under eighty dollars. I got there around three PM and caught a cab to the port of New Orleans. I showed the shipping documents that I had for my Z and the guard told the cab driver where to take me. When we pulled up, I paid the cabby and walked into the terminal where my Z was. There were hundreds of cars, mostly new ones. When I saw my Z, it was filthy, but what could I have expected for it being gone for over two months.

The guy that took me to my Z had a golf cart type of vehicle, and it had a battery in the back. When he handed me my keys, he had me open the hood, and he connected battery cables to my battery in the Z, it fired up easily and I left it running while I signed all the paperwork.

I had stickers all over the driver's windows and the left side of the windshield, I could still see out of the windows, but they were filthy. He said I could take most of them off except for one that was a shipping label letting the police know I had just picked it up. I had to show him my insurance papers, and then he signed one of the documents and I was almost ready to go. I asked him where the nearest gas station was and he drew a map for me and also how to get to the Interstate Ten highway.

It was cold outside, but I let all the windows down. My car had a slightly funky smell from sitting in the different ports and then on a ship for the ride to New Orleans. The gas station was close to the port facility where I picked up my Z and it also had one of those drive-thru car washes, I was glad of that. After I filled the gas tank, I took it right through the wash and when I went inside to pay for the gas, I brought some of those things you hang on the rearview mirror for the smell along with a pack of cigarettes. I checked the oil stick and it was fine, I was ready for the three-hour drive down to Pensacola, Florida. I would drive past on the I-10 through Louisiana, then Mississippi and then to Florida for a little over two hundred miles, the speed odometer in my Z was in kilometers per hour, not miles per hour.

I kept my speed at 96 kph, which was near sixty miles per hour once I got on the I-10 heading east. I had water and cigarettes, enough to last me for the three-hour drive, plus my car hadn't been driven in almost three months. I was doing good and making good time, listening to my cassettes with the speakers blasting. I had to put the heater on after I got on the I-10 as it was in the forties or low fifties. I had on my dress blue uniform and was just cruising and had just gotten off of a long assed bridge when my lighter stopped working. I checked in my center console, but no extra lighter or matches. I was on my fourth cigarette. I looked down for the lighter that was in the car when I left it at the port in Japan, but the lighter was missing just a hole where, the lighter should have been. I got pissed, I didn't want to make any stops except for gas and dinner, that plan was out of the window.

I saw a rest stop sign for gas near a place called Slidell, I had never heard of it, but I pulled off the I-10. All I needed was a cigarette lighter and to use the restroom. There was a little restaurant there and I decided to see if they had any matches. There were two Louisiana Highway Patrol cars there, so I figured this would be a good place to stop. Was I wrong or what?

I asked the waitress if she had any matches or a lighter I could buy. She looked at me like I had no right to talk to her at all. She didn't say a word. I just turned around and started walking towards the gas station, which is where I should have gone in the first place, then one of the patrolmen walked out to my car. I kept walking to the gas station and went in a brought a lighter for a dollar, normally they were twenty-five cents, I paid and walked back to my car, both of the officers were standing near it looking in the windows.

When I got back to my car, one asked me, "Boy, where in the hell did you get a car with the steering wheel on the wrong side?" I told him I just had it shipped in from Japan, and he said, "Yeah, right." I asked him if it was okay to get him the shipping documents that were in the center console. He said, "Go on!" I slowly opened the door and reached inside to get the paperwork along with my insurance. I handed him the paperwork he didn't even look at it. He just looked at my insurance papers, handed the papers back to me and said thanks.

I got in the Z and slowly drove off, put my seat belt on and lit up a cigarette. I was wondering if, together, the two of those officers could count to ten. I was back on the I-10 when I noticed the patrol cars lights coming behind me real fast, I pulled over and it was both of the same officers that were at the restaurant. I just shook my head, I let the window down, one came on the right side of my car and the other was standing behind it with his weapon drawn. I asked the officer what was going on and he said someone with a car like mine was known to have drugs in it. While he was talking to me, a tow truck pulled in front of my car. The next thing I knew, I was in handcuffs and my car was being towed.

I asked when they got me to the jail if I could make a call to the base and let them know where I was and that I would be late getting back. I was told I could make a call when they decided I could make a call. I didn't say anything else to any of the officers.

Two hours later, I was released. They had pulled up my center console. It only had four screws that held it in place. They didn't bother unscrewing it. It was cracked where they must have used a crowbar or something to pull it up, all the shipping documents were laying on the floor and everything that was in the glove compartment was on the floor also. My keys were in the ignition, they gave me back my wallet, watch and my wedding ring which I still wore and the officer just told me goodbye. I didn't say anything I just signed the paper saying this is what I had, I checked my wallet and I still had my one hundred and fifty dollars in it. I looked the officer in the eye, grabbed my stuff and left.

I got back on the I-10 in about ten minutes. I was really pissed off. Two and a half hours after I got my car, I still had over two hours to go. Instead of getting back to base around seven or eight, it was going to be around nine or ten. I reached in the back for one of the bottles of water I had, but there were none. I lit a cigarette and kept going. An hour later, I saw the signs for Mississippi. I got nervous and slowed down to around what I thought would be near fifty-five miles per hour in the slow lane, it wasn't much traffic and I was just cruising with the cruise control on. An hour later, I again had lights directly behind me.

I was thinking to myself, "Oh, hell no." I pulled over, this officer just wanted to check out my car, he was cool. I told him about my last stop and he laughed. He said he had heard of Fair Lady Z's, just never saw one. I showed him the straight line six-cylinder engine that was fuel injected, and he must have been a mechanic or something asking me all kinds of questions. I just looked at him and said, "I don't know," he laughed and told me to have a good evening, that lasted another thirty minutes, at least he was cool.

An hour later, I saw a sign for Mobile, Alabama, I was starving, I didn't want to stop, but my stomach was making gurgling sounds. The last thing I had to eat was some peanuts on the plane, plus I didn't have any water and I was just under half a tank of gas. Mobile, here I come. I pulled into another rest area that had a gas station and a McDonalds, I filled up the gas tank first and then pulled into the drive-thru to the window, the only problem was I was sitting on the wrong side. I had to get out to order. The lady at the window lost her mind. She called her coworkers to come and look at this little car with the steering wheel on the wrong side. After they all got a good look, I was able to order my Big Mac with fries, a coke, large fries and a bottle of water all for less than three dollars.

I ate my food as I drove, I was listening to jazz, but I was getting tired, so I put in some Earth Wind and Fire and kept cruising. I still had another damn near sixty miles to go. I sped up to ninety-six kilometres per hour and an hour later, I was at the Florida state line. Another thirty minutes and I was at NTTC Corry Station. My car ran perfectly. When I pulled up to the front gate on Chiefs Way street, one of the guys standing duty just looked at my car. I showed him my ID card and got a temporarily base pass until Monday. Now I still had the Japanese license plates and the shipping stickers on my Z, but it was awesome. I drove straight to the little base car wash and I grabbed the water hose and rinsed the Z down, took a towel from one of the racks and dried it off, headed to the barracks, but the car covered over the Z, went up to my room and took off my dress blues and crashed out. That little more than a three-hour drive took me to damn near seven hours to get back to base and I was done.

I was awakened around two-thirty that night by my new roommate, he was a new E-5 also and he looked as tired as I was, he took off his dress blues and just jumped on his rack. He didn't bother to put sheets on it or anything, I said hello to him and went back to sleep. I woke up Saturday morning around nine. My roommate was still asleep. I woke him when I opened my locker to get my soap and shaving gear, his name was Joe, he was Hispanic and cool as hell, he was also in my class. I told him I was going to get something to eat off base if he wanted to come with me and he jumped out of his rack and grabbed his gear also. We went to this little restaurant that did breakfast like Denny's. We both pigged out, bacon, eggs, sausage and toast with large glasses of milk. He had driven down from his parent's home in Texas while I was driving from New Orleans, I told him about my issues with the highway patrol, and he laughed his ass off and said that's why he brought a Ford Bronco. We both laughed.

After we got back to base, I called my new lady friend Glenda and asked her if she wanted to go back to that club, I met her, and she said, "Yes." She asked me what time I would be there to pick her up and it said around nine that night and she said she would be ready. She had a southern accent and that was for sure. I hung around with my roommate Joe and took him to the bowling alley. This guy was as crazy as I was. While we were at the school, I would say he was my best friend there, him and bugeye.

That Saturday night, I did my three S's and put on my burgundy three-piece suit with my burgundy and black shoes, and a black shirt with a burgundy tie, went to Bugeyes room and said, "Let's go," I told him I would meet him at the club and then I left the base and went to pick Glenda up at her house. She lived in the part of Pensacola where most of the blacks lived at that time. It was a little house built on a block of cement and the house was made of wood, most of the places I had seen were made of brick, her house was better than my room in the barracks and when I pulled up, she was waiting for me by her front door. She had on a nice black dress that really showed off her cleavage and those lovely long legs and I was glad she was with me.

I walked her to the car and opened the door for her. She couldn't believe that the steering wheel was on the other side. It took her a few minutes to get used to sitting on the left side of the car and in a two-seater, it only took about ten or fifteen minutes to get to the club. I pulled up in front of the club, got out and opened the door for her. As I was doing that, I heard one lady that was standing by the door say that she wished her man would do that for her.

She waited for me at the front door while I parked my Z, then I walked back to her and I paid the eight dollars for each of us to get in. Some of the gang from the base were there and she had some friends there also. The party was on. Bugeye and Joe were hanging out at the bar. I think Joe was married because all he wanted was beer, Bugeye, on the other hand, had his eyes on one of Glenda's friends, but I don't think he was the guy she wanted for the night. We all sat at a table in the back of the club, and I ordered the first round of drinks, two pitchers of beer and the party was on.

The music was awesome, songs by Tina Marie, Kool and the Gang, Rick James, and most of the new eighties dance music. I taught Glenda how to do the Cha-Cha the way I did it as a teenager and she loved it. I also showed her how we slowly danced back in Los Angeles back in the day to the song called "You Don't Have to Cry" by Rene and Angela. I held her so tightly and she had her arms around my neck. I was hoping the song would go on forever. I didn't want to let her go. Bugeye and Glenda's friend partied, but he left alone that night. The last dance for Glenda and I was a slow song by Evelyn Champagne King, 'Love Come Down', and we did the, 'Cha-Cha' to it. We finished off another pitcher of beer and Joe left. It was just after eleven, and Glenda and I left a little bit later.

After I opened her door and got in the Z, Glenda said she didn't want to go home. She wanted to stay with me for the rest of the night. I smiled and started car, and we drove south towards the Pensacola beach area. The moon was perfect as we could see the Gulf of Mexico waters and it looked as smooth glass. We were just talking about the fun we had at the club and she told me how jealous her friends were. I think we drove around for thirty or forty minutes until I saw this little motel right on the water. I went in and paid for the room. It was in the back and had a perfect view of the water. It was more like a bungalow. It had a little kitchen, bathroom with a shower, only no tub and TV, we spent the night there and neither of us was disappointed.

Glenda had a shape like Bella's and she was probably a few inches taller. She had shoulder length hair and it was in the big hair style of the nineteen eighties that curled up on her shoulders. I loved that look on her. We stayed in the hotel until check-out time the next morning. After we left, we stopped at the McDonalds for lunch and then I took her home. She had three kids there waiting for her, she invited me in and I did go inside for a few minutes. Her kids ranged from three years to. I think the oldest was a boy and he was around ten years old. I would get to know all of her kids and they really didn't care too much for me. They missed their father. I drove back to base thinking about last night, her partying with me and the time we had in the motel. I liked it. I would see her again. Monday through Friday evening I spent on base, but after study time on Friday, I would have my bag packed in the Z leaving for Glenda's place. Time was flying by for me, school was good (most of the training I had been doing for years), so it was kind of easy, Joe, Bugeye, and Randy would show up at Glenda's house, and we would hang out there on the weekends, they would pass out on the couch or her chairs and spend the night.

One day as I was leaving her place, her husband pulled up and walked toward my car. I reached under the seat to grab the little crowbar I kept there. I was sitting in the car and he said he wanted to speak with Glenda and didn't want any problems with me. I just looked at him and said cool, just don't give her any of your bullshit. Glenda had told me he left her for this little blonde girl that was probably eighteen years old and that he hadn't given her any money for the kids in over a year. I hated guys like that, and my thoughts were if you leave, at least pay for the kid's clothes and food.

But I stayed out of their business. I helped her with the food, especially since my friends spent most weekends there. One weekend we had a bar-b-que. All of the guys were outside drinking beers and just standing around the grill. Glenda's husband drove by with one of his friends in his car and when they saw all of us, they just kept going. I never saw him again. One Friday, just as I got to Glenda's house, she was crying. I thought it was a problem with her husband, but it was with the police, they had come over to her house to take her son to the police station to identify some guy that had robbed a store or something, but they wouldn't bring the kid home.

Bugeye had followed me over to her place, so we went in his car to pick up her son. When we got there, the office at the front desk looked up and saw two black men in dress blue uniforms and didn't know what to say to us. I told him I was here to pick up my friend's son that he refused to take back home. He told me to wait a minute, then Bugeye and I were asked to follow him. He took us to this room that had pictures of black wanted criminals. Each picture had just the face of the person and a red circle around it with one red slash going through it, and below each picture were the words, "A head shot is a good shot." Bugeye and I both looked at the pictures and busted up laughing. We couldn't stop. When the officer brought the kid in the room, Bugeye just pointed at the pictures and said, "Really?" then I grabbed the kid by the arm and still laughing. We all walked out of the room and left, just as we got to the front desk. I asked Bugeye "Do you believe this place," we both laughed again.

The next week Glenda could not go to the club, and I had promised the gang I would be there, so I went with Joe, Bugeye and Randy. Bugeye was not having any luck with the babes. Randy, Joe and I were busy drinking the pitchers of beer. I knew Glenda was waiting for me as soon as I got out of here. Randy and Joe left around ten that night. They had enough to drink. Bugeye wanted to stay and I said, "Only for a little while," I was finally able to get him out of there around thirty minutes later. When we got outside, Bugeye was damn near running to his car and left, I had to walk to the end of the street where I parked my Z, but I headed back to the base instead of Glenda's house. I just wanted to make sure he got back to base okay. I got halfway there and I saw Bugeye's car. He was pulled over by the police. I stopped and got out of my car and let the officer know Bugeye was one of my guys and what he was being charged with. I just knew it was drunk driving, but it wasn't. At the front of the officer's car was this very thin looking black female. She had both her hands on the hood of the patrol car. Bugeye was just sitting in his car.

The officer looked at me and said that we could listen to his speech or he would take Bugeye to jail. I told him we would listen. I leaned on Bugeyes car and then the officer looked at the female and said, "Sam, get your ass over here." Bugeye and I were both looking for a guy to come walking towards the car, the female walked over with her head down. I looked at Bugeye, then the officer pulled the female's wig off. I couldn't believe it, when Sam came closer you could see the stubble of a beard, fake long eyelashes and he was wearing a mini-skirt, his feet were bigger than Bugeyes and he just smiled at Bugeye.

I was trying not to laugh. I didn't want Bugeye to go to jail. Then Sam spoke and I couldn't help myself. I busted out laughing. His voice was deeper than mine and Bugeye's voices put together. I was dying laughing so hard, the officer was trying to keep a straight face, but his face was getting redder and redder. Bugeye looked like his eyes were going to pop out of his head. I almost fell over. I was laughing so hard. Then the officer gave us his speech. It was about not everything being what it appeared to be. I really busted up, then the officer told us about how paying for sex is against the law down here in Florida. I really lost it then. Bugeye was just staring at Sam. He couldn't believe Sam was not a woman.

Then the officer let us know that oral sex is the same as normal sex and still against the law if it is being paid for. I couldn't help myself. I had to turn around. I couldn't look at Bugeye, the officer, or Sam. After the officer finished his speech, he put Sam in the back of his car and drove off. I couldn't even walk to my Z. I was laughing so hard. Bugeye was just staring at me. His lips were quivering like he wanted to say something. All I could do was tell him to start his car and take his crazy ass back to base. Instead of going to Glenda's house, I followed him to the base and watched him get out of his car and go up the stairs of the barracks and in the door.

I didn't see Bugeye that weekend, but on Monday at class, he pulled me to the side as we were walking to class and asked me not to tell anyone. I told him that was his business and we let it go at that. I wanted to know if he had finished, but then I started laughing and just walked away from him. Our time at NTTC Corry Station was almost over and we were having our after-graduation party at the base club, we did party and we moved our tables into the middle of the dance floor. It was on after that. Some air force guy started complaining that we shouldn't have our table in the middle of the dance floor and Joe screamed at the poor kid, saying, "Shut the fuck up and sit, your no dancing ass down," that was the last anybody complained. Glenda and her friends were there and we had a great time. I knew It. It would be the last time. I wanted her but not her kids and their issues with the father.

I stayed with Glenda that night and the next morning, Joe and I left for Homestead Florida over five hundred and thirty miles. Joe was driving his Ford Bronco and I was in my Z, the speed limit was around sixty-five miles per hour, Joe was barely doing sixty and it was over a eleven hour drive taking the I-10 east to Jacksonville then the I-95 south to Miami and after that, the 1 freeway to Homestead Air Force Base.

NSGA Homestead December 1987 – January 1989

Joe and I arrived at Homestead Air Force Base that night around nine PM, we only made stops for gas, and that was at larger rest areas that had someplace to eat or restrooms. I made sure I had two brand new cigarette lighters, several packs of cigarettes, a six pack of beer and a couple of bottles of water in my little Styrofoam cooler. I didn't drink beer while we were driving, but at the rest stops, we would both get out and stretch our legs and have a beer or two.

When we got to the main gate at Homestead. We were both done, tired and sleepy, we were given directions to the navy barracks and the quarterdeck. We drove to the quarterdeck in the navy administration building, turned in our orders and were told to check in at the barracks by the petty officer, that was standing on his Officer of the Day watch (OOD). He said welcome and then told us that Miami was insane. He told us to hurry and put in our request to move off base and that the request would not take long to be approved. Then he gave us a map, each showing us how to get to our base off of Card Sound Road. Now from Homestead Air Force Base to Card Sound Road was not too hard to find our little base, but it was over a thirty-minute drive. NSGA Homestead was just like NRRF Imperial Beach. It only had the antenna array and our building in the middle of the array. There was a lake behind the base, but that was it. If you stayed on Card Sound Road, you would end up in the upper Keys of Florida.

I put in a request for off-base quarters the next day. After leaving the cold air of Misawa, Japan. I was now in the sub-tropics of southern Florida and it felt good to be warm again. No more snow and freezing my ass off. This was going to be a good duty station. Joe and I both had Saturday and Sunday off and we explored the Air Base. It was almost as big as the air base in Misawa, like Misawa also had a golf course on the base and I was told it was one of the best, and all the generals and admirals loved to go and play on it. I didn't like golf, but I was in one of the best places in the world to do what I liked to do and that was fishing.

I spent the weekend checking out the base, finding the cleaners, laundry, chow hall and PX. The base was something else, the air force had all kinds of planes there, just like Misawa had at its base. I had gone back to the quarter deck on Sunday and checked out the command listing of all the personnel on board and I found a name that I knew very well from NTTC Cory station in Pensacola, Florida. After bootcamp, he was one of us in the original crew, he was really quiet back then, but he did hang out with us a lot when he wasn't chasing the ladies.

I left a message for him several times to let him know that Dino was looking for him. On Monday morning, I was dressed in my blue dress uniform. I was told later in the day on Sunday that I was to report to the Commanding Officer at 0800 on Monday morning. After I got to the work site, I had to check in and get my badge along with everything else I needed to get inside the building, the command master chief was waiting for me and he took me to the CO's office after I was checked in. I knocked hard on the door and was told to enter.

Our commanding officer was a navy commander. After I entered, I started my rank and name CTR2 Jackson, reporting as ordered sir and stood at attention. The CO stood up and looked directly into my eyes. Then he checked out my uniform and my medals. I was a little bit nervous. I was trying to think if I had done anything wrong. He told me to be at ease and to be seated. I stood at ease and then sat down. He had my personnel records on his desk. He said, "There are three things I need to understand and I am asking you and no one else about them." I said, "Yes sir," he asked me about the captain's mast and about the Air Force Sargent and also about my shipmate's statements, and he wanted to hear my side of the story. I told him as briefly as I could, I was there with my shipmate, who was trying to help me get over my wife and child leaving me. We had about six beers apiece and my shipmate was not able to drink anymore. The Japanese self-defense guys wanted to arm wrestle with us and we just wanted to leave and go back to base, I managed to get my shipmate out of the bar, but I got kicked when I tried to get thru the door, then the fight started.

He said, "There was another witness to that fact." I said, "Yes, sir, an Air Force Sargent." He asked me if I knew the Sargent and I said, "I had never seen him before." The CO then asked if I made the payments for the Japanese medical and dental. I replied, "Yes sir," he then said, "I see here, you passed the drug and alcohol program. I said, "Yes, sir." The CO asked me if I still drank alcohol and I told him that I did have one drink after my captain's mast right before I left Misawa. He asked why and I told him the entire base was celebrating the CO's departure from the command, he shook his head.

The second question was about me leaving NTTC Cory station after A-School and knocking out a shipmate, I told him that story. The Commander told me if I have any racial problems, to let the Command Master Chief know immediately. I said, "Yes, sir." The third question was about how I felt about going out to sea and that I had volunteered to go each time. I quietly said, "Yes, sir," he said, "I wanted the truth," he asked how many times I was volunteered and I told him three times. He smiled and said this command would be sending CT's and that I was going to be one of the TAD personnel going, I smiled.

He asked if that would be a problem for me and I said, "No sir." The last thing he asked was about my prepping for OCS (Officers Candidate School) and I told him that was dropped prior to my captain's mast. I didn't think anyone knew about that. He stood and I stood also. He told me "Welcome to NSGA Homestead!"

Then he said a commander is only as good as his crew and that he was glad to have me and to tell the CMC to come in on my way out. Then he said you are dismissed. It stood at attention and did an about face, and went out the door, the Command Master Chief was waiting for me and I let him know the CO wanted to see him.

There was a seaman waiting for me. He was to take me into the spaces to meet with our supervisor and the watch chief. The seaman looked like he was afraid of me, I just smiled at him, and we walked through several doors and were in the work area, where I met the watch chief and the supervisor. The first thing my new supervisor asked me was if I had done any report writing and I let him know that was all I did at Misawa. He smiled at me and said, "Good," we needed someone with experience in technical reporting and briefing and I was that person for section two.

My new supervisor's name was Joseph. He was a little bit shorter than me, he wore these cool little round glasses and it was like they were all waiting for somebody with my experiences with tactical writing and HFDF experiences. We had an assistant supervisor and she was the second black female that I had seen with the rank above a third-class petty officer. She was also a senior second-class petty officer. She was awesome at work. They both were good people to work for. The only problem that I had with her was she was a total stickler for detail. She just wasn't sure what the important details were.

I finally ran into Kevin. He came up behind me at the PX and just grabbed my arm and looked me straight into my eyes and said, "I never knew you as Dino. What the hell happened to dancer?" I told him about my breakup with Sharleen and that I kind of stopped dancing after we broke up; I also was dating a lot of the new babes in navy, army and air force, that was when Billy called me a dog, like Dino on the flintstones. He told me he thought Sharleen and I had gotten married.

Kevin was an E-6, he made it the same time I made it, but instead of him being a CTT he was now a CTI (linguist) first-class petty officer. I told him about my captain's mast. He said he had heard rumors about it, but it was my real name and the rumors were not what I had just told him. We both laughed. I told him rumors were a Mother, and we both laughed again.

He told me he spent most of his time over in Europe in Rota, Spain, England and Germany. I told him I spent all of mine on both sides of the Pacific, from Misawa, Japan, down to Imperial Beach in California. He said, "The frocking ceremony would be sometime this week." I told him, "I knew." Kevin told me about all the brothers on the base, which ones I could trust and the ones that weren't even worth talking to. Kevin had two cars, one was a really cool black jeep and the other was a fairly new Cadillac. He worked straight days but could be called into work, if needed. He gave me his phone number and told me to call him during my 80-hour break. I told him he knew I would. He asked if I had been out in Miami and I told him I was waiting to catch up with him first. He gave me his home phone number, grinned at me and said, "Boy, are you going to have fun?"

He told me he had to leave, he had a girlfriend that was a stewardess and she was due to arrive that evening. We gave each other the short dap and he took off. I was glad to have found him. At least I would be able to hang out with someone my age. I went back to the barracks and walked past the front desk on my way to the pool room. This one white second-class petty officer came over and told me he worked in the admin office. He knew that I had left Misawa and wanted to know about Japan and the command.

I told him about the vending machines on the sides of the roads where you could buy everything from candy to beer and the fake plastic police officer posters on the side of the roads and also the love motels. I did not mention anything about the command. He shook his head. I told him he was going to a whole new world when he gets there. The guys and ladies in my section were pretty cool. I was the third highest petty officer in the section, but I really didn't have any extra things that I needed to do like I did in Misawa as a senior E-5 and then an E-6, no writing people evaluations, no training them. I did have to give the morning briefs after my supervisor was told that I did that job in Misawa and that took a big chunk of his morning time. He put me in charge of setting up the briefs for our two-day watches. I was good with that.

Kevin and I got together on my first day off. He said we were going to his apartment, which was in a place called Cutler Ridge in the south Miami area, not too far from the city of Homestead, where the air base was located. I asked him if we were going to hit any clubs and he said, "Hell yeah!" I took my black suit and grey and black shoes along with a black shirt and tie. I showed him my Z, and he said it kina looks like a little Chevy Corvette and it did. He laughed at the steering wheel being on the right side of the car and asked, "How in the hell you drive it?" I laughed and said, "That's the way it is in Japan and I had to get used to it fast." Once we got to his apartment, which was a one-bedroom with a nice size living room, kitchen and bathroom with lots of closet space. I knew where I was going to move as soon as I could.

I told Kevin about getting my car in New Orleans and what I went through getting back to the Pensacola. He laughed and told me, "It aint easy being a black man," and we both laughed and headed outside on his little slab of cement right outside his living room through a sliding glass door. He had his bar-b-grill out there and a little round table with four of those plastic chairs to sit in. He told me if this was the summertime, it would be too hot to sit out here, but in the winter, it was always in the mid to upper seventies. I knew I was going to have a good time here, in this part of Florida.

That night we hit a club that was maybe five minutes from Kevin's apartment and the party was awesome. For every guy, there must have been at least three ladies. I was in heaven. Kevin just looked at me and said, "How long has it been since you were in a club that wasn't on a base or overseas?" I told him about the one in Pensacola, but other than that one, probably six or seven years, he smiled and said, "Let's party," I ended up with this very nice looking dark skinned sister with long straight hair. She had on this short gold colored dress and I knew she needed to spend the night with me.

She said she was born and raised in Miami, she and I danced for quite a while. Kevin hooked up with this really fine-assed babe from Cuba. We took them both back to his place and they spent the night with us. They both drank wine while Kevin and I worked on the Chivas Regal, they both wanted to know if we had any coke while Kevin was driving us back to his place. We nicely let them know that we don't do drugs and that there would be no need for any as there was plenty of alcohol. They never mentioned it again. The next morning, we took them both back to the club where the lady I was with left her car. I kissed her goodbye and that was it, I never saw her again.

She gave the lady that was with Kevin a ride home. I asked Kevin how many times had he been to that club, and he said that was his first time. He smiled at me and said it won't be his last time either. We both laughed and headed for this little restaurant. He liked to eat breakfast, he said that both of them wanted us to take them to breakfast, but he wasn't feeling it, and neither was I. They were nice but not who I would want to see again. I was checking out the waitress at the restaurant, she looked like the Cuban babe Kevin had last night and she kept staring at me also. That's when I got one of many lessons from Kevin and one was never ever mess with someone that works where you eat. I asked him why and he said she works here, and if you hook up with her and things don't work out will you want to eat here again?

I thought about it, this place was only minutes from the apartment complex and it was good and cheap. I said, I understood. Kevin had a small afro, and I had the high and tight and the hair I did had was curly. I didn't have to wear a do-rag to make the curls they were natural. When I left a tip, the waitress came over to me and said she liked my hair, Kevin smiled at me and we both laughed. We went back to Kevin's place, and he said he would like me to kick it with him, but his stewardess babe would be back this afternoon, and they liked to be butt naked in the apartment. I winked at him as I said, "I definitely understand."

I went back to the barracks, took a shower, got dressed and headed out of the main gate. The gate guard stopped me, stuck his head in my window and said he had just gotten orders to Misawa Security Forces, I smiled and him and slowly drove thru the gate. Once, I got on the main street, I put my Z in second gear and stepped on the gas pedal. The car peeled out. I let up off the gas and put it in third gear and cruised toward South Beach. I cruised around the beach for a while, then I started looking for spots to go fishing. I planned on making up for all the years I couldn't fish and I was in one of the best places in the world to do it.

On my way back to the base, I stopped at a liquor store to get a six-pack of Budweiser and I thought to myself it felt good to be back in the real world. I knew on Monday morning I needed to have my butt at the tax office to get my car registered. That was number one on my list of things to do. I had gotten the phone number from Kevin for his apartment complex, and that was going to be the second thing I was going to do, find out about vacancies and prices for a one or two-bedroom unit. I did both of those things, then I drove over to the woman's barracks. There was one lady I met at work, and I wanted to take her off base and see if she wanted to hang out with me.

She had practically said that to me when I first met her, when I got to the barracks. I went to the front desk and asked what room was she in and the petty officer at the desk called her and told her I was here to see her. For some reason, she declined to come down the stairs to talk to me. I was confused. I asked if I could talk to her on the phone and was told, "No."

I turned and walked back to my car, got in and drove off base. I went to McDonalds, but I pulled into the drive-thru. What the hell was I thinking? I had to get out of my car to get my order. The lady that took my order was freaking out because I was sitting on the other side of the car. I drove to the front and parked and went in to get my order.

I didn't do that again. I drove back to base and ate my burger and fries afterward I went down to the lounge to watch some TV. This brother walked in. As soon as I saw him, I, for some unknown reason, hated him. He was dressed like Eddie Murphey, had a short jerry curl and I was trying not to laugh at him. He walked over to me and said, "Did you just try to get my girl to go out with you?" I laughed at him. He had baby teeth. I politely asked him to please move out of my view of the TV, and he said, "No!" I stood up and asked him if he wanted to have a problem with me. He was just a little bit shorter than me. My nose was damn near touching his. Then I backed up and said, "Look, I didn't know she was you girl. I don't need your bullshit, so please get out of my face."

He stepped back. This other black second class petty officer stood up and told the guy to tell me what was up and why she wouldn't talk with me when I went to the barracks to pick her up. It seems he told her I was drunk in Misawa at a club, and I hit an old female bartender with a chair and that's why I got busted from E-6 to E-4. I asked the guy if that was what was the scuttlebutt going around, and he said something like that.

I looked at him and said, "Do I look like someone that would hit a woman?" He said, "You hang out with Kevin, right?" I said, "We were homeboys back in Pensacola when there weren't many black CTs," he looked me in the eyes and said, "I heard about you guys having race riots in the base club because you were dating white chicks because there were no black females." I said, "You got it."

Then he asked me what really happened and why did I get busted. I said it just doesn't matter, but that was not the reason why I sat down and finished eating my burger and fries. The next time I saw George, that was the asshole that told her that I hit a woman with a bar stool or chair. He always tried to stay out of my way.

About two weeks later, just before I was getting ready to move off base, I almost got into it with one of Georges's friends. He was a little bit taller than me and bulky, I drove up to the bar-b-que area of the barracks to meet Kevin and this guy started talking a bunch of shit to me. I tried to ignore him, I was just getting ready to move off base and I didn't need any problems, but he and one of his friends just kept getting in my face. He wanted me to drink some cheap ass whiskey he had and I told him I couldn't drink that stuff and I wouldn't. He got pissed off and walked over to me. He said he didn't trust anybody that wouldn't drink with him, I told him I didn't give a damn. That's when his buddy stood up and walked over to me.

Kevin stood up and said he would put his money on me with either one of them one on one, but since there were two of them, he would be by my side to even this issue. There was no doubt in my mind that I would have hurt both of them with no problem. Kevin later told me he didn't want me to get busted again. He was there with his stewardess girl and one of her friends before I drove up, then Kevin looked at George and told him to be a man and stop trying to get his buddy's asses kicked just for him, and the other two backed down.

I looked at Kevin and said, "I know I can beat the hell out of both of these assholes with no problem for me except for the captain's mast," then I said, "At least I won't have to pay for their medical bills the navy would fix whatever I broke on them for free." They both sat down, Kevin's and his lady said, "Let's go," I told them we were staying here for the bar-b-que as I chipped in for the steaks and if somebody doesn't like it, well!

We stayed and ate bar-b-que and then the other lady that showed up with Kevin came over to me and said let's get out of here and she kissed me. I said, "Let's go, Kevin." His girl got in his caddy. Her friend went to get in my Z and I told her unless you can drive this, you want to get in on the other side. She looked and saw the steering wheel on the passenger side and smiled and said, "I better let you drive." We all laughed. Once I had her in the car with the seat belt on, I got in and we slowly drove off the base. Once we got off base, I was still in first gear, and slammed on the gas and we burned rubber for a few seconds and shot past Kevin and his girlfriend. My girl's eyes looked like fifty-cent pieces. I let off the gas and we headed to Kevin's place, the lady I was with was about five foot six inches tall and she looked like she could have been part Native American. I could have fallen head over heels for her, but she had the marks of a wedding ring on her finger. I didn't say anything, I just wanted to be with her that night.

Kevin headed toward the beach instead of his place and we followed. I pulled in front of him as we couldn't find any parking and we went to one of the spots I found for fishing. We all got out of the cars and grabbed the chairs that we brought for the bar-b-que and just sat there watching the ocean and the sunset. The lady with me, grabbed my hand and she held it until we left. Once we got to Kevin's place, both of the ladies ran to the bathroom we all had to go badly. All that beer and steaks and more beer, once we left the bar-b-que, but watching the sunset in Miami, was awesome.

Kevin had a nice little color TV and we all watched it for a while, drinking more beers until around ten PM. Then Kevin and his girl left and went into the bedroom, then he came out and told me the couch let out to be a bed. I gave him the evil eye all the time I spent there and he never told me, we pulled the lever and the couch was almost a queen-sized bed, my girl and I both smiled at each other. I asked her if she wanted to take a shower, and Kevin and his girl had earlier.

She said oh yeah, we took off our clothes and got into a nice warm shower. After the shower, we had fun in bed. Then she put her head on my chest, and I pulled the sheet over us and passed out. We were awakened by Kevin, and his girl at about eight AM. They had a flight out at ten AM, my girl got on top of me and just held me, she told me she didn't want to leave me, but we both knew she had to. I told her I understood and that I hoped to see her again, she kissed me like we knew we would never see each other again. I knew we wouldn't. She told me in the shower, "If things were different, she would not leave me." I smiled at her and said, "I know."

Once we were dressed, we all went to Kevin's Caddy and I kissed and hugged her. They drove off to Miami International Airport. After we got back to Kevin's place, I got in my Z and headed back to base. I had found an apartment on the other side of the complex where Kevin lived and I was going to surprise him later that day after I had moved in.

A friend in my section at work was waiting for me at the barracks with his pickup truck, I only had my stereo and my mama san and papa san chair and couch along with the speakers and stereo. I was able to get the stereo and one of my speakers in my Z. The rest went into his truck. I had brought a bedroom set for five hundred dollars, a queen-size bed with headboard and two nightstands along with a good size dresser and it was delivered about noon. After the bedroom furniture was delivered, I got into my z and went and brought kitchen stuff, a couple of pots and pans, some decent plates and silverware, which I got from on base at the PX. I took it all back to my new apartment.

The last thing I did that day bought groceries. I was on the other side of the complex from Kevin's apartment. I was on the first floor in a one-bedroom apartment. It had a decent-sized little kitchen, the one-bedroom. When you walked into the front door, you could see thru the living room to the little piece of the patio, which was a slab of cement that was the size of the sliding patio doors, just enough room for a bar-b-que grill and maybe four little chairs with a very small table exactly like Kevin's place. I had my new home and I was happy. I was able to see my Z from the bedroom window, so I was totally good with that, and plus, I had a very serious alarm system on it. I had it installed a couple of months before I had it shipped from Japan.

My neighbor who I met the next day was a female marine sergeant. She was blonde with hair down past her shoulders, a perfect body and those green eyes that drove me crazy. She came over and introduced herself with a bottle of wine, wearing only shorts and a t-shirt with no bra (her nipples let me know that). She was absolutely gorgeous. I mean perfect. I think she had a one-night stand with Kevin and she knew it wasn't going any further because she was just a booty call. I think they both liked it like that.

She and I both felt comfortable around each other, I just wanted to have sex with her, that never happened and don't get me wrong. I did try and several times, I came very close, but I realized I had a female friend and that was all it would be. Sometimes, she would introduce me to her girlfriends and they would party with me before going to her apartment to have a good night.

It didn't take me long to realize she would be just a good friend. I think she was kicked out of the marines because she liked to smoke her weed. She left about three months after I moved in, I missed her leaving as I had to go on my first temporary assigned duty (TAD) on board the USS Forestall, but before she left, she and I were pretty good friends.

After I moved in the apartment, I felt so much better. Living in the barracks at my age was not a good thing. Music blaring at all hours and it was mostly rap or country and western. I was still hooked on my oldies but goodies and jazz. All my furniture and stereo equipment was put in place the same day I moved in. Kevin had his flight attendant girlfriend over, so I knew I wouldn't see him for a couple of days. It just felt good having my own place again.

My TAD orders came in and four other sailors and myself drove from NSGA Homestead to Mayport Naval Station in another one of those old beat up navy vans. A drive that should have taken a little more than six hours took us seven and a half hours, the driver didn't want to go more than sixty miles per hour and I, for one, was glad he didn't. None of us was sure we would make it that far in this van. We made it with two or three stops for gas and one for chow.

Once we arrived at the main gate for the navy base, we were all tired of sitting in that van. We asked for directions to the pier for the Forrestal. When we got to the location, I noticed they were loading supplies. I told the driver to turn around and get us off the base. They all wanted to know why and I explained in as nice of a way as I could that I was the only E-5. The rest of them were two E-4's and two E-3's. All hands were to help with supplies! It took a minute for the information I gave them to sink in. Then I told them supplies for a little over five thousand personnel would be an all-night operation. We decided it would be better to get two hotel rooms for the night off base.

I took the junior E-4 as my roommate and the rest had another room. The place was a dump but it was clean, and we could rest. There was a McDonalds within walking distance, so that was where we had dinner. Some of them wanted to party. I said, "It would probably be a bad idea, getting on the carrier hung over would really suck for us." We found a Circle K liquor store and brought a couple of six packs of beer, took them back to our rooms and that's where we stayed until the next morning. I had everyone up at 0630 hours and we headed back to the base and straight to the quarter deck.

We had parked the van on the far side of the pier, where it stayed until we returned. We reported to what was called Z-Division (part of the communications division) with a radioman chief as our new boss. I reported to him if we had any problems. It was a thirty-day assignment on board and it went as planned for our little team.

It took us a while to get used to the places and spaces on board. I also had to set up the watch schedules we would all be standing, and it was to be twelve hours on and twelve hours off for each of the team except for me. I would be spending from 0600 (6:00 AM) to 1600 hours (4:00 PM) for the day watch and then I would go back to the spaces at 2100 hours (9:00 PM) until midnight every day we were underway. We had to decide who would go to breakfast, lunch, and dinner first, so each position stayed manned. Our crew would receive head-of-the-line privileges, so they could get in the chow hall and out as quickly as possible so the other guys on watch could get their chow.

We left Mayport and headed east. The ship was conducting flight drills. The air wings started landing on board after about thirty minutes out at sea. There were fighter jets and bombers landing one after the other. I believe there were more than sixty or seventy aircraft that landed on the flight deck that morning. It was awesome to watch them landing. Our berthing (sleeping quarters) sounded like we were just below the flight deck, but we were actually three levels below it.

Being on a carrier was totally different from the other ships I had been on a lot more sailors, the noise from the flight deck, the continuous communications over the ships speaker systems was unbelievable, and the smells of jet fuel, diesel, and over five thousand sailors were going to take some time to get used to. Now the funny nickname for the Forrestal was the Forrest fire. The other nickname was the FID (first in Defense). It was also the ship's patch. The Forrestal (CV-59) was over thirty years old. She was commissioned in 1955. The Forrestal was the first supercarrier, and she could carry a lot of different types of aircraft, from jets, bombers, and communications aircraft to search and rescue helicopters. It was a proud ship, and the crew was proud also. Our first few days on board were spent trying not to get lost finding our way from berthing to the chow hall and workspaces.

The showers in our berthing area were set up as stalls and I wore flip-flops when I got in the showers. The water from each of the stalls splashed into each of the other stalls. You had a hand-held shower head that you needed to push a button on it to let the water come out and when you pushed the button on, the water felt like you had something else in it, and it felt slimy. I kept trying to rinse it off, but that didn't happen.

One of the radiomen petty officers told me it was probably JP-5 jet fuel in the water lines. I didn't know if I believed him or not, but I can tell you this none of our little crew had any problems going to the toilet. After the first week, we were pretty much settled in and doing our jobs.

Someone had put a sticker on the outside of our door that read, "In God, We Trust All Others We Monitor," and it had a picture of the little spy cartoon character of the sixties and seventies. Our thirty days went by quickly. We stayed mainly south of Key West Florida and off the coast of Cuba. The Cubans didn't like that too much and there were always old Russian MIG-21s jets flown by the Cuban Revolutionary Air Defense Forces. I think it was both Russian and Cuban pilots, but none of them would come close to the Forrestal. Our jets kept them well away from the carrier.

At this time, there were no female crew members allowed on combatant ships, but that would change in the nineteen-nineties. There were pictures from Playboy, Penthouse and Hustler magazines in a lot of the spaces on the ship and especially in the little racks we slept in. You could see naked babes everywhere. I thought it was just like all the other ships I had been on but with a whole lot more pictures. Our thirty days on the Forrestal were done before we knew it, our work was done and our crew did a good job. We all received evals from the division officer that I only met once, and we all received 4.0, the best we could get. Just as we were getting used to all the noise on the carrier. Our time was up, she was pulling back into Mayport, Florida and we would be departing.

We all brought some kind of souvenirs before we left cigarette lighters, ball caps, t-shirts and sweat suits from the ship's store. Our crew worked well together as a team, but I would not have the same crew after this trip. Once we got back to Mayport, we had the dreaded drive back to NSGA Homestead. The van was waiting where we left it and the tank was filled. Once the Forrestal docked, we were ready to depart, but like all ships departing was by highest ranks first, so once our senior E-5, and myself got off, we had to wait for our E-4, and E-3's and that took about twenty minutes. There were lots of wives and families waiting for the ship's crew. All we had waiting for us was a van and a long drive back home. Most of us slept damn near the whole ride back to base and it was dark after nine PM when we did get back once at the quarterdeck, we were informed that we would have two days off after the next morning's debrief. We were told to show up at our base at 0800 the CO, XO and division chief would be there.

I would be the one answering all the technical and tactical questions. The rest would just be there to answer questions about how they felt about being out to sea and equipment questions, did the equipment work as planned. That next morning, we arrived on time and went to the debriefing, the CO and XO were very excited. We answered all their questions and we were out of the debrief in less than thirty minutes which meant two days off and party time. I got in my Z and hauled ass down the Card Sound road headed back to my apartment in Cutler Ridge, South Miami. While I was out TAD on the Forrestal, I didn't bother to mail my rent in and I told the apartment manager I would be gone for thirty days she said, "No problem, just pay it when you return." That was the first thing I did after the debrief. At the time, I didn't know it but paying rent when I was TAD was going to be a real problem later on.

Once that was done, I stopped and got a bottle of Chavis Regal and went straight back to my apartment and ran a warm bath. I then sat in the tub and washed all that JP-5 fuel oil off and kept drinking. I think I stayed in the tub for a little over an hour, and when I let the water out of the tub, there was a black ring in it like I hadn't had a bath in weeks. After I cleaned the tub, I took a shower. I needed to know I was clean again.

Shortly after that, I passed out. It felt good to be able to stretch out in my bed. I woke up and went looking for Kevin at his apartment, he had just got off work and was telling me about the club we went to before my TAD trip and that we had to go back there that night. I just smiled and said, "You're on." We sat around in his apartment listening to jazz and talking about being on a carrier. Kevin said he didn't think he would like being out there with no females and all that noise and we both just laughed. He also told me about some of the new females that had arrived on base while I was gone. I told him, "I might have to check some of them out," we both laughed again.

That night he drove his caddy and I was in my Z heading to a club in South Miami. I don't remember the name of it and when we got there, it was packed. We already had a good buzz from a couple of six-packs of Budweiser and drinking was not high on my priority list. I know it wasn't on Kevin's either. We both parked in a lot about a block from the club. I didn't want to do any valet parking in case the drug dealers started shooting the place up. We could just sneak out the back, run to our cars and get the hell out of Dodge. A lot of clubs were off-limits just for drug problems. Uncle Sam didn't want his folks getting shot up while trying to get laid, so the most notorious clubs were strictly off limits to us.

It cost $20.00 to get it, but I thought it was well worth it, everybody was dressed to party. I had on my burgundy silk suit with my burgundy and black eel skin shoes, and Kevin had on a dark blue suit with shoes to match. We both walked up to the bar. I had my normal Chivas Regal on the rocks and Kevin did the rum and coke thing.

We were standing at the bar checking out the ladies when two very nice looking Cuban babes walked over to us and asked us to buy them drinks. Kevin and I both started laughing and told them to buy their own drinks, one just walked away, the other one started talking shit, we just walked away from her, within minutes we were dancing with two nice ladies, Kevin and I were both in our early thirties and Miami was one of the cities to be in for the parties. There were black, white, Cuban, Porto Ricans and Colombian babes everywhere. The one I had that night was Porto Rican. She was about 5'5" with long black hair and a really hot body to go along with a beautiful face and a smile that kept me dancing with her most of the night. Kevin hooked up with another stewardess that was about 5'8", long legs, big boobs and a kinda flat ass, we brought them a couple of drinks found an empty table and the rest of that night we partied. The lady I was with told me her name was Layla, we basically did the danced the Cha-cha all night long, her and I both smoked, so I was able to get her out of the club a couple of times. We talked and she told me she was born and raised in San Juan Porto Rico and had just come to Miami.

I never told her I was in the Navy and I don't think she cared. We just had a great time together. After the club closed, we walked to our cars and agreed to stop at Kevin's place for a few more drinks both the ladies were drinking rum and cokes. I knew I had rum at my place, but I wasn't sure I had any coca cola left. Kevin and his girl stopped at my car and I heard him tell her to watch me. I opened the driver's side door for Layla and told her to get in. She looked at me and said she didn't have a Florida driver's license yet. I told her it was ok because she wasn't going to be driving. That was my job, when she looked inside my Z and the steering wheel was on the other side, she had the 'what the hell happened to your car' look, I told her, "I brought it while I was visiting Japan." After she got in the car, her mini skirt showed how much of a mini skirt it was.

I closed the door and walked over to the right side of the car, got in and fired my Z up. As soon as I turned the key, the song 'I can't wait' by Nu Shooz came on and I turned the volume down so we could talk. I waited for Kevin to pull his caddy out and we shot past them and headed back to his apartment. The lady Kevin was with was leaving in a couple of days to fly back to New York and Layla was leaving the next week to go back and visit her family in Porto Rico. I asked her about growing up on an island and she said she loved the beaches, but the cities were poor, nothing like here in Miami.

Layla had another drink and I took her to my place. We talked for a few more minutes and then it was bedtime. The next morning I took Layla to her place, where she grabbed some clothes so she could stay with me for a couple more days. My two days off just happened to be the last two days of my shift, so I ended up having five days off and believe me, I didn't mind spending them with Layla. After a couple of days, I did tell her I was in navy and she just smiled and me. I took her down to the south beach and we stayed on the beach for a while. The sun was just too hot for me, so we ended up at one of the little bars and had lunch and a few beers. I really liked her, but I knew she wanted to go back to Porto Rico to be with her family, and I really just wanted to have fun with her.

She could cook very good and liked to laugh, along with looking good, she was perfect. I took her fishing on the third day, but a swarm of mosquitos ran us both back to the Z. We waited for them to leave and had a few beers in the car. We couldn't leave because we left the tackle box and rod and reels outside of the car. Once they were gone, we ran and got the gear and put it all in the back of the Z and drove off. We were both laughing so hard about being run off by a bunch of blood-thirsty flying bugs. We did manage to catch a few fish. Once we got back to my apartment, I cleaned the fish and Layla cooked them.

We had fish, rice and beans. It was all good. The next day, I took Layla to the Air Force base for lunch and we had a very good time. I loved watching her see things that were new to her, like all the people in uniform and all the jets on the runways, we went to the bowling alley, and some of the navy folks that I worked with were there, so we hung out with them for a while. Like me they were all wanting to know about Porto Rico, she was kind of the center of attention, and she handled it very well. She was a perfect lady. She couldn't bowl very well, but she had never been to a bowling alley and when she threw gutter balls, she just laughed with the rest of us.

One of the females that worked with me told me she thought Layla was beautiful and that we were a perfect couple. I smiled and thanked her. Layla just smiled at her also. After the bowling alley and a few beers, we headed back to my place. I asked her if she wanted to go to one of the nightclubs and she said no, she just wanted to stay with me until she had to leave, she told me her grandmother was very sick and that was the only reason she was leaving. We stayed at my place that night, watching TV and talking. I was only going to have one more night with her, so I wanted to be with her alone.

Kevin came over and hung out with us for a couple of hours, then he left and we were alone and happy. I woke up the next morning and she was not lying in bed next to me. I checked the whole apartment. I found a note on the kitchen counter. The note read she could not stand to say goodbye to me, and she knew if I had taken her to the airport that, she probably would not have left. It also said it was really her mother and that her mother was dying. She knew she would have to take care of her father, brothers and sisters.

It also read that she had fallen in love with me and goodbye. She took a picture of me in my dress white uniform that was taken after I made E-5 the second time. I just hoped that each time she looked at the picture, she remembered the fun and love that we had for each other. I got TAD orders to go back out to sea for two months on board USS Saratoga the day I went back to work and I had a decent group of guys to go out with me. Our crew consisted of two E5s, three E4s, and one E3, we hit some awesome ports. Well, they would have been awesome if not for the racial problem we had in St Martine.

The ship put in for X-X-number of rooms at one of the local hotels. When they showed up, they did not want to rent rooms to the black sailors. They were informed it would be all US sailors or none, so they tried to put the black sailors in what was less than any of us wanted. That place lost over one hundred and forty customers for six days that would have been paid for without any questions. This was the mid-nineteen-eighties, to hell with that part of the island. We all ended up spending the day checking out the beaches, which were topless or nude and none of us got into any trouble. We did have an incident where we did not make the last ferry boat back to the carrier and had to spend the night sleeping on the ground at the park, one of the marines settled for a park bench. Later that night, I heard chanting coming from the area of the bench. Several of the guys were standing around watching what was going on. I stood up, walked closer and saw one of the natives putting some kind of voodoo or root (whatever you call it) on the marine that was sleeping on his bench.

I didn't say anything or do anything neither did the other guys. Whatever it was, I didn't want any parts of it. I lay back down and went to sleep. The next morning, we all caught the first ferry back to the ship, got cleaned up and went back out again. We asked the cab driver to pass by the hotel we were supposed to have been in and it looked empty. We all hung out at a couple of the bars that were wide open on the beach it was awesome. We ended up on the Dutch side, that's where we should have made room reservations.

The Dutch people were cool as hell. I guess they had figured out that money is money no matter what the color of the person spending it was. We headed back to Mayport shortly after departing the Caribbean and our TAD trip was over. After our long ass drive back to NSGA Homestead, we were debriefed and sent home with 3 days off, it was in the middle of my section shift and I was glad that I fired up the Z and cruised to the post office. I had about ten letters from Gabby. She was back in England living with her mother and needed to get away. She put the phone number in each letter.

I called her while I sat in the bathtub, soaking and trying to get clean. We only spoke for a few minutes. She would be coming to the states in six months after she had saved up enough cash for the trip. I told her that I missed her and would be glad for her to get to Homestead. I met one of my new neighbors that had moved into the complex. She and her son were directly across from my apartment on the second floor. I noticed her immediately and the reason was she was maybe 5'1" tall, but her chest was huge and I couldn't help but smile at her the first time I saw her and she smiled back at me. Her son was around eight years old and kind of short for his age.

I asked her if she would like to go to lunch one day and she said yes, she was from Jamaica, she had that little body with those large breasts, she was awesome the only problem was that she had a child and I was not ready for that, we became a little more that friends what is called booty call friends today. We just liked having sex with each other, I'm not sure how she did it, but she was on welfare and not an American citizen, but then again, lots of people from other countries were doing the same thing. I took them both fishing a couple of times to show the kid there were things he could do besides sitting in their apartment watching tv all day. I gave them all the fish that we caught and she cooked them for us. I had to let her know that I didn't want to eat any fish with the head still attached. She laughed and said, "Okay, no head on the fish."

We lasted about three weeks as friends, then she found a guy that wanted to be with her all the time. She told me he made her happy. I understood and wished her and her son the best of luck. They moved out a couple of days before I went to sea again. It was going to be a short trip, only twenty days along the southeast coast and into the Gulf of Mexico. I was glad to be getting a short trip. You just cannot imagine how glad.

Our crew drove up to Mayport Naval Base and boarded the U.S.S John Rogers DDG-983. It was a Spruance class destroyer and she was a lot smaller and newer than ships. I had been previously assigned to. The crew was awesome and we had a radioman chief that we reported to. It was a good cruise. We headed down the east coast around the Keys and into the Gulf of Mexico and back to Mayport. We did not hit any ports during the cruise. We spent most of our time between Texas and the Mexico border, then headed back east toward Florida. We did hang out a couple of days near the Mexican border. We stayed at a station, close to Texas and Louisiana (cruising along the coast), then we headed back to Mayport.

The chief in charge of us was so cool, as we were pulling back into port, he called me over to the port side of the ship and told me to wave at his wife and kids, they were on a fishing boat about fifty feet away from the destroyer pulling into port. We didn't realize until we pulled into port that our return orders were not until the next day and the van would not be there until then, we had a free day in Mayport.

Our crew all knew what we needed to do and that was catch a cab to the base club. It was Wednesday and the club was open to civilians (mostly females came to the enlisted men's club). The only table left big enough for all of us was near the hallway leading to the restrooms. We were having a great time drinking beers and making fun of each other until this woman came over. She had to be about 5'9", weighing in over two-hundred and fifty pounds with this yellow mini dress with black polka dots. She was looking at our table and heading our way, I felt this uncontrollable laughter starting, but I held it in check. She had huge arms and breasts, blonde hair and enough makeup that if she would have sneezed, I would have been white. The worst part was she had this really determined look on her face and I wasn't sure what the hell her problem was, but when she got to our table. She looked straight at our youngest guy and told him he was taking her home for the night. He turned red and looked at me as to say, 'help me', I was still trying not to laugh at the poor kid. He was probably nineteen years old and we all knew he was still a virgin, but the look of fear in his eyes was almost too much for me to handle. She grabbed him by the arm and they were gone. The rest of us just looked at each other for what seemed like two or three minutes, then we all busted out laughing. The kid was making little whining sounds as she dragged him off. Now, if she would have been a guy, I would have helped him, but there was no way I was going to get my ass kicked by a big babe that just knew she was hot.

We all laughed for a good ten or fifteen minutes none of us could stop. One of our guys hooked up with a really nice lady and they left. I reminded him that we would be leaving tomorrow, so he needed to be back on base and near the ship as soon as he could. He smiled and said he would be back. The rest of us left the bar around ten PM and found a hotel not too far from base. We got two rooms and crashed out there.

Both of the guys that got lucky the night, before beat us back to base, and the van was there waiting. It must have been just after noon. We were all ready to get back to Homestead. We teased the young guy about the big girl. He never said a word, he only smiled at us. We didn't tease him for long. Once we were back at NSGA Homestead, we were instructed to be at the base the next morning for debriefing and then we would have two days off. My watch section was on their last eve-watch, so it meant I would have both the day watches off for the next string of watches after the eighty-hour break.

Like usual, I went back to my apartment, opened a bottle of Chivas Regal, ran some bath water and just soaked and drank. After that, I called my family to let them know I was back in the states. It always made my mom's happy when I did call. She claimed her hair was turning gray because of me going out to sea so much. We both laughed when she said that. The next morning, I went to check my mailbox, and as usual, it was packed with junk mail. I did, however, get a new sears catalog which was very important for me as I did order stuff from it, usual boots for work and some underwears.

There were also a lot of letters from Gabby that made me happy. I couldn't wait to see her. I had promised to take her fishing and she really wanted to try it. Homestead Air Force Base rented out these little skiffs (twelve-foot boats) with fifteen horsepower engines and a ten-gallon gas tank. You could be out there in the water near the base for hours with those boats as long as the weather was good. I loved fishing in them. The only problem was that if you caught something too big, it was a hassle getting it in the boat because the fish would flop around like crazy and you could possibly get hurt from the tail of a big fish. I had heard stories of that happening to other folks so I usually took my hammer or a pistol with me when I went out there. You needed to kill the big ones before you could pull them in the boat with you.

I had already brought Gabby a rod and reel. I had all the tackle that we would need. I just needed her to get here to me. I went to a couple of clubs and hooked up with a couple of ladies, nothing serious. Once they found out I was in the military, they kind of shied away from me and I was good with that. One young lady that I met could have been a keeper except that she had a very young daughter, and the second time I went to her house, the little girl asked me if I was her daddy, that freaked me out, and I never went back.

I had two daughters I surely didn't need another one. After that incident, I kind of stayed away from the clubs. I did date a couple of the Air Force babes but not seriously. I managed to stay off of ships for about two months, and during that time, my oldest daughter came to stay with me for a while. I loved having her with me, but I think she was a little bit afraid of me and some of my friends, most of the guys treated her like she was their niece or something, she had lots of toys that all my friends and myself brought for her.

I had to find a babysitter and I did. The lady was awesome and sexy. She was from Trinidad, she had one hell of a nice body. I ended up dating her as she watched my daughter so much while I was out to sea. The last time I went out to sea while my daughter was with the babysitter, southern Florida had a really bad storm, not quite a hurricane, but winds strong enough that all military personnel and their families were brought on base. Some of my guys came and got my daughter and the babysitter along with her two kids, and they stayed on base at the shelter, which was the gym.

I got back the next day and I couldn't find them. I drove my car all over the place looking for them, then one of my crew members told me his family was at the gym and that's where they were. I drove them all the way back to our apartment complex in my Z. I really liked the babysitter. The only problem was that I had with her was that my daughter started speaking in her accent and her oldest daughter was eighteen years old and going through the pre-adult issues with boyfriends and drugs that were so common back then in Miami.

We stayed friends after the storm until she and her husband got back together. After that storm, my daughter's mother wanted her back home, so she left. I was sad to lose her, but I knew it was for the best. I went back out to sea on the USS Forrestal again, it was only for two months and we stayed off the coast of Porto Rico and then down to the Caribbean area. The water was so clean and clear you could see the fish swimming and of course, we still bet on the flying fish, which one would stay air-born for the longest time and which one went the farthest.

It was a good trip. Only one person got hurt and it was a guy replacing a rubber ring around a hatch. I don't mean to be cruel when I tell you this but it was his fault. The actual hatch weighed over a hundred pounds, there was a heavy latch that held it open and there was one a little bit bigger than the ones that are on the typical screen doors. He only used the little one. He had his legs inside the hatch, so he was sitting down instead of kneeling outside of the hatch. We hit some rough water and the little hatch broke. The weight from the actual hatch bent him in two from his waist to his neck, he lived for about thirty minutes. His leading petty officer and division chief both got in trouble for that accident if they felt sorry for all three of them.

Once we got back, we got the usual three days off and it was my section's second day watch which meant I would go back to work on my last eve watch. I was really good with that I still had almost a month before gabby got there, so I hit a couple of clubs on and off base. I had a good time. I picked up two air force ladies one night and drove them to my place in my Z. They were flirting with me and each other the whole way home. They both stayed with me for a couple of nights. They took care of me, then each other and then me, again and again, each and I have to tell you we had a really, really good time.

The first morning I took them to breakfast and then to the grocery store. I brought three steaks and some red potatoes and stuff for a salad, and we barbequed our dinner. All the neighbor's wives were just staring at us while I was barbequing. Both of them took turns kissing me while they were watching just to let them know that they were both with me. The next morning I took them both back to base and I needed some rest and beer. I still had one string of work before Gabby arrived and it seemed as if it was taking forever. I had put in for two weeks of vacation time and it was approved quickly. I was surprised.

My chief told me he was wondering when I was going to request some time off and we both smiled at each other. Gabby arrived at the Miami International Airport right on time. We went to the bar at the airport as soon as I found her and had a drink. I figured she would need one and she did. We both had a couple of drinks and then it was back to my apartment. She slept for damn near fourteen hours. It was a long flight, but it was a two-hour drive to get to the airport from her little town in her sister's car. I only woke her to eat dinner, and after that, she went right back to sleep.

The next morning, I made bacon, sausage, eggs and toast for us. We stayed in the apartment most of the day, just talking and catching up on what we had been doing since we last saw each other. She had a new baby niece and the last thing she told me was that her ticket was only one way. She intended on staying with me. I was kind of shocked, but I didn't let her know it. I just smiled and kissed her. I was thinking the same thing as she was. AIDs had come out, and the horror stories were starting and I knew I didn't want anything to do with that STD. Settling down seemed like a good idea to me. Gabby and I enjoyed ourselves, we loved being together and she was the best fishing buddy I could have had. We went fishing a lot and rented the little skiff most of the time. Once we stayed out so long just cruising the little boat and we ran out of gas.

I waved a red flag that was on the boat for emergencies and these really nice people in a forty-foot cabin cruiser threw us a line and towed us back to the base. Their yacht was awesome, I was hooked on civilian yachts after that. Their yacht was like a small apartment, the guy that owned it said they usually go to the Bahamas at least once a year for a couple of months in the winter time. They were awesome folks.

I also took Gabby to the base during my off days and we hung out with some of my friends from work. She wasn't the best at bowling, but she liked going to the bowling alley just to chill out and bowl a couple of games. It was always a good time and it got her out of the apartment. We also went to South Beach, but mainly to the little restaurants. Gabby liked just walking around and seeing all the little shops and all the bright colors of the buildings.

I took Gabby to some of the clubs near the apartment and we danced and partied until the clubs closed. She really enjoyed that. After my vacation was up, I had to go back out on the TAD trips. The drug problem in Miami was really starting to get out of control, cocaine was everywhere and the dealers were starting to kill each other over territories to sell their drugs in, there was one guy killed near our apartment and the police had our whole street locked down for hours. They even flew in a helicopter with DEA agents in for the investigation.

Gabby came from a small town in England and had never seen anything like this. I was getting ready to go TAD again and she was a little nervous after the shooting. The next morning, I took her to the Miami animal shelter and we got a puppy. He was a pointer and Labrador mix. When we walked into the shelter, I looked at this German Shepard puppy. I put my finger in his cage and he bit it. I wanted him. Gabby was looking at the pointer lab mix puppy and wanted him. She was going to spend a lot more time with the dog then I was, so we got the one she wanted. The puppy had just been neutered and was still shaking and scared. She named him Shakey. As soon as we got him in the apartment, he went behind the couch and stayed there, we kept moving the couch and putting him in the middle of the room and he kept going back behind the couch. I told Gabby he just needed time to settle in and just having had his testicles removed. He probably doesn't like people too much. We left him alone behind the couch.

We had a box for him to sleep in with a towel inside it. I put him in there and he went straight to sleep. While we were at the animal shelter, we brought Shakey a collar and a leash, we went to a pet store afterward and brought him two bowels, one for water and the other for his food. Shakey was all set. He was not potty trained and that needed to be done. Gabby tried putting paper on the floor, but he just sniffed it and pissed right next to it. After a week, she was getting frustrated.

One day I was watching tv and he just walked right in front of the TV and lifted his leg, getting ready to pee on the floor. I took my tennis shoe and smacked his nose, then I put his nose in the pee. After that, I took him to the patio and tied him to the barbeque grill for a few minutes. He stood up and walked to the grass that was off the side of our cement slab of patio and took a poop. I untied him, brought him back inside and gave him a doggy treat. He never pissed or pooped inside the house again.

I went out to sea for two months, and when I got back, Shakey knew how to sit and lay down by command. He didn't know how to roll over yet, but Gabby said he would know soon. I liked this puppy. I brought him a wind-up mouse toy and he would chase it all over the house. After he was potty-trained at night, he would sleep at the foot of our bed on a little pillow.

Shakey was like a child to us. We took him with us most places that we went to. If we went to one of the outside restaurants. I would just tie his leash to my chair and he would lay down while we ate. He did have one bad habit and that was any bird that was on the ground. He wanted to chase and bark at it and he didn't care where we were.

He did keep the birds from our bait while we were fishing and that was awesome because the seagulls and pelicans like to steal the bait, especially the shrimp that we kept in a bucket of water. I was back out to sea for two weeks on board the Forrestal just to do an equipment check and when I got back, Shakey had learned how to roll over and give me a high-five with his right or left paw. Shakey had it going on.

I asked Gabby to marry me after we had been together for almost half a year. I put in for leave as we were going back to her little town in England to get married. I was told that even if I was TAD I could still take my leave as my commanding officer. I was good with that. By now, I had been to most of the islands off the southeast coast, and at least half of the Caribbean islands, one of my friends from work was going to stay at our apartment and take care of Shakey while we were gone for the two weeks.

Our command was to send to different crews out for what was called fleet week back then. One crew went to New York City on one of the old carriers, I chose the battleship and our division chief laughed. He said he knew I had enough of the carriers. He named all four of the ones I had been TAD on and he shook his head and laughed again.

I went TAD on board the USS Iowa, that ship had a better ride than the carriers I had been on. I liked the ship, the thirteen-inch guns and most of the crew. I wasn't too impressed with the guys that worked down in the engine room. We called them 'cannibal humanoid underground dwellers' after the movie 'CHUDs', most of them were in so much of a hurry they didn't bother to clean up just a little before they left their workspaces and they were sweaty and oily. We couldn't blame them, but to sit down and eat with their poopy suits down around their waist with hands and arms covered in oil and eating like they were starving was something else to see.

When we left Homestead, Florida the temperature was in the mid-seventies in February. We boarded Iowa at port Miami and headed over to the Gulf of Mexico. From there, we entered the Mississippi river through the Mississippi River Delta with a civilian pilot and two coast guard escort ships. We were headed for New Orleans. None of my crew, including myself thought to bring any types of cold weather gear. All we had were our dress blue uniforms and dungarees. Going up the Mississippi, the crew manned the rails about five miles out from New Orleans. Since we did not have the proper uniforms, we didn't have to man the rails (standing at parade rest while the ship entered port.)

Once we got near New Orleans, the temperature was in the high fifties, which was damn near freezing for us Floridians. Once we docked, most of the crew was allowed off the ship, we had to wear our dress blue uniforms the first day. Our little crew stayed on board that day. On the second day, we got off the ship in civilian clothes and went to find a place to buy some kind of jackets.

Once we had brought new jackets, we were off to Bourbon Street in two taxis. Once we were near Bourbon Street, the taxi stopped and let us out. We were in the crowd and it was wild. The street was packed damn near like boot camp, what was called nut-to-butt. It was like once the person in front of you took a step, then you could move. If the crowd stopped to watch some babe on one of the balconies flash her boobs for the crowd. We all stopped and yelled. Bars had folks outside selling large plastic cups of beer for five dollars. We had plenty of those.

About a third of the way down Bourbon Street, we went into a strip club that had female wrestling. We got thrown out, it was a wrestling match between the club's female champion and a challenger. The champion was gorgeous. The challenger looked like she was in her late fifties and hadn't aged well at all. She had little saggy boobs, and her nipples were aiming at the ground, and she had very bad stretch marks on her belly.

When they came on the stage, they were wearing bikinis and once the bout started, the champion snatched the challenger's bikini top off. Two of my guys, myself and another guy in the bar, were just taking sips of beer when that happened. I spit my beer out of my mouth and the guy at the table next to us spit him out. We all were laughing like crazy, then one of my guys threw his empty cup at her, the challenger had Band-Aids trying to cover her nipples and that's what really got us laughing. Somebody threw a half-empty cup of beer at her and the bouncers asked us to leave. They said one of us threw the cup. I asked him if he had ever heard of a sailor wasting beer. He laughed and pointed at our youngest guy (our guy claimed he didn't do it). Our whole table was kicked out of the bar. We were still laughing as the bouncer escorted us out.

Once outside, we did what sailors do, get more beer. We saw lots of breasts, nice ones, not nice at all and some really huge ones, we threw them the most beads, all the beads we had we picked up off the ground. What can I say we wanted to spend our money on beer. The police were parked on side streets and some were riding horses down the streets. The only problem we saw was what one officer told us and it involved the Crips gang and some redneck college kids.

I liked the parts of the city that we had seen, not the crowds but the buildings and the sounds were cool. We made the walk from the bottom of Bourbon Street to the top and it took almost six hours, stopping at a lot of the little bars and listening to the music of New Orleans. We stopped at one other strip joint, mainly to use the bathrooms. If you just walked it to go to the toilet, there was a five-dollar charge. We figured if we were going to pay that amount, we may as well buy a beer, sit for a while and listen to some music and watch the strippers. When we reached the top of Bourbon Street, we all had to pee badly. We noticed this building on a side street. It was a big building, fairly new and all the windows were tinted. It looked like it was closed. We all went to it pulled out our hookups and pissed like crazy. Then lights came on in the building, and we could see people eating and some were staring at us.

We ran like crazy to the next street over and caught two cabs back to the ship. Just as we were leaving, we could hear police sirens and they were headed toward the building we were at. Four of us wanted to go to a club since I was getting married and would be leaving the ship soon. We stopped one of the taxi drivers and told him that we wanted to go to a club that was safe, so we could meet some babes and dance. He laughed and said he knew the place, it was in one of the roughest parts of New Orleans, we didn't stay long maybe a couple of hours, in that time there were three fights. We left and went back to the Iowa and crashed out.

The next day I had the duty in our spaces, so most of our guys stayed on board. We were kinda worried about the new building we had pissed in front of and the police. There was a mall near where the ship was docked and we went there on the third day and hung out. It was cool and I loved the Creo look of the ladies. They were beautiful. I never talked to any I just looked. I had Gabby and that was enough for me.

The next day we left New Orleans with our coast guard escorts and headed back into the Gulf of Mexico. We had a call about some drug boats hauling ass our way, the captain launched one of the helicopters with a gun crew and they ordered the boat to stop. That boat was doing over forty miles per hour and it just kept going. The boat was hailed three times and it never answered or stopped, we fired one round at it and when the shell hit the water, the boat was swamped. The water that splashed up from the shell caused the boat to flip over. Some of the packages of cocaine were floating near the boat, and the four guys that were driving it were sitting on the bottom part of the boat, waiting to be rescued. The coast guard arrived about thirty minutes later to rescue them.

We left the gulf and headed for the Caribbean. Much to my dislike, we hit St Martins again. I did go ashore and went to the Dutch side with two of the crew and caught a cab to Happy Bay Beach. It was a nude beach, we didn't get naked, but it was fun sitting in water that was almost eighty-six degrees and looking at the nude ladies while drinking beer. We stayed there for a while, then went off to explore the St Mateen area that was within walking distance of the ship. We all brought little souvenirs, I brought a shell necklace for Gabby and this really thick piece of rope that had wooden pieces weaved into it for Shakey.

We left that area in the middle of April and headed for a small island near Porto Rico called Vieques, which at the time was used for target practice by the US navy and air force. During the time we were in the Vieques area of Porto Rico, the ship fired most if not all of the heavy guns. I volunteered to be part of the snoopy team (taking pictures team) with this really cool camera the navy had. It took a lot of pictures automatically. I was on a shelf outside the ship on the eighth level up with a chain attached to my belt, above the big guns to see if I could capture a picture of the shell leaving the barrel. It didn't work. As soon as they started to fire, the wind shifted, and the flames from the guns came up and right over where we were standing, it only lasted a second at the most, it was enough to singe my mustache, eyebrows and it blew my ballcap right off my head. It looked I had a serious suntan, once they came up to check on us, the one second class petty officer told me to come down.

I told him my butt cheeks were holding me in place. He laughed and helped me to the latter get down, I couldn't hear anything for several hours, and I had ear plugs and these big ear muffs over my ears. The only pictures I got were all orange, except for the toe of one of my boots. I never volunteered for the snoopy team again. A couple of days later, we were cruising right off the coast on the west side of Puerto Rico, and we saw this gorgeous lady riding a horse on the beach in her bikini and we were not the only ones that saw her, of course, I didn't have my camera then.

We headed over to the northern side of the island and cruised around there for a few days. On April 17th, I caught the supply helicopter from the ship back to the carrier, and then I was on the supply airplane, a Grumman C2 (COD) to Naval Air Station Key West and a bus to Homestead Air Force Base.

Gabby and I left on April 18th, 1983. We got married at her town's justice of the peace offices. Gabby's mother, sister and brother-in-law were there, along with her niece and nephew. After the wedding we got a room above a pub called the Cock and Bull, it was awesome, that is where I learned that I did not care for Guinness after we unpacked our luggage I went down to the pub to get a beer, all the locals stopped talking and stared directly at me. Once I ordered a Guinness, they all went back to their normal activities, darts and drinking.

One came over to tell me a joke about us Yanks. He told me the only thing wrong with Yanks "Is that you are overpaid, take our women and over here." They all started laughing. I would have laughed also, but I could not. I was trying to swallow the Guinness beer. I downed the whole thing there and ordered a Budweiser. They all went back to laughing and telling each other jokes.

I went back up the stairs to our room and just as I got inside the door, my stomach made this loud growling noise. I barely made it to the bathroom. I don't think I ever drank a Guinness beer again. I didn't care too much for our breakfast. I didn't mind the sausage and ham (which was called bacon), but the beans on the toast with mushrooms. I just wasn't ready for that. That night we went back downstairs for dinner. We had steaks with mushrooms and baked potatoes and a salad. I remember because it was probably the best meal I had for the two weeks we were there.

That night after we got back into our room. I turned on the TV and got the news channel. To my surprise, the news started with USS Iowa suffering an explosion. I was supposed to be on that ship, but I came to England to get married. I was worried about the crew. There was no news about any casualties yet. I knew our work area onboard was above and behind the massive three forward sixteen-inch guns. I hoped they were all okay.

After the third day, we stayed with Gabby's Mom, and I got to know her family better. Gabby and her sister did not look alike except for the large boobs and being just barely over five feet tall, that was it. Her mom looked more like her sister. Gabby's Mom was a true believer of the royal family. One day we were watching a British comedian called Bennie Hill and he said something bad about one of the royals on TV. Her mom got up and turned the TV off. She did not want it back on until the offending show was over, she could have changed the channel, but she didn't want the tv on until that particular program was over. The house was awesome. It had the old fashion heaters on the walls. It was a two-bedroom, one-bath home on a quiet street. It rained a lot while we were there, and the weather was nice and cool, the air was fresh, and the town was surrounded by woods. It was beautiful. Some of the houses had thatched roofs on them. They looked awesome. The main street was just two blocks away and they had a very good bakery and all kinds of shops, even a Chinese restaurant which we went to a couple of times.

Her sister came over with her oldest daughter and son, the girl was around eight years old and the boy was near six years old. I asked Gabby where the bank was, and the little girl said she would show me, so I went with the two kids to the bank. They were good little ones and I liked them a lot, when we got back all the lights were off in the house it was a fuse in the breaker box. They did not use the same kind of fuses as we had in the states. Theirs were just a piece of wire. When there was a problem, the surge would break the wire, Gabby had changed them a lot of times. I had never seen anything like it. Her mother would only let me change it, not the girls, so I had to ask Gabby how to change it and she showed me. That was the best that I could do.

She thought it was a man's job to change fused or change a light bulb. The last night we all went to dinner. It was a good dinner, none of the ladies cried at dinner, but when we got back to Gabby's Moms' house. The tears started, I was with Gabby's brother-in-law. He was trying to be a tuff guy and said straight out that if I hurt her, he would fly over and kick my ass. I told him to stop dreaming because we both knew what would happen if we got into a fight. He looked like he was going to pass out when Gabby came into the room she asked him what was wrong he told her nothing. She sat on my lap, and I kissed her, looking straight at him. I never cared much for him and I just wanted to pimp slap his ass, but I didn't out of respect for Gabby's Mom and being in her house. I don't think I ever saw him again and I know it was good for me. I did like her sister and her sisters' children. They were well-mannered and I just loved hearing them speak with that little British accent.

The next morning, we caught a cab to Heathrow Airport and headed back to Miami International. It was a long flight, but Miami is three hours behind England, so it was just getting dark when we landed and got through customs. We had a drink at the bar in the airport, then went to the parking lot, got in the Z and headed back to our apartment.

As soon as we got there, Shakey was wagging his tail and happy to see us. The apartment was just as clean as it was when we left and my friend was ready to get back to his room in the barracks. He told me that my family had been calling like crazy. I forgot to let them know that I wasn't on the ship when the explosion happened. I did call immediately after he left. Shakey jumped into my lap as I was telling Mom that I was getting married in England when the explosion happened and that I was back in Miami now with my new wife.

My entire family was double shocked, I never told them what ships I was going on and I never told them about Gabby. I can't begin to imagine what my mom was going through, thinking I could have been on the ship that had an explosion on it and then to find out she had a new daughter-in-law that was from another country. I told her that I had been on that ship, but I got off two days before the explosion, she asked me what had happened, and I told her I really didn't know and to be honest, I really didn't.

Mom was so happy that I called. I guess she called most of the family that she knew I liked or that liked me and we got calls from them all night congratulating us and saying how glad they were I was not on the ship. I didn't really want to think of the explosion because I had met some of the ship's crew and they, for the most part, were good, hard working sailors, most of whom were proud to be on that ship, just like most other US Navy crews.

My time at NSGA Homestead was coming to an end and it was time for me to have two overseas duty stations. I filled out my dream sheet and put in for Spain and then England. That way, Gabby would be close to her family and she was happy with my choices. I did let her know that I never got any choice that I made overseas. Did she look and me as if to say, then why fill out a dream sheet?

We both started laughing. I really loved this little woman. I had four more months left and I got my last TAD orders from NSGA Homestead. I was to do a cruise on board the USS. It was the newest aircraft carrier I had been on, she had just finished having a lot of work done on her and I was to do a two-month cruise around the east coast while the pilots conducted flight operations (flight ops), then we headed to Rota Spain. The ship had flight ops damn near the whole way and like on the old Forrestal and Saratoga. The birthing I had was just a couple of decks below the flight deck. I had learned a lot from being on the older carriers, America was bigger and faster, but most places I needed to go to were basically in the same locations.

At night when I couldn't sleep, I would go up and watch the flight ops. There is nothing that could compare to watching an F-14 Tomcat taking off at night. The flames from the engines afterburners were awesome and then in just a few seconds. It was air born and ripping through the dark night skies. I will never forget those sights. Once we pulled into Rota, Spain, I was to have a couple of days off and then catch a flight home back to Homestead Air Base. That didn't happen, there was some bad weather over the Atlantic Ocean that prevented any flights going to Homestead.

I called my chief back in Homestead and he told me there was nothing that I could do to enjoy Rota. I did for a little over two weeks. I was stuck in the place I wanted to be stationed. I had gotten a room in the Rota Naval Base Barracks and I had a roommate that was an old marine. He was a Gunnery Sargent, his feet were giving him some serious problems and he was retiring out of the Marines after twenty-one years. He wanted to get twenty-four years in, but his condition wouldn't allow it. He could either get the normal retirement or a medical discharge, he took the regular retirement as it paid more per month. Once he was retired, he could claim his medical conditions and get extra monies.

He was cool as hell, I was happy to be here, but not able to get home to Gabby sucked, but Gabby and I partied during the day. We would catch a cab off base and get to this club I can't remember the name of it, but it is now called the 'Bullring'. We would get there around noon, just as the locals were getting off for their siesta. They would get off work around eleven or twelve and stay off work until five or six PM. Most of the ladies would be at the beach, and back then, a lot of those ladies went topless. Gabby and I would just chill outside the little beach bars, check out the ladies and drink lots of beer.

Gabby had a wife back home in Virginia and he was glad to show me pictures of her in her negligee when he got drunk. I would just do a quick glance and then get him on another subject before he started telling me about his sex life with her. I didn't want to hear it. I wanted to be home with Gabby having my own sex life. I'm pretty sure I could have gotten lucky in Rota, but I had just gotten married and that was not how I planned this marriage to go. After the second week, we were able to catch a MAC flight back to NSGA Homestead. Gabby caught another flight up to Virginia and we shook hands. I left the terminal and got to my Z. It was time to go home. It took me twenty minutes to get home. I hadn't called Gabby to let her know I was on my way. She still thought I was in Spain. When I opened the door and dropped my sea bag, Shakey was the first to greet me. He had gotten bigger, but he still liked to jump up in my arms. He was trying to lick my face, then Gabby came in and shouted for him to get down.

I let him go and grabbed Gabby. She ordered pizza that night, enough for the three of us, there was still plenty of beer in the refrigerator and I still had a bottle of Chivas Regal in the kitchen cabinet. She went running my bath water and put the Chivas bottle near the bathtub. Just as I finished undressing, she turned on the shower and I got in. I really needed to shave and get my hair cut, I didn't care and neither did Gabby. The pizza arrived not too long after I got out of the tub and the three of us ate dinner together. Finally, after almost three months, we kidded each other, played with Shakey and then watched TV. Around eight PM, I was done and ready to pass out. Gabby had other ideas. Shakey had to sleep in the living room.

The next morning, I went in for my debriefing. I thought I was going to get three days off. My chief started laughing. He said you just got back from a two-week vacation in beautiful Rota, Spain and you want time off, I smiled he said I would get two days off after I went in on the last mid-watch, so I would have to do the last two eve watches and then I would have my eighty hours off with two additional days off, I was pleased.

Then he handed me my new orders to NSGA San Vito, Italy. It wasn't what I had asked for, but it would be awesome to be stationed in Italy. I would be going to another A-School for three months for more advanced analyst training in San Angelo, Texas. Gabby would be staying with my family in Los Angeles as I wanted them to get to know her.

I went home and told Gabby. She had a big smile on her face. We both thought we were going back to the Pacific side of the world. Gabby asked if she would be going with me and I told her, yes and no. I had a school in Texas that I would be going to for six months and after that, we would all be together again and heading to Italy. I hugged both her and Shakey. I kissed her and we did a barbeque that evening as I would be working the next two eve watches, then we would have five days together. It was the end of February and we were ready to leave Shakey didn't know what was happening when the moving folks came and picked up our furniture. He lost his mind, barking at them. I had him on his leash the whole time they were there.

I called my moms and let her know that I had orders to a place called San Vito, Italy, but I had to go to another school for three months and I asked her if Gabby and Shaky could stay with her for a couple of months and then Gabby would go back to England with her family until I finished the school. Of course, Mom said, "Yes" and she would be glad to have Gabby and Shakey.

I had one week of leave and we flew to Los Angeles, California, to spend time with my family. It was great to see my family all together, and my little nephew Little D. It took pops some getting used to Shakey, but once Gabby made Shakey do some of his tricks, pops was okay. Little D loved Shakey so did Mom.

Gabby got along great with both of my sisters and it was all good from then on. I would wake up and Gabby and my sisters were off to the mall or somewhere. I just smiled. I knew she would be okay with them. She wanted to go and visit a friend of hers that was in Misawa for my last month in A-school. I told her as lone as she and Shakey were going to be safe, I was okay with it. What neither of us knew was the fact that her friend's husband, who was in the air force, was getting out of the military. His wife didn't know either. I don't know the reasons why he got out, but I do know he was a total asshole, which I found out later.

I hugged everybody and slowly kissed Mom on her cheek. I didn't want her to think I was going to bite her cheek again like I did when I was leaving for Okinawa. She gave me that you better not bite me look and then she smiled at me. I knew my wife and dog were in good hands.

Pops drove me to the Los Angeles International Air Port and dropped me off at the front entrance. I grabbed my sea bag, which also had a little thirty-two pistol he had given me on the top of it. (back then, there was no hard-core screening of passengers at the airports). I was in my dress blue uniform as it was winter uniform time. I handed the lady behind the counter my tickets and put my bag in the space for her to put it with the rest of the luggage for the flight. She smiled at me and said she had never been to San Antonio.

I told her I hadn't either, she smiled and said enjoy your flight and I said as long as they have been on board,.I would be okay, she laughed and I walked to the gate and sat down. Now in 1990, not many people had laptops or smartphones. We had laptops in the military and they weighed around twenty pounds. They were slow and built to be dropped without any damage to the screen or the internal parts, so most people read the newspapers or magazines. I went and brought a book about Italy and read that while waiting to board my flight.

I don't know if I mentioned this, but I am not now or never have been big on being in airplanes, but I do know that if I used a credit card with the travel miles. I would have had plenty of them. As soon as we boarded and the plane took off. I noticed that this flight had a guy as a flight attendant. I think they used to be called stewardesses. Now, they were called flight attendants. Times were really changing and changing fast in the United States. One of the attendants was a black man. I read my book and had a few beers, okay more than a few beers and I slept for two of the almost three-hour flight.

NTTC Good Fellow - San Angelo, Texas March 1990 – June 1990

The plane arrived in San Antonio, Texas, around ten fifty-five that night. I got my sea bag and went out for a smoke, grabbed a cab and the driver asked me if I wanted to go to the base and I said, "Yep, to San Angelo," which I thought would be the next town. It was not the next town, it was nowhere near San Antonio. It was over one hundred and eighty miles away. The driver told me that there was a bus I could catch if we hurried up. The bus station was out in the middle of nowhere and it was dark as hell. I was glad I kept a couple of hundred dollars on me for an emergency. Whoever typed my orders put San Antonio instead of San Angelo, I was pissed and I mean really pissed. The person I purchased the bus ticket from told me I would have to wait for the bus at the bus stop out the gate and across the road. The bus station was probably about a quarter of a mile from the main road. It was pitch black outside. Did I mention I was really pissed off at whoever typed up my orders? Well, I was just pissed off.

I was told it would be around a five-hour trip. I tried not to show how mad I was and I thanked the man that sold me the ticket. I put my sea bag on my back, and started walking, then I sat it down, opened it and took the pistol out just in case. I was told the bus would be here in about an hour and to be standing by the Greyhound sign or it wouldn't stop.

I didn't see any cars or anything for that whole hour I was waiting. I could hear things out there and they were not human sounds. I put my sea bag on the bench and sat on it. I did not want to mess up my dress blues sitting on a dirty bench. I had never been in this situation before, a place that I could not see more than thirty feet in front of me with no houses or anything, just the road and dirt all around, and it was just a little light above the bench, so the bus driver could see if someone was there. I made sure the pistol was locked and loaded. I kept hearing all kinds of sounds. I wasn't scared, but I wasn't happy either. The longer I waited, the more noises I heard, like animals chasing other animals.

My biggest fear was the snakes and scorpions that Texas has. After the first thirty minutes, I was ready to walk back to the bus terminal and change the ticket for the next day, so I could get a room somewhere, but I stuck it out. The Grey Hound bus was right on time and I could see the lights from the bus getting brighter and brighter. I checked the ground because I had been sitting on my sea bag and didn't want to jump down on any animal or bug. I put my pistol back in the sea bag, and the driver stopped the bus, opened the door, and took my ticket. He told me I was the third person that month that had the same orders. Then he told me to make myself comfortable as we had more stops on the way. It was going to be a little over five hours to get to San Angelo.

I would say the bus had maybe fifteen or twenty people on it, I went to the back and put my sea bag on the back seat and I stretched out next to it. I was able to get a little bit of sleep, but the driver would announce each little town we stopped at. I probably got about two hours of sleep and I had taken my top off and folded it so it wouldn't be wrinkled when I did get to the base in San Angelo. When I got off the bus, it was after four am, and there was a taxi at the front of the bus station. I told the cab driver I wanted to go to Goodfellow Air Force Base. About fifteen minutes later, I was there, the cab ride was like six dollars and I was at the front gate.

Once I got out of the cab, I walked to the gate guard and asked where the Navy quarter-deck was located. He told me to hold on one second. He went inside the little post and made a call. About five minutes later, one of the old white navy vans showed up. The driver was a third-class petty officer. He was pretty cool. He drove me around the base showing me all the facilities, the px, chow hall, church and where I would be going for classes in the restricted side of the base. He then told me about the club and how some of the officers are brand new right out of their different academies and they had strange ideas about how things should be run around here.

I smiled at that thought, he pulled up to the quarter deck and we both got out. I went to the front desk and when I looked around, the driver was gone, probably back to his rack. The chief that I handed my orders to looked at them and just sighed. He said you were sent to San Antonio, I said, "Yep I was." He shook his head again and said the important thing is that you made it here okay and that I was the fourth person sent to the wrong base. He told me that I wasn't expected for another two days and I told him, "I like to get to my duty stations a day or two before ordered." He smiled and said he was the same way. He handed me a room key and told me I was billeted on the second floor and I would have one roommate. I thanked him, found my way to the stairs and went up to my new home for the next three months.

As soon as I got into the room, I opened my sea bag and took everything out, put it all in the locker, then I took off my dress blues and hung them up. I put the pistol back into my sea bag, which I folded up and put in the bottom of the locker. Both of my roommates were passed out. I tried to be as quiet as I could, but when I got into the rack, it made lots of squeaking sounds. I passed out almost immediately.

I slept until about one or two PM, got up and went looking for some chow. I hadn't eaten anything since I left Los Angeles. I took a very long shower, brushed my teeth and shaved. I needed a haircut also. I would take care of that after I put some chow in my belly. I got dressed, went down to the Quarter Deck and asked where the chow hall was. There was a very pretty third-class petty officer sitting behind the desk, she was a student also, she was just assigned to the front desk until her class started. I asked her where the chow hall was and also the barbershop, she gave me a map that was easy to read and I could make out most of the places I would be interested in going to.

Air Force bases were something else. They had everything. There was a little fast food place for people like me that slept thru breakfast and lunch. The uniform shop was right next to the px along with the barbershop. In an hour and a half, I had filled my belly with a cheeseburger and fries, went next door and got my little afro back to a high and tight. Then I went looking for other sailors and I found some at the bowling alley.

The training we went to was mentally challenging, and we did do a lot of PT (physical training) at least once or twice per week and we would run on the weekends. Goodfellow Air Force base had all the different branches of the military there. The Marines and Navy got the same classes, Army and Air Force each had their own training programs. You had to go through two security checkpoints to get into the classes and I will tell you, security was tight here. If you failed a test in one of our classes, the instructor would put a red brick on your desk. None of us wanted to walk in and find the brick on our desk.

Some of the training was really outdated and I let this one instructor know that this doesn't work anymore. I outranked him, so he tried to explain that this is the curriculum that he was given and it is what our test would consist of. I sat back down and shut up. One of the other second-class petty officers came over to me and said just go with the flow, bro and the whole class, except for the instructor, laughed.

Our accommodations at Goodfellow Air Force were beyond what we were used to in the navy, our barracks held the sailors and marines, there were no female marines so the marines had less than a third of the barracks, female sailors were on the top or third floor and they only took up half of that floor the rest were male sailors. The rooms only had two people in them, not the three or four that we were used to. The Air Force had it made, they had someone come in and clean the floors for them, get their uniforms cleaned and it was much better living conditions than us sailors, marines and soldiers were used to.

In the back of the barracks, there were a couple of bar-b-que pits, benches, plenty of room to have a nice party and we partied every weekend. Someone always had something to drink and boy did we drink. Most of the folks I hung out with were married except for one female, she was very nice looking and all the guys wanted to be with her. She and I clicked like a big brother and his little sister. We hung out all the time with another guy named Gary. He had just reenlisted and brought a brand-new mustang, so it was Teresa, Gary and me hanging out all the time when we were not in class.

PT was done in an area specifically for PT and nothing else. I liked all of it but the mile and a half run. There was a female chief that was in charge of us during PT. She seldom ran with us as she would run in the mornings before most of us were up for classes. If there was a serious straggler, she would run back to find him or her with the radio just in case she needed to call an ambulance.

The night before our runs, I would hide beer and cigarettes behind some of the trees for a quick break. I was amazed that I never got caught, we would lag behind all the lower-ranking personnel and then take a few seconds of a break and we always made the run on time. The younger kids would make fun of us and laugh. We didn't want to comment back as we had beer on our breaths.

One day I got a runner's high. It was weird. I kept running and went an extra mile like I said it was weird because I hated the idea of running long distances. After the run, Gary and I went to the chow hall. We had both missed breakfast and were hung over from the night before. When we got there. We got our trays stood in line and picked out what we wanted to eat and sat down at a table that had some Army folks. Halfway through the meal, Gary started nudging me with his elbow. I was shoveling food in my mouth. I was starving.

Then he started laughing, I looked at him and he was red as hell. I quietly asked him if he was alright. He shook his head slowly and whispered no. I asked him what the hell was wrong with him, and he got up and said to come with him, so I did. Once we left the table, he broke out laughing and I mean that hard laugh that brings tears to your eyes. I said what is so funny and he told me to look at the female sitting at the end of the table. I had been so busy shoving my food in my mouth that I hadn't noticed her. She looked like she had a hell of a set of breasts on her, but her face looked like a horse. I giggled, Gary stopped laughing, and we went back to the table and tried to finish our lunch. That's when all hell broke out. Gary grabbed a sugar cube and tossed it at the female soldier that looked like a horse, and then he made a sound like a horse snorting and I started laughing like crazy. Well, the guys there didn't find that shit funny at all. I was holding my sides when Gary grabbed me and said run.

They chased us until we got to the barracks. We went to Gary's room and laughed for quite a while. After that, we found Teresa and told her about the lady with the horse's face. She said she had also seen her and tried to be stern with us about the sugar cube and all. Gary and I looked at each other and burst up laughing again. Teresa turned her back to us then she started laughing.

Gary and I went totally downhill from there. We should have never met. The next day the three of us decided to rent fishing gear on base, buy beer and try our luck at Lake Naseworthy or, as we called, lake Nasty worthy. We got there and opened the beers and Teresa pulled out her foldout chair and sat back to watch. We were using live worms for bait and not having any luck. I decided to walk further down and try my luck there. While I was casting, I heard a rumbling sound like nothing I had ever heard before, then I saw them, about twenty or thirty cows were running as fast as they could to get to the water. I just stood there staring at them, and that was when Gary grabbed me and we took off running back to Teresa and the car. He said, "Fool, you could have gotten trampled. Haven't you ever seen thirsty cows and a bull leading them?"

I said, "Hell, no, damn it. I'm from Los Angeles. When I see a cow, I think of steak and milk."

They both laughed their asses off at me. We got back in the car, went back to the base and returned the fishing gear. We started one of the bar-b-que grills and had hamburgers.

I had put my uniform in on a Friday and it would be ready on that Saturday, so after PT, while everybody else was partying. I grabbed one of the ten-speed bikes that were sitting around and not used, rode up the hill to the base cleaners, and got uniform, then I went and brought more beer and headed down the hill. That hill was pretty steep, so I just took my feet off of the pedals and let the bike take me down the hill. I took my hands off the handlebars and opened one of the beers and started to drink it. When I got about two-thirds of the way down, one of the Air Force Security guys pulled behind me. I didn't think anything of it.

Then he pulled on the side of me and told me to pull over just as I was taking another swig of my beer. I looked at him like he was crazy and kept going. I had a slight turn to make, so I put the empty can back into the bag with the rest of the gear. I had my uniform in my other hand and it was on a hanger covered in clear plastic. I leaned into the curve and shot right in front of the guard's car and onto the pavement in front of the Navy barracks. It looked like everybody in the barracks was out front drinking and when Teresa saw me coming down the hill being chased by the police car. She told everybody to check this out. When they saw it was me, they were all laughing and screaming, "Go, Dino, go!" I stayed on the bike until I hit the sidewalk, slowed it down and jumped off the bike, tossed the beers to Gary and ran through the front door, hit the stairs and put on jeans and a Navy t-shirt.

I knew he never got a good look at my face as I was wearing my navy hat and the big aviator sunglasses. He called for backup instead of chasing me into the barracks. I came back down the back stairs and grabbed a beer from Gary and started shouting and laughing also. The other car came, and the two guards talked for a few seconds, got back in their cars and left. I guess they didn't want to mess with a bunch of drunk sailors and marines.

Teresa told me that I was the only person in the world that could outrun a car on a ten-speed bike and come back down and make fun of the officer. We all busted up laughing and continued to party. There were two new marines in the barracks and one of those guys should have been the Marine Corps Poster dude. Teresa was in lust as soon as she saw him. Teresa, Gary and I were all at least twenty-four years old. This marine was probably nineteen or twenty, she said she didn't care. The party was still going strong and the two new guys were introduced to the gang. The poster guy was cool as hell. His buddy had that why are we partying with sailors attitude. Everybody ignored him. They were both brand new corporals, they were both handed a beer and we got back to partying. We ran out of beer, Gary told everybody that had any booze in their rooms to bring it down. I had a bottle of Mad Dog 20-20 that was almost full, and Teresa had a couple of bottles of wine. Gary brought some whiskey and other people brought all kinds of booze down.

Gary grabbed one of the fifty-gallon trash cans and poured the trash from it into another trash can. He then went to the supply closet in the barracks and came back with one of those big black plastic bags used for grass and weeds. Teresa, the new poster guy and I went to the ice machine and got as much ice as we could carry and put it all in the bag that was now inside the trash can (we never washed the can out). Then Gary asked if anybody had any kind of fruit juice. We all had some of that in our rooms. We poured all the booze and juice into the trash can over the ice and Gary told us all to wait just a few minutes for the mojo to cure. I looked at Teresa and she looked back at me. We both said fuck that, took our cups and dipped them into the can and so did everybody else. The party was back on.

People that had girlfriends in the navy started pairing off and heading back into the barracks a little before midnight. We were all toasted and should have all just gone to bed. Gary left for a few minutes, came back and we both staggered over to his car. I asked where we were going. He said he had just called this little Pilipino babe he met in town that looked like his wife and she wanted us to come over. I said, "Cool," we got in the car and drove about twenty minutes to some apartment complexes. She was standing outside and he was right. She was very good-looking. We went inside. She offered us some beer, I took mine and Gary asked where your friend was. She said her friend couldn't make it. I told them to go ahead ill just watch some tv.

About fifteen minutes later, Gary came out of the room. He looked pissed and kind of scared. I was damn near passed out when he said let's go. I asked what the hell was going on. He mumbled something while he was putting his clothes back on, and she came out of the room naked as hell crying. I was confused, really confused and we were both still drunk as hell. We got into his car and headed back to base.

Now Gary had just left Misawa, Japan, where I had been before and he was still getting used to driving on American roads on the left-hand side of the roads. I was nodding in and out of consciousness. The police officer asked Gary for his license and then told him to get out of the car. The officer asked Gary, "What the hell is your problem?" He was driving on the wrong side of the road speeding and Gary told him the biggest bull shit story I ever heard. Gary told the officer that he had just gotten back into the states after leaving Japan and tomorrow, he would be leaving for Oklahoma to bury his mother and dog. She was driving home from the vet's office when a truck t-boned her car, killing both his mother and dog, then he broke down crying. I was trying not to laugh and stay conscious at the same time. The officer peeked into the car and asked if that was correct. I nodded my head, trying to stay awake.

He made Gary do the drunk test where you have to walk a straight line, one foot in front of the other. He only made two steps. The officer told Gary he was only going to give him a warning. Then he asked me if I had a driver's license again, I nodded. The officer told me to drive the car back to base. Gary was grinning his ass off and I was trying not to stumble getting out of the car and make it to the driver's seat.

The officer must have gotten a call on the radio because he peeled out, made a U-turn and was gone. Gary said, “Let’s go,” I put the car in drive and we took off halfway there. Gary told me to pull over and I did.

He said, “Dude you’re driving worse than I was. I’ll drive the rest of the way.” I was so happy. I got in the passenger seat and passed out, Gary got me to my room and I passed out again.

The next morning around nine am, somebody was banging on my door like crazy. I screamed that I wasn’t home and tried to get back to sleep, but the banging started again. I got up went to the door and opened it, it was one of the new marines, the little one and he was pissed. I asked him what did he want, and he said he couldn’t find his buddy, and they had an inspection and it was my fault that he couldn’t find him. I slammed the door in his face and tried to lay back down.

He banged on the door again. I was pissed off now and ready to give him a knockout punch so I could get back to sleep, I opened the door and he told me if his friend was late to the inspection, he would not be a corporal for long. I looked at him and shook my head, I asked him when was the last time he had seen his friend and he said around midnight. I told him, “At midnight I was in town with Gary watching TV.”

He asked about Teresa and where her room was and to be honest, I didn’t know where her room was, she was always down here in my room or Gary’s room. I put on shorts, and a t-shirt walked to the front desk and grabbed the room list, found her room number and we both went up the stairs to her room. We had to bang on the door for a long time before she opened it, she squinted both her eyes and asked what was going on. I told her and she said he is sleeping in her bed. The poster boy was out cold. I just winked at her. His buddy just pushed past both of us and started yelling for his friend to wake up. He went to the sink and filled a glass with water and poured it over his friend’s face. That woke him up real fast and he was pissed.

Teresa and I both stepped back a few feet in case he grabbed his little friend and bent him in half. He yelled at the poster boy that they had an inspection in forty-five minutes, the poster boy stood up, put on his clothes, kissed Teresa and they both ran to his room.

I looked at Teresa and called her a cougar. We both laughed. I kissed her on her cheek and said lunch at twelve. She nodded her head and took off her robe, and got back into bed. If I wasn’t married, I probably would have joined her. I slowly turned and walked back down the stair, made it back to my room and hit the rack. Teresa knocked on my door a little after noon, I was getting ready and she asked me what the hell happened. I told her that the marines were having some kind of inspection and that the poster boy and his friend were getting promoted.

She said damn, nothing else was mentioned about it. On the way down the stairs we met Gary, he wasn't mad anymore and as soon as he saw me, he started laughing. Then we walked to the chow hall. Teresa asked where did we disappear last night. I told her as much as I could remember and Gary told her the rest. She couldn't believe it. I told her I was driving back, trying not to pass out, and we all laughed.

We ran into the two marines while we were leaving the chow hall, poster boy asked Teresa if he could speak with her, and they walked away. The little guy walked up to me and I was ready to sock the hell out of him, but the first word out of his mouth was an apology to me. He thought I hooked Teresa and poster boy up. Gary told him that we left way before everybody stopped partying, and the little marine told me that poster boy had told him that and he was sorry for his behavior. I shook his hand and Gary and I walked back to the barracks. Teresa caught up with us and asked me if the little guy had apologized and I said, "Yep." We made it back to the barracks and nobody was outside. Gary said that was probably the best party we had to date. We all laughed and went to his room, his roommate left a week ago and he didn't have a new one yet. He had a little TV and we all sat on his rack and watched it. After a while, I got up to call my wife. I needed to know how she and the puppy were doing. When I called, we were both happy to hear each other's voice, we really missed each other, she asked me if I was still partying, I told her the truth that I was but nothing else, just getting wasted a lot.

I told her she was mine and I was hers. She didn't have to worry about me cheating on her because it just wasn't going to happen. Then she told me about her friend and her husband getting out of the air force. I didn't say anything, I just told her everything would be okay. I told Gabby they were teaching us stuff that doesn't exist anymore, and she laughed and told me to do my best and hurry up.

The parties kept on going. One day, I asked Gary if I could borrow his car because Teresa and I wanted to get off the base for a while just to get away. He had to study for the next test and was going to be in class until later that evening. He told me to stay on my side of the road and handed me the keys.

Teresa and I drove down to lake Nasty worthy, where we had tried to fish earlier. When we got there, some air force folks were there partying and told us to join them. One of them had his father's ski boat. His family lived not too far from the base, so he borrowed it for the day. It was four guys and a female. The female was not the best-looking girl, but she was fun and partied like the guys. Teresa told them the story about the base police trying to pull me over on the ten-speed bike and one of the guys said, that was you. I nodded at him. Two of them were base police and they told me the guy that tried to pull me over was a rookie and that he got straightened out as soon as he returned to their security center. We all laughed.

The guy with the boat asked us if we skied and I said I could. Teresa didn't want to, so I took off my shoes and got in the water. I yelled at Teresa that I hadn't water skied in years, and she yelled this should be funny, I gave the ready signal and the boat took off. I still remember how to ski, I was wobbly at first, but it was like riding a bike. Once you did it, you couldn't forget. The girl sat in the back of the boat with the red flag in case I went down. She would wave it for other boats to let them know there was someone in the water near the boat. There were none in our area. I skied for about four or five minutes. Then we headed back to shore. I got my feet out of the skies and sat in one of the little cheap fold-up chairs that Teresa and I brought along.

We had a couple more of their beers and then we noticed the girl walking to the truck and she took off all her clothes and laid down on her back. Each of those guys took turns having sex with her. Teresa and I got in the car and drove back to base. The only thing she said to me on the way back was, I didn't know you knew how to water ski and did we just see what we saw, then we both started laughing.

When we left, the guys that were not with the girl were setting up tents and pulling sleeping bags out of the back of the truck. Teresa said that girl is going to be busy tonight and we laughed again. When we got back to base, we headed to the chow hall. Gary was there with several of our group eating. When he saw us, he asked about the lake. Teresa and I got our food and sat down with them and told them what happened. Everybody's eyes were wide open. They just couldn't believe it, the new marines were there and the little one said sloppy seconds. We all laughed and finished our meals.

I handed Gary his car keys, and he, Teresa and I got in the car and drove back to the barracks. We still had a little over a month left at Goodfellow Air Force Base and I was beyond bored with it. I called Gabby and she told me that she wanted out of there, I let her know we only had a little over a month to go. She said she knew that, but a friend's husband was a real asshole. She was paying them a little over a hundred dollars a month for her and Shakey's food. I told her not to worry about him, but if he put his hands on her, I wanted her to kick him like I taught her, right between the legs as hard as she could. We both started laughing and after a few more minutes, I told her it wouldn't be much longer and we would be a family that was back together again and that I loved both of them.

If you failed two tests at school, you were dropped from the class and could request it again in a couple of years. I had no plans of requesting to go back to Goodfellow Airbase. We continued with our parties for the rest of our time at the training. During our last month, all E-4s and above in the classes got extra duties on the weekends. Gary and Teresa went to help with stranded animals, and I got to help with feeding the homeless at a church in San Angelo. There was an air force E-4 that I was working with at the church. The church was a decent size. I thought it could probably hold around fifty people in it. It was an old church, but it was well kept. The kitchen was a good size and was very clean. We cooked mainly some kind of stew which the air force guy said stretched the meals. The first meal we cooked barely had any meat in it, which surprised me. After we finished serving the meals, I walked back into the kitchen and caught him putting more than half of the beef in a big zip-lock plastic bag. I told him to take the beef out of the bag and put it back on the butcher's block. He told me he was an E-4 and we were going to do what he said, "I told him I was an E-5 and we will be doing what I say unless he wants me to report him for stealing food for the hungry." I went out and told the folks we made a mistake and had to work on their plates. None of them had started eating as the E-4 did one thing right. They all had to wait until the said grace before they could eat.

I made him go out and get all the plates from all the families that showed up for the free meal. I took the chunk of beef and cut it into small, thin pieces. I put the pieces in the microwave oven for about three minutes. Then I gave each of the plates nice helpings of the cut beef. After that, I told the E-4 to put each plate in the microwave for one minute. There were almost twenty plates that needed to be reheated. As soon as the plates were reheated, we served everyone. I could see the looks on their faces, it was a racially mixed group and they all looked happy to see real meat on their plates. I made the E-4 slice the bread and butter each piece and put the pieces in the microwave for just long enough for the butter to melt.

There was lettuce and tomatoes in the refrigerator. I chopped that stuff and made them a little salad. I found some of those little white sugar donuts in a bag that had potato chips and everything in it all packed up. This E-4 was going to take the stuff home to his family. I was pissed, but I did let him take a little of the stuff home. I put salads out for each of the folks sitting down and each one got a few of the little donuts. They looked kind of happy when I went back in to pick up the plates. The E-4 didn't look too happy. He was worried that I would report him. I let him know that I understood. I knew he had a family and how hard it was for him even living in base housing. But to take food out of homeless families' mouths was more than I could stand.

The E-4 and I worked together again two more times, he did what he was supposed to do and the folks that came into the church were happy. I had told Gary and Teresa about him and they were like me, understanding. It was a shame that we would have to steal from a church to feed our own families in the US military and in the United States at that. They both agreed that I did the right thing, not reporting him.

We were all ready to leave NTTC Good Fellow Air Force Base in San Angelo, Texas and head off to our new duty stations. Gary was heading to Misawa, Japan. Teresa and I both were going to San Vito, Italy. I know I was excited about leaving and getting back with Gabby and Shakey. Gabby had flown into San Angelo the day before I left San Antonio and got a ride with Gary to San Angelo. He dropped me off at the hotel Gabby was in. We shook hands and we wished each other good luck promising we would stay in touch. We never saw or heard from each other again. Gabby, Shakey and I headed for the San Angelo Airport and were on our way to Italy. Gabby told me that the vet gave her some pills to put Shakey to sleep during the long flight, so I gave him one just before we put him in his plastic cage and he was off to the baggage and loaded on the plane. Gabby and I barely had time to hug and kiss, but we were now ready to board the plane and start a new adventure in San Vito, Italy.

NSGA San Vito, Italy June 1990 – January 1993

Once we landed in Rome and got off the plane, we went to collect our luggage and Shakey, he must have just woken up and his mouth looked like it was foaming. I needed to get him some water quickly. I went to the kiosk near the front exit for our flight and there was a huge crowd around the kiosk. No line or anything, just people shouting in Italian what they wanted and the little guy behind the desk was trying to accommodate everybody.

It was just out of control. I walked to the cooler that had water and juices in it and grabbed three bottles of water and a little plastic cup. Two of the bottles were for Shakey and one for Gabby and I to share. I left three US dollars on the counter and just walked away. Then I lugged Shakey's cage and most of the luggage out of the door. Gabby had the rest. We got outside and had a smoke. I put the leash on Shakey and let him out of his cage. He just laid down on the ground. Gabby was pouring water into the plastic cup and he drank both bottles of water.

These were some of the rudest people that I had ever seen. We were sitting on a bench with Shakey between both of us, and I had to put my feet way out in front of us to stop people from stepping on Shakey. Those drugs we gave him were kicking his ass. The poor dog was still groggy from them. I spotted a Navy van and walked over to it. There was another couple in the Van and the driver said they were waiting for us. I walked back to Gabby and Shakey, and I grabbed his cage along with most of the luggage and walked over to the van, put all the stuff in the back, and went back for them.

After we were all in the van, the driver took off, he was driving like a crazy man, but he got us out of Rome and headed south. It took us at least four hours to get to the base in Naples, where the other couple was dropped off. We all had a break and got something to eat and had bathroom breaks. I took Shakey for a walk and he only peed. I was trying to urge him to take a poop, but he didn't need one.

We stayed on the base in Naples for about ten minutes while the driver filled the gas tank and then we were off again, heading south towards San Vito Dei Normanni. I found out from the driver that once I got a car in this country. I needed to make sure I filled it with gas on base as the off-base gas was sold in liters and it would cost almost three times as much. That held true for most places in Europe. Once we were out of Naples the countryside was breathtaking, there were lots of mountains, lush greenery, lots of olive trees and grapevines all along the sides of the mountains. The air was clean and fresh. It was just beautiful.

Shakey laid in my lap in the van, he just slept most of the way. It was late when we arrived at NSGA San Vito, so we were driven to the quarterdeck and the van driver stayed outside in the van. After I handed over my orders, I was told the van would take us to temporary housing, a place where we would stay until we found off-base housing. I was also told there was nearly a three-year wait for on-base housing. I said isn't that something, so just before we leave, we can get on base housing, the petty officer just shook his head.

We were driven to a place off base. It was sort of like a hotel, but the rooms were like a very small apartment. It had a small kitchen, bedroom, a bathroom and a sitting area, directly outside of the front door was a small patio area. The place was completely furnished, we stayed there for almost a month.

That first night Gabby and Shakey both went to sleep. I decided to watch some tv, of course, I couldn't speak Italian, but it was fun just changing the channels to see what was on, boy was I surprised. TV in Italy during those days had all kinds of shows, including late night porn and a show called Culpo Grosso. I hope that is how it was spelled. It was some kind of game show where the ladies and couples answered questions. If they answered the question wrong, someone on the show had to disrobe.

I was definitely going to show that Gabby the next night, we had a few beers left in our luggage and I was finishing the last one for the night before I crashed out. I woke up the next morning with Shakey scratching on the door and whining. I jumped up out of bed, put on jeans and a shirt and had his leash on him in seconds. I also took the newspaper we took from the flight over to Italy, I just knew he was going to poop and he did. The look on his face was one of pure relief when he was done.

That first morning I did not have to report in at all, we had three days off and it was awesome. I just wished my Z was there so we could do some traveling. Around mid-day, we had a visitor. A second-class petty officer showed up in civvies and told us he was our sponsor. I had never had a sponsor before, his name was Greg and he explained what his job was for us as a sponsor. Basically, he would be taking us to the commissary on base, showing us where everything on base was located and just to see if there was anything we needed. He also had an off-base housing list, and we both started laughing when he handed it to me.

I didn't know where any of the places on the list were. Gabby and I knew that we wanted to be within a forty-five-minute drive to base at the maximum, but not close to the base. We wanted to live among the Italians. We were going to be stationed at San Vito for three years and we wanted to enjoy living there. The foods, the sights, sounds, and the people. We both wanted to learn a language we had never really learned.

Most of the folks we hung out with were military-like us and the Italians wanted to learn English. Greg lived in San Vito. He let me know a lot about living in Southern Italy. It was totally different from the north, very different back then from northern Italy. Southern Italy during the time we were there was totally laid back, the beaches were something else, some of them were clean as hell, others were not, clear blue water of the Mediterranean Sea and you could just feel how warm the water was compared to the Pacific Ocean, the sand was smoother and softer than the Pacific Ocean, but I had a few things to learn about being at the beaches, especially with Shakey. My car arrived after our third week and I was happy as hell to have it. Gabby and I both had to learn how to drive in Italy. There were two speeds as fast as you could go and dead stop. The Italians back then saw driving as their right, not a privilege. They would drive down a one-way street, going the wrong way. A four-way stop sign meant whoever thought they got to the stop sign first would just go. No one stopped, but it was okay for them to do so. Most of the streets in the little towns down south were very narrow as the towns were hundreds of years old, cars hadn't been invented when these towns were made, there was so much history in this country and we planned on seeing lots of it.

Soon after my car arrived, Gabby got a job on base as a chef at the officer's club and she would fill in at the enlisted club when she was needed. They loved having her. That woman could cook. She was happy with having a job and so was I.

We brought a Chevy Chevelle that needed work done to the steering column, we got the steering fixed on the Chevy Chevelle, and she would drive to work just before lunch and stay until after the dinner shifts. It kept her happy, but Shakey found himself alone for a couple of hours each day in the little hotel room, and he would always let me know he didn't like it too much by jumping on me as soon as I got home.

My first week at work was getting used to my new section and the second week was lectures on living in Italy. We were told about the town meetings with the folks that don't like Americans and to just avoid them, we also learned a little about the country and its people from Italian civilians that worked on the base and they had a lot of information for us. The dos and don'ts while in Italy like the differences between the police, there were the regular police and the Carabinieri, which are like military police, then about driving in Italy and insurance for our vehicles.

I had never had any information about any of the different duty stations until we got to Italy. It was awesome and very much appreciated. During the end of our first month in San Vito at the hotel, we finally found a place where we wanted to live. It was in a village that was a five-minute drive from a city called Cellino San Marco in the Puglia region of Italy.

Cellino was southeast of Brindisi, which was the major port city in southern Italy. We actually lived in a walled compound that they called a village (Villaggio) that was owned by a very famous couple, the husband Albano Carrisi is a famous tenor singer and actor that was born in Cellino, his wife was an American her name was Romina Powers also a singer and actress, her father was Tyrone Powers a very famous actor in the United States in the nineteen thirties through the nineteen fifties.

They had four children. The couple had made a deal with the base commander for some of the navy personnel to live in their village and that their kids would go to school on the base. It worked out well for the military families in the village. I believe the village was called De Bosco. At the end of the village was his mansion. His brother had a mansion right outside of the village. Out of my fourteen years in the navy, this was the best place I had ever been stationed, Gabby, Shakey and I loved it, fresh air. A view that was beyond awesome and all the different little towns and cities that were twenty to thirty minutes from each other.

There is a lot of history in that area. I was told by one of the Italian civilians that gave us lectures about southern Italy that the city of Brindisi was where the gladiator Spartacus and his army were defeated by the Romans. Some of the villages looked the same as they did in the Roman era.

To get to our village from the base, we had to take the roads that were called Strada Provinciale's (SP), which ran from city to city and were usually only two lanes, one each way. We drove south from San Vito for about twenty minutes to a city called Mesangne through it. Then south again once we went through it for another fifteen or twenty minutes on the SP 365 to SP 51, made a right on it, stayed on it for about two minutes and we were at the gates to the village.

Once you left the cities, it was all agricultural with farms and olive trees everywhere. Driving through the cities was very challenging, especially if you had a large American car because the roads were narrow and some of the cities were hundreds of years old. San Vito, I was told at one of the lectures, was established in the late tenth century.

The village was totally walled in with at least twenty-foot brick walls, it was a place where the folks that used to work in the vineyards lived, but Albano turned them into luxury apartments (villas), each had three bedrooms and two bathrooms. A huge fireplace that you could bend down and walk into to clean it out. The kitchens were very spacious, with normal American-sized refrigerators and stoves. The bathrooms had both a shower and tub along with a regular toilet and a bidet. All of the floors in our villa were a nice light brown colored tile. Fans were in almost all the rooms. The one thing that I really had to get used to was no closets and screens on the windows.

There were, I think, eight or nine buildings that were built in the old Mediterranean style and all were white, along with the walls that surrounded the village. The huge gate was dark green. Each of the buildings held six units, one on top and the other on the bottom, we had the bottom unit on one of the corner sides, there was a restaurant, lots of pine trees, the only problem was that you had to take your trash outside the village to a dump, most of us did that on the way to work.

If you had the top unit, that meant you had the little one-car garage, but the bottom unit had access to the rooftop and I loved it up there. We had the view. There was a four-foot railing completely surrounding it, and at the back of the building and from your neighbors' parts of the roof. There were no windows on the back side of the villas as that was also part of the wall. On the roof, you could see the vineyards and farm areas and beyond that was the sea.

On the back side of our villa was a path that the sheepherders used to get their sheep to the main road. It was awesome to see stuff like this. The weather was basically like southern California without the smog, but it had the dry heat. Most of our neighbors were military, but there were some Italians that lived in the village. Those of us that had the bottom floor villas had covered parking spaces and that was nice to have.

We moved in the night before our furniture arrived so we slept in two sleeping bags on the hard-ass tile floor in the front room, we were lucky to have a corner unit because we had windows on two sides of our villa. I really loved it there.

The next morning we were up early. Shakey needed to go outside and take care of his morning chores. He had a lot of space to run around and have fun. I took him out the gate of the village and it was nothing but pine and olive trees and about fifty feet past the village was the dump. I didn't let him get too close to it. I wasn't sure what kind of animals were in there and I didn't want him getting bit by any of them. Our walk outside the gate was about fifteen minutes then we went back inside the village and walked around it, at the back near the left side of the village was a huge chain link fence with a door in it. On the other side was a basketball court, a tennis court and a volleyball court and at the end was Albano and Romina's mansion. There were some little American kids playing there, and they all ran over to see Shakey, they asked his name and I told them they wanted to know if he could stay with them and play. I remember telling them that he didn't have his breakfast yet, but he could come back outside after he had something to eat. They all smiled at me.

After we left that area I let Shakey off of his leash and he stayed by my side. I threw his little tennis ball and of course, he chased after it and brought it back to me. We played outside for a little bit longer, then went back to our villa. Gabby was waiting for us, we had brought groceries and had plenty of kitchen cabinets and they, along with the refrigerator, were full from our shopping the day before we moved in. I picked Shakey's front paws up and put them on the door latch and let go. The door opened, he looked at me, then again I put both of his front paws on the latch, and again the door opened when I let go. He knew what I was trying to teach him and that was how to get out the front door if it wasn't locked so he could go and do his business. It almost looked as if he smiled at me.

When it was time for him to take care of his business, he went outside of the gate across the street into the olive groves. He was awesome in the village. The kids would come over and ask is Shakey could come out and play, and most of the time, we would let him go.

Once our furniture was delivered, we went back to base and picked up more pots and pans and kitchen stuff like a new coffee pot (the old one was damaged during the move) and skillets and pans. We also brought a new double incliner couch with two coffee tables in the city of Mesagne. It was this thick blue material with little red flowers. Gabby liked it, I didn't care as long as it reclined, I was happy. It took us three days to get all of our stuff unpacked and put away the way Gabby wanted it. Luckily, it was on my eighty hours off.

When I got back to work, three of my old friends were at San Vito. They arrived a couple of months after Gabby and I got there. It was Teresa, a not too close friend named Frank and another guy named Will. I went to the barracks and found all of them. I gave them my work phone number and let them know I was there for them.

Teresa stayed at our place for a few days. Gabby and she got along very well. I guess Teresa felt as though she had known Gabby forever, listening to me talk about her all the time while we were in San Angelo. I had met a few of the neighbors, we had an air force officer, and his family there were cool and another air force sergeant that was cheap as hell, I mean cheap. His wife told us about her having to wear second-hand clothes all the time, and that they usually only brought food that was of reduced price (that was usually food that the sale by date was going to expire.) then, I met most of the Italian neighbors, there was one we called Poppy, he was pretty old probably in his early seventies and tall as hell probably about six foot eight inches and wore a size fourteen shoe, then there was Glenda, she was German and was married to an Italian but later divorced she had a tall skinny girlfriend that I called big bird, and last was Cesare. I knew he was in the mafia. He became my best Italian friend, he drove a two-seater Maserati and that damn thing was fast.

One night on my way home from the base, I was coming up on the city of Mesagne. I noticed that my rearview mirror had some headlights. I stepped on the gas until I was moving close to one hundred and ten miles per hour. The lights in my mirror just got bigger and bigger, then all I saw were tail lights. The car that passed me had to be going at least one hundred and fifty miles per hour. When I got to the village, Cesare was waiting for me with the biggest smile. It was his car that had passed me on the road home.

That night I invited him home for a beer. When I walked in the door, Shakey was waiting to go out as Gabby was still at work, I told Cesare to have a seat, and I told Shakey to go outside, Cesare sat down and Shakey opened the front door and went outside, Cesare just kept staring at the door, when I came back from the kitchen with two beers he was still staring at the door. I whistled and called Shakey in two minutes he opened the front door and came back inside the house and sat next to me on the floor, Cesare couldn't believe a dog could open the door and go out by itself.

It took Cesare a few tries before he could pronounce Shakey's name right. Once he got it right, Shakey walked up to him and put his paw out. That really freaked Cesare out. He kept looking at

Shakey the whole time he was in the house. Cesare didn't speak much English, but he wanted me to teach him and I wanted him to teach me Italian. We got along well.

A couple of weeks later, we got a new sailor in. He was the same rank as I was, but he had a different job. We were on the same exact schedule, so we always were outside smoking and we finally started talking to each other. I was a CTR2 and he was a CTT2. We were both going up for the first class test, so that was what we talked about all the time. The test, being an R-Brancher, it was harder to make the next rank because there were so many of us, and for Freddy, it was just starting to get hard. He made it during that test cycle; I had to wait for the next one before I got my E-6 rank back. Freddy was the only guy that I considered my real brother. He was younger than I was, but he was cool as hell. He looked like the guy on the Marlboro cigarette posters. He was somewhat of a red neck, but he was cool as hell. We kept each other laughing all the time.

One day one of our female CTT's had Captain's mast. None of us really knew what it was about. She always kept to herself, especially in the smoke break area, but we eventually found out why she had to see the Captain. Her husband was a drunk pot smoker, and he damn near burnt the on-base house down with their two children in it while she was on a mid-watch.

She started male bashing all men one day while she was out at the smoke break area. After a few minutes, I couldn't take her shit anymore and I let her have it. I told her it was her fault for marrying a drunk pothead, and I'm not sorry he had a small pecker (which was another problem she had with her husband). I told her she needed a monster-powered sex toy that takes two people to hold it for her, and everybody outside started busting up laughing. Most were coughing as they were trying to smoke when I said that to her.

Her husband and kids were sent back to the states, and she had to move into the barracks, so naturally, she was pissed off. I didn't know about anybody else, but I had enough of her shit. After I did that, Freddy would just look at me and bust up laughing. We became best friends. Freddy moved to a town called Latiano. It was maybe a fifteen-minute drive from the base. He moved above a car repair shop. The apartment was very nice, with three bedrooms and two bathrooms.

Most of the buildings in our part of Italy were not much to look at from the outside, but the insides were very nice. The tile floors and the huge fireplaces were just beautiful. After our third month in the village, Gabby and I started to invite people over for bar-b-ques. We would provide hamburgers and hot dogs, but if anybody wanted something else, they would have to bring it.

Gabby, Shakey, and I would usually have steaks, Shakey would get some of both of ours, and he was always happy.

At one of the bar-b-ques, I took my old bow tie from my old tuxedo and put it on Shakey. From then on, if we had a bunch of people over for parties, he would walk to my wardrobe and stare at it until I put the bowtie on him, then he would go either outside or up to the roof to hang out with everybody.

Cesare came to the second Bar-b-que and he was hooked. Every time we had a bar-b-que, he would show up. Gabby and I treated him like a brother, so we didn't mind. Most of the time, he would bring some expensive vodka or wine and it was all good. One day he brought Albano over, and his girlfriend, Albano, grabbed his guitar and sang one of his songs for us. That's when Albano, Cesare and I became good friends.

Freddy was finally able to talk his wife into coming to one of our bar-b-ques. After that, I knew why he seldom showed up, and when he did, he didn't bring her, she was beautiful, Spanish and they had a pretty little girl, but his wife was jealous as hell if any of the females walked over to talk to Freddy you could see her face turn red from anger, I thought it was funny and so did Gabby.

On my days off, when Gabby was at work, Shakey and I would go to the different beaches and the first time we went to the beach near our house, I learned a serious lesson. The lesson was that we were in Europe, not the good ole USA. I took a lot of stuff with us whenever we went to the beach, a big ice chest with beer, water and ice, a boombox with cassettes, a folding chair, and a small blanket for Shakey, along with some of his toys and his small basketball. It usually took me 2 or 3 trips from the car to the beach to unload everything and again to load it all back into the car once we were ready to leave.

The one thing I was never told about the beaches was that in the southern part of Italy during those days, being topless and or nude was no big deal. I had to lay on my belly on Shakey's little blanket for the first twenty minutes we were at the beach. I didn't notice anybody at first because I was so busy unloading my Z, and I had things stuffed behind the passenger seat and in the back, so I was really busy trying to get everything out and I picked a spot away from the crowds because I didn't know how Shakey would act around a lot of people. Once I had everything where I wanted it, my music turned on (not too loud). I grabbed Shakey's little basketball and threw it in the water. He ran after it and brought it right back to me. When I bent down to get in the water, I put my foot down on a rock. I picked the rock up and threw it in the water. Shakey ran after it and put his head under water and brought the rock back to me. I had never seen him put his head under water. I was amazed and when I looked up, lots of people out there were watching him. That's when I noticed most of the ladies were topless.

It took a minute for my brain to register what I was looking at, not staring at it. I opened the ice chest, grabbed a beer and laid down on Shakey's little towel. I had to stay there for another beer before I could get up and sit back down in my chair. Just when I thought I was safe and ok down there, this mother and her twenty-something-year-old daughter got right in front of me, both carrying only those little mats and a bottle of water, put their mats down and stripped butt naked in front of me, I almost lost my damn mind, my hookup got so hard so fast I didn't know what to do, I was glad they were both facing the water, I had a big problem, Shakey was laying on his blanket looking at both of them and I needed to lay on it. I took the rock and threw it into the water. He took off after the rock and stuck his head again under water and grabbed the rock. I was so glad in those few seconds I had gotten down on his blanket with no one noticing I had an erection from hell, or at least I thought I did. When Shakey brought the rock back, he was huffing and puffing, I knew he needed water, but I still had my issue going on. I opened his bottle of water and poured it into my hand. I couldn't get up to look for his water bowl, so I did that a couple of times. Then I poured some of his cold water over my head, which immediately helped my big issue.

As soon as I was able to get back in my chair, I tried not to look straight ahead of me, but no matter how hard I tried, my eyes kept going to the two ladies laying naked directly in front of me. This was not funny. I wanted to move to another spot, but then the daughter came over and asked me, "Canni namo." I knew she wanted to know Shakey's name and I told her Shakey. Just like Cesare, she had trouble pronouncing it at first, and after the third try, she got it right and he looked up at her and put out his paw for her to shake it. That was almost more than I could bear. This your woman was beautiful and had thirty-six, twenty-eight, thirty-six shapes. The perfect curves for me to look at, I was trying to look her in the eyes when we talked and I put that ice-cold can of Budweiser between my legs as I pointed at him. That's when she helped me out, she reached her arm up and when she did, the afro under her arm popped out. I almost laughed. I was able to take the cold can of beer and take a sip. My erection died immediately.

I wanted to thank her, I handed her the rock Shakey kept bringing back and pointed at the water she threw it and he took off. She laughed and said something to her mother and the mother rolled over to look at her daughter. When she did, I got a double eye full of everything, but again I was saved. All I could see was lots of dark hair all over the place, between her legs and under her arms. It was time for me to jump into the water and cool off. I got up, took off my t-shirt, which was soaking wet and I called Shakey. I grabbed his little basketball and ran to the water. He was already in the water, waiting for me to throw the ball. I threw it as soon as my feet hit the water. I ran a few more feet and dived in.

I stayed underwater for a few seconds and then I came up. Shakey was right next to me with the ball in his mouth. The girl was sitting down, waving at us. I went back underwater. After playing with Shakey for a few more minutes, I got out of the water, walked past the two ladies and opened another beer. The oldest one looked at me and said, "Bello bronzo." I had to remember that so I could ask Cesare what it meant. I offered both a beer and the mother came over and got them, they were both laying on their stomachs and it was almost too much to bear. Then they came over and told me their names, the mother was Maria and the daughter's name was Dallia, I think.

I will never forget them. After they finished the beers, they both stood up slowly, bent down, grabbed their towels, put their bikinis back on and waved goodbye to me and said chow Shakey. I just stared at them as they walked away. I was the one that gave them a beer, and they didn't even remember my name, but they did remember Shakey's.

I laughed and finished my beer, I threw the rocks to Shakey for a little while longer, then I looked down the beach and all the topples and nude people were damn near gone. I didn't know it, but they also had a siesta like the Spanish. I now had another reason to love southern Italy.

When Shakey and I got back to the Village, we ran into Cesare. He was out by his car. I had a book on how to speak Italian and I showed it to him. He smiled and read out of the book that he was going to buy a bigger car. He wanted one for all his new American friends to fit in. I didn't know it at the time, but he had the hots for one of my co-workers. She was a black woman with nice breasts but kind of a flat ass, she had a pretty face and that was all he needed. Gabby came home a few hours after Shakey and I got home,

I told her about the beach and she busted up laughing. She just couldn't stop. At first, I didn't think it was so fun being out there and scared to move because I had a raging erection. She just laughed again. After a while she said she was sorry and she should have told me about the beaches, she only thought they were topless, then she started laughing again, so did I.

We had some really good sex that night, better than normal. I passed out afterward. She got up and let Shakey out, and when he was done, she came back to bed and passed out. We were both off the next day and we decided to check out some of the cities that were nearby. We had been through and seen most of San Vito. We wanted to check out the towns south of Cellino San Marco, so we went down to Squinzano, but we had to go up and over to San Pietro first. They were all little towns no bigger than Cellino in San Pietro. We went to the museum Parco Della Memoria Storica. It was an old castle turned into a museum and it was badly damaged during WWII.

We stopped and got a drink in one of the sidewalk cafes, then headed south to Squinzano, which was twice the size of Cellino. We wanted to stay on the main road because it was easy to get lost and we did for about 5 minutes. We did stop at a café and had a couple of beers while we laughed at ourselves for getting lost so quickly. We left Squinzano and kept south and ended up in Lecce, one of the biggest cities in that area. We got lost immediately and just drove around until we needed to find a café with a bathroom. We drove around looking at all the old buildings and the narrow streets. It was fun getting lost and then finding our way again. We started heading back around three o'clock. It was a good distance to get back to Cellino and the village.

We made it back just after dark and Shakey needed to go outside very badly. That night our friend Bev came over. She was the one person on base that we would trust to watch Shakey if we were gone. She would come over and hang out just to get out of the barracks. Neither Gabby nor I minded. Sometimes Gabby would stop by the barracks and pick her up and we always had a good time with her over for visits.

What I didn't know was that she and Cesare had a thing going on, he was usually there when she was, but for some reason, no one wanted me to know. I let Gabby know how I felt about that and then I let Cesare and Bev know that I was not her father. I did outrank her, but this is her personal life, and if she wants to have sex with somebody. It's just not my business unless it's happening in my house, they all apologized and all was well in the village again. Bev spent the night with Cesare.

They were a thing after that I was happy for them until I found out that he had a fiancé, but I was cool with it. She didn't want to marry him, just get off base and have sex. I didn't see a problem with that and there was none. After a while, Freddy started hanging out more and more with me. I had to ask if things were ok with him and his wife, he said no. he was jealous of everybody and everything and that he was tired of sleeping on the couch. At least at my house, he could sleep on a bed, we laughed.

I didn't mind Freddy hanging out with me. He, Cesare, and I would get in Cesare's new Maserati and cruise down to Lecce, and he would get us into all the clubs, and everything was always free. People would come up and introduce themselves to him, and he would just smile at them, that's when I knew for sure he was in the Mafia.

Once I was in the car with Cesare, and he saw a guy riding a bike and without any warning. He ran into the bike and damn near killed the guy. I was thinking, *what the hell am I going to do?* Cesare just smiled at me and said he said he fuck my sister, so I hurt him we went back to the village in Cellino and he parked his car, about thirty minutes later the police showed up. I went inside and watched out the window as Cesare talked with them. The only thing that happened was they took his driver's license, the guy didn't die and Cesare went to Lecce and got a new driver's license the next day. I couldn't believe it.

Freddy said, "Dude, we are in Italy!" Gabby and I both had the next two days off, so we decided to go to our nearest beach and Shakey loved the idea. Once he saw me grab the ice chest, it was on. He ran straight to the Z and sat down. The only problem was we were taking Gabby's Chevy because it wasn't enough room for the three of us to be comfortable in the Z.

After we ate breakfast and got our beach stuff in her car, he jumped in the passenger seat. It took a while to get him out of the front seat and into the back seat. He was used to being in the front seat when he and I drove to the beach in the Z.

It was beautiful outside and a little bit warm, surprisingly. The beach was clean, not the usual trash all over the place like normal. We parked right on the beach, maybe ten feet from where we put our chairs and Shakey's towel, I had his little basketball and threw it into the water while he was swimming out to get it Gabby and I unpacked the car.

The ice chest was full of beer, water, and our lunch, three ham and cheese sandwiches, and a plastic jug filled with water for Shakey. As we got situated, the beach was starting to get crowded, most of the ladies, including Gabby, were topless and a few were totally nude.

A couple of the kids wanted to play with Shakey and he was okay with that. They were playing soccer. He used his nose to push the ball around. His only problem was he would push it into people laying on the beach. Gabby and I were laughing so hard. Then he ran in one of the kid's fathers, who got pissed and did a little swat at Shakey. I stood up, but Gabby grabbed my arm and told me to watch what Shakey did. I watched, each time Shakey got the ball, he ran into the same guy. We couldn't stop laughing, then the guy got up and walked toward us. I stood up again and put my beer down just in case the guy needed assistance laying down, but before I could do anything. Shakey was between the both of us and he was growling at the guy. Everybody was watching. The guy threw his arms and called me a stranso (Ass hole). I repeated it back to him so he could hear it, but he kept walking and went back to his matt and laid his ass back down. He didn't mind his kids running around kicking sand on everybody and I didn't mind Shakey pushing the ball and running into him. Gabby was still laughing. She called the guy a wanker and we both started laughing again.

I took Shayk's ball and put it under my chair. Then I threw a pebble in the water. Shakey took off to get it. Gabby and I took turns doing that and playing with him in the water until we were too tired to play with him, he just lay next to Gabby and she poured him some water in his bowel. He was panting pretty good, trying to cool down.

We had lunch shortly after that and a few beers. Shakey was relaxing and finally chilling out. I took him for a walk so he could take a poop in a grassy area near the car. I did pick it up and put it in one of the paper bags we kept in the cars just for this reason, then I threw the bag into the trash can and we both walked back to Gabby.

Gabby and I started using the phonetic alphabet to describe people. Bravo Tango Bravo = Bathtub butt, Whisky Tango = wonder tits (we wondered what happened to them), and our favorite was Foxtrot Alpha (Fat Ass). She used that a lot for the guys that had huge bellies and all the gold chains wearing the little speedo's swimming trunks.

We did that for about an hour, had a few more beers and decided it was time to leave. Gabby cleaned up and put all the paper into the ice chest. We put everything in the car and headed back home, but it was such a nice day. The three of us were having such a great time we decided to stop in Torchiarolo, a nice little town on the way home. We pulled up at one of the little pubs and went in to get some ice cream (gelato). We left the windows down in the car and told Shakey to sit and stay, we walked in and I ordered three white gelato's (Vanilla Ice Cream), got back into the car and drove home. Gabby fed Shakey his with one of the little spoons we got from the bar. We were amazed at all the bars near the beaches selling booze and ice cream.

After our first year at San Vito, Gabby and I decided to go on a vacation. It was like one of those Sandals' all-inclusive vacations. It was located in Otranto, Italy. We really needed this vacation. I was still working the two-two-two and eighty-hour schedule and she, as usual, was doing double shifts at both the officers club and the enlisted club cooking meals, so we booked two the vacation for two weeks at this all-inclusive resort (sorry, I cannot remember the name of it) and we took her car and drove to the resort.

We probably should have taken the Z, but we didn't know where the car would be parked and if it would be broken into or not, so we drove the Chevy. It didn't take too long to get to the resort, just a few minutes over an hour. We listened to music on our boom box with the cassette player all the way. We were laughing and giggling like little kids going to the park and we had a couple of beers on the way.

One of the ladies that worked with me stayed at our villa to take care of Shakey. The other girl had left San Vito and was in Imperial Beach. The new girl wanted a break from living in the barracks. She was like a little sister to me. We knew Shakey was in good hands.

For two weeks, it would just be the two of us. We had all food and drinks paid for in the package deal we brought. I did some double checking, and back then, all-inclusive meant the free continental breakfast (fruit with bread and eggs and dinner was cooked outside in this big open area near the pool. You just walked up and pointed at what you wanted. It was the same for lunch.

We were going to have fun. We brought our old kodak camera with us, but I don't think we ever used it. We arrived at the place around one in the afternoon. We should have driven the Z. The place was totally secured. It is beyond beautiful with the plants, trees and the view of the Adriatic Sea. The property of the resort surrounded the sea on three sides. We didn't know it when we first arrived, but the center portion of the beach area was for families and the left and right sides were for clothes optional. I love Italy!

Once we checked in, we were taken to our room which was on the first floor and had a view of the sea. It was relaxing just to sit on the bed and look out the sliding glass door at the water as soon as we unpacked our clothes, we put on our bathing suits. Gabby handed me a gift-wrapped box and told me to open it just as I was ready to walk out the door. I stopped and looked at her, then I walked over and gave her a kiss, opened the package and told her, "Hell no!" I threw it on the bed. She couldn't stop laughing. It was the speedo swimming trunks for me (a damn G-string). I turned around, looked her in her beautiful eyes, took off my trunks and put the Speedos on. The first step I took, one of my testicles popped out. I pushed it back in and tried to take another step, the other one came out, and Gabby could not stop laughing and now I was laughing with her. I'm not sure how guys wore them back then, but my hookup wouldn't stay put.

I asked her what size they were, and she said medium, we both laughed as I took them off and put my navy swimming trunks back on. I grabbed her and kissed her. Then we walked towards the bar that was outside just before you reached the beach. We were issued tickets for drinks and food. Gabby told the guy at the concierge desk to give us extra tickets for the booze and he did.

We used one ticket per drink and headed toward the beach. There were no lounges left, but we both had our beach towels. I also had the little boom box and a couple of cassettes, mostly Michael Jackson and Earth Wind and Fire type of songs, along with some of Gabby's music from England. We were ready to just relax and chill out until dinner.

I remember it being pretty warm, so I was in and out of the water trying to cool off (I already had the perfect tan). Gabby rubbed sun tan lotion on each other, and just as I was finishing her. This family walked down to the beach. The father was a short and extremely huge-bellied little fella, the wife was Gabby's shape, and height and they had a boy and a little baby girl that could barely walk. I had my back to them as they came down to our part of the beach. The father was making funny sounds with his mouth. I guess he was breathing hard because of the twenty-foot distance he had just traveled. The wife had all the towels and toys for the kids. He looked so red I thought he was going to have a heart attack.

Gabby pointed at the little girl and told the mother she was beautiful. The lady said thank you with a really harsh accent. Gabby told me she thought they were South Africans. I just shrugged and smiled at them, laid on my stomach and started reading a GQ magazine I brought on base. I wanted to see what the new men's clothing styles were and the articles were pretty good also. Gabby was looking through the Sears catalog. She loved looking and ordering stuff from it.

The father was still huffing and puffing as he sat down. He waited for his wife to put a towel down for him. I guess he couldn't bend over to do it by himself. That's when he noticed me. He growled something at his wife. He was almost shouting at her. Gabby and I both looked at him. She just smiled and turned red.

Gabby looked at me and said, "This is going to be fun."

I looked at her and said, "What?" she explained about the white South African. I listened very carefully to her. I couldn't believe it. She also told me he called me a keffa (not sure how to spell the word). Gabby looked nervous. I told her, "We are here to have a good time and I will let that slide, but only once." I didn't want to stay out in the sun too long on our first day and neither did Gabby. We wanted to explore the resort and we did just that. It was made to look extra tropical with the plants and the little streams. There was also a very large pool with a bar that you could swim up to for drinks and lots of staff to serve the customers.

The pool area was also one of the places where the nightly dances were held. I liked that a lot, Gabby and I could just go dancing and cool off in the pool. This was going to be one of the best vacations ever.

We chilled out the rest of the first day in the room until dinner time. That's when I saw the South African family. I grabbed Gabby's arm and damned near dragged her to the seats right next to him, the dining area was filling up fast and we got there just in time. That fat ass didn't notice me as he had two plates full of food. They served everything from small steaks to hot dogs. I told Gabby that I would get our dinner and asked her what she wanted. I got both of us the same thing baked chicken, french fries, and a cheese burger.

I went back to my seat and Mr. South African was saying something to one of the resort folks. When I got there, the guy he was talking to just shook his shoulders and smiled at me as he walked away. I scooted my chair closer to Mr. South African, grabbed my knife and fork, laid the napkin in my lap, and stared at him for a few seconds. Then I started to eat. His eyes looked like they were going to bulge out of his head, his wife looked very nervous, and I just smiled at her.

Now I had a goal for my most awesome vacation besides relaxing. I was going to piss off Mr. racist South African every chance I got. Hell, Nelson Mandela was in prison for speaking his mind. This guy was not going to be happy for as long as Gabby and I was there. Gabby could hardly eat. She wanted to laugh so badly. This fat pig of a man was making noises as he ate, so I started making them too. I felt so sorry for Gabby. While I was making his noises, I would look at her and raise and lower my eyebrows. I just knew It was killing her, trying not to laugh. It was killing me also, but I didn't want to choke on my food.

Mrs. South African still looked so nervous. I kind of felt sorry for her, but not too sorry. I kept this up all during dinner. I ate slowly just so I could sit next to him the entire dinner. I knew I should have given him a break and left. When he made his wife go and get dessert, I did the same thing. I told Gabby to get me some ice cream and chocolate cake. He was horrified that we didn't leave. He was making slurping sounds when he ate the ice cream and so did I. This went on for about ten minutes. I was full and couldn't eat anymore. He had his wife go back and grab another piece of cake to eat. I was stuffed, and Gabby couldn't hold the laughter back anymore as I sat back in the chair and pushed my stomach out as far as I could and started rubbing it.

I would look at him and raise and lower my eyebrows and Gabby just busted up laughing and got up to leave. I acted like I was mad at her and told her to sit her ass down while I raised and lowered my eyebrows and she took off running and laughing. I finally got up and looked at Mr. South African and told him to enjoy the rest of his meal. Then I busted up laughing and ran after Gabby.

We sat in the room and had a few beers, watched some tv in Italian and crashed out. I couldn't wait for the next morning. Gabby and I got just in time for breakfast. It was served like on the ship. There were eggs, Canadian bacon, potatoes, every kind of fruit you could think of and pastries. Gabby grabbed the eggs and bacon, I did also but I also tried one of the pastries. I did not see my new friend from South Africa.

One of the guys serving spoke English and he came over and told me that the South African complained about me sitting next to him last night. He also said that the manager let the guy know that I paid to be here just like he did and there was nothing they could do about where anyone sat or went on the resort.

Then he just laughed and walked away. Oh, it was on now. I was going to seek out Mr. South African every chance I got. This was going to be so much extra fun. After breakfast, we went back to the room and got ready for the beach. We were going to go to the side, whichever side didn't have a lot of people, that was Gabby's request. I had taken my snorkel and fins with us, so I planned on doing some snorkeling. We ordered four beers and headed to the beach. Gabby said she just wanted to see what was in the new sears catalog and relax. I promised her I would behave, or at least try to if you know who showed up. Gabby was topless laying on one of the towels we took from the bathroom. I must have been in the water just floating around for about twenty minutes.

The water was crystal clear, warm and smooth. There were not many fishes to see in the area I was snorkeling in, but lots of small crabs were going crazy down there, fighting amongst themselves in the sea grass. Once I got out of the water, I noticed I had floated quite a ways down the beach. I was now on the right side of the cove and Gabby was sitting near the right side but still, in the center part of the cove. I stood up and guessed who I saw as I looked around, Mr. South Africa and his family. I knew this guy didn't like me, but what happened next really pissed me off to the point that I wanted to slap the hell out of him over and over again.

Once he spotted me, he started screaming and hollering at his wife, who was barely standing in the water with her two little children. He was bright red and just screaming in their language that I didn't understand. I looked at her and she quickly grabbed her kids and headed out of the water to where he was sitting. Once she got it, he slapped her and made her put her biking top on.

Gabby was looking at me with that worried look when she knew I was going to do something stupid like fighting, but I didn't. My mind was trying to figure out why he would do something like that and both of the kids were crying along with his wife. A few minutes later, I walked back to Gabby. I didn't realize I had been staring at him like I was. I walked back to Gabby and sat down. She let out a little sigh of relief. After a few minutes, she got up and went into the water as I watched Gabby, along with most of the women on the beach, was topless, so I still couldn't understand why he slapped his wife.

After a few minutes, I got up, looked over at him again and just got in the water long enough to cool down. Gabby and I splashed water on each other and I grabbed her and kissed her. Once we got out of the water, Mr. South Africa allowed his wife and kids to get back into the water.

Gabby noticed that as soon as I got in the water, he made his family get out. I spent a good two hours getting in and out of the water just to mess with him. Gabby and I were supposed to get drinks by the pool, but I chose to stay near the beach instead. Gabby finally dragged me off the beach and over to the pool, where we stayed until the time. It was time for dinner. We got toasted and she couldn't stop laughing at the day we had with the South African family.

We didn't see them again for the rest of our stay at the resort. I guess they left. I kind of felt sorry for the lady and the kids and I didn't want to spoil their vacation. Gabby and I partied the rest of the time. We were there mostly by the pool. She had a really great tan by the time we left there.

At our little village, she hardly got any sun as she was always working on the base. She couldn't wait to tell our friends about the South African family and how I interacted with them, that was a story told at the weekly bar-b-ques. Out last night at the resort, there was a toga party. Most folks just had on sheets from their rooms. Gabby and I did the same, the drinks were back to back and they played lots of Greek music, which was pretty cool and they had some Greek dancers there to show us how they danced. It was awesome.

Gabby and I got pretty good at Greek dancing and we had a really good time. We left the party early, around midnight, and headed back to our room and packed our clothes so after our showers in the morning we could just check out and be on our way back to our little village in Cellino San Marco.

The drive home took a little over two hours. We stopped at a pottery shop in Lecce, a really nice city and did a little bit of shopping. Gabby found a few vases she liked. I saw what looked like a beer mug. We did get lost in the city for a few minutes, but we did see a sign for Brindisi. We headed north from Lecce and we easily found our way home with a quick turn-off at the entrance to San Pietro.

When we finally got home, it felt like I needed a vacation from our vacation. Luckily, we both still had two days off. I think I drove home with a two-day hangover. The lady that was staying at our place was still there and she was both happy and sad to be leaving the village. She told us that Albano had taken all the kids and Shakey to his mansion and sang songs to them while they played on his tennis court. She mentioned a lot of Albano's fans would come over and knock on our front door to see if we knew where Albano was, I told her I forgot to mention that to her as it was a fairly common occurrence, they would come over in tour busses.

Albano's Mansion was completely closed off to them, so they would come to our area of the village looking for him or Romina. They would actually come up to the villas and look in the windows. Sometimes, you had to be a little bit mean to them so they would get the idea that this was your personal space and that Albano and Romina did not live in this section.

Shakey would not leave my side for the entire first day we came back. She told us he slept by the front door every night. He did, however, go out and play with the kids and their dogs. Gabby drove her home later that day as Ceasera had come over and we both went to his villa. Gabby and I slept for a good three or four hours that day. Gabby forgot to mention that we were going to have a bar-b-que the next day and that she had invited most of our gang over. I never had a problem with having the guys and their girlfriends over. It was always fun and I got to know them better when we were all off base.

The next morning, we were up and getting everything ready for the grilling session, we still had plenty of beer, most of the guys would bring beer and if they wanted steaks or something else put on the grill, they would bring it. We always had plenty of hot dog's hamburger meat and chicken wings just in case we wanted to put something quick on the grill. Gabby's friends showed up. Both were air force wives that worked with her in the kitchen on base and they both brought their husbands. At first, the guys seemed nervous, but once they got to know us, they figured out we were all pretty good people.

One of Gabby's friends had the hots for Ceasera, and it didn't look like she was trying too hard to hide it and Ceasera was checking her out also. She was a pretty blonde with a nice body and a pretty face, but she was kind of loud and liked to be the center of attention. We had two new people in our section one was a beautiful little second-class petty officer she was the third black woman in our section. She was shorter than Gabby, probably four feet eleven inches tall. Gabby was just barely five feet one inch tall. All the ladies hung out together.

We had the music blasting and as usual, most of the neighbors showed up. Ceasera was there with Poppi. We had new neighbors, a mother and her daughter. Both were beautiful as hell, the daughter was only seventeen, but she looked like she was in her mid-twenties. Most of the younger troops were trying to talk to her, then I let them all know her age, most of them backed off immediately like I said most, but one guy didn't. I told him again, and he told me he just didn't care and that she was awesome. I had to admit she was, she wanted to learn to speak English and he was happy to teach her.

Most of the guys headed over to the basketball court that was also used as a tennis court. Albano was invited and as usual, he showed up for about fifteen or twenty minutes with his younger children. Shakey was having a natural born fit and nobody could figure out what was wrong with him. He was in the house barking near my armoire. I went downstairs and put his bow tie on him and he was all good to go (anytime we had a guest, he liked to have the black bow tie on).

This had to be one of the biggest bar b ques that we had and it was awesome, we had all kinds of music from soul music, rock to British rock and roll. We were jamming on the roof. We even had the air force neighbor and his wife over, probably because she wouldn't stop bugging him to come over (he never wanted to be around anybody and was cheap as hell). They didn't bring anything, but they did help themselves to the beer and burgers.

(I didn't put cheese on theirs like he requested and Gabby cracked up laughing, it was our joke). Once I put the jazz cassette in the stereo, all my guys knew what that meant, it was chow time. We had borrowed a long table with some chairs from Albano's restaurant and had it along with all the chairs from our dinner table, which was about eight of them and Ceasera brought four of his chairs over. Some of us just stood near the edge of the roof without plates and beer on it.

The new second-class petty officer was named Kisha and she brought her two-year-old dog with her, we all thought it was a newborn puppy. It probably weighed a little over one pound. I was a little nervous about letting Shakey near it and I didn't want him to accidentally kill it. Kisha cut one of the hot dogs into little pieces and put them on a paper plate, the dog stood on the plate while it ate the hot dog pieces she puts on the plate.

Shakey just stared at it and then he would look up at me as if to say what is that! There must have been at least thirty people up there on the roof. Just as we were almost done eating, this sheepherder and about ten sheep came down the little dirt road that was on the outside edge of the village directly below us. I asked in Italian if he would like a beer. We were running short on Budweiser's, so I grabbed a Michelob and held it over the edge directly above him. He had both his hand directly over his head when I let the bottle go. Everybody was watching.

The bottle dropped straight down and he missed it. It hit him right on the forehead. It looked like his body jumped up and then he dropped straight to the ground. The sheep kept on walking around him. At first, we were all quiet, not a sound, just the jazz playing from the stereo. One of the air force wives screamed, everybody thought he was dead, he didn't move, now we had been drinking since around 1 PM after she screamed Ceasera and I ran down the stairs. I got into Gabby's car and drove it over to the body. Ceasera was already by the guy. He had a two-inch cut straight across his forehead. I shouted up to Gabby to throw down the medical kit and I put a large dressing on his head and taped it in place.

Ceasera and I picked him up, laid him on the back seat and took him to the hospital in Cillino. I was freaking out, the dressing had leaked blood onto the blanket that we kept in the back seat for shakey. I was thinking, I hope I didn't kill him. Once we got him inside, he came to and he looked around and started yelling he didn't want to be in the hospital. Ceasera gave him the equivalent of fifty dollars, we both winked at the lady at the front desk and we left him at the hospital. Then I had to drive to the guy's home where Ceasera told his family what happened and to go and get the sheep before they went onto the main road.

Once Ceasera and I got back into the village, Ceasera busted up laughing. I mean, he was crying and laughing so hard, then I started laughing. We barely made it back up the stairs to the party, and when they all saw us laughing, everybody on the roof busted up laughing. They were pointing at me a couple of the guys acted like they were asking someone if they would like a beer then they dropped beers over the edge onto the dirt below and we all started laughing again.

The laughter lasted most of the night. Ceasera explained as best he could that some people don't like the hospital and he was one of them. We all busted up laughing. A little bit later, Albano came back over, and Ceasera told him what had happened, he tried not to laugh, but he couldn't help it, and we all started laughing again.

Ceasera told me Albano would take care of the accident and not to worry. Before Albano left, he managed to say don't give anymore beer and he walked towards the steps and started laughing again. Needless to say, everybody thought that was the best bar b que we had had to date. The incident was all over the base the next day when I got to work.

My chief asked me when he stopped laughing to try not to kill any of the natives. Gabby said all the officers busted up laughing when she got to work the next morning and that the next time we have a bar b que, they wanted to be invited. There was a captain in the air force at the party I guess he told all the officers. All of the navy officers knew me and they also said they wanted to come to the next bar b que, we all laughed.

I was in my dress whites that morning as I would have to stand at the podium and give my portion of the morning brief, which meant I would be at work at least thirty minutes early so I could go over the report from the day before for the operations that I worked, just as I got in the command master chief came right over and said follow me, I did straight to our commanding officer's office. The Commanding Officer, Executive Officer, my Division Officer and Chief were all there. I was asked what exactly happened yesterday at my party, only the incident with the civilian.

I told them exactly what happened. "I explained that it was hot and I saw this sheep herder with his sheep. I asked the sheep herder that was on the outside of our building, approximately fourteen feet below us, walking his sheep past. I asked if he would like a beer and he said yes. I held a Michelob bottle over his head, he put both his hand up as if to catch it and I let the bottle drop. He missed catching the bottle and the bottle hit him on the forehead, causing a two-inch cut across it. Then I, along with one of my civilian neighbors, ran down the stairs. My neighbor ran to the guy the bottle hit, and I drove up with my wife's car. I yelled up for my wife to throw down the emergency medical kit. I used it to bandage his wound as I learned to do a battle dressing, we, my neighbor and I drove him to the hospital and carried him in.

The civilian that the bottle hit came to and started complaining that he didn't want to be in the hospital, my neighbor paid the equivalent in Italian lira of fifty dollars, and we left and when we got back, Albano came over and said, "It was all taken care of and not to worry."

Everybody in the room stared at me as if they couldn't believe it, the commanding officer said and Albano took care of it. I said, "Yes, sir." He told me since Albano had it under control, it was not going to be a JAG matter. I said, "Thank you, sir, I have been through that before."

He said, "I know and if it had been, you would not lose any stripes." and said, I was dismissed.

Just as I closed the door, they all busted up laughing. I smiled and went to work. They were all smiling at me when I gave my portion of the morning brief, I knew they could just picture me dropping the bottle and the lady screaming and me thinking I killed a civilian. After the brief, I had the same conversation with my section officer and he was crying and laughing. When he stopped, he said try not to kill any of the civilians and winked at me. I finally got my E-6 rank back and it was almost time for us to leave San Vito. Gabby and I were both hoping that we would be stationed at NSGA Rota, Spain, we had four or five more months left, we were supposed to leave in March of nineteen ninety-three, then we got word that our base was to be disestablished in January nineteen ninety-three, none of us could believe it, no one could. There was an Air force officer that lived in the village with us along with his family. They were very good people, not stuffy like the other air force folks that were there. He and his family came to most of the bar b ques we had and usually brought something good to add to the grill. His kids loved Shakey.

When there was no school, they were the first kids to come over to see if he could come out and play with them. I will never forget the day that the large green gate into the village was left open and a pretty good-sized cat just casually walked into the village like he owned it. Shakey and the other dogs went crazy. Most of the neighbor's dogs weighed less than thirty pounds. Shakey was near fifty pounds, and I must say when he ran up on that what we called a bob cat which was a lynx, he got his ass kicked.

I had just gotten off my first day watch and was getting out of my uniform. I still had on my work trousers and boots when one of the air force kids came running to my front door saying

Shakey is fighting a really big cat, and later we found out it wasn't fully grown. It probably weighed a little more than Shakey, but it was a lot faster.

I grabbed my baseball bat and ran to where they were fighting, Shakey had grabbed it by the left rear leg and was trying to rip its leg off, the lynx was really fighting back and it had scratched Shakey's nose, gave him a deep gash and it was bleeding badly, he wouldn't let go of the lynx's leg, the lynx was almost adult age, but I have to say in all fairness my poor dog got his butt kicked, I yelled at Shakey and he let go, the lynx ran out of the gate hobbling as fast as it could, I grabbed Shakey and put him in the back of my Z. I went into my villa and got some dressings for his nose. I drove him all the way back to base and took him to the little base hospital. They stitched the scratch on his nose back and gave him a couple of shots. He had been put under before they did the stitching. By the time I got home and put him on his pillows. Gabby came home and that was our first real fight.

She was mad at me for not coming to her job to take her to the hospital with us. I tried to tell her I was really worried about his nose bleeding, but she did something I had never seen before. She lost her damn mind and started yelling at me saying I should have been keeping my eyes on Shakey. I didn't say anything to her until we got home then she acted as if nothing had happened.

I didn't know it at the time, but she was going thru menopause and it got worse as the months leading to us leaving San Vito ran down. San Vito was the one duty station I could have made my entire career at, but like so many of our CT bases, it was closing down. I had to make arrangements for Shakey to fly to our next duty station, which was going to be NSGA Edzell, Scotland. As soon as I got the orders, I found a flight for him.

He would arrive two weeks after I got there. The air force officer that had moved into the village with his family agreed to take care of Shakey until his departure, the air force officer and his family were just awesome people and we knew we could trust them with Shakey.

On one of our normal visits to the little towns near us after our first mid watch, Fredd. I and a friend of ours named Greg, who had just made E-7 (chief), decided to go to the beach at the town of Torre Santa Sabina and check out the beach. It took us over forty-five minutes to get there and then another hour to check out all the little clubs that were open and selling beer.

We finally got to the beach and went to one of the outdoor bars and started drinking again. The bar had bowls of pistachios at each of the tables outside and we ate them while drinking our beers.

After a while, I put my head on the little table and went to sleep. Freddy and Greg we still awake and drinking. They started spitting the pistachios shells on the ground. One of the Italian guys started mouthing off about them spitting the shells on the ground and he woke me up. Freddy and Greg just ignored him. I was pissed that he woke me up, I asked Greg what the hell was going on and he told me. I grabbed one of the pistachios and threw it right at the guy. The pistachio hit him right on the forehead and he jumped up out of his seat. At that time, I stood up along with Freddy and Greg. The Italian wife or girlfriend grabbed the guy's arm and told him to sit back down. He did, then Freddy kept winking his eye at her, the guy got really mad and stood up again then he grabbed her arm and they left. We, along with some of the Italians that were spitting the pistachios shells on the ground, were laughing our asses off.

During our last year at San Vito, Gabby's mom came down from England to visit for two weeks. Gabby and I drove the Chevy up to the Naples airport, which was over a four-hour drive each way, and by the time we got her to our place in Cellino San Marco, all three of us were totally exhausted. I had learned to drive like the Italians and Gabby's mom was freaking out in the back seat. Every time she whined or twisted in her seat, Gabby would just smile.

When we finally made it back to Cellino San Marco, we were all totally done for the day. We went to the restaurant in the village and had dinner. Then it was beer time for Gabby and I. Gabby's mom hit the sheets as soon as we got back from the restaurant, which we probably a few minutes' walk from our villa. The old girl was done. Gabby had taken two weeks' vacation time off and I took one week. That way, someone was always there with her mother.

During the two weeks, Gabby's mom was with us. We would take her to all the towns and cities near us. The third day after she arrived, we went to San Pietro Vernotico for lunch and dinner at Torchiarolo. For the rest of the first week, we visited Brindisi and Ostuni, where her mother brought little Italian nick knacks for her kitchen and living room. Gabby's mom's last couple of days were on my eighty hours off, so we took her on next to her last day to Ostuni for some small pottery pieces that she brought. The last place that I went with them was to Bari and to the Bark Castle (Castelli is the word for a castle in Italian).

The week that I was working, Gabby drove her to Lecce and Cupertino, where they had lunch and wandered around the cities. Her moms got to meet some of our friends while she was there. Albano and Romina were off doing their singing engagements, so she did not get to meet them, but Ceasara was there with Poppi, and some of our friends from base met her during her last week as we had one of our bar-b-ques and her mother loved it.

Gabby left San Vito three weeks before I did. She went to her mother's house in England. I was glad she had time to spend with her family before she came to Scotland after I found an apartment.

I left San Vito in the very beginning of January and went straight to Scotland, which I soon began to call Snotland (my eyes and nose were always running).

NSGA Edzell, Scotland (United Kingdom) January 1993 – January 1996

NSGA Edzell, Scotland was a whole new chapter in my military life, I had never been anywhere that was this cold, not even Misawa, Japan which I thought was one of the coldest places in the world other than the north and south poles and Russia. I was really in for a big surprise. I caught a civilian flight from Rome, Italy, to Edinburgh, Scotland, in nineteen ninety-three. There were a lot of things to get used to besides the chilly days and nights. There were days when the sun was out when I got up and past midnight and the other had nights that lasted forever.

I do have to say I have never seen a country that was so cold that had so much green grass and trees. The day I arrived it was snowing, I was glad I still had my parka from being stationed in Japan, it was water proof with fur and it had a hoodie with fur in it, that kept me warm as hell with the long johns and thick socks.

All of us new arrival personnel had a week of learning about the country and its history, one of the instructors claimed that damn near everything that was invented and useful was done by a Scotsman. He was funny. I had to get used to driving on black ice again.

Gabby sold the Chevy and I had shipped my Z out three weeks before I left San Vito. It came to Scotland three weeks after I arrived. I lived in the barracks for about two weeks. Some of the old gang got there just as I arrived, so we were all in the classes about Scotland together and all off at the same time.

The village Edzell had maybe a population of about six or seven hundred people. I think when I was there. It did have base housing which made up a good portion of the population. It was a quiet little village and most of us in the military lived in the surrounding cities and towns. For a place to be called a city it had to have a cathedral. I lived in the town of Brechin which does have a cathedral, but it is called a city 'Go figure'.

I had never seen so many pubs like I did in Scotland, our crew, all of us new guys to the command, went to Edinburgh to try what was called a pub crawl. The crawl was on a street that had pubs on both sides of it and the street was nearly a mile long. I think there were seven of us that went from the old gang and about six or seven other folks from the base. We took a tour bus to what was called Rose Street and it was full of pubs (bars), some only big enough for maybe ten or twelve people others you could really party in, we all tried out best to hit all the bars, somebody said Rose street was the best place to party, I couldn't doubt it.

I cannot remember how long we were on Rose Street as I was back in the tour bus passed out after about three or four hours, the idea was to have a drink in as many of the pubs as we could. We all thought we could handle our liquor. The Scots taught us a lesson. We were beginners compared to them.

I laugh, thinking about how I thought I could drink a lot. I don't remember much after the sixth pub I remember we were all singing as we went from pub to pub and holding on to each other. I guess in a place like this. Pubs are necessary to keep warm. One of the guys said it was the best night he couldn't remember. None of us went to jail or got in trouble, so I guess it was a good time. Like I said I couldn't remember much after getting to Rose street. I kept the ticket from the tour and that is the only way I even remember the name of the street the pubs were on.

The first couple of weeks were cold as hell, and there was no longer any smoking in the buildings on U.S. military bases, so we had to stand outside by the dumpsters and smoke and at the time I was doing analysis and reporting if that didn't make you want to smoke anything would. I had a cool supervisor. He was a senior first-class petty officer ready for chief. We all knew he would make it. He was coming up on his twenty years and he retired as soon as his time hit the twenty. I think he had a job with the US post office waiting for him dealing with computers and he just couldn't wait to get out.

I was still a new first-class petty officer and there was one other guy there that out-ranked me so, I was sitting a position again, quitting smoking was not going to happen for me doing that job. It was fun as hell but super stressful. I cannot speak for anybody else about their stress issues, but the analysis was it for me. I took smoke breaks whenever I could and that was often. The third week in Snotland, Freddy showed up. His wife was in Spain visiting her family with their daughter, so he and I partied like crazy.

I found a flat on the third floor above the meat market in the city of Brechin (Bre-kin) on the High street (the high street was the main street in the city), and the building was built in the sixteenth or seventeenth century. There was no one on the second floor as that floor looked like it would cave in if you put a couch or something kind of heavy on it. The building consisted of just the meat market on the first floor, the empty apartment (flat) on the second floor, and the flat on the third floor, which I moved into. There was no elevator and I had to climb some steps to get up to my flat.

The key to the main door downstairs was huge. It would not fit into my trouser pockets. It did fit in my coat pockets but just barely. The flat had new carpet and those old-fashioned wall heaters that didn't really heat like a heater in the US would. The water in the apartment and the heater for it worked but I had to wait a while for the water to heat up for the shower and it was also a bath in the bathroom with no screens on the windows. (I used to put my six-pack of beer outside the window on the window sill to keep it nice and cold.) This was a two-bedroom flat; I knew Shakey would like it, I wasn't too sure how Gabby would feel, I would find out in another month that she wanted to stay in England with her family a little longer and that was fine with me.

High street had all the main shops located on it, except for the grocery store that was a couple of blocks away, but I think there were at least four pubs on just the part of High street I lived on, there was a Chinese restaurant, jewelry store and a few clothing stores. There were no American fast food places like McDonalds. But I had the butcher shop and a bakery right below me. There was no heat in the stairway, so the steps would get icy and that was really tricky to deal with drunk or sober.

When my furniture arrived, most of it had to be hoisted up to the third floor with a winch-type device outside and above the living room window. I had brought a nice couch with double incliners and a love seat to match. We also had three-bedroom sets, a kitchen table and basically all the appliances for the early 1990s.

Gabby and I only had one VCR, but we had lots of videos that my family sent to us in Italy. When Shakey arrived, I had to find him. I was told he was misplaced by the folks at the airport, but I later found out he wasn't misplaced. They took it into the office and fed him, and he started doing his tricks and they fell in love with him. I basically had to make them give me my dog back. I was informed that I would have to put him in quarantine for six months at the cost of the equivalent of ten dollars a day. I was choking and coughing with that news, but he was my family and I agreed to pay. He was taken to a place near Brechin and put in a kennel.

I took some of his toys, but they told me whatever toy I gave him would have to stay after he was released, I kept the little basketball and gave him one of his old chew toys, he looked so happy to see me, I was allowed to play with him for about fifteen minutes, he started doggy crying when I had to leave, I felt like crap for leaving him, I could only visit once a week and with my schedule two-two-two and eighty, it wasn't easy to get to him as visiting hours were from eight to four, so one of my days off was spent visiting him.

Gabby forgot to tell me about the quarantine. When I called her at her mother's house, I let her know about Shakey's situation. It sounded like she was going to cry. When all the furniture arrived, like I said, it was hoisted up to the third floor and thru the front room window. The flat had three windows in the front room, all facing the High street, so I could see into the neighbor's windows directly across from me and they could see in our place if the curtains were open.

I usually kept them closed it helped to keep the heat in. To get to the stairs leading up to the flat, you had to walk between two buildings and on the side was the entrance. It was a dark blue door once the movers arrived with our furniture. We stuffed the two bedroom sets into one room until we were able to sell one of the sets, the Italian company that packed and moved out furniture packed the trash can with the trash in it.

We were lucky there was no food in the trash. This was probably the only military move that nothing was broken during the delivery. I had the apartment situated pretty good when Freddy arrived at the base. I had the guest bedroom set up but it was full of the other bedroom furniture. You could make it to the bed and back out of the door. Freddy stayed there once he checked in. Neither Freddy or I was too terribly impressed with the weather, but the pubs were everywhere and we both liked that part.

I had met the manager of the pub directly across the street from my flat it was called Amigos and it was always packed. The pubs were nothing like the bars in the United States, during the daytime they served lunch and dinner and after dinner it was pure party time. I met a babe in Amigos and told her my brother would be here soon. She was excited, she and I had partied a couple of times, but she had lots of dogs and their fur was all over her and her clothes. She had a hell of a nice body, and like I said, we did party.

I called the base from Amigos and got Freddy at work. I told him to come straight to the pub as the doors would shut after ten. He got to Amigos a little after ten and the manager a really cool Scottish guy who I had become close friends with let Freddy in after Freddy told the manager he was my brother. I was sitting at the bar playing one of the slot machines (all the pubs had them. The Scots called them bandits) when Freddy walked over to me and ordered a drink. I saw the babe and went over and whispered in her ear to kiss Freddy and grab his hookup. She was a little tipsy and walked right over to him and did what I had told her.

But she didn't do anything else with him, this other lady saw her and she came right over to where Freddy and I were seated at the bar and the next thing I know Freddy wanted the keys to my flat. I gave him the spare key. I didn't lock the bottom door as it was too hard to get it open and I didn't like carrying that big assed key around, Freddy and the lady left and I was left to pay for his drink. I talked with the lady that I told to kiss and grab him and we later went to my place also. The next morning both of the ladies were gone, and damn, Freddy and his new friend had drunk all the beers I had in the refrigerator. He didn't know I usually left a six-pack outside on the window sill.

A couple of weeks later, Gabby came home and we sold the other bedroom set. Freddy stayed with us for a few more weeks until he found a place a couple of blocks north of High street. It was in a quiet neighborhood and he was happy with it. It was like a duplex with two bedrooms. One night our little crew went on a pub crawl in Brechin and we got totally drunk. None of us drove. Everybody was going to stay at my place that night and then they would drive back to the base the next morning. We hit the disco that had females from all the surrounding cities bused to their club. They actually had a bus that would hit the nearby towns and bring the ladies to their club.

All the guys from Brechin, along with us sailors, would be there. They played that 1980s and early nineties house music. There was no stop between songs. It was okay to go there once in a while, but I just didn't like the place too much, mainly because there were always fights and even if you didn't want to get involved once the police came, we sailors could still get into trouble and lord knows I didn't need that in my life, but that was the first place we went to and we stayed there maybe an hour or so, there were eight of us, three ladies and the rest guys. Freddy didn't like the place at all, one of the ladies stayed there and we didn't see her until the next morning, so the seven of us left and hit the pubs. We had way too much fun. By the time we were ready to leave, we were walking by this beautiful old church. It had a fence along the back of it and then we had to go down the next street, which was downhill. Freddy decided to jump the fence. Before I could tell him it was damn near a twenty-five-foot drop, he climbed it and jumped off. We heard some crashing sounds. We all looked around and took off, running around the corner and down the hill.

We heard Freddy screaming, it was pitch black outside, but we found Freddy, he was scrapped up and holding his head, we got him up and brushed most of the mud off of him, he was still dizzy and thank God he was drunk as hell, or he would have killed himself. Once we started walking back up the hill heading to my flat, Freddy looked at me and asked how come I didn't tell him about the little cliff. We all busted up laughing.

Once we got near my place, they all saw the club, Amigos. We spent the next few hours there, Freddy had forgotten his near-death experience and went back to drinking. I had a few beers and told them I would leave the door open. I had had enough to drink. I forgot to tell them that after eleven at night, the doors at Amigos were locked and no people could enter, only leave. Freddy made it to the men's room, where he threw up all over and in the toilet. I was told that when they all came back to my flat, he sat on the couch and tried to lay down. We wedged him on his side just in case. Then I handed out a few of my sleeping bags for two of them to use and the rest all passed out in the spare room. The next morning we all said we would have to party like that again. I don't think we ever did. At least I don't remember all of us partying again. We all were in different sections at work, so that was that.

Once Freddy's furniture arrived, his wife and daughter left Spain and came to Scotland, Freddy's wife did not like Scotland one bit. I don't think she liked too much of anything. Gabby's mom did not want to come up to Snotland to visit at all, Gabby would go down to England to visit her and those were my party days. Gabby got a job on base again cooking in both the clubs. Edzell was a pure navy and marine corps CT base, there was only a British Royal air force officer there as a liaison officer and a contingent of the Royal navy's version of CT's. The Scottish version of hippies would protest outside the front gate, they were harmless and usually high as hell, chanting that our base was a secret submarine base with nukes. The damn base was about six miles from any water and high on a hill. They wouldn't try to stop us from entering the base they just stood outside on the grass with picket signs, I would wave at them and keep driving.

The road leading to the sight was covered by these trees that seemed to have connected over the road to the base. In the fog, it was kind of weird, looking like being in a haze through a tunnel.

Once my Z arrived, I had to put chains on the tires and drive really slow, or it would just lose traction, and I would slide all over the place. I eventually took it to a friend of mine in the British Royal Navy, and he put it in his garage, where it stayed for almost two years. I would go over to his place and start it every now and then. I had to put blankets over the hood to stop the engine from freezing, did I mention this place was cold? Freddy used to always say he hadn't seen his balls since he landed in Scotland because they went up in his belly where it was warm.

I think that was the way most of us felt that we were not used to continuously cold weather. It could rain, snow and the sun would come out all on the same day. Gabby came back home and Shakey was finally out of quarantine and we were a happy family again, but the day I went to pick Shakey up and bring him home, he looked at me like he was totally pissed off. Gabby was at work when we got home, the first thing Shakey did was walk right in front of the TV, lifted his leg and piss on the legs of the TV stand. I was mad, but he was not punished for it. I just cleaned up his mess and told him not to do it again. He never did.

That evening he sniffed the entire apartment, and when I took him out to do his business, he loved being in the snow. He was hopping around like a rabbit in the one foot of snow on the ground and barking. I had a tennis ball and through it. It went into the little river and he ran to get it. Once his front paw hit that freezing water, he let the ball go. I laughed and he ran back to the apartment.

I felt as though I was turning into a really serious drunk while stationed in Scotland. While I was there, only one in four Scottish people had a car. The gas was so expensive just like the rest of the country and Europe. Gabby and I were starting to get along much better and we made friends with a few of the locals, mostly the ones that were regulars at Amigos Pub, three of them along with Gabby and I, decided to go on a vacation together.

We all wanted to go to Ibiza, one of the islands in the Spanish Archipelago. It is pronounced (I-be-tha) because the king of Spain at the time had a lisp and couldn't pronounce the letter Z correctly. At least, that is what I was told by one of the club owners I met when we got there. We rented a two-bedroom apartment on the second floor near all the clubs, Gabby and I were still in our 30Ss, so we were still able to party with the youngsters.

Just like in Italy, most of the beaches in Spain at that time were topless or nude. Gabby and I rented a little car, just big enough for the five of us, and we went to a few of the beaches off the beaten path. There were three guys and two ladies in our little group, and when we hit the beaches. Gabby had no problems being topless, but the other female in our group did. She was nineteen and had very big breasts. Gabby had good-sized breasts that were perfect for her size but not as big as our friend's.

On the beach, damn near everybody was topless and the young guys just stared at our female friend. One guy asked her if she had implants and still had the scares? Because she was wearing a bikini top, she got upset, and the rest of us just laughed.

On our second night, the local police came to our room as we were getting ready to go out and start partying. We thought it was because our little boom box was too loud. They wanted one of us that spoke English and an American if possible, that was me. I asked why and they told me an American kid that was there on summer vacation had passed away from drinking too much. I asked what that had to do with us. He said he would explain on the way and that there was no foul play in broken English.

I went to the little police station and they explained it all to me. They called the poor guys parents and there was a letter that they wanted me to read. I didn't feel right calling some poor mother or father. Ibiza has a six-hour difference from the east coast of the US and this was like ten at night. I had told Gabby and the rest of the gang to go on and party. I would catch up with them after I was done with the police.

I asked the police officer how the kid had passed and was told that he had passed out from too much alcohol and his friends laid him on his back. The poor kid drowned in his own vomit. I was trying to figure out in my mind how to tell someone that their child had passed away in a country over four thousand miles away, the police handed me the phone and the father answered. I told the father my name, explained that I was here on vacation with my wife and friends and also that I was a petty officer in the US Navy and then I just told him that his son had passed away while here in Ibiza, the father told me this joke is not funny.

I asked him one question and that was, "Sir, with all due respect, how do you think I feel? The police found me by my passport, which is a military passport, I was supposed to be with my wife and friends and I did not ask the police to let me call someone I don't know to tell them his son had died?"

He told me this was not a funny joke then I told him something that let him know it was no joke, "In my job, one of the worst things I could think of would be to have to write someone a letter or someone writing my family a letter that a loved one was lost. Now I am calling a young man's father a kid that probably had a really good life ahead of him and was just on vacation and I had to tell his father his son is dead."

There was silence for a few minutes, then I heard a woman cry, the father said he would be on the next flight he could get to Ibiza, he then thanked me and I could tell he was crying when he hung up. I told the police what the father told me about being on the next flight to Ibiza, they all looked sad and the one that spoke to me with his broken English thanked me. I felt like a giant piece of shit. I didn't go out with the gang. I went back to the room, opened the bottle of Chivas Regal I was going to share with the gang and drank until they got back. I sat on the balcony looking at the ocean and I felt like crap thinking about the kid and his family, along with what I had to say to the father to get him to understand that it was no joke.

When the guys came back, they all wanted to know what happened and I told them. Gabby and the other lady had tears in their eyes. One of the guys said that his friends were stupid for laying the kid on his back. I told him they probably just didn't know any better. We were all silent for the rest of the night, all sitting on the balcony. I poured them all a drink and I went to bed. Gabby was right behind me. I told her that I let the police know how hard that was and they didn't say a word as I was leaving. The next morning was a beautiful day. The sun was up and we weren't freezing our balls off in Scotland. I got them all in the car and we headed for a beach called

"Aguas Blancas" (white water) had mud that was supposed to be good for the skin and it was a nudist beach which I had to promise the two guys we would at least go there. We had brought breakfast food when we first got into our apartment along with toilet paper, so we ate breakfast before leaving for the beach, where we wanted to go was on the northern part of the island with cliffs surrounding it. I had heard there was good snorkeling there. Once we finally got there and found our way to the beach, Gabby started laughing. The guys were ready to walk the beach. The other lady didn't want any part of a nude beach. Her, Gabby and I stayed near the car. The two guys walked along the beach and then came back claiming everybody was covered in mud, I busted up laughing along with Gabby. We got gas for the little car and drove back to Ibiza town, we laughed at the two guys for being pervs and the lady for being such a prude, we stopped at a couple of little shops on the way back, brought some fresh bread and ham slices for our lunch.

Our stay was only four days and after the last night of partying. I was ready to get back to Snotland and Shakey. The same lady that watched him in San Vito was in Edzell also and she jumped at the chance to watch him while we were gone.

That was the last good vacation Gabby and I took together, we did drive down to England to visit her family a couple of times, but we were falling apart as far as husband and wife. She cried a lot for no reason and was always mad at me. The last little bit of fun we had was one of the locals that worked on base invited us to her party, she asked Gabby to invite some of my friends and she did, only three guys showed up and when we got to the party most of the locals were already drunk and still going strong, we brought a case of Budweiser and a bottle of vodka, that made them happy as hell because they were running out of booze as soon as we walked into the house the mother of the birthday girl took a look at the four military guys and started shouting let's get this party started, she grabbed a dish towel and put it around one of my guy's butt and pulled his body against hers and she started grinding on him, her daughter looked shocked, we all started laughing except for the guy she was grinding on. She had to be in her early 60s and he was barely twenty years old. He gave me that save-me look. I just shook my head and kept laughing, Gabby grabbed a beer and handed it to the old girl, and she had to let go of the towel with one hand and my guy took off to the other side of the room.

There were plenty of younger ladies and he practically grabbed one and danced with her. The mother was chugging beers down like crazy and basically chasing my guys around the room, trying to grab their hookup. It was all funny until the old girl stopped really quickly and ran to the bathroom, we could hear her throwing up through all the loud music, we all tried to pretend we weren't hearing it, but she was loud as hell.

She was in there for about five or six minutes and when she came out of the bathroom, she walked straight to her daughter and whispered something in her ear. The daughter looked shocked and she walked over to Gabby and said something to her I couldn't hear.

Gabby couldn't help herself. She busted up laughing. I mean, she had tears in her eyes from laughing. Gabby grabbed my arm and told me to follow her, but she kept stopping because she was laughing so hard. None of us had a clue as to why she was laughing, then the daughter started laughing. I asked Gabby what the hell was going on and she said you would see. I followed her into the bathroom. It didn't smell too good in there. Then Gabby pointed to the toilet and said the old girl was puking so hard she blew her teeth into the toilet and then flushed it.

I looked at Gabby for a few seconds and then my brain finally understood what she was saying. I started laughing. I had to put the seat down on the toilet just to sit down while I was laughing, then I heard all the people in the front room laughing and Gabby started laughing again, which in turn made me laugh even harder.

Once we stopped laughing, Gabby asked me if there was anything we could do to get the false teeth back. I started laughing again and so did gabby. Once the laughter subsided, I asked her to see if they had any wire clothes hangers. Maybe if the teeth were stuck in the trap we could get them out. As soon as I said that, Gabby busted up laughing and so did I.

Gabby finally went out of the bathroom and found the daughter. A few minutes later, she came back with the clothes hanger and we tried to see if the teeth were in the trap, but that didn't work, so I asked the daughter if she had any tools. Her father who had passed away years ago, had an old toolbox and it had a wrench in it. I used to remove the tap after I turned the water off. The false teeth were not there. The old girl went through the rest of the party with no teeth, and she just drank more once she started with the "does anybody want a gum job" we laughed so hard we had to leave.

I had never heard of anybody puking their false teeth out. When I think of it to this day, I still laugh uncontrollably for a few minutes. The mother had to go through the whole week waiting for new false teeth. I felt so sorry for her, she was having the time of her life that night and once she found out they were gone, she didn't let that stop her. She just kept on partying.

Gabby and I were not doing well together at all. I stayed in the flat on High Street and she moved out to I don't know where. We split the furniture up and I kept Shakey. I met Freddy one night at Amigo's and he told me he was getting a divorce. His wife had enough of him partying and coming home drunk all the time.

I left went to the flat and left a note for Gabby telling her I wanted a divorce and then I went back to Amigo's and got pretty drunk. When I got home, the note was gone. Gabby would just come over when she felt like it and take Shakey for walks and play with him.

The next morning at work, Freddy and I were leaning against each other, trying to stand up while outside in the smoking area. I remember feeling very rough, my stomach was making gurgling sounds and my eyes were red as hell. Freddy had gotten lucky and moved into base housing. After his wife and daughter left, he had to move back to Brichen in the same spot he had moved into when he first got to Scotland.

Things were changing for us CTs and changing fast. We got word that our base was closing along with NSGA Torri Station in Okinawa, I still had close to a year left to go at NSGA Edzell and the worst part of the changes was that it was getting really hard to make higher rank, like only two or three E-6's were making E-7 (chief petty officer) per year and that really sucked for most of us that were E-6's and in all honesty. We knew our chances of making chief petty officer were too far out of reach for us and I still had almost three years before I could retire at the twenty-year mark. I sucked.

Freddy found a new girlfriend, she was a bartender in a pub on the other side of Brichen. I went to the bar with him and she had a friend that was just absolutely hot. She and I got together and we all partied.

I had a friend that I liked to hang out with. She was a model, and the locals in Amigos called her Perky, she was beautiful, but she liked smoking her weed and I couldn't deal with that. During one of my eighty-hour breaks, Freddy and I decided to go to Glasgow. I left first and picked up Perky. Freddy came later. Perky and I checked into the hotel and had some fun in the room while we waited for Freddy to arrive. He finally showed up about two hours later, we all left the hotel and found a couple of pubs to hang out at, and we all ended up back at the hotel in its main lounge. Freddy had found this lady with orange-red hair. Every time I looked at her, I just started laughing. She was kind of pretty with a small frame. Freddy was drunk as hell, he had been drinking Snapp's and beer all night and he was out there, so was the lady with the hair. Perky told me she was sleepy and smiled at me.

That was my cue to get back to our room for a quality, fun time. The next morning, we got up and checked out. I told the desk clerk to put our room and drinks on Freddy's bill, she smiled at me, and Perky and I left. It was over two hours to get back to Brichen. We laughed all the way. It was one of the few times the weather was nice enough for me to drive my Z and Perky loved it.

I dropped her off at her mother's place and went back to my flat, Freddy showed up later and he was pissed, I laughed and handed him the money for my room and drinks, then I opened the window and grabbed one of the beers I kept on the window sill, he smiled and sat down looked me right in the eye and asked me what he had done last night, I told him the truth about the red-orange haired lady, he smiled and said he had to wake her up and get her out of his room, he didn't want anything else to do with her and I busted up laughing.

We went back to that hotel one other time we both drove our own cars again and this time I went alone and so did Freddy. We had fun and ended up at the hotel's lounge area again and Freddy had met these three ladies. They sat with us and ordered a couple of drinks and it was late when Freddy took one of them to his room. I told the other two ladies good night and went up to my room. None of us were attracted to each other they were both bigger than I was and I just wasn't ready for that.

When I got up to check out the next morning, the desk clerk told me that Freddy had already left and charged everything to my bill. I was pissed. The whole drive back home, I was gonna choke him to death when I got to his front door, he opened it laughing his ass off and handed me the money and a beer, I started laughing and he said payback is a bitch. We both started laughing and drank more beers.

Perky and I probably lasted a couple of months longer. I decided that I wanted to go to one of the Greek Islands and I asked Gale (Freddy's girlfriend's best friend) if she wanted to go with me. She was blonde, about five foot six inches and had one hell of a nice body and a very pretty face. We got along really good, so we went on a four-day vacation. I remember it was in early November, I paid for the flight, and she paid for the apartment rental and we split the food and drinks. She was awesome the first day. We spent half of it in bed having quality time. We hit one of the bars on the beach, we both ran from the bar and jumped into the water right off of Mykonos and our apartment was maybe one block from the beach.

We had to buy our own toilet paper and breakfast foods like ham and eggs. We also brought the Greek bread loaves. We later found out it was cheaper to order breakfast and dinner at the little restaurants that lined the streets leading to the beaches.

Our little apartment was like and efficient apartment. It was made to just shower in and sleep. It had a little two-burner stove, a tiny refrigerator that was just big enough for the breakfast food and two six-packs of beer, a double bed and the frame had pieces of it sticking into the mattress. I put the frame on its side against the wall and we slept on the mattress. The water was heated by solar panels on the roof and if you didn't take a shower while the sun was up. Well, it just wasn't a good thing like we found out the first day.

The shower just had a little lip around the floor of it and it was just big enough for two people to stand in. It had a shower curtain that went around it in a circle. We tried not to splash any water as there was only a two-inch lip around the bottom of it to stop the water from getting on the rest of the floor.

There was a little plastic table with two plastic chairs and a few cabinets and that was it for the apartment. On our second day for, Gale tried some of the really hard bread and it cracked one of her teeth. We spent most of the day looking for a dentist that spoke English and would accept credit cards. The dentist had to remove the whole tooth as it cracked from the top down under her gums. If I remember correctly it was damn near fifty dollars in American money, she was in some serious pain, so it had to be pulled.

Gale was given some meds for the pain, along with a couple of beers and she was happy again. We found one little bar that was about fifteen or twenty yards from the beach and we hung out there. We met a couple from England that were newlyweds and hung out with them that night. Around eleven o'clock I was ready to go back to the room. Gale stayed and danced until she came back to the room an hour later and passed right out. We hung out and partied the next two days at the same little bar near the beach.

The island was beautiful, clean, clear blue water of the Aegean Sea. The water was getting cold and we only went in it once or twice out of the four days we were there. We did not rent a car as we could walk to the beach and to all the little shops in the town of Mikonos, just about all the buildings were whitewashed. It was cool to be there. When we got there, most of the tourists were gone and it felt like we had most of the beach to ourselves. Just like most of the European beaches a lot of the ladies were topless.

We spent the last day at our little apartment swimming pool, it was not very big, but we didn't have to walk far to get to it and we were both burnt out with drinking and the beach, in Snotland I only went to the beach two times and that was in the town of Arbroath. We flew back to Edinburgh the next morning. We both had a great time and started seeing more of each other over the last six or seven months that I had left in Scotland.

I was starting to drink more than normal, totally getting wasted on my days off and I knew I needed to slow down, but as soon as Freddy and I got together, it was party time. Another one of Freddy and my friends really came into play during my last four months at Edzell came into play. We called him G-man. He was awesome, a white male about five feet six inches and he loved the Sista's, as he called them.

He was in the middle of breaking up with one that lived in Atlanta, Georgia and he was having a rough time with it. When he got around Freddy and I, he would chill and go with whatever flow we had going on and he usually had lots of fun, he would hang out at my place and I would come home from the pubs and find him sleeping on the couch or either he was with me at the pubs. I was invited to Perky's Mother's birthday party. I really didn't want to be there as her mother worked with Gabby on the base. I stayed for about twenty minutes and decided to leave. Her mother said she would walk me to the door, she grabbed my hand and walked me out past the gate, then without any warning, she started kissing me, I mean tongue in my mouth and she started trying to unzip my trousers, then we heard her husband calling for her from the front door, she was on her knees and I pulled her up and left as fast as I could.

I never saw Perky again and I was fine with that. I didn't care that she was as gorgeous as she was. I was done with her. G-man and Freddy hung out with me all the time as my time in Edzell was getting shorter. I had lots of one-night stands with a lot of the females in other cities around Brechin. I met several in the town called Arbroath, it was a fishing village and they also had a box factory that made the boxes for different companies like Chivas Regal and the likes.

I met one and she was a total party animal. I went to a club called Flicks in the town I lived in, it was just after my last eve-watch and I was supposed to meet up with some of the guys from the base. I rushed to get home, put on jeans, long sleeve shirt, a leather jacket, and my work boots along with my Los Angeles Raiders ball cap. I barely made it to the club in time before they closed and locked the door. I was standing in line to get a beer when this short little Scottish guy turned around and gave me an angry look. I just ignored him, I needed a beer. It had been a long string of two-two-two work weeks and I was ready to start my eighty hours off. I wanted a Budweiser and to find a seat and wait for the guys, not any problems with this little guy.

While I was in the line, I noticed three ladies sitting near the bar. They were staring at me. I smiled back, walked over to their table and asked if they needed drinks. Only one said yes she was a cute little brunette with short hair, a small chest and a very pretty face. I got back in my place in the line and just as I did, the little guy again gave me a dirty look, thenn he got on his tiptoes and head-butted me. I had my ball cap on so his nose hit the bill of the cap, he screamed and yelled, I heard his nose make a cracking sound, he fell to the floor and the guy behind me said, "If I was you mate, I kick the hell out of him."

I had on my steel-toed work boots, so I gave a good kick to his ribs, stepped over him and ordered two Budweiser beers from the tap. Just as the bartender handed me the first beer, I just barely got it to my mouth, waiting to take a sip and the bouncers grabbed me. I was put down by the door and was told I was banned for one month. They knew my name as I knew the owner of the club, I was pissed. All I wanted was that beer.

As I was being escorted to the front door, the little cutie was yelling, "He didn't start it." They grabbed the other guy and tossed him out the door. I felt like kicking him again, but he was still bleeding from his nose and holding his side where I kicked him. I took the back alley towards my place and hit the club across the street, Amigos. I knocked really hard on the door. Then I kicked it a couple of times and the manager opened the door, looked at me and smiled. He told me to hurry up and get my ass in the door. He always said that.

I walked over to the bar and sat down, ordered another Budweiser and took a sip. Just as I did, one of the ladies I had seen at the club I was just escorted out of came over to me and told me her friend really liked me, then she turned and walked back to the table the same three ladies I had seen and smiled at in the other club were sitting there all grinning, the little brunette was just staring, I noticed they were all drinking beer, so I ordered a pitcher of Budweiser from the tap, walked over to their table and sat down, I told the brunette which I called cutie that I would probably be taking her home for the night and I did, we stopped at what she called the beach in Arbroath. It was a normal cold as hell night and my car was the only one out there. We had fun for a while and then I took her to her flat. It was nice and clean.

She didn't have any children, that was a plus in my book. I spent the night with and got up the next morning and drove back to Brechin. Shakey was waiting at the door for me. I had left the bottom door open and he ran out to take care of his business. I closed the door and when he was done, he barked one time. I opened the door and let him in. I was cooking my breakfast bacon, eggs and toast with strawberry jelly. I opened his can of dog food and he ate all most all of it. He always saved some in his bowel for later. After I ate, I watched TV for a while lying on the couch. He was on the floor right by me, Freddy showed up later and I told him about the new babe I met in Arbroath, he just smiled.

I showered and got dressed while he watched TV with Shakey. After I got dressed and came back out to the front room, Freddy said lets hit Amigos. The three of us got up and went down the stairs, crossed the street and walked into the put, Shakey sat by my chair and Freddy ordered a pitcher of Budweiser. The manager asked if I wanted water for Shakey.

I laughed and I bet him that three other Scots that my dog would only drink Chivas Regal, not the other whiskey, the three of them all bet me twenty pounds apiece. The manager Pete poured three little bowels with three different whiskeys, the one on the left had the Chivas Regal, Shakey went straight to it and finished off the little bowel, and walked back to the table where Freddy. I were sitting and laid down. Freddy just shook his head. The guys handed over the money and with the sixty pounds, we had lunch and drinks until we left. The one meal both Freddy and I liked was the French fries with gravy and cheese over them.

Both Freddy and I were hooked on the bandits (small slot machines) that were in all the pubs that day. Freddy hit for eighty-five pounds. While we were in Scotland, it cost one dollar and sixty cents for one pound. We were both pretty excited that day. We hung out in Amigos until around six that evening, checked out all the babes and watched three houses wife's beat the hell out of a lady that took money from their husbands while they were drunk the night before. She promised them all sex and took the money and ran out of the back door behind the lady's room.

She got hit on the nose with a beer bottle and then smacked around until Pete ran over and stopped it. I think while I was stationed there, I had seen just as many female fights as I did guys. What a place. All the ladies in the club were yelling at the one that got her butt kicked. Freddy and I left and went to the pub his new girlfriend worked at. As soon as we walked into the pub, his girlfriend called Gale and she came right over.

Freddy and I brought them both dinner and we partied with them for the next two days. Gale had brought some sausages and pork chops at her place, so we went on base and brought some charcoal and we grilled food outside, along with some salad and beer. We were all set. Gale had two daughters. One was better looking than her mother and was the youngest of the two and the other was not. I liked the youngest daughter.

The oldest daughter didn't care for me at all, Gale was a nurse or nurse's aide, single and like I said before, very nice looking, but her oldest daughter was a pain in my ass. One day I had the quarterdeck watch, which was twenty-four-hour duty on the quarter-deck (after work, along with three other lower-ranking petty officers, we would have to stand watch on the quarter deck). I had told Gale that was where I was going to be that night and I would see her the next day. Her oldest daughter went out that night and told her she had seen me at one of the clubs in Brechin, the one I had been banned from.

Gale called me at the quarter deck and was pissed. I waited for her to stop talking and asked her what phone number did she call me on. She was silent, started to cry and said she was sorry. I told her not to worry. I would see her the next day after I got off of duty. The next morning it was the start of my eighty hours off, so I went home, showered and went over to Gales' house. The daughter that I didn't like was gone. We hung out with Freddy and his girl for the rest of the day, Freddy had brought some steaks from the base and we grilled them outside and had a good dinner.

I hung out with Gale for the rest of that day and night. The next morning, I went home, took care of Shakey, grabbed some clothes and Shakey and I headed for the base. I brought cigarettes (what the Scots called fags), beer, vodka, a six-pack of coke and steaks from the base before I headed to her place. Shakey loved going on the base. Everybody liked to pat him as he was a little attention whore.

We stayed on the base for a little over an hour and we headed to Arbroath. When we got there, Cutie had the lady that had told me Cutie liked me at her place, it was light snow on the ground and I took Shakey out for a walk. He didn't mind the light snow. He just didn't like the deep stuff, what could I say he was from Miami, Florida, not the cold north. The food I brought filled Cutie's little refrigerator. I put two six-packs of Budweiser out of the window on the sill. I kept some of Shakey's food in the car just in case we went somewhere and spent the night, so he was all set. Her friend was a hottie with a really nice little body, but she had a little girl and I didn't need anybody else with kids. I already had Gale with her two daughters.

Cutie would do just fine. I hadn't seen Gabby in months, I did worry about her, but I knew she was a survivor and could get a job anywhere as a chef. That night Cutie and her friend were recovering from hangovers and I showed up with all that booze. We were all drunk in a few hours and having fun. We asked each other questions and if you didn't know the answers, you had to do something really stupid. I had them both on their hands and knees, sniffing the furniture like dogs and lifting their legs like Shakey did when he had to pee.

I didn't know one of the answers and had to go outside naked and run around the three cars in the parking lot. Thank god I was full of liquor. They were both laughing at me for the rest of the night. The next day Cutie took me to her mother's place a couple of blocks away. We left Shakey at her place and walked instead of driving. It was as usual, cold as hell outside. We took the bottle of vodka with us and shared it with her mother and stepfather. He was a real piece of work, a real dick head. He called me a darky. I let him know how I felt about that in the kitchen. He didn't call me that again, at least not to my face or where I could hear him say it.

We stayed until it got dark. It was probably in the high twenties outside when we walked to her mother's house, it was in the low teens when we walked back to Cutie's house and of course, Shakey needed to go outside as soon as we got there. He was back inside in no time. Shakey and I stayed with Cutie for the next two days and headed back to our flat in Brechin and the weather had gotten colder with a forecast to be in the low teens for the rest of the day.

Our time in Scotland was getting close to an end, and I decided to take one last vacation, I had so many vacation days on the books I really needed to use some of them, or I would lose some, so

I decided to take a trip out of the United Kingdom and headed for Amsterdam. I put the word out on base that I planned on going there and about four others said they wanted to go. Only one actually brought a ticket. We stayed for four days and three nights, the flight was close to an hour and thirty minutes, we flew out of Edinburgh straight to Amsterdam, Netherland and surprisingly it was nice weather when we arrived. I left with another black sailor named Sawdog, he was cool as hell. Our only problem was that he worked the opposite shifts from mine, so during my eighty hours off, I also took an extra four days of leave which gave me seven days off.

We left on a Friday and returned on Monday. We had made reservations to stay at the Botel Hotel, only a couple of miles from the center of the city. We arrived at Schiphol Airport, went to change American Dollars for the Dutch guilder and then we took an underground shuttle into Amsterdam, from there a quick taxi and we were at the Botel Hotel. It was an old cruise ship that was anchored and turned into a hotel. It was weird but fun. Our room had two full-sized beds and one bathroom with a shower, sink and toilet. There was a little two-person table in the room and that was it. Sawdog and I left the room right after we unpacked our clothes and headed out to check out the city of Amsterdam. It was beautiful, especially the architecture. Some of those buildings were hundreds of years old from the 17th century, according to the pamphlet I took from the Botel lobby.

Once we left the motel, the first thing I noticed was there were bicycles everywhere and just like a lot of the European cities I had seen, there were no front yards, just sidewalks and the buildings that people lived in and or worked in, but Amsterdam had the canals. There are one hundred and sixty-five canals and one thousand and eighty-one bridges.

I felt hungry after a few minutes and that was because I had a buzz from all the weed that you could smell everywhere. We got on one of the tour boats or water taxis that took us around the most notable parts of the city that you could reach by the canals. The weather was a little bit chilly and there was no sun shining, kind of dreary, so we both were in jeans, boots and leather jackets. The ride was around seven dollars each and lasted for about forty-five minutes. The boat we were on was open but had the capability to have been covered. The driver or captain greeted us as we boarded. There were probably about seven or eight people that got on board with us.

The wind was not too bad and so the water in the canals was kind of calm, not much rocking or rolling. Once we pulled into the canal, the captain took his shoes off and steered the boat with his feet, Sawdog looked and me and we both had that is this going to be safe look on our faces.

The captain started telling us about the buildings and what they were used for. We stopped on the street that had some really expensive jewelry and clothes. Then we went past two places that we both wanted to see and that was the home of Ann Frank and the red light district. I was glad when the tour was over as it started getting colder and I was ready to get something to eat. There were little coffee shops everywhere, and they sold more than just coffee, WEED, it was sold in all the coffee shops.

When we were there, you could buy seeds and have them mailed to where ever you wanted back in the states. Neither of us wanted to try that or to smoke any of the weed. I did not want to get busted by a urine test back in Scotland. I think we went to the Kentucky fried chicken restaurant three times the first day that we were in Amsterdam. Having the munchies was something else and it lasted until we left that city. We were both glad we didn't get tested when we got back to Edzell.

The next morning, we got a cab to the house where Ann Frank stayed in hiding from the Nazis during World War II. It was something to see the place where her family and others hid for two years from the Germans and her diary, which was a serious part of history.

Later that day, we went to the red-light district. I think we got there too early in the day as most of the ladies we saw were not anyone we would not like to take home. I'm pretty sure the hottest babes came out later at night. The ones we saw were older than us and not as good-looking as we expected. We walked around there until it was time to hit night club. The first one we went to we were turned away by a female bouncer. She was a tall, thick woman who looked like she needed to be wearing one of those Viking outfits. She was cool as hell, though. I saw about six or seven beautiful ladies walk into the club and I just wanted to get inside. She told us, "Your kind are not allowed inside." At first, I was pissed, then she said follow me, we did and when she opened the curtain it was nothing but fine ladies, then it hit both Sawdog and myself at the same time. This was a club for lesbians only, I felt like crying, then the bouncer told us a club to go to where she knew we would have a good time, we went there and the place was going crazy Sawdog and I both found a couple of hotties, but some little Scottish guy started a fight, got his ass kicked and started throwing bottles and stuff, the police came and dragged his little ass out of the club, both or ladies left when all the fighting started.

Sawdog and I both just moved out of the way of the folks that were fighting. We left, went back to the Botel hotel and called it a night. The next morning, we went to the needle park, that was where all the heroin users went to take the medicine the Amsterdam government gave them to help them get over their addiction. It was a good thing we were wearing boots, there were used needles everywhere in the grass, on the sidewalks and on the tops of the trash cans.

We went back to Kentucky Fried chicken for breakfast and then back to the hotel to check out and head back to the airport. Once we went back to the airport, we went upstairs to the casino, we knew we didn't belong there and it was not like Las Vegas. We were in jeans and leather jackets. The folks in there were dressed to impress. On the way up on the escalator, we were behind this lady that had a skirt on which was so short well, we will just leave that there, it was a lovely view, she turned and looked down at us, smiled and walked into the casino. We walked to the escalator that went down, went to our gate and headed back to Scotland.

I have to admit most countries I went to, I tried to either buy or take a shot glass, but I didn't have any luck in Amsterdam. Once we landed back in Scotland and were back on base, Sawdog and I hung out a little during my last few weeks stationed at Edzell. Freddy threw me a going away party, which was something else I was told by him and several others. The party was over when I was drunkenly staggering to the bathroom and had to get between Freddy's glass table and this one lady that was a barmaid at one of the pubs that Freddy and I went to a lot. She had very large breasts, which I had the pleasure of seeing one night when she was drunk and decided to remove her blouse and bra.

I needed to get past her and I was doing a good job when she turned suddenly and her hip knocked me off balance. I grabbed for whatever I could, which was her big tits and when I did grab one, she pushed me away. The next morning, I ended up going to the ATM at the bank and getting Freddy the money for the glass table as I fell into it butt first and glass went everywhere, that was what Freddy told me had happened and I couldn't remember any of it, so I paid him.

I did see Gabby before I left, we talked for a little while and she told me she had found someone that wanted to marry her. I told her I was happy for her. She could not take Shakey where she was staying. She couldn't have a dog. I promised her I would take care of him. She knew I would. We kissed and I left. I had driven my Z to a port called Cromarty Firth not too far from Inverness, which was a little over an hour round trip. Freddy followed me, and of course, we stopped at a few of the pubs in Inverness, and then we headed back to Brechin, where I stayed with Freddy until I was taken by the navy van to Edinburgh for my Flight to Los Angeles, California.

I was able to get Shakey on the same flight that I was on, but he had to travel as luggage in the storage compartment of the plane. I had put his blanket inside of his cage and given him a pill that knocked him out for almost twelve hours, and when he woke up, we were in Los Angeles, California, at my parent's home. He slept through customs in Atlanta, and when he came to, there was plenty of water for him to drink, which he lapped up like crazy. There were also three other dogs on the property, two of them stayed outside, and the other, like Shakey, was allowed to stay in the house.

The was going to be a new experience for Shakey, he was used to being the biggest dog in the neighborhood and the only one in the house, all that changed when we opened his eyes. He would have to get used to a new pack, no longer would Gabby be there, he would have my mother and sister mainly to hang out with and my father when he was in the mood to play with the inside dogs.

One of the outside dogs was part Irish wolfhound and some other breed mixed and the other was some kind of Labrador mixed breed, both bigger than Shakey. The wolfhound was almost twice Shakey's size with twice the hair, which made it look bigger than it was. When Shakey saw the two dogs outside, his fur went up on his nape and so did theirs. We all knew he would have to stay inside with the poodle, the poodle was my mother's favorite and all living in the house and the yard knew it.

Once the effect of the pills wore off Shakey that evening, I locked the other two dogs in the backyard so Shakey and I could sit on the front porch. I needed him to get used to the new living situation. There would be no snow. It was no longer freezing cold outside the house. I was sitting on one of the two chairs that were chained to the front porch (so they would still be there in the morning), and my father was sitting on the other chair. We both had beers in our hands and I had a bowl of water in front of Shakey. He had to get used to this new environment, cars going up and down the streets with their music blasting in English and Spanish, old cars that had smoke coming out of the tailpipes, all that kind of stuff. My father told me that they would take good care of Shakey until I found a place. My little sister wanted to keep him with her and told me not to worry and to take my time finding a place.

I let her know that I would have to live in the barracks until I found a place. My brain did not count on how much it would cost now to live in the states instead of being overseas where rent was nowhere near what it cost back here in the States, especially in California, which had some of the highest costs of living than most other states.

I stayed with my parents for almost a week. Then I caught a bus from Los Angeles to San Diego. At the bus station, I found a navy bus that would make runs to the main Navy base on thirty-second street and then the one to I checked into Imperial Beach four days early. I rented a car for a few weeks until my Z arrived. I would turn it in after my second week in Imperial Beach. I would catch the base bus until my Z arrived.

NSGA Imperial Beach, California October 1996 - February 1998

NSGA Imperial Beach was my last duty station. It was no longer called NRRF (Navy Radio Receiving Facility) Imperial Beach. I didn't know it at the time; I was hoping to stay in the navy for another four years to make chief (E-7) and get another overseas duty station.

NSGA Imperial Beach had changed since I was last there, and for me, it was not for the better. It was for the command. It was just not what I expected or wanted. I was to be an analyst again, only this time a sea-going one that would be temporarily assigned duties on ships again. As a leading petty officer and analyst, those were my duties and I was okay with them.

I walked into the Coronado Navy base quarterdeck and handed my orders to another first-class petty officer. He was cool as hell. After he read my orders, he instructed me to the right part of the office that handled us CTs, and then he asked me about Scotland. I told him if he liked the cold weather, it would be the place for him, but the base was closing. He shivered and said that was all he needed to know. I smiled at him and walked to the other side of the office where I saw the CTA emblems on the sailor's uniforms and handed my papers to the chief that was sitting at the first desk I came to, which was the check-in desk, he looked at me and smiled, read my orders and told me that I was early, but there were rooms open in the barracks so I wouldn't have to worry about rushing to find a place to stay off base,

I asked him who was the commanding officer and he smiled at me and told me our CO is a female captain and she is awesome. I said, "Thanks." He logged me into the command and gave me a map of the base, showed me where the barracks were located and told me to go to the site on Monday morning at 0700 hours. I explained I had been stationed there before, and he shook his head and said most R-branchers tried to stay away from this place it has really changed. I smiled at him and said I had my two overseas tours and they wouldn't let me stay out for the third time. He shook my hand, said welcome to NSGA Imperial Beach.

I smiled at him and grabbed my sea bag, threw it over my shoulder, grabbed my suitcase and orders then I walked to the barracks. I showed my orders to the second-class petty officer at the front desk of the barracks. She asked me if I wanted to be on the first or second floor. I told her I would prefer the second floor. She smiled at me and said I was one of the first that they were expecting from Edzell. I told her there would be about twenty of us. She took a key from a small key holder on the wall behind her and said follow me. My room was ok, I would not have a roommate and I was good with that.

There was twice the amount of female CT's than we had in Edzell here and most were awesome. I was put on straight days, which made me happy for the time being. I stowed my gear in my new room and headed out to check out the Coronado Navy base. It had changed a little from my time in the nineteen eighties here. I found the chow hall and was right on time to get some dinner.

There seemed to be more navy seals there then I remembered, and now there was a large portion of marines that I don't think were there when I was there. After I ate, I went and found The Acey Deucy club (first and second-class petty officers club). I sat down and had a few beers. I pulled out my little notepad on things that I needed to do, rent a small car, find out the status of my car and furniture were first on the priority list. The second was to find a place in imperial beach, get through the week or two of command Indoctrination and find any old friends if I could.

That Monday morning, I was standing outside the door to NSGA Imperial Beach. I rang a buzzer and the chief came out and walked me in. He took my orders and walked me to the CO's office. I sat there for a few minutes, then at 0700, I knocked on her door hard two times, I heard the order to enter and I opened the door and walked to the captain's desk, the command master chief, and the executive officer was also there, I told her "CTR1 Jackson reporting as ordered. She looked at me, then she stood and told me to be seated. She walked to another little desk in her office and took my record off the desk. She to me to be seated and I sat down.

She looked at my record again, frowned and then looked me straight in my eyes and said, "First I want to welcome you to the command. This is your second time here."

I said, "Yes, ma'am." She smiled and said we are a much different entity than your last time here as we have expanded our mission".

She then told me that we actively support the fleet and the fleet force marines. You have more sea time than most of the folks we have here, so we need your knowledge and support. Can we count on you for that?"

I said, "Yes, ma'am."

She said other than the problem that you had in Misawa, your record is all 4.0 and that I had leadership positions in San Vito and Edzell, and I looked at her and said, "Yes, ma'am."

She said, "Your leadership will be very important here also." Then she looked at the XO.

Then he said, "We demand your best one hundred percent at all times and your honesty."

I looked at him and said, "Yes, sir."

He looked at the command master chief and told him that petty officer Jackson is all yours, master chief. The captain stood and I stood. She shook my hand and said, "Welcome aboard, petty officer Jackson. The master chief will fill you in on what will be doing in his office." I stood at attention as she dismissed us all and I followed the master chief to his office.

We talked for about fifteen minutes. He asked about the incident at NSGA Misawa and he wanted to hear my side. I told him everything and he just shook his head, then he asked me about the one in Corry station when I socked the asshole that liked to call me names and run. I told him the truth. He looked like he wanted to laugh.

He said there would be more sea time for you. Then he called in a second class petty officer that would show me around before I left. He told me the XO has plans for you. I smiled and said I hope there are good plans, he just smiled and said that would be all.

The base looked as though it had been painted inside and out since my last tour there, but the outside looked almost the same, sand dunes and the beach. I found myself thinking about Bella and all the fun we had here. I wondered what my youngest daughter looked like and how she was doing in school. Whenever I thought about her, I would get sad as hell and it usually took a few stiff drinks to get out of feeling so low. I knew she would be fine as Bella was a good woman and that I would see her again. I just knew I would.

The base indoctrination lasted for just under a week. We got information about clubs in San Diego that were off limits to navy personnel due to gang and or drug-related incidents, the best and lowest cost places to rent apartments, where to go to get your car registered, and all the stuff I really needed to know about.

The rest of the folks from Edzell slowly started drifting into the base, and by the end of my first month, all were there and checked into the command. My car came in a week after I turned in the rental car. I had caught a bus back to Los Angeles so I could get my father to take me to San Pedro, California, where the Z was sitting.

I was still in my working white uniform, a white short sleeve shirt with ribbons, rank and rating badge on it. On the bus to Los Angeles from San Diego, people just stared at me. A few guys asked me what all that stuff on my shirt meant. I just looked at them like I didn't want to be bothered and they got the hint.

I arrived at the Los Angeles downtown bus station a little after seven that evening, my father was waiting at the station for me and I saw him as soon as I got off the bus. I just had a small backpack with enough clothes to last me for two days as I would be leaving that Sunday morning. I got there on a Wednesday night and spent the night at my parent's house. Shakey was doing well, he looked healthy. He jumped all over me just as I walked into the front door. Everybody was glad I was home; both my sisters were there and my oldest daughter was there with her mother. I grabbed my kid and hugged her so tightly that I had to let go so she could breathe. She was a teenager now getting ready to leave what we called junior high school, now known as middle school.

She was a very active member of the church and had great grades. What more could I ask of her? I was so proud of her. She and her mother stayed for a couple of hours and then left. My oldest sister left shortly after they did and then my nephew came in. He was trying to be a rap star, and we all thought he was awesome and we all knew he could make it as a rapper if he stuck with it. He was graduating from high school and had stayed away from the gangs, which made me very proud of him.

After talking with him for a few minutes, my father and I went out on the front porch and sat in the chairs with Shakey between my legs, drinking beers. We decided to leave early as it would take about thirty-five to forty minutes to get to the location of my Z, so we crashed early and were both up by seven the next morning, ready to go. I told my father I was treating him to breakfast, so we went to a Denny's that was on the way. We got there just as the gates to the dock opened. There were hundreds of big American diesel trucks waiting in lines to grab containers from container ships. I knew I was home. My father pointed out places we used to go fishing when I was a kid, right near the docks. Once I got all the paperwork filled out, we were taken to the location of my Z. Just like all the other places it had been shipped to. It was filthy, just dust covered from bumper to bumper. The shipping tags and stuff were put on the right side of my windshield, which I had to remove and put on the left side so I could see out of the window to drive it.

I had to show proof of insurance and my driver's license again before the guy gave me my keys, I asked him where the nearest gas station was and he was able to point it out to me. It was just about a quarter of a mile away and it had a drive-through car wash. I was really glad about that car wash. Inside looked just like it did when I dropped it off. It even had my cassette tape in it. I brought some more with me in my backpack. I got the Z reasonably clean after I filled up the gas tank. My Z had a speed odometer that was in kilometers per hour instead of miles per hour, so I had a conversion cheat sheet that I wrote for myself. Sixty miles per hour was almost ninety-seven kilometers per hour, so I kept it between ninety-seven and one-hundred and twenty kilometers per hour, which meant I was going between sixty and seventy-five miles per hour.

I remember it was almost one pm by the time I got to highway five heading south to Coronado and then to the base. It took almost four hours because I got stuck in rush hour traffic once I got close to San Diego. I didn't care. I was in no rush and on the 5 freeway. It was an awesome drive heading south along the southern California coast. I cruised through Dana Point, San Clemente, Ocean Side and Carlsbad right on down to San Diego, then about another twenty minutes south on the I-5 to Coronado and the base.

Seeing the Pacific Ocean from the coast was awesome and listening to my music, I felt relaxed, I only made one stop and that was at a gas station outside Encinitas, which was almost halfway between Carlsbad and San Diego. I grabbed some candy and water and filled up the tank, which was only half empty. I didn't want to have to fill up in San Diego. I wanted to stay on the freeway until I hit the Coronado bridge and then the base.

Once I got to the base, I had to get a temporary base sticker for 1 day. Then I headed straight to the chow hall. After I ate, I came outside and there were a few people looking at my Z. I just smiled at them, unlocked the door, fired it up and drove to the barracks. When I pulled up to the barracks, there were a few guys sitting outside and one of them came up and asked me where I got the car. When I told him about Misawa, Japan, he looked at me like I was crazy. I locked the car turned on the alarm and walked up the stairs to my room. I was tired and needed a couple of beers which I had plenty of in my little refrigerator. After a couple of Budweiser's, I went to the head and took a nice long shower and I needed a shave.

After I was done with my shower and shave, I got dressed and drove over to the Acey-Deucy club. I needed a few more beers, then I noticed someone that looked very familiar from the back sitting at the bar and it was G-man. I waved over to him and he shouted my name. I told him to get his ass over here. I brought him a beer. He was a new second-class petty officer. I was proud of him.

He told me he had checked in Wednesday night, and I told him I left and went back to Los Angeles to get my Z and it was outside. We hung out for the rest of the night. He told me Freddy had orders to England. I was pissed, I could never figure out how he got another overseas tour and I had to go back to the states.

G-man also mentioned a couple of the ladies that I knew and how they were doing. He said the base when he left was damn near a ghost town, and a lot of the civilian locals lost their jobs on the base before it closed completely and he said he hadn't seen Gabby. I knew Gabby could and would find a job at any of the pubs as a cook, so I really wasn't too worried about her.

Then he told me that both apartments of the building I lived in at Brechin had been condemned, but the butcher shop was still open when he left Brechin. We both laughed at that. G-man asked me about living in Imperial Beach and I let him know that I was ready to start looking for a spot and if I found any in his price range, I would let him know.

I found a really nice townhouse in Imperial Beach, I could walk to the beach and the little fishing pier, and with the extra money I got from the military for living off base, I could afford it. My furniture had already arrived in the states and they just needed an address to deliver my furniture.

I still remember the day the movers came to get my furniture. They opened the front window and with a hoist, lowered my couch down three floors and onto the waiting truck. This would be nothing like that if I was back in the United States. This townhouse couldn't have been more than five years old, and it was full of enlisted military, mostly mid to senior enlisted with their families.

I had to pay the security deposit and one month's rent in advance. The only thing wrong was I could not bring Shakey. No pets were allowed when I moved in there. I tried to explain that he was a good dog and wouldn't bite anyone. I even told them I would pay extra, still the answer was no.

I called home to let my family know and my youngest sister said she wasn't going to let me take Shakey anyway. I was so glad to hear that. I knew I would be going out to sea and I didn't want to have to find someone to take care of him for months at a time. I didn't think I could afford it, and I knew he would have problems with that, so my sister took care of those issues for me and I think he was happy living with her and my family.

I signed and paid for a corner townhouse that was close to the beach. It was really nice, two bedrooms both upstairs with a full bath up there and downstairs was the front room, a half bath with only a shower, toilet and sink. The kitchen was a nice size and the living room was good size. There was a fenced-in little yard area that had a cement deck with a little storage room that was accessed through the sliding door in the front room, it was a really nice place, I think I paid seven hundred a month and most of the time it was worth it.

Across the street was the Tijuana estuary, which borders the United States and Mexico. It's basically a saltwater marsh, with lots of birds and some snakes, one of my neighbors had to call animal control to remove a big ass rattlesnake that was sunning on her front porch. She would not leave her place until it was gone, she had a young son and neither of them wanted to go out of that door. She would drop her son off at another of the neighbor's house that was married and had school age kids. The kids would all go to the bus stop together.

I couldn't blame her, I'm not a snake fan either. After that incident, I would look out the front window before I left in the mornings to go to work. I didn't mind the birds, but the snakes were just not my cup of tea.

I got back into fishing once I moved into the townhouse and I needed that to help me relax, so I slowed down on my drinking and partying. I was damn near forty years old, I had kept in touch with both of my lady friends in Scotland, Gale and Cutie and they both wanted to come down and visit. I was good with that. I really wanted to bring Gale down here as she was a nurse I was hoping she would want to stay. I knew she was a new grandmother and loved the baby, but there was always hope and plus, she was a nurse. I knew she could pass whatever test in the states that was needed to become a nurse. It was something I had been thinking about.

I had G-man come over and help me unpack the moving boxes a week later after I had moved into the townhouse, we had plenty of beer and I had brought one of those Weber bar b que grills for nineteen ninety-nine, so we had burgers, beer and potato chips for dinner, when It got dark we were done putting most of the stuff up. I just needed to hang a few pictures, I still had the painting from the Philippines, which was of Marvin Gaye singing at a juke joint and that was going in the front room over the couch.

G-man hung out with me for a couple more days and then I got orders to go out on a ship that I had ridden a long time ago when it was only five or six years old when I got on board it for the first time, back in the late nineteen seventies that was almost twenty years ago. It was the USS

Blue Ridge LCC-19. It was still a command and control ship. It was supposed to be a two-month TAD (temporarily assigned duty) just to check out the new equipment that was installed for CTs onboard, but it turned into nearly four months before our little crew got relieved by CTs from NSGA Misawa, Japan.

I had only left three checks with the management for my townhouse. I didn't want to mail them a check and the reason was the way the mail worked from ship to ship until it reached a place that it could be taken to, like a US military base or a US consulate, via helicopter and then put in the US mail system from overseas.

Just like the first time I was on the Blue Ridge, I got lost. The ship was two-thirds as long as the old aircraft carriers I used to be assigned on while I was stationed in NSGA Homestead. I had forgotten how big this command ship was. It was the flagship of the Seventh Fleet and had the admiral's flag, which means it was his ship to command the entire fleet from.

The changes that had been done to it since my last time on board were amazing, where I worked once I got on board was a mini version of the normal land-based sites for CTs, with the ability to get the information to the Admirals staff in real-time (as it was happening).

There was a chief on board that came down to get our crew and show us around, he was pretty cool and he and I both knew some of the same folks in the CT world. Once we left San Diego, we headed northeast toward Hawaii. We had a few days in port Pearl Harbor on Oahu. When we pulled in, we passed the USS Missouri monument. While entering port, it looked the same as it did almost twenty years ago on my first visit to Hawaii. Being a first-class petty officer, I had the liberty for both of the days we were in port. A few of my guys and I went to a couple of strip clubs and got drunk, then headed back to the ship the first day. On the second day, another first class and I took a tour around pearl city and then to Pu'uloa Beach Park. We hung out there for a while, then we found a Kentucky Fried Chicken restaurant for a late lunch and headed back to Pearl Harbor and the Blue Ridge.

The next morning, we were headed east for about two weeks toward Taiwan and pulled into port in Keelung and caught buses to Taipei for another two days of liberty. We did our normal port thing, which was to hit a few bars, get a little bit boozy and head back to the ship. After that port visit, we headed south towards the Philippines and then west. Most of the time we were cruising, my crew and I was checking and testing all the different equipment in SSES (Ships Signals Exploitation Systems, which is what the space we worked in was called - look it up online).

A lot of the equipment was new to us and it was awesome learning what equipment was in there and how it worked. After the third month out there, we were told this trip was going to be extended for us an extra couple of weeks. None of us minded, really, the food was good, and as on most ships, no one really bothered us. There were probably over a thousand sailors and marines on board and I never saw anybody have issues with anybody else. We were part of the Admiral's staff, so everything was good for us, there was no shore patrol duty or any other collateral duties. We only had to do our normal jobs, which was working in SSES (Ships Signals Exploitation Systems.)

We headed back to Hawaii and caught the first flight back to San Diego, that was probably one of the best TAD trips I had while stationed at NSGA Imperial Beach for this tour. Once we landed back in San Diego International Airport, our command sent a van to pick us up, I had four guys with me and they all had a great time with that TAD trip.

When we pulled into the quarterdeck at Coronado Navy base, I felt tired as hell. I forgot while on board the Blue Ridge, I was normally working fourteen to sixteen hours a day while we were underway. I worked the day shift and two or three hours on the mid-shift. After we took our sea bags out of the van and checked back in at the quarterdeck, I went straight to my Z and took off for Imperial Beach and my Townhouse.

I poured about one-quarter of the tub with warm water and then turned on the shower. I just soaked in the tub until it was almost full, drinking a couple of shots of Chivas Regal. Once I was done with them, I pulled the plug in the bath and scrubbed with more soap than I needed to use and got myself clean, dried off and just walked around my place with nothing on but my towel. It felt good to be home.

I had gotten several letters from both Gale and Cutie, and I definitely wanted to see them both again. I felt like time was flying by, I had been in NSGA now for a little over six months and it all seemed to go such a fast hell. I would be going on forty-two years of age pretty soon and that made old man in the enlisted ranks of the military and me. I called Gale and Cutie and I was able to get ahold of Cutie. We planned for her to come down to San Diego in the next couple of months.

I had a new job when I came back. I was now the leading petty officer in charge of setting up the commands email system. In other words, we were getting the internet. I had absolutely no clue about how to set it up or even where to start. I was allowed to pick the part of my staff of forty people. The first thing I did was ask if anybody had their own personal computers. I found six guys that did.

I put them to work. We knew that we needed computers. We needed cabling to go from a router to each of the different offices and also to a couple of workspaces. Back in those days, AOL was the email of choice and that was what we went with. We had a budget that was not much, but we were able to get a bunch of used machines and a small group of new ones for the commanding officer and her staff.

It took a good three months just to get all the equipment and parts that we needed, we also needed instructions, and we grabbed any books that we could about the internet. Windows 98 was the operating system we used on all the computers and that took a while to set the computers up. Most of them only had thirty-two or sixty-four megabytes of memory. They were slow but back in the mid to late one-nineteen-ninety's, what we had was kind of the going thing. It was completed in four months.

I had been seeing this one lady, but it was nothing serious, just a mutual booty call. I left on a Monday evening and headed to the San Diego International Airport. I didn't have a long wait as Cutie had cleared customs in New York. Her first stop was in Amsterdam, then to New York, Atlanta and finally to San Diego, she was tired, but I had a large Mcdonald's cup filled with vodka, coke and ice waiting for her.

It didn't take us long in the baggage claim area and her suitcase was there, going around with the rest of the passenger's luggage. She pointed it out to me, I grabbed it and we walked out to the parking area where my Z was parked. It took damn near an hour with all the traffic to get back to Imperial beach and my place.

She drank the whole cup of rum and coke. She had a nice buzz by the time we got home and I knew she was ready to pass out. I put her in my bed and went to McDonald's and got some burgers and fries. I woke her up, she ate and went back to sleep. It was a good thing I had this whole week off so I could spend lots of quality time with her.

I lay down with her for a few minutes, then I went back downstairs and watched TV until I was ready to sleep. The next morning was crazy, we went to Denny's for breakfast and then we drove up to Coronado Beach and hung out. Cutie loved it. We were near the Coronado Hotel just sitting in the sand. A couple of F-14 jet fighters flew past and they were hauling ass, then they went vertical and disappeared into the clouds. Cutie had never seen anything like that and she was really impressed.

After an hour or two on the beach, we headed south and parked the Z on the United States side of the border. I had told Cutie that morning to keep her passport with her at all times when we left the house and she did. We went through customs, caught a cab to Tijuana and hit one of the clubs on Revolution Boulevard. I ordered 2 Budweiser's and told Cutie to keep her eyes open, it was probably about five or six in the evening and the place was jumping. It wasn't totally packed but it was a good crowd.

After our third beer, one of the waiters came over and asked Cutie if she wanted a tequila shot, she didn't know how the shot would be done and I nodded at her to take the shot. She said, "Okay." The waiter pulled her head back and poured the shot straight into her mouth then he picked her up, put her on his shoulders and spun her around about three or four times, that was the last drink we had in Tijuana that day, I could see Cutie was really tipsy, so I paid for our drinks got a cab to the border and went back through customs, all I needed was my military identification card (ID), but Cutie had to pull out her passport which of course she had trouble finding in her purse.

We finally got through customs, walked out to the Z and Cutie practically passed out. It was only a ten-minute drive home. I got her out of the car and had her put on her bikini. She laid on one of the chaise lounges on the patio and fell back to sleep. I went to the kitchen and got the pitcher of cold water, walked upstairs, opened the window that overlooked the patio and poured the cold water all over her. I quickly closed the window and ran downstairs just as I heard her screaming and cursing in her Scottish version of English, I tried not to laugh, but I couldn't control myself and I busted up laughing. She looked at me for a few seconds and then she started laughing, we had a good day.

The rest of the week was spent hanging out with friends of mine and partying. The second week of Cutie's visit, I had to work and I was on straight days, Monday through Friday, like a normal work week. I would leave at 0730 and be home no later than 1700 (5:00 pm) and that was awesome. We did go back to Tijuana, Mexico, once more to party and we were back across the border before sunset. I took her all around San Diego, Chula Vista, and National City, and on next to the last day of her visit, we went to the beach by the San Onofre Nuclear power plant. We didn't get in the water, but we did have two six-packs of beer. It was a nice drive up to it and back to Imperial Beach.

We had a bar-b-que after we got home, just some burgers and some beans with a salad. The next morning, we were in the traffic heading to the San Diego International airport and Cutie was on her way back to Scotland. I enjoyed her company and we got along well together; I was going to miss her. At work, we were a new division called Direct Support (DURSUP). We were trained to go on board ships as needed.

We were also responsible for the base internet support. The only problem that I had was we were mainly temporarily assigned to gator freighters (troop transports) for the marines and most of those ships were old and slow with very little protection. The next trip I was going on would be on an amphibious transport dock (LPD). The navy figured out that we couldn't always take over the ship's radio room, so they built our own ship's signals exploitation space and it could be fitted on different size ships as long as they had a clear space on deck for it to fit. It was about twenty feet long and about ten feet wide. It had cables coming from it, and they connected to the ship's internal systems like communications and power. It was painted grey, just like the ship and it held all of the equipment we needed to do our job.

And because it was ours, only personnel with the top security clearance that was elevated for our job could come inside it. On LPD-6, USS Duluth, our SSES van, was put on the starboard side of the flight deck where helicopters would bring in supplies and also transport the marines and navy seals. We had two weeks to check all of our gear and equipment after the van was installed.

I was able to find a little bit of information about the trip I had on board from Wikipedia that summarized part of the mission we were on, and it is the only mission that I will write about before we leave for our TAD on board the Duluth. I had a few crew issues and they were with a warrant officer that I knew from my past in Pensacola, Florida, during my A-School days. Let's just say he and I didn't get along at all. He had a few E-6s that just didn't have to go TAD because they laughed at his jokes and were his friends. I had an E-4 whose wife was having problems with her pregnancy and he was a nervous wreck. He needed to be with her and not on board a ship thousands of miles away from her. I explained the situation to the officer and he told me lots of our people had wives that were pregnant while they were TAD. I was pissed, very pissed off. As I was leaving, I heard him tell his buddies that I didn't know my place in this command.

I knew from the moment he was put in charge of the DURSUP division I was going to have problems with him, but I thought the problems would be between him and I, not our crew. We only had three days left before we would be checking in on the Duluth, I know I said I was pissed a couple of times, but I was beyond that after I heard them all laughing.

After I left his office, I went to the base Chaplin on navy station Coronado and explained the situation. The next day I was told to pick a replacement for the guy with the pregnant wife when the officer told me that he looked madder than I was the day I went to the Chaplin's office.

I smiled at him and said, will do (not yes, sir). I never called him sir and that probably added to his anger. I just didn't care. I was close to my twenty years and I was getting burnt out. I could feel it. I was the leading petty officer on the trip. We had a lieutenant junior grade (LT JG) who was in charge of our crew. There were eight of us leaving for the TAD trip, I was still an E-6, I had one other (CTR), a senior E-4, three E-3s that were (CTO) and a first for me. I also had an E-5 maintenance Tech (CTM2) his job was to maintain all the equipment on and in the SSES which included our own air conditioning unit, which meant he was on call twenty-four hours a day, every day we were TAD.

The night before, our TAD trip was to be started. I invited some of the crew over to my place. My youngest sister, along with my nephew and one of his little friends, were there. Both of the kids were young teenagers. The party started around 6:00 PM, most of the guys showed up around noon that day and they brought beers and what they wanted to put on the grill. I think I started the grill around six pm and by then, I, along with all the rest of the guys, had a serious buzz going from all the beers we drank. We knew we were headed to a part of the world where alcohol was forbidden, so we were going to get a good buzz before we left. That night one of the CTOs that I didn't think would show up came over with his new girlfriend. He said she was a dancer. We all knew what he meant.

About eight that night, most of my guys were sitting in the living room, we had burnt the steaks and damn near everything else we put on the grill, but we ate what we cooked. I noticed some of my neighbors had come in and were partying with us, they were just as drunk as my guys and I was. One of my neighbors told me the bathroom thing was awesome. I didn't know what the hell he was talking about, so I got up and went into the bathroom. The guy that brought over his new girlfriend was passed out on the couch. His girlfriend had opened up shop in my downstairs bathroom, giving blowjobs for twenty dollars a person. When I found out I was pissed, I took half of the money she made and told her to grab her boyfriend and get out. I used that money for one of the few ship parties when we hit one of the ports that visited that served alcohol.

We were briefed on our mission the morning before we left. I thought we all were (the LT didn't have a clue about the mission or our job, which we found out on the first day that we departed from San Diego). It was May of nineteen ninety-six when we left NSGA Imperial Beach and headed for naval station San Diego and boarded the USS Duluth. By the time we got to the ship, the marines were already on board and the ship had left the dock that morning. Our crew maintained twelve hours on duty and twelve hours off. The hours were from 0800 to 2000 hours (eight am to eight pm), the LT agreed to it and it was all set. This would be a six-month TAD trip for us. The weather sucked that morning and the next two days.

We headed out in kind of rough weather and the next couple of days. It turned into what was called Tropical Storm One-E now. I have to explain that the Duluth was a flat bottom vessel at the rear of it. It held tanks and troops that could and would be put ashore where and when needed. There were probably around fourteen hundred of us on board, mostly marines with about six hundred sailors. Once the storm got really bad, the front end of the ship sliced through the waves, but the ass end was bouncing around like crazy. I would say two-thirds of the crew were seasick to the point that all they could do was lay down and throw up. In our SSES, we had a video camera and I went around recording a few of the guys that were puking their guts out. Most carried big plastic bags so that they had a place to throw up. If they didn't have the bag, then they had to clean up their mess.

The weather did cause some damage to the Duluth one of her shafts for the propellers bent, which meant we could only use one engine; we were now way behind the rest of the fleet with only one propeller working. I normally worked from 0800 through 2200 hours, but that night I damn near worked a little longer. I needed to make sure my guys were ok and they were. Some didn't look too good, but I don't remember any of them throwing up. I think our maintenance guy just stayed in his rack during the storm. I didn't see the LT at all. Once we were out of the storm, the weather was beautiful with warm and clear skies.

The LT showed up in our spaces and changed all of the frequencies on most of the equipment that was set up by the NSA and probably several other intelligence agencies that we assisted whose name ended with an A. Then he told us if we knew our jobs we could figure them out, none of us said a word as no one could believe what he had just done, I pulled him to the side and explained the problem he had just created for us.

He turned red and sat down in my chair. I just stood there looking at him. I couldn't cuss him out as he was in charge of us. After a few minutes, I just shook my head and told him we would have to figure something out. after a few minutes, he stood and tried to get control of the SSES, we all lost any and all respect that we should have for him and he would not get it back from any of us during that trip.

He told us there would be inspections of the SSES and us twice a week and he wanted to be called if anything deserved his attention. I had to figure a way to keep him out of the SSES and out of our sight. One of the guys found out he was allergic to Lysol. That was our answer every morning, I would have the guys wipe down the front end of the SSES van with Lysol and that was the only cleaning solvent that we had it was all good.

The next morning when the LT walked into the SSES, we were waiting for him. His eyes turned red immediately. I was doing my best not to laugh. Then his nose started to run. Yep, we found our solution for the LT, he wanted us outside for inspection, and I let him know that the positions had to be manned at all times, so I would come out and he could inspect me.

Most of us had our hair cut really short before we left Imperial Beach and we all wore the blue coveralls, which were called poopy suits. We cut the sleeves off and half of the length of our T-shirts, and I don't know if anybody worked skivvies. I was free balling (no underwear) once we hit the Gulf of Oman, the Persian gulf and the rest of that area.

A couple of days after the storm, we got a new captain, he was cool as hell and the crew members I met liked him a lot. The new captain had his change of command ceremony on the flight deck and it was awesome. The old captain gave him the Duluth, they both saluted and the ship and crew were his. The old commanding officer left the ship via helicopter. The news was a commander. The executive officer was a different issue, he had to play the role of a hard ass and he did it well.

We had lots of cigarette smokers on board the Duluth and probably doubled the number of folks that chewed tobacco. They liked to chew tobacco and spit it on the outside decks or just throw the cigarette buts on the decks, the executive officer would have a fit when he stepped in that stuff and I didn't blame him, he put the word out about his dislike of stepping in wet slobbery chewing tobacco, they kept spitting, he ignored it for a while.

We smokers would just throw the butts in the ash cans that were placed on the deck in the smoke break areas, but the executive officer (XO) didn't distinguish between any of the tobacco products. He hated all of it. We went to Thailand and Singapore for our first two port visits. Singapore had really changed since the nineteen seventies when I was last there. They had white signs with red circles and a red slash through the circle with the 'do not do things like spitting on the streets, staring at the females, etc'. An American kid got six strokes of a caned there for keying cars two years earlier for theft and vandalism (sounded like a good thing to me), so I let my guys know that this country didn't play around with any stupid stuff. They all got the hint and understood.

I had arranged for half of the crew to get off on the first day. My senior third class CTR would be in charge of them. We called him Big-T. He looked like a smaller version of the Los Angeles Lakers Shack. He had two of the others with him, the two CTOs, Ryan and Jeff. Ryan was a bit of a whiner and Jeff was awesome. He wanted to see and try almost everything and I never heard him complain during the trip.

Ross, our CTM, and Phil, the other CTO, would go off the ship with me. Our CTI joined us just as we got to Singapore. His name was Tony and he was cool as hell and had made E-5 on the last testing. He also went out with me. Big-T came back with the guys and they were a little bit tipsy but had not gotten into any trouble. I told him to take them below and to get some sleep and they did.

We had been out to sea for nearly twenty days. Other than Big-T, none of them had been on a ship. I had a fairly good group of guys and I was happy with each of them so far. After Singapore, we went through the Malacca Strait and headed up by India and then into the Gulf of Oman. Going through the Gulf of Oman, the Iranian's defense systems went crazy. They knew what a0 US troop transport looked like and they knew we had a lot of marines on board.

After we got past the Gulf of Oman and entered the Persian Gulf, we headed straight to Abu Dhabi and refueled. We spent the next three months cruising around between Abu Dhabi, Doha and north through the Persian Gulf to Kuwait City. Once we pulled into Kuwait City, they didn't want us in their city. So, we had to hang out on the pier of Kuwait City for three days, someone got ahold of one of the major beer companies in the US and we had beer tents set up the next morning.

Now during this time, I started having problems with my little crew, one of my guys got a video of his wife and kids, another one of my guys got of his girlfriend's worn panties and both of them wanted off the ship immediately. Before we left port in San Diego, I told my little crew in front of the LTJG that if they got any kind of mail or packages to put them away, do not leave anything out inside the van like food or letters. If you got a video, let me know and I will arrange for you to go into the back of the van and watch your video there. I guess these two guys forgot.

I was going to have to crack down on those two guys and I did. The one that got the underwear in the mail just put them back in the box and left them on his position in the van of course. Somebody looked in the box and hung them up on the inside of the door with tape. Now had the lady's panties been a normal size, most of us would not have minded, but they were on the extra, extra-large side and were blocking the map. He actually had the nerves to get upset when he came in and found them hanging up!

The guy with the video didn't really care for me and I never tried to figure out why, but he thought he was god's gift to everybody. I just thought he was full of shit and needed some mental help, we all knew he cheated on his wife as he bragged about it all the time and when his wife sent him a video and he took it down to the galley and put in to be watched. It started out with his wife and kids, then his wife putting the kids to bed, then she was on the phone, and the next shot was in a see thru negligee and she was opening the door for two black guys. The rest you can imagine. Her husband lost his mind and tried to get to the VHS to take the tape out, but the rest of the ship's crew wasn't having that. If you put a tape in, it stayed in until they all agreed to remove it and they all liked watching his wife taking care of two huge guys. The rest of that video lasted about fifteen minutes. He was crying while two guys held him down. By the time I got down there, the video was over and guys were going over to him asking for his phone number.

I got the video and him, walked him back to our berthing quarters and handed him the video. He didn't say a word the whole time we walked down there. He did give me that look like he was waiting for me to say I told you so. A lot of guys saw that video and I knew he was as low as a person could get, but there was nothing anybody could do. He put in a request to get off the ship and go home, but the LTJG denied his request.

All of a sudden, my crew's morale was low. I had to figure something out, I knew I couldn't help the guy with the video, but I could get the rest of them back. We were getting ready for a port visit in Jordan and I knew it was going to be hard to get them off of the ship, but there was a trip that we could get really cheap to Petra and I would go along also. I knew I had two guys that would want to see it, so I set that up, the others would be glad to stay on board with the ship's air conditioning.

The weather was insane. We had sand storms and scorching heat. If you wore glasses, as soon as you stepped out of the inside of the ship, your glasses would fog over, like sticking your face near an open over, the normal temperature was near or over one-hundred and five to one-ten degrees, while I was walking topside (out on the deck) if felt like I was walking in bubblegum (the soles of our boots were melting) and they wanted us to wear some sort of cover (hat) while out on the deck, most of us cigarette smokers did just that.

We were still in the Persian Gulf and heading south for the Arabian Sea, the Gulf of Aden and Djibouti for refuel. We stayed in Djibouti for about six hours. I thought Tijuana, Mexico was poor. While we were refueling we were instructed to take the ship's garbage to the dumpsters about twenty feet away from the ship. We formed a line and passed each bag through to the dumpsters. After about five minutes, we had to get the Djibouti police to stop the people from trying to take the bags from us, (once the bags were in the dumpsters, we didn't care what happened to them, the police came and moved the people away from us and they took the trash from the dumpsters. I did feel sorry for those people.

The Duluth was supposed to fill up in Djibouti, but they only had one fuel hose and we would have been there for a couple of days to get topped off. We stayed for about five hours and then we headed north into the Red Sea and then to Jeddah in Saudi Arabia to finish refueling. The Red Sea was packed with allied warships, from our Aircraft Carriers to French frigates and Russian Aircraft, taking pictures of all the ships.

This went on for months. We traveled up and down the coast of the Arabian Sea, freaking out the Russians and whatever country that we came close to with all the marines on board. Our morale was at an all-time low, the marines were going crazy, the rest of the crew were constantly on edge and our little crew was done. One morning everyone got relieved on time except for one guy. I went down to our berthing area and the person that was supposed to have relieved the man still on watch was in his rack crying, saying he wanted to go home. I did a general Patton on his ass and started slapping him. It was a good thing Big-T came down and stopped me as I was starting to lose my damn mind. I let them get away with almost anything but not coming in to relieve the guy that you were supposed to relieve was unforgivable to me.

This kid was actually crying, saying he wanted to go home! Hell, we all wanted to go home, but we had a job to do and he was going to do his part. I never had that problem with him again. I think the guy he was supposed to relieve gave him a slapping also. We finally pulled into port in Aqaba, Jordan. There were females in the water with the full burqa (dressed from head to toe). I don't know if it's still the same, but as soon as our guys saw that, we were all ready to go somewhere else.

But we were in Aqaba and would be here for three days. The first day was when we had the trip to Petra scheduled. We caught busses to Petra, the only problem was our driver was talking to one of his friends and didn't have the bus running with the ac going, we all yelled for him to finish, and he basically ignored us, one of the guys closed the door and started the bus leaving him outside in the heat (probably around one-hundred and ten degrees, he started yelling we started laughing, after a few minutes the door was opened and he got in and we took off.

And you wonder why we are known as ugly Americans. It took a little over two hours to get to Wadi Musa and Petra, we did see Petra and walked around a little inside, took pictures and that was it. We got back on the bus. The driver was waiting for us and we headed back to Aqaba. We couldn't wait to get back inside the ship for the air conditioning. We all went straight to the SSES van and cooled off in our own a/c and it was good to just sit and be in seventy-eight-degree temperature.

The next day the ship a/c died and most of the marines and some of the sailors slept outside on the deck where ever they could find space for their mattresses. We just went to the van and slept in chairs or under them. The third day in port finally came and we went back out into the gulf and did the same patrols, but our six months were nearly over and everyone on the ship was getting excited about that and the fact that Big-T made a second-class petty officer. The guy that was crying in his rack made a third-class petty officer and three of my crew re-enlisted for four years each and each two of them got a ten thousand dollar re-enlistment bonus.

That cheered those guys up. I still had to deal with the one that got the video and the LTJG. About two weeks before we were set to depart the gulf, we got a flash message for the commanding officer's eyes only. I was there when it was decoded, so I knew exactly what it said. I told my guys not to say a damn thing to anybody about the contents of the message after it was decoded. I walked to the captain's quarters. It was after midnight. There was hardly anyone out and about on the officer's deck.

I knocked on his door hard three times and announced who I was. The captain got up and opened the door. He looked me straight in the eyes and asked me if he was going to be happy after he read the message. I just handed him the message and waited for his reply. He was one hell of a good man. All he said was, "Damn!" and told me to let them know he acknowledged the message.

USS Duluth's current tour in the gulf was to be extended for three more months. The next morning the captain let the crew know that we would be extended in the Persian Gulf and surrounding areas for approximately three more months. He didn't give a reason why only the fact that we would be staying longer than anticipated.

You could hear the crew moaning all over the ship, nobody wanted to be there, but orders were orders. We had two more port visits for the next three months. My guy whose wife made the video was beside himself. He wanted to go home, I had sent a letter back to one of my friends in Imperial Beach that knew him and the responding letter said his wife and kids had left California and had their furniture sent somewhere in the northeast United States. That was all he said about. He did go and let my landlord know that we had gotten extended on our trip and was told it was all good by the rental office.

That was a relief for me. We pulled into Manama, Bahrain, for a little over a week and a lot of guys were able to let off some steam. Big-T spent some of his re-enlistment money on a couple of babes and a nice hotel room. He was gone for two days. The other guys mainly just stayed on board the ship. I had one guy that volunteered to help paint the part of the ship that had the huge white numbers on it, as we had frequent sand storms which were so intense that they actually sanded one side of the ship to the bare metal and the number six was completely removed, so they hung a harness over the side and he along with three other guys repainted that part of the ship grey again and the number back on it while in over one hundred degree temperatures.

I had three guys I could really depend on. One was the guy that helped with the painting, Big-T and the maintenance guy. Our air conditioner died on us and we could not even go into the van during the last days of our first month's extension, we ordered a new one and it arrived four days later. It came into Doha, Bahrain and was delivered by a helicopter, which set it down on the roof of our van. Big-T and I assisted our CTM2 with the installation of the new air conditioner. None of us had ever done anything like it before. We had our air conditioner up and running in a little over three hours. I think that was the hottest I had ever been and again. My boots felt like I was walking in bubble gum as the soles of them were slowly melting away.

It was so good to be able to get back into the van again and have that ac. It was awesome. We didn't turn on any equipment for at least six hours until the inside of the van was back down in the mid-seventy-degree range. Two days later, we headed back to the Red Sea and ended up back in the Gulf of Aqaba, where we stayed for a couple of weeks. Again the ship A/C went down and the marines were sleeping on the decks outside, but at 0400, it was early morning prayer and it was blasted over loudspeakers all over the city.

The worst part of this port visit was that at night we could see the city of Eilat in Israel and they were partying at night; you could see the bright lights from the clubs and big hotels. Here we were in a country where alcohol was against the law. Now there were people that would try and sell you wine from grapes that were crushed by their beautiful sisters' own feet for fifty US dollars, those guys were usually cab drivers who would sell you the wine and then turn you into the police who would then give then the bottle back to the guy that sold it to you if it hadn't all been drank and the process would start all over again and we would have to pay to get our guys out of jail.

We did go to the gold souk (jewelry store) in Aqaba and just about everybody in our little crew brought someone back home some kind of gold necklace or bracelet. They also had perfume, lots of it (probably knock-offs), but you could buy little boxes full of small bottles of all the most expensive perfumes for around thirty dollars. I brought five of those boxes, had them all wrapped up together and put them in our safe in the SSES van. I was going to give one to each of my sisters and one to moms, one to Gale and one to Cutie.

On our last day in port Aqaba Jordan I had heard of a restaurant where we could go and get some beers, I got Big-T, my CTM and the little guy that I could count on and we caught a cab and headed for this place. The place was full of reporters from all over the world and the only beer that was served was from the Netherlands and it was served at room temperature, and cost sixteen U.S. dollars per bottle, now I was never a big fan of that particular beer, but even at room temperature it was better than anything I had in a long time, we stuck around long enough for each of us to have two bottles and headed back to the ship.

The next day we just barely went into the Gulf of Oman and turned around and headed back down into the Red Sea. I have to tell you, in most parts of the world, while cruising on a ship and looking toward the land, you will see some type of vegetation on land, be it grass or trees, even weeds, in the Red Sea and the Persian Gulf. All you saw was sand and sand dunes. Dubai was just beginning to lay the giant stones down for the man-made island of Palm Jebel Ali. I believe they are still working on it to this day.

I know those people in Dubai have more money than most countries, but why in the hell would they want to build anything in the Persian Gulf, with Iran, Iraq and Saudi Arabia as nearby neighbors. I just couldn't understand any of it. We pulled into Port Sudan and refueled near the end of our extended stay. We headed south in the Red Sea and entered the Gulf of Aden, and passed Djibouti into the Gulf of Aden. The next morning, we were cruising down the Arabian Sea. A week later, we entered the Andaman Sea, heading south into the Malacca Straits. We had our first port visit on our way back to San Diego and it was in Pelabuhan Klang (Port Klang) for five days. Most of us caught the train to Kuala Lumpur. It was nice beautiful and green, nothing but hot jungle between Port Klang to Kuala Lumpur, Malaysia.

It was not as hot as the countries surrounding the Red Sea or the Persian Gulf, but the humidity was something else. While riding on the train, the damn thing stopped. It was electric. My guys and I got a little bit nervous, the country of Malaysia had its own terrorist in the nineteen nineties and they were known by US military as the Tamil Tigers. They were not people to be around or get involved with as they would kill or capture anyone that they thought could help their cause.

The train started back up in about an hour. We were relieved about that and also that the air conditioning came back on. The trip without the hour wait was supposed to be a little over an hour. With the stop, it was well over two hours. We got to Kuala Lumpur just as the sun was setting and we needed to find a couple of cheap hotel rooms, we found a hotel not too far from the train station. The rooms were around thirty-five US dollars. The currency in Malaysia was called ringgits, they were paper and smaller than an American Dollar and one dollar would get you, if I remember right, eight ringgits, could be more or less. After we got our hotel rooms, we caught a cab to a place the cab driver called Bukit Bintang (the only reason I remember that is I found a receipt with that name on it and a bar that we went to, the drinks were kind of expensive, but the food was reasonable and almost like the food in the Philippines. The ladies were little and cute, just like the babes in most countries in Asia, small and petite.

But at least we could see what the hell they looked like; it was good to be out of the Arab countries where it was shameful for a woman to show her beauty. We made the cab driver stop at the first bar we came to. All I wanted was beer, preferably an American beer. You already know BUDWEISER!! I think I paid close to eight American dollars for my Budweiser. I had about four of them, then I told the guys I was going to find a place to eat some American food. I left by myself, my guys wanted to check out the ladies, so I walked out of the bar and our cab driver was still there. I told him I wanted some American food. Fifteen minutes later. I was in a Kentucky Fried Chicken place and was happy as hell. I remember ordering a four-piece meal with the biscuit and I actually had two little packets of honey. I was happy as hell. I bet most of the people in there were amazed looking at me eat. I was making sounds like my friend from South Africa, and there was nothing left on the leg bones, and I killed the chicken breast. I had a large coke to go with my meal.

God, that food was great. In the Persian Gulf and the Red Sea, we got food from the surrounding countries that we had normal relations with as part of the Status of Forces Agreements made back then. When the ship ran out of regular milk, we went to the Carnation canned milk and then if we had it powered milk and no milk unless we wanted goat's milk and that just didn't work with corn flakes.

I was glad to be in a country where I could find the food I wanted to eat. I did like the dates in Arab countries, though. After I left Kentucky Fried Chicken, I needed a smoke. As soon as I got out the door, all I saw were no smoking signs. I jumped back in the cab and lit a cigarette, handed the driver one and I must have smoked three of them during the fifteen-minute drive back to the bar I left the guys at.

When I got there, only my CTM2 was still there. His name was John, and he was married and would not cheat on his wife, especially after seeing the CTO's wife's video. John and I stayed at the bar until around 2200 hours that night, then he left, I stuck around a little bit longer and one of my smoke break buddies from the ship showed up. He was a radioman first class. His name was David.

David and I hung out while smoking and we worked out in the makeshift gym on board the Duluth a lot, we didn't do much weight lifting, but sit-ups and push-ups were all we did. He was also in the first class lounge a lot of the times I was there. He was married and not looking to hook up with any of the local ladies, he did say we had been out there for nine months and if the opportunity did arrive, he would probably take it.

We both laughed. I told him where my room was near the train station. He had gotten one in the same place on the third floor and I was on the second floor. We both knew my next port visit was going to be Manila in the Philippines, then Hawaii and back to San Diego. Neither of us told anyone about that info. It was classified. We hung out for a little while I told him about Kentucky Fried Chicken, and he said, "Let's go." I laughed and told him I would catch him the next day as I wanted to get to my room and take a bath and sit and have a drink of whiskey. I left and went straight to the hotel and my room. I didn't want to pay the amount they were asking for whiskey in the hotel bar, so I ordered two shots which room service brought to me. I did my normal thing and sat in the tub with a little bit of water in it and the shower on me, just cold water. The second shot of whiskey did the trick. I got out and just hit the sheets.

It was a good sleep. The room didn't smell like sweaty feet and ass like on the ship. I was content for that night. That next day David and I went to check out the city. Kuala Lumpur was kind of expensive for us. If we were getting paid what the military folks get today, we would have had a great time, beer was expensive for us and we both knew our next port visit would be Manila in the Philippines.

We went and had lunch at KFC, then headed back to the train station and back to Duluth. Both David and I stayed on the ship and let our guys get off the ship. I made sure my guys had more days off than I did because when we pulled into Manila, I was taking four days off.

After we left the Malacca Straits, we headed for Manila. It took us four days. There were a couple of civilian yachts not too far from us. The yacht owners liked to be near military ships when traveling through the straits during those days due to the pirates. They knew they were safe as long as a military vessel was nearby.

We pulled into Manila bay, where we would be in port for seven days. I let the guys pick the days they wanted to have off duty. I explained that all the days were like Friday and Saturday. It was always party time when I was here in the Philippines in the late 1970s, and the late 1990s and a lot had changed. Mainly, the price for beer was less than thirty cents in the seventies. When we got there, it was close to two dollars at the cheap bars and five at the better places.

The room rates had gone up also, but after nine months in the middle east, I didn't care and neither did any of the rest of my crew. Once we pulled into port, I had the last four days of the port visit off, and so did my buddy, David. We had everything planned out to the T. Big-T left with two of our CTOs. They had two days off each and were happy as hell just to be getting off of the Duluth. Once they came back, our CTM and one of the other CTOs would Take off. I didn't ask the LTJG what his plans were. I just didn't care.

The three days I stayed on board was spent checking all equipment, the safe contents and work order request with the CTM and cleaning the van inside and out. On the third day, I was out of there at 0800 hours and I know I had a smile on my face. David and I met up at the quarterdeck and then we were off.

It felt good to be leaving the ship even though it was our temporary home. We caught a taxi and David told the driver to take us to an area where we would not find many sailors, but it had to be close to the port. About twenty minutes later, we were sitting in a nice bar and no sailors or marines in sight. We had decided before we left the ship that we would find our rooms after we had a few beers.

As soon as we got into the bar, we saw about eight or nine ladies and a couple of benny-boys all talking together. We sat at the bar and ordered Budweiser's. I remember telling the bartender I wanted them as cold as possible. He smiled at us and said no problem, he handed us two ice-cold buds and we were happy. After the second bee. One of the ladies came over and started talking to us. She wanted to know where we were from in the states, David was from Iowa and well, I was from California, and as soon as I said that, she wanted to know if I was from Los Angeles or San Francisco. I told her Los Angeles, she smiled and asked me to buy her a drink. She looked pretty and had long hair down to her butt. I brought her a beer.

I turned and asked the bartender where was a good place to get a couple of rooms. Of course, he knew a good place for us, not too crowded and not too expensive. That's when another girl came over and just sat in David's lap. He looked at her like she was crazy, but I guess he liked her sitting in his lap because he brought her a beer and they started talking.

After the third beer, I was ready to go. We needed to find a place. I needed a real bath and a shot of whiskey. I looked over at David and said let's go, both of the girls tried to get us to stay there, but David told them we would be back later that night. The bartender knew of a place that we could rent. It had two bedrooms, one bathroom, a small kitchenette and a little living room with a 3-person couch and a small love seat.

The price was close to thirty-five dollars a night. I told David about it. It was on the second floor of a three-story building, and it was within walking distance to this bar about two blocks away. When we got there, we both thought it looked like crap on the outside, with bars on all the windows and graffiti all over the walls, on the outside, but the inside was okay and there was a small balcony. We had found our spot for our four days away from Duluth. We were again happy.

We passed a mom-and-pop store on the way to our little place and as soon as we unpacked our bags. We made a bee-line for the store. We had to buy toilet paper, soap, beer and munchy foods. We both walked back to our little spot with two or three paper bags and put all that stuff away, David wanted to drink more beer and I wanted a bath. I had brought some Crown Royal in the airplane-size bottles at the little shop. David only drank beer, so I kept the four little bottles for myself, I had two while I was taking my bath/shower and that's when I heard David scream, "Oh hell no!" really loud. I had forgotten to tell him about the giant roaches in the Philippines. When I got out of the bath, he had a rubber band and was shooting paper wads at the roaches. I guess they stayed hidden until they figured out who their neighbors were.

We both walked back to the little store and brought some bug spray. I sprayed the bedrooms and David sprayed the rest of the place, then we left and went back to the club we had been at earlier. Neither of us wanted to be in there with the smell of all the bug spray we sprayed. I had told David to keep his money in his pockets at all times and do not leave it in the little apartment. He said no problem. We both put most of our cash in our shoes and enough for the nights drinking and partying in our wallets.

We were ready for some fun. We walked back to the bar we had stopped at earlier that day and went in. We were surprised that there were not more of us sailors in the place all together. There were probably only about fifteen Americans in the place, a few bits were there and that was it. We had our choice of dance partners that night. I picked this lovely lady with very long hair and a nice slim figure, if it wasn't for her very pretty face I wouldn't have chosen her, but I did like the way she danced, she knew how to move with the music, slowly gyrating to the rhythm, and she looked really good doing it. She was going to be mine for that night and she was. We stayed in the club until I had spent around twenty-five or thirty dollars on our drinks, then I told her, "Let's go."

She said, "I had to ask mama-san."

I looked at her with that 'what' look on my face, then I remembered where I was, we had been kissing and dancing all night, she wasn't falling for me, this was business. I walked over to mama-san and said I wanted to take number twenty home with me, it cost me fifteen dollars and it was well worth it. We left the club with David and his girl her number was seven. He said it was his lucky number, we both laughed, he paid his fifteen dollars also. We walked to a little restaurant that was on the way to our apartment and got fish and rice for dinner and took it back to our place.

We had a good night. David and I woke up before the ladies did. We both checked the spots where we had stashed our money when we got them home and it was still there. We both let out a sigh of relief. Both of us smoked cigarettes as soon as we woke up and were in the little front room on the couch chilling. After we finished our smokes, we woke the ladies up. My girl and I took showers first, and then David and his girl went in after we got out.

The girls showed us a little place off of an alley where we could get bacon and eggs with toast for cheap, like two dollars each plate, so we had a good breakfast and it was time to go sightseeing in the capital city Manilla. We walked back to our street and caught a cab to the Manilla Hilton, where I had spent a couple of days with my mother and sister. We all got out of the cab and just walked around for a little while.

Neither of the girls had been to that part of the city, so we walked around looking at the shops. I looked at David, and we both wanted a beer, so we hit this little bar and got four beers, and of course, we stuck around there for a few hours, getting a nice buzz. After we left the bar, we decided to take a carriage ride on this really cool-looking horse-drawn buggy. It was a nice ride until the driver started really beating the horse with the whip that he had. I had to stop David from smacking the driver. We paid him and got out of the carriage and walked back to the Hilton hotel, which was only a few blocks away.

When we got to the Hilton we went down to the club and it was jamming, the band was playing stateside music and we partied until around midnight, caught a cab back to our part of the city and went straight to a little restaurant for something to eat and back to our little apartment. The next morning, we just spent most of the day in the apartment, we did go out for beers and food, but that was it. The ladies took good care of us. David and I both dreaded the next day as we would have to return back to the ship before 6:00 PM. We made the most of the time we had left. We both owed Mama san some money for keeping the girls for more than three days.

The next morning we packed our clothes, got the girls and their clothes together and walked them back to the club down the street, had a couple of beers and then caught a cab back to the pier where the Duluth was berthed. Neither of us wanted to get back on board, but it was what it was.

The next port would be Hawaii and that was going to be a little over two weeks as the Duluth was just cruising at sixteen knots and was doing maneuvers and communications exercises with a couple of the ships that were also heading back to San Diego. Once we were near the Hawaiian Islands chain, most of the fleet kept going heading for San Diego. The Duluth, along with two

Destroyers, pulled into the Pearl Harbor Naval Base. As we entered, we manned the rails (most of the crew standing at parade rest along the edges of the ship) in working white uniforms. We passed the Arizona Memorial and then we were at the pier where tugs came out and helped the Duluth pull into its place along the pier. We had three days off in Hawaii. At first, we had to get all the documents that needed to be shredded together and into huge bags that looked sort of like our sea bags. We had six in total, I think. Once we had everything stuffed into the bags, I took Big-T and one of the CTOs with me, there was a van waiting for us to take the documents to be shredded.

We went to NSGA Kunai. I was hoping to see someone I might have known. I was trying to think of anyone I would have known that was stationed there when all of a sudden, the driver stopped the van. There were two other vans taking material like ours to the base, but one of the van's back doors opened and there was classified material blowing all over the road. We all got out, chasing documents and holding up the traffic. We had two sailors on both sides of the road stopping traffic while the rest of us were chasing paper.

That took about fifteen minutes then we were back on the road for another fifteen minutes. Once we were at NSGA Kunai, we signed documents to release the bags to the base for shredding. The drivers had us get back in the vans and took us right back to the Duluth and the other ships, I was a little bit upset I didn't get to check out the base, but once we got back to Pearl Harbor, we were able to shut down the van and most of the crew left the ship, I stayed on board the first day and only left to find a place to get something to eat.

There was a McDonalds at the Navy Exchange and I ate like a pig. I forgot how at that time, I liked McDonald's. I caught the base bus back to the pier area and just walked around for a while. Then, I headed back to the ship, watched some TV and just relaxed in the first- and second-class lounge until it was time to hit the rack.

I was trying to save my money for getting back home to Imperial Beach. I stayed pretty low-keyed until our last night in Pearl Harbor. I went out with Big-T and David to a strip joint. I lost my damn mind. The dancers were beautiful. There were black and white ladies with tits and asses. I didn't know what to do. I had only taken forty dollars with me. I forgot how expensive Hawaii was for us poor sailors, the drinks were like seven or eight dollars apiece, and I had planned to get blasted. I also forgot about tipping the ladies. I borrowed twenty from Big-t and started my night. I went through the forty dollars I brought with me in about two hours, tipping the ladies and drinking Budweiser's, I had a seat not too far from the stage and I was content as hell.

The guys wanted to go to another club further down the street. I told them I would stay here. I ran out of money and walked out. I couldn't find the guys, so I started walking, trying to hitchhike back to the base. I was toasted. I had my thumb out as I was walking and a car actually pulled over, it had two guys in it and when I got in, they were giggling like young girls, one asked me where I was heading and he had a very high-pitched voice, when I told him I was going to Pearl Harbor, they both got quiet. I told them which pier I needed to go to and then they both let out a sigh of relief and went back to giggling again.

The driver's father was stationed on the base but on the other side of the pier area from where I wanted to go, I was ready to pass out by the time we arrived back on the base and at the pier. The driver stopped the car and I slowly got out, like I said, I was toasted. I could feel myself staggering when I got out of the car. Both of the guys waved goodbye to me and were giggling just like they did the whole ride to the base.

I tried to straighten up as I got to the gangway. I grabbed the rope with one hand and slowly made my way up to the ship. I really took my time. Once I got to the top, I saluted the flag and the officer of the deck and asked for permission to come aboard. I had my ID in my other hand and I showed it to the second-class petty officer. He smiled and said permission was granted. As I was stumbling toward the hatch to get inside, I heard him tell the other petty officer to hand over the money. The other petty officer had bet him that I would either fall on the gangway or into the water.

I woke up the next morning feeling like two tons of cat poop and still in my civvies, shoes and all. I got up, went to the shower and washed up, went to The Acey Deucy Lounge and made myself a ham and cheese sandwich, sat down and looked around. I wasn't the only one in there hung over from hell and I started laughing so did most of the guys in the lounge.

After I sat there for a little while, I went back to my rack, took off my uniform and passed out again. I woke up around 6:00 PM and went to the van. Big-T asked me where did I go last night as they had gone back to that club looking for me. I told him I hitched a ride back to the ship a little after midnight. He started laughing, saying they didn't get back to that club until after 2:00 AM and that they were pretty drunk also.

The ship left late that evening and we were on our way back to San Diego and for our crew down to Imperial beach. It was a long twelve days getting back to the United States. We were basically shut down in the van except for the CTOs as they continued to communicate with our base in Imperial Beach and other sites that we worked with. We cleaned the van every day and worked out in the make-shift gym. It was a slow trip back because we wanted to get off the Duluth, we were on it for more than nine months and that was the longest single cruise that I had done. I wanted to be on dry land and in my townhouse, it was like I couldn't wait. Once we got close to the United States, we could see two large brownish-orange colored clouds, they were Los Angeles and San Diego, it was all the smog that was trapped in those two areas.

We traveled a little north of San Diego to unload the marines at Camp Pendleton, California. They had tanks and all their stuff to get off the ship. We would not get home until the next morning and that is when we pulled into San Diego Naval Base. Once the Duluth was docked, our little crew was packed and waiting to disembark, we had boarded the Duluth in San Diego, California and headed west, past the Hawaiian Islands chain, past the Philippines, into the Celebes Sea, through the Makassar Strait into the Java Sea and into the Singapore Straits, through the Malacca Straits and into the Andaman Sea into the Bay of Bengal and into the Arabian Sea, through the Gulf of Oman and into the Persian Gulf and up into Kuwait City then back out of the Persian Gulf to Abu Dhabi, Dubai and out of the Gulf of Oman and into the Gulf of Aden to Djibouti then north up into the Red Sea and into the Gulf Of Aqaba to Aqaba Jordan with the return through those same Seas back to the Pacific Ocean to the Philippines, Hawaii and then back to San Diego California, it was over nine months long and we were all exhausted, just ready to be back in Imperial Beach. We all had brought some kind of gold trinkets and perfumes for the ladies in our lives. As usual, getting off the ship was highest ranks first down to the lowest ranks, it only took about ten or fifteen minutes and we were in the white navy van taking us south of San Diego back to NSGA Imperial Beach.

We had been out to sea for over three hundred days. That was the most I had done on any single temporarily assigned duty on any ship to support operations near Iraq. I had put in for Big-t and the CTM2 to receive Navy Achievement awards and when I told the (LTJG) he kind of balked about it. I told him that I would also put it through the Duluth's commanding officer (CO), so it would look good to our (CO) at our base's next awards ceremony, he didn't really want to sign off on it, but he did, god I didn't like him at all and if I had any inkling of respect even a little for him, it was all lost at that time.

The ride from San Diego Navy Station took us about twenty or thirty minutes and we were back at our base in Imperial Beach. All of us looked happy, at least I was, until after the debrief and I got my evaluation from the lieutenant junior grade (LTJG). Instead of getting my normal 4.0 which is the highest mark I could get, I averaged a 3.6. That low mark would stop me, along with the problem I had in Japan from making chief (E-7) and I knew it.

I basically handled everything we did on the trip. What a dickhead the (LTJG) was, they were only making 2 CTR chiefs a year and I was coming up on my twenty-year mark next year. I only thought about it for a few minutes, but I was really pissed. I just had to get over it.

I was not a happy camper. I just looked at the (LTJG) and signed the evaluation. I did put a few comments on it about how I managed just about everything and did keep our officer in charge up to date on what was happening during the trip. I thought to myself that it should sting him really badly if the Captain took a look at my evaluation, and I knew she would want to know what happened on the trip and I would tell her everything.

After that, we all said goodbye and each of us headed back to either the barracks or our apartments off base. I walked out of the building and started up my Z. It was filthy as hell. After sitting on the lot for over nine months, you can imagine how bad it was. I reached in behind the driver's seat and grabbed one of the towels I kept there and tried to clean the front windshield so I could see good enough to get to the nearest car wash.

After I cleaned the car and dried it off, I headed home, my cd player was playing the last song I had listened to before we left and that was a song by Kool and the Gang it was called 'Summer Madness', it felt good to hear it again while actually driving my own car heading home.

It took me about five minutes to get home and just to see my townhouse made me happy as hell. I called Mom to let her know I was back, and she must have called the rest of my family because just as I was turning on the shower, the phone calls started, and both of my sisters and one of my aunts, along with a couple of my homeboys called. After an hour, I opened my whiskey decanter and poured a large glass full of Chivas Regal whiskey and just sat down for a few minutes.

I finally got in the bathtub with the shower running for about thirty minutes, slowly sipping on the Chives Regal whiskey, savoring each sip. After I got out of the tub and dried off, I felt drained and hungry. I got dressed and went to Taco Bell and ordered four tacos, a large coke and headed back home. After I ate, I got in my bed and passed out. I slept for a good five or six hours.

I put all the uniforms and clothes I had taken with me on the Duluth in my sea bag and then I headed for the Coronado base laundry. My dress whites I took to the cleaners and the rest all went into washing machines at the laundry. I was probably there for an hour and after that, I hit the base club for a few beers and I headed back to the imperial beach to do some grocery shopping.

My youngest sister came down once a month while I was gone and took care of my place (I had left checks for her to pay the bills, electric and rent). She loved being there. It was a retreat for her and she kept the place clean and threw out a lot of the food I had in the refrigerator, I was glad she did that for me, she had sent me letters letting me know when she had come down to my place and stayed for the weekend, I had filled out checks for car insurance and the electric bills along with the rent for six months.

I called Cutie and then I called Gale. Both were happy to hear from me. I knew I would have them come down and visit me soon. I had saved a little bit of money while I was deployed and it felt good to have funds in the bank like that, I had a little over five thousand dollars saved after over nine months out to sea, so I knew I could pay for both of their plane tickets. Seeing them again would be fun, more than fun. I chilled out for the next two days, had my little bar-b-que just by myself and relaxed. It really felt good being home again.

I filled up my Z with gas and headed off to Los Angeles and my family and few friends that were still alive. Out of thirteen kids that grew up together, only five of us were still alive. That was really something to think about. The drugs, gangs and police were taking a serious toll on my friends. I had called to let my mother know that I was heading her way and that I wanted to stay there for a couple of days. She was happy and so was I.

Everybody was glad to see me and I got home bearing gifts from different parts of the Orient and the Middle East. My mother and sisters got perfumes from the countries of Jordan and Kuwait, my father smoked with pipes and I brought him two new pipes (he had a collection from a lot of the countries that I had either been stationed at or visited), then I found out he quit smoking.

I had brought a painting of an Egyptian woman that was painted on a sheet of reef paper. No one was interested in it. I was glad about that, I also had brought a carpet from Jordan for moms, she loved it. I got there on a Wednesday and planned on leaving that Friday morning. I drank a lot of beer with my father and my friends and just chilled with them the first day. The second day, I visited my great grandmother. She was in her mid-nineties and I just loved hearing her stories about her life and the rest of our family, her and her sister both lived in the retirement home, I stayed with them for a little while and then I just drove around Los Angeles, the place had really changed since the riots, my landmarks were practically all gone.

I did go and visit some of my biker friends and hung out with them for a while until they started smoking weed and doing their drugs. It was time for me to leave. The last night of this visit, I stayed at this lady's house I had met and we had a good night. She wanted to keep in touch with me and I told her we would be good friends. The next morning, I went back to mom's place and stayed there until they all came home from work. I left Los Angeles about six and got back to Imperial Beach around seven-thirty that night. As soon as I got home. I called Gale and we made arrangements for her to come and visit for two weeks the next month.

I couldn't wait to see her. Between her and Cutie, she was the one for me. The next day I hooked up with Big-t and his fiancée. I didn't like her one bit, he had other ladies that liked him and most of them looked better, but this one made him happy and that was that. I started hanging out with one of the guys that came down from Edzel. No one had heard from Freddy. I wondered about him a lot, he was just as crazy as I was and I often thought of all the fun we had in Italy and Scotland.

I was back to work, the base's internet install was completed and now our spaces were just for DIRSUP (direct support) training, that is what we did when we were not out to sea. My crew got nine days off after our return from the last trip, I know I needed it.

We had an ungodly amount of new people at the command and they were needed. There were new things that the navy was pushing and some not so new, like weight. No longer would there be any overweight sailors in the navy. If you had a baby, you had six months to lose the weight. If you had a normal weight problem, you had six months to get it under control. Drugs were not tolerated. If you popped positive one time, you were out unless it was doctor prescribed. Drunk driving was another issue that you could only get one chance at.

The new navy wanted new lean, sober sailors. No parties like back in the eighties in the barracks. People stayed late at work trying to overcome their problems with work-related issues. For me, it meant no drinking and driving. That was going to be tricky as everywhere you went out to have fun back in the 19s there was drinking. I knew I had to be careful.

Gale finally arrived and did I have fun with her. We went all over San Diego and Tijuana, Mexico and had a really good time. I took her to the base on Coronado and we had a slight problem, one of the racist sailors, along with one of his friends, walked over to our table in the club on base while I was away getting us a couple of beers and asked her what in the hell would a beautiful lady like her be doing with a nigger, boy did she let him have it, she told him, "My man looks better then the both of you two red necks asses put together, he knows how to treat a real woman and he is respectful." They were both just standing there looking at her when I walked back to the table with their mouths wide open. I asked them what did they want, and one of them started to say something, and the other one told him who I was and my rank, they both left.

I introduced her to a couple of my friends and they both told me that she is a total keeper. I smiled and said I know. G-man hung out with Gale and I while she was visiting. He was going through a rough time with his ex-wife. She would call and ask for more child support and tell him she was moving and taking the kid with her and he would not be able to see his kid. He was really upset. The only problem with him wanting to come over so much was that we were hardly dressed when in the townhouse and we liked it that way.

Gale stayed with me for two weeks and unless I was at work, we were never separated. Even If I was watching something on tv that she didn't want to see, she would still lay on the couch with her head in my lap while reading a magazine. We grilled a lot of chicken on the bar b que along with steaks that we brought on base for damn near half the price we paid off base and always had a good salad. Gale said we ate good when we were together. G-man was there for all the grilling. Once he came over with some fresh fish he brought on base, I was a little mad because I hadn't taken Gale fishing. I just never thought of it. The next day, she was standing on the pier next to me fishing and she caught the first fish. It was a small croaker (they made croaking noises when you pulled them out of the water) and she was excited as hell. We both caught enough fish to have a fish fry that night along with some of those frozen french fries that come in a big plastic bag and you had to put them in the oven for forty-five minutes. We put them in the oven and waited about thirty minutes before we fried the fish, all the while drinking beer.

That last morning neither Gale or I wanted to get up to take her to the airport so she could go back home to Scotland, but it had to be done, we almost stayed in bed too long as we were a few minutes late at the airport, she had to run after we got her bags checked in, we quickly kissed and she was off. Gale called me when she got back to the airport in Glasgow the next morning, we were both sad, but she had to leave.

When I got back to work, I was told to be ready to pack my sea bag for a two-day trip in two months just to check the equipment along with one of the CTM's. It was a quick trip and all we did was inspect all the equipment in the SSES van on another LPD, I was glad to go and glad to get back. My time in the navy was getting close to being over. I only had three months until my twenty-year mark. After we did the debrief, I was called into the division officer's office and he informed me that I shouldn't unpack my sea bags as I would be going back out on another TAD trip for six months. I looked in the right eye and said that I did not want to go back out for six months as there were several other E-6s that needed the sea time and experience. I knew they were his friends and he was not going to send them out.

He asked me if I was refusing to go. I asked him when the trip was to happen and he said next month. I let him know that I was refusing to go out to sea again as I still had fifteen days leave and at the time I was retiring, you got twenty days plus a few days for travel, which meant that just before he wanted to send me back out to sea, I would put in my retirement request which usually took a couple of days for the commanding officer to approve. His face turned red as hell. I turned and walked out of his office, I could hear him yelling at the CTA first class. He wanted to know when my twenty years would be up.

I smiled and left work a little early that day. I took along my request paperwork to retire. I wanted to read everything I could about it and I wanted to try and get in touch with Freddy. I had his sister's phone number in Texas to call her and find out where he was. I read everything I could about the retirement and the ceremony that went along with it twice, then I called Freddy's sister and she refused to give me any information about Freddy, which made sense. I called her back and mentioned Freddy's ex-wife and daughter's name. She told me to call back the next day.

Retirement Ceremony February 28 1998

The next morning, I put in all my paperwork for retiring. I was told an appointment with the Commanding officer was needed before it was approved and that would be in two weeks. That even gave me more time. I was also informed about all the things that go along with retiring and the classes that I would be given prior to my retirement date, stuff like how to fill out a resume, what type of jobs were compatible with what I had been doing during my career in the navy, and who I wanted to set up all the things needed for my ceremony. I had over a month to figure all of this out and mainly nothing else to do, I would go to the base and for the first two weeks. I would get this little old navy pickup truck, throw my rod and reels in it and go fishing. I took the radio in case they needed me for anything.

On my first day after fishing, I called Cutie and told her to cancel her trip to San Diego as I was coming to England to visit Freddy for a couple of days, then I would go down to Scotland to visit her and some of my friends in Brechin. She sounded funny like she was disappointed, but she said she would cancel her trip. I called Freddy's sister again and was told where he was in England. I called the base there and was lucky enough to get someone that actually knew him. The guy gave me the phone number Freddy had on record for his off-base residence. I would call him when I got to Gatwick airport in London and surprise him with a visit.

At the end of my first week, I had to have my physical and it was a full one, from dental, eyes, hearing and the ole finger up my rectum. God, I was glad when that was over. I got a clean bill of health from the doctors. The third week on the first day, I had my appointment with the commanding officer, she asked me why I wanted to retire and I told her the truth. Things were getting hard for me to understand and about the division officer and his choices for going TAD and taking orders from people that I could not respect, herself not included.

I told her out of my twenty years. There were only four commanding officers I would have followed to the gates of hell with and she was one of them. She smiled at that and then she asked me what she could do to fix the low morale in the DIRSUP division. I told her it's not my place to belittle an officer, but getting rid of the division officer would be a great start. She wasn't smiling. Then she asked me about the trip on the Duluth and the officer in charge of our team, I told her about the mistake he had made, but due to the fact that the part of the mission those frequencies were set for was canceled before we would have been able to use them, it was nothing we could not overcome.

She looked at me and smiled. She asked me where I wanted my retirement flag to come from and I told her I thought long and hard about that the other night and I decided I wanted it to come from the Arizona Memorial in Hawaii. She smiled again. She asked me what I wanted to do when I got out and I said I really didn't know. We both laughed. I will never forget what she told me before I left her office and that was, "She had never heard me say I or met. When it came down to my crew, it was always WE." She stood and I also did. Then she put her hand out and told me it was her honor to have worked with me. I said it was my pleasure. I did and about face and walked out of her office. After I shut the door, I felt like I was letting her down, but there was no way I was staying in, knowing I didn't stand a chance of making chief and dealing with asses that had their own interest at heart instead of the crew.

I requested the commander be the orator at my ceremony, I had worked for him in Homestead and he was beyond a great officer. He was one of the ones I told the captain I would follow to hell. I had a fellow E-6 set up the ceremony. He was awesome and said he appreciated the fact that I chose him. He was smart and very thorough with everything he did, plus I liked him. His name was Craig. Craig and I went to the last navy day ball that I attended and had a good time. I won't go any farther than that about the ball. I will say this much, though. It was one of the best Navy Balls I had been to, right on par with the one in San Vito. Everybody was dressed in winter dress uniforms. It was awesome, all medals shining, and no one that I saw got out of control and it was quick and easy. Craig and I left with one of the female sailors that used to work form me in the DIRSUP division. As I was retiring, I was no longer in any division.

All my work days consisted of going to the administration building on Coronado Navy Base and filling out papers and going to medical appointments. Other than that, I was usually somewhere in San Diego fishing. My normal day started at 0800 and usually ended around noon. I did that for almost two months. Every chance I got, I would drive to NSGA Imperial Beach just to see if I could see the ex-division officer. I never saw him again and I was alright with that. I received my new identification card that read on the bottom of it, "US Navy Retired," and there was no expiration date on it.

Craig would come over to my apartment and we would go over exactly what would happen at the ceremony. I pretty much had it memorized after the second time he came over, and after the fifth time, I let him know that, "I got it." Craig said he just didn't want anything to go wrong.

Two weeks before I retired, one of my new friends, since coming back from Imperial Beach, retired. It was a cool ceremony, he was allowed one request and if it was reasonable, it would be granted. All he requested was that some of the officers that he didn't like were not allowed to attend his ceremony. I knew my request would be different and better. And I knew the officers I didn't like would not want to attend.

He requested the captain to orate his ceremony. She named his first enlistment date and all the duty stations he served in, along with two ships that he was TAD on. After the captain finished, she saluted him and handed him his retirement flag, which was folded and placed in a wooden box that was squared from top to bottom on three sides. The top was a triangle shape on three-sided and glass covered the form. Below the flag was his name, rank, all his medals and the names of the two ships he had been on. I was to have the same thing. I believe his flag was flown on one of the ships he was on.

At the end of his ceremony, he walked through the middle of twenty sailors, ten on each side saluting him. As he made his walk, he kept his salute up until he reached the Harley Davidson Motor Cycle and then he turned, removed his cover (hat), put on his helmet and fired up his Harley and drove off the base. It was awesome.

G-man came over damn near every day asking me how I was doing and if I was sure I wanted to get out and he always got the same answer and it was Hell Yeah, and that I have done enough and seen enough. That was usually good enough for him and then we would open a few beers and toast the folks that we not there with us. It was good having him there with me.

My oldest daughter came down from Los Angeles to visit me and she would be there for the ceremony. I thought it was a good idea. The rest of my family was working and couldn't get the days off. I was glad she was there with me. I had completed all medical, vision and dental tests and signed all required documents. I had to list all the ships I had ridden as there were no records of the ones I went TAD on in Homestead, the base wasn't computerized at that time, so when hurricane Andrew, a category five, obliterated our little base NSGA Homestead, a lot of records were lost. Go figure. I had to try and remember all the ships that I was temporarily assigned to. I was just glad I didn't have to remember the dates.

My daughter was dropped off by her mother two days before I retired. That first night we went and had dinner at Taco Bell, which was a good change for me. I had been eating so much at McDonald's that I was wondering if I should get a job there after I retired.

My day arrived and I was ready. My dress blues were still in the plastic that your clothes come in when you pick them up. We no longer shined our shoes as we wore these patent leather shoes. Mine was brand new. I had the cleaners attach my medals to my jumper blouse, and my necktie was tied and ironed, so the tips were flat. I only had four good conduct medals, not the five I would have had, had it not been for my problem in Misawa, Japan. I had overseas ribbons, sea service deployment ribbons, armed forces expeditionary medals, overseas medals and national defense medals.

Before the ceremony, I had to go to the base on Coronado and sign my Certificate of Release or discharge from active duty form (DD214), which meant that I was transferred to the fleet reserve inactive for ten years. My retirement pay would start the next day, which was March 1, 1998, and I would be paid half my normal salary for the rest of my life unless I screwed up and went to prison or something. I had been TAD to over ten different ships, a couple of them I served on more than once. I had done enough. That morning I had taken my Z to the car wash and paid to have it cleaned and it was sparkling. You could see your face in the paint, it was awesome, my daughter had a new dress and she wore it to the ceremony.

I had requested that all the sailors that came to my ceremony voluntarily would get the rest of the day off, my ceremony was held at NSGA Imperial Beach and it was a nice cool day, not too windy and if I remember the temperature was in the high 60s the weather was perfect for an old sailor to end his sailoring career. I believe at least two-thirds of the command personnel showed up, including the commanding officer and the new division officer.

At 1100 hours on February 28th, 1998, I walked up and stood at attention in front of the podium that the commander was standing behind. He looked at me and smiled. He started reading the list of my duty stations, accomplishments, awards and the list of ships that I had served on, then he spoke about the time when he and I were stationed together. It was here in Imperial Beach I had made E-5 and he was a new lieutenant. Then he said something that made me stick my chest out a little bit farther and that was, "Out of the five years I served with this petty officer, I never heard him say me or I, it was always We."

Then the commander took a step back and saluted me. I returned the salute, turned towards the commanding officer and saluted her. The commander walked from behind the podium and handed me a Certificate of Appreciation signed by the president at that time, Bill Clinton and my Fleet Reserve Certificate that certifies that I was transferred from active duty to the fleet reserve of the United States Navy after twenty years of service on this day, signed by the commanding officer. I smiled and thanked him.

I did an about-face and that's when it really hit me. The same feelings I had on the first navy bus I rode on to boot camp on May 7th, 1975, I saluted all the way to my car and I almost stopped my walk to my Z, but I didn't. I held my head up high and kept going. As I was saluting the commanding officer at the end of the commander's speech, Craig escorted my daughter to my car. After I reached the end of my walk, I dropped my salute and turned around to take one last look at my crew. They were all standing together, still at attention, right behind where I stood in front of the commander. I smiled at them, removed my cover and got into my Z, fired up the engine and slowly drove off the base just barely under the fifteen miles per hour limit listening to my music. Once I got off the base, I burned rubber putting my Z into second gear and drove myself and my daughter to my townhouse.

Acknowledgments

Links to see pictures of some of the places and ships in the book:

Images for nsga hanza okinawa Japan:

https://www.pinterest.com/pin/720576627612874 35/

USS Oklahoma City (CL-91) - Wikipedia

https://www.okieboat.com/Ship%27s%20history.html;

https://www.okieboat.com/The%20Ship%27s%20Crew.html

USS Forrestal (CV-59) - Wikipedia

https://en.wikipedia.org › wiki › USS_Forrestal_(CV-59)

USS Saratoga (CV-60) - Wikipedia

https://en.wikipedia.org › wiki › USS_Saratoga_(CV-60)

USS Duluth (LPD-6) - Wikipedia

https://en.wikipedia.org › wiki › USS_Duluth_(LPD-6)

USS Blue Ridge (LCC-19) - Wikipedia

https://en.wikipedia.org › wiki › USS_Blue_Ridge_(LCC-19)

USS America (CV-66) - Wikipedia

https://en.wikipedia.org › wiki › USS_America_(CV-66)

Thinking about the time I spent in the navy as a CT while I was writing this book, only my immediate family (mother, father and two sisters) were as close to me as most of the characters in this book were. I could not have written this without them, as that part of my life would not have existed. I, along with the characters in this book, saw things, places and people that are not the same today as what we experienced during our time in those places overseas. I know I missed a lot of things here in the United States while I was serving overseas, like tv shows, car models, and civil unrest in some of our major cities that helped change some things in my hometown and other cities in this country. However, the experiences like living in Italy and Scotland, along with all the travel that I did on my own during my time off and vacation times, most people will never have the chance to know what things in those countries were like during those times. The hardest things about being in the military for me were deciding to leave and go into the navy and missing my family during holidays like Christmas and New Year, along with birthdays. Racism was another big issue. I had some in the navy but mostly in the cities and towns here in the United States and other major countries like England and being away from your family, worrying about them.

You want to know what my regrets were? The first would be not marrying the woman I loved so much in Pensacola, the second was getting into the unavoidable fight with the Japanese Self Defense guys in Misawa and the last was not seeing my second daughter for all of those years, which I am trying to make up for today.

My last thoughts about what I have written were about the way technology changed everything, who would have thought that what was called a communicator in the tv show Star Trek which was written by Gene Roddenberry would come to life as a flip phone? Most of the racism I witnessed in the navy has been dealt with and corrected, it is probably a small amount still there but hidden as it should be. And I want to make this one thing clear this book is not about racism. It's about myself and my friends and the times we shared good and bad during our off-duty times.

I would like to thank several people that encouraged me to start and finish this book. Foremost is my mother, she told me that this book would be a story like no other for the times it encompasses. Next would be my two sisters for their help and guidance, my father for telling me a few of his stories as a sailor. Also, a few people that I have kept in touch with since retiring as they kept me going wanted to read more. And last but not least the men and women in the United States Military, especially those I considered to be family. I know all of them have gotten out of the military, most retired as I did. I really want to thank a good friend of mine, Ramiro for the book cover. He is awesome.

Lightning Source UK Ltd.
Milton Keynes UK
UKHW050658041222
413255UK00005B/122

9 781088 062951